The Cambridge Companion to Nathaniel Hawthorne

The Cambridge Companion to Nathaniel Hawthorne offers students and teachers an introduction to Hawthorne's fiction and the lively debates that shape Hawthorne studies today. In newly commissioned essays, twelve eminent scholars of American literature introduce readers to key issues in Hawthorne scholarship and deepen our understanding of Hawthorne's writing. Each of the major novels is treated in a separate chapter, while other essays explore Hawthorne's art in relation to a stimulating array of issues and approaches. The essays reveal how Hawthorne's work explores understandings of gender relations and sexuality, of childhood and selfhood, of politics and ethics, of history and modernity. An Introduction and a selected bibliography will help students and teachers understand how Hawthorne has been a crucial figure for each generation of readers of American literature.

THE CAMBRIDGE
COMPANION TO

NATHANIEL HAWTHORNE

EDITED BY
RICHARD H. MILLINGTON

CAMBRIDGE
UNIVERSITY PRESS

PUBLISHED BY THE PRESS SYNDICATE OF THE UNIVERSITY OF CAMBRIDGE
The Pitt Building, Trumpington Street, Cambridge, United Kingdom

CAMBRIDGE UNIVERSITY PRESS
The Edinburgh Building, Cambridge, CB2 2RU, UK
40 West 20th Street, New York, NY 10011–4211, USA
477 Williamstown Road, Port Melbourne, VIC 3207, Australia
Ruiz de Alarcón 13, 28014 Madrid, Spain
Dock House, The Waterfront, Cape Town 8001, South Africa

http://www.cambridge.org

First published 2004

Printed in the United Kingdom at the University Press, Cambridge

Typeface Sabon 10/13 pt.   *System* LATEX 2$_\varepsilon$ [TB]

A catalogue record for this book is available from the British Library

Library of Congress Cataloguing in Publication data
The Cambridge companion to Nathaniel Hawthorne / edited by Richard Millington.
p.   cm. – (Cambridge companions to literature)
Includes bibliographical references (p.) and index.
ISBN 0 521 80745 X   ISBN 0 521 00204 4 (pbk.)
1. Hawthorne, Nathaniel, 1804–1864 – Criticism and interpretation – Handbooks,
manuals, etc.   I. Title: Companion to Nathaniel Hawthorne.
II. Millington, Richard H., 1953 –   III. Series.
PS1888.C355   2004
813′3 – dc22   2003064044

ISBN 0 521 80745 X hardback
ISBN 0 521 00204 4 paperback

For our colleague, Gillian Brown

CONTENTS

ACKNOWLEDGMENTS

My first debt is to the contributors to this volume. It has been a pleasure to learn from their work, and it is an honor to serve as its presenter. I am especially grateful to Robert S. Levine for his excellent advice along the way, and for the example his Melville *Companion* provided. My thanks to Ray Ryan for the invitation to edit this book, for his careful and astute reading of the typescript, and for his heroic exercise of that noble virtue, patience. Jackie Warren, the book's production editor, and Audrey Cotterell, its acute and eagle-eyed copy editor, performed their tasks with great skill and good humor. Richard H. Brodhead introduced me to the study of Hawthorne some twenty years ago; I am grateful for that, and for the still vivid example of his teaching. The last debt I wish to acknowledge is at once the deepest and the most oblique: my father, Bill Millington, died as this volume neared completion. I thank him for all the gifts a good man's life confers.

NOTE ON REFERENCES

Unless stated otherwise, all references to Hawthorne's works relate to *The Centenary Edition of the Works of Nathaniel Hawthorne* (Ohio State University Press, 1962–97), and are noted parenthetically in the text by volume and page number.

CONTRIBUTORS

GILLIAN BROWN is Professor of English at the University of Utah. She is the author of *Domestic Individualism: Imagining the Self in Nineteenth-Century America* (1990) and *The Consent of the Governed: The Lockean Legacy in Early American Culture* (2000).

EMILY MILLER BUDICK, Professor of American Studies at the Hebrew University of Jerusalem, has written three books dealing with Hawthorne: *Engendering Romance: Women Writers and the Hawthorne Tradition, 1850–1990* (1994), *Fiction and Historical Consciousness: The American Romance Tradition* (1994), and *Nineteenth-Century American Romance: Genre and the Construction of Democratic Culture* (1996). She is also the author of *Blacks and Jews in Literary Conversation* (1998), and *Emily Dickinson and the Life of Language: A Study in Symbolic Poetics* (1985).

CHRISTOPHER CASTIGLIA is Associate Professor of English at Loyola University, Chicago. He is the author of *Bound and Determined: Captivity, Culture-Crossing, and White Womanhood from Mary Rowlandson to Patty Hearst* (1996) and the forthcoming *Interior States: The Romance of Reform and the Inner Life of the Nation*.

ALISON EASTON is Senior Lecturer in English at Lancaster University, Lancaster, UK. She is the author of *The Making of the Hawthorne Subject* (1996) and has edited the Penguin edition of Sarah Orne Jewett's *The Country of the Pointed Firs and Other Stories* (1995) and *Angela Carter: Contemporary Critical Essays* (2000). She is the coeditor of *Women, Power and Resistance: An Introduction to Women's Studies* (1996).

KRISTIE HAMILTON is Associate Professor of English at the University of Wisconsin, Milwaukee. She is the author of *America's Sketchbook: The Cultural Life of a Nineteenth-Century Literary Genre* (1998) and of essays on eighteenth- and nineteenth-century American literature and culture.

T. WALTER HERBERT is Professor of English and University Scholar at Southwestern University in Georgetown, Texas. He is the author of *Dearest Beloved: The Hawthornes and the Making of the Middle-Class Family* (1993), *Sexual Violence and American Manhood* (2002), and two books on Melville: *Moby Dick and Calvinism: A World Dismantled* (1977) and *Marquesan Encounters: Melville and the Meaning of Civilization* (1980).

GORDON HUTNER is Professor of English at the University of Illinois and the editor of *American Literary History*. He is the author of *Secrets and Sympathy: Forms of Disclosure in Hawthorne's Novels* (1988), editor of *American Literature, American Culture* (1999), and coeditor of *National Imaginaries, American Identities* (2000).

ROBERT S. LEVINE is Professor in the Department of English at the University of Maryland, College Park. He is the author of *Conspiracy and Romance: Studies in Brockden Brown, Cooper, Hawthorne, and Melville* (1989) and *Martin Delany, Frederick Douglass, and the Politics of Representative Identity* (1997), and has edited a number of volumes, including *The Cambridge Companion to Herman Melville* (1998), *Martin R. Delany: A Documentary Reader* (2003), and the forthcoming Norton Critical Edition of *The House of the Seven Gables*.

RICHARD H. MILLINGTON is Professor of English at Smith College and President of the Nathaniel Hawthorne Society. He is the author of *Practicing Romance: Narrative Form and Cultural Engagement in Hawthorne's Fiction* (1992), the coeditor of *Hitchcock's America* (1999), and has published essays on Hawthorne, Willa Cather, and Alfred Hitchcock.

JOEL PFISTER is Professor of English and American Studies at Wesleyan University, Middletown, CT. He is the author of *The Production of Personal Life: Class, Gender, and the Psychological in Hawthorne's Fiction* (1991), *Staging Depth: Eugene O'Neill and the Politics of Psychological Discourse* (1995), and *Individuality Incorporated: Indians and the Multicultural Modern* (2003), and the coeditor of *Inventing the Psychological: Toward a Cultural History of Emotional Life in America* (1997).

LARRY J. REYNOLDS is Professor of English and Thomas Franklin Mayo Professor of Liberal Arts at Texas A&M University. He is the author of *European Revolutions and the American Literary Renaissance* (1988), editor of *A Historical Guide to Nathaniel Hawthorne* (2001) and of Margaret Fuller's

Woman in the Nineteenth Century (1998), and the coeditor of *National Imaginaries, American Identities* (2000).

KAREN SÁNCHEZ-EPPLER is Professor of English and American Studies at Amherst College. She is the author of *Touching Liberty: Abolition, Feminism, and the Politics of the Body* (1993) and is completing a book on children in nineteenth-century US life and imagination.

BROOK THOMAS, Professor of English at the University of California, Irvine, has authored four books: *Cross Examinations of Law and Literature: Cooper, Hawthorne, Stowe, and Melville* (1987), *American Literary Realism and the Failed Promise of Contract* (1997), *The New Historicism and Other Old-Fashioned Topics* (1991), and *James Joyce's Ulysses: A Book of Many Happy Returns* (1982). He is the editor of *Plessy v. Ferguson: A Brief History with Documents* (1997), and has written many essays on American literature and society.

1804 Born Salem, Massachusetts, July 4, second child of Nathaniel Hathorne, a ship's captain, and Elizabeth Manning Hathorne, member of an enterprising Salem family. Descended on father's side from prominent Puritan colonists. Sisters: Elizabeth (1802–83) and Louisa (1808–52). (Hawthorne will add the "w" to the family name in his early twenties; his mother and sisters accept the emendation in 1837, with the publication of *Twice-told Tales*.)

1808 Father dies of yellow fever in Surinam (Dutch Guiana); family joins Manning household. Begins schooling.

1809 Sophia Amelia Peabody, later Sophia Hawthorne, born September 21 in Salem.

1813 Injures his foot playing ball; suffers from lameness for the next fourteen months. Is tutored at home.

1818 Moves with his family to Raymond, Maine. Attends school briefly but enjoys considerable freedom, hunting, fishing, reading, and running "quite wild."

1819–20 Returns to Salem, living with his Manning relatives while his mother and sisters remain in Raymond. Attends school, then prepares for college under the tutelage of a Salem lawyer.

1821–25 Attends Bowdoin College in Brunswick, Maine, where he forms lifelong friendships with Horatio Bridge, Jonathan Cilley, and Franklin Pierce (fourteenth President of the United States) and meets Henry Wadsworth Longfellow, who becomes a good friend in later years. An admittedly "idle" student, he is fined for card-playing and begins writing fiction. Graduates eighteenth in a class of thirty-five.

1825 Returns to Salem after college graduation. Lives in Salem with his mother and sisters for the next ten years, working to establish himself as a professional writer and traveling to early tourist destinations in New England and New York; several of these sites find their way into tales and sketches. While some of his best stories are written during this period and his reputation grows, he struggles with the conditions of an immature and unremunerative literary marketplace, abandoning ambitions to publish thematically linked collections of his tales and sketches and burning one such manuscript.

1828 Publishes his first novel, *Fanshawe*, anonymously and at his own expense. Later repudiates this book, destroying his own copy and eliminating it from all accounts of his career. (Unsold copies of the novel burn in a Boston bookstore fire in 1831.)

1830 Publishes first tale, "The Hollow of the Three Hills," in the *Salem Gazette*.

1830–33 Other early publications, all anonymous. The sketch "Sights from a Steeple" appears in *The Token*, an annual gift book, for 1831; the 1832 *Token* includes the extremely popular "The Gentle Boy," "My Kinsman, Major Molineux," and "Roger Malvin's Burial."

1834 Proposes a collection of tales and sketches, "The Story Teller," to Samuel Goodrich, who refuses it. The contents of the projected volume will be scattered among various gift books and magazines.

1835 Contributes stories and sketches, including "The Minister's Black Veil" and "The May-Pole of Merry Mount," to *The Token* for 1836; "Young Goodman Brown" appears in *New-England Magazine*.

1836 Moves to Boston to edit, with the help of his talented sister Elizabeth, the *American Magazine of Useful and Entertaining Knowledge*. Resigns editorship when publisher goes bankrupt, and returns to Salem. With his sister he works on *Peter Parley's Universal History, on the Basis of Geography*, part of a popular series for young readers, which appears the following year.

1837 Succeeds in publishing *Twice-told Tales*, a collection of his earlier work, when Horatio Bridge, without his knowledge, agrees to secure the publisher against losses. A favorable review by Longfellow helps establish Hawthorne's reputation as a promising American writer. Meets Sophia Peabody, his future wife, and her sister Elizabeth (a friend of Emerson and a powerful presence in intellectual circles and reform movements), who begins her support of his career.

1838   Befriends John L. O'Sullivan, editor of the *United States Magazine and Democratic Review* and later promoter of the idea of "manifest destiny." Hawthorne will publish frequently in this notable magazine, associated with the Democratic Party, during the next seven years. College friend Jonathan Cilley killed in a duel with a fellow congressman; Hawthorne writes memorial essay in the *Democratic Review*.

1839   Accepts appointment as measurer in the Boston Custom House; becomes engaged to Sophia Peabody, to whom he addresses the first of a remarkable series of love letters.

1840   Publishes *Grandfather's Chair*, the first of his books for children.

1841   Leaves Boston Custom House. Joins Brook Farm community (the model for the utopian community depicted in *The Blithedale Romance*) in April, becoming a trustee and director of finance. Hoping to establish a home for Sophia, purchases two shares in project, but leaves the community in late October.

1842   Publishes second, expanded edition of *Twice-told Tales*. Marries Sophia Peabody, July 9; they settle at the "Old Manse" in Concord.

1842–45 The "Old Manse" period. Encounters Transcendentalist circle gathered around Ralph Waldo Emerson; friendships with Emerson, Henry David Thoreau, Margaret Fuller, and Ellery Channing. Writes many tales and sketches, including "The Birth-Mark," "Rappaccini's Daughter," "The Artist of the Beautiful," and "The Celestial Rail-road," later collected in *Mosses from an Old Manse*.

1844   Daughter Una (1844–77), named after a heroine of Spenser's *Fairie Queene*, born March 3.

1845   Edits Horatio Bridge's *Journal of an African Cruiser*. Cash-strapped, the family returns to Salem, where they move in with his mother and sisters. Seeks political appointment through influential friends, Bridge and Franklin Pierce; nominated for position of custom house surveyor by Salem Democrats.

1846   Appointed surveyor in the Salem Custom House; publishes *Mosses from an Old Manse*; son Julian (1846–1939) born, June 22.

1849   Removed from surveyorship in June by new Whig administration; considerable public controversy ensues. Mother dies, July 31. By September is "writing immensely" on "The Custom-House" and *The Scarlet Letter*.

1850   *The Scarlet Letter* published by Ticknor and Fields (the latter a
        key figure in the promotion of American literature), who remain
        Hawthorne's publishers for the rest of his career. Having
        resolved to leave the "abominable" Salem for ever, moves family
        to Lenox in the Berkshire Mountains of western Massachusetts,
        an early summer resort. Meets Herman Melville; the two form a
        profound friendship. Melville publishes "Hawthorne and His
        Mosses," a manifesto for a distinctive American literature, in
        The Literary World.

1851   Publishes *The House of the Seven Gables*, *A Wonder-Book for
        Girls and Boys*, a new edition of *Twice-told Tales*, and *The
        Snow-Image, and Other Twice-told Tales*, which contains
        uncollected tales and sketches, including "Ethan Brand," "The
        Wives of the Dead," and "My Kinsman, Major Molineux." For
        the first time, earns enough from his writing to support his
        family. Daughter Rose (1851–1926) born, May 20. Melville
        dedicates *Moby Dick* to the "Genius" of Nathaniel Hawthorne.

1852   Publishes *The Blithedale Romance* and *The Life of Franklin
        Pierce*, the presidential candidate's campaign biography. Returns
        to Concord, Massachusetts, purchasing Bronson Alcott's former
        house (renamed "The Wayside"); sister Louisa dies in a
        steamboat accident on the Hudson River, July 27.

1853   Pierce appoints him American Consul at Liverpool, one of the
        most lucrative posts in the Consular Service; his fee-based salary
        will make him a rich man. Publishes *Tanglewood Tales for Girls
        and Boys*. Family leaves for England in July.

1853–57 Lives in England, performing his consular duties conscientiously
        and traveling in the British Isles; records his impressions of
        English life in his notebooks. Publishes second, revised edition
        of *Mosses from an Old Manse* in 1854. Last visits with Melville
        in the autumn of 1856 and the spring of 1857.

1858–59 Hawthornes travel to France and on to Italy, living first in
        Rome, then in Florence, then again in Rome. Records
        impressions in notebooks; becomes friendly with members of
        British and American expatriate artistic community, including
        Robert and Elizabeth Barrett Browning, Harriet Hosmer, Louisa
        Lander, and William Wetmore Story. Begins writing *The Marble
        Faun* in July, 1858, finishing rough draft in January 1859.
        Daughter Una contracts malaria in October, 1858 and becomes
        gravely ill; near death in April, 1859. Family returns to England
        in May, where Hawthorne finishes revising *The Marble Faun*.

1860   Publishes *The Marble Faun* (released in England under the title of *Transformation*). The Hawthornes sail for America, returning to Concord and The Wayside. In the four years until his death, will begin and abandon three new romances, "The American Claimant," "The Elixir of Life," and "The Dolliver Romance."

1862   Visits Horatio Bridge in Washington, D.C.; meets Lincoln. Publishes an essay on the Civil War, "Chiefly About War Matters," in the *Atlantic Monthly*; several pieces on England appear in the same magazine.

1863   Publishes *Our Old Home*, based on *Atlantic Monthly* sketches on England; dedication to Franklin Pierce, now seen as Southern sympathizer, is harshly criticized.

1864   His health deteriorating, he leaves with Pierce on a carriage tour of northern New England. Dies in his sleep at Plymouth, New Hampshire on May 19. Buried in Sleepy Hollow Cemetery, Concord, Massachusetts; pallbearers include Longfellow, Emerson, Alcott, and Holmes. Pieces of his last work appear in the July *Atlantic Monthly*, under the title "Scenes from 'The Dolliver Romance.'"

RICHARD H. MILLINGTON

Introduction

Item one. In the "College" episode of the brilliant HBO series *The Sopranos*, mobster Tony Soprano finds himself sitting in a hallway at Bowdoin College, waiting for his daughter Meadow to complete her admissions interview. We have just watched Soprano set aside his role as bourgeois dad while he garrotes a gangster-turned-informer he has discovered in a nearby town. The camera then shows us the inscription chiseled into the wall above his head: "No man can wear one face to himself and another to the multitude without finally getting bewildered as to which may be true." The author, of course, is identified as Hawthorne, and as the scene ends an undergraduate walks by, informing Tony that "He's our most famous alumnus."

Item two. Dr. Leon R. Kass, the head of President George Bush's Council on Bioethics, assigns the members of the council – a body established to advise the President and the National Institutes of Health on the moral questions raised by controversial research initiatives like cloning – to read Hawthorne's story "The Birth-Mark," and opens the council's first meeting with a discussion of that tale of a scientific enthusiasm gone perversely awry.

Item three. "The Connection," a call-in program on National Public Radio in the US, devotes a show, featuring a panel of Hawthorne scholars, to a discussion of the 150th anniversary of the publication of *The Scarlet Letter*. They take a call from Carolyn, in Boise, Idaho: "I would just like to say that I identified with the book because I was an adulteress, I was a single mother, and I had to raise my children by myself. I make no excuses for that, but because I not only had the shame but the children, I had to become more able, stronger, better at other things . . . I believe that this is the essence of America: that one can overcome inauspicious beginnings. If you make mistakes you can change, you can overcome. Sometimes people don't let you forget it – that's their problem – but I love this book because you can identify with Hester: she made mistakes but she went on." There is a moment of stunned silence as the assembled scholars take in this unexpected fulfillment of the English teacher's dream: a direct and moving testimony that literature matters.[1]

Taken together, these episodes from the life lived by Hawthorne's texts in present-day America give us the figure of Hawthorne that belongs to literate mainstream culture – to the descendants (in a cultural rather than a genetic sense) of Hawthorne's first readers. This Hawthorne, as my examples reveal, has written works to which we return for ethical guidance, for an acknowledgment of life's moral complexity, for encouragement in difficulty. (Indeed, in the scene from *The Sopranos*, Hawthorne operates almost as an icon of the moral, inviting us to take the measure of the ethical confusions of current American life.) We imagine this Hawthorne as the espouser of values we may think of as "universal," time-tested, foundational, and we think of him, in this guise, as a literary master, in full artistic control of the emotional and moral subtlety his works exemplify.

Readers of this *Companion* will encounter a different – though not, finally, an unrelated – writer, the Hawthorne of the colleges and the universities, the figure (or figures) that emanate from the current moment in academic discourse: from classroom discussions, from doctoral dissertations, from scholarly essays like the ones this volume contains. Where the "literary" Hawthorne taps into shared feelings and timeless themes, the "academic" Hawthorne possesses a particular and specifiable relation to the historical moment he writes in. Indeed, many currently practicing Hawthorne scholars would claim that the value of Hawthorne's texts lies precisely in the opportunity they offer to understand a clearly defined and bounded historical moment, while others might argue that the capacity of his texts to illuminate the lives of his current readers derives not from his command of universal human truths but from the fact that the middle-class cultural formations he saw coming into being are still powerfully with us. The "literary" Hawthorne is often imagined to be "above" politics, while the scholar now sees Hawthorne's texts as inevitably and variously political, and the question of whether his texts tend to resist or reinforce the particular ideological orthodoxies of his era has become almost tediously central. Finally, where the traditional Hawthorne's insights – ethical, emotional, psychological – were felt to be the products of a masterfully wielded artistic intention, our new Hawthorne's acuity and value as a cultural analyst is most often understood as the effect of his very embroilment in the conflicts and contradictions, the yearnings and anxieties, of his experience.

While my main purpose here is to introduce the essays that form this volume, I want to take a little time to consider the relationship between the Hawthorne of my opening anecdotes and the Hawthorne we are now studying, and to describe, a little more fully, how their estrangement came about. One might begin by observing that the relationship between these apparently contemporary Hawthornes is historical. The Hawthorne evoked on public radio or discussed in the halls of government is the academic Hawthorne of a previous generation, the author taught in universities to many of the teachers now teaching American literature in US high schools. What split the scholar's Hawthorne from his more mainstream brother was the changing sense of who authors are and what books do that emerged out of the re-encounter between American literature and American history that began in the late 1970s and came to dominate academic writing and training in the eighties and nineties. Out of this encounter came a complex description of conditions of artistic creation, in which institutional structures and ideologies join the imagination as generators of texts and guarantors of artistic reputation, and what writers evade, fail to see, or defend themselves against becomes as revealing and representative as what they do see. Several academic Hawthornes emerge from influential studies of this period, ranging from a remarkably astute analyst of a fast-changing culture (the historicized version of the earlier generation's master) to a figure whose intentions are irrelevant to the value and interest of his texts – which now consist in the access they give us to otherwise submerged ideological narratives that shape American life. Yet, in whatever form this encounter with history has taken, Hawthorne has remained central, an indispensable figure both for those who would defend old verities and those who would demonstrate the validity of new kinds of argument. Let me turn now to the chapters that make up this *Companion*, to the Hawthorne they bring to life, and to the arguments they offer for the value of reading Hawthorne.[2]

In the chapter that begins the collection, "Hawthorne's labors in Concord," Larry J. Reynolds gives the contextual turn in Hawthorne scholarship a local habitation and a distinctive personal intensity. Reynolds demonstrates that Hawthorne's experience of living in Concord, especially his first years of marriage and his relationships to Emerson and Margaret Fuller, profoundly shaped his writing. Concord – as the capitol of Transcendentalism, the most intense field of Emerson's magnetic influence, and an incubator of political and social reform – presented Hawthorne, in bodily form, with the pressing questions – ethical, social, sexual – that he would interrogate in works like "The Birth-Mark," "Rappaccini's Daughter," and *The Blithedale Romance*. The concreteness and specificity of the links Reynolds establishes between life and text make this chapter a rich, compressed literary biography, while the complex emotional life of Hawthorne's Concord, along with his investments in and withdrawals from that life, resonates as revealing cultural history, setting the scene for the chapters that follow.

In "Hawthorne as cultural theorist," Joel Pfister makes the case that Hawthorne was long ago brilliantly engaged in a task that his critics have recently adopted: the delineation and exploration of an emergent middle-class ideology, particularly as it found expression in the emotions and attitudes that form and express the self. Through readings of a wide range of Hawthorne texts, Pfister makes the case that Hawthorne is one of America's "most complex, self-reflexive, daring, and artful cultural theorists." Like many of his fellow contributors, Pfister sees Hawthorne's relation to the ideological processes he explores as complex and ambivalent. While he acknowledges that in some ways these texts assist in the establishment of a new middle-class emotional orthodoxy, Pfister demonstrates how *much* Hawthorne sees, especially about the elusive – but, when seen, revisable – social processes that, in profound and specifiable relation to economic change, make us ourselves. Pfister's Hawthorne, then, serves us less as an object of cultural analysis than an incisive model of how to conduct it.

T. Walter Herbert's "Hawthorne and American masculinity" provides another exemplary case of the possibilities and ambitions of Hawthorne criticism at present, as he uses Hawthorne's characteristically conflicted acuity to write the inner history of American masculinity. Because Hawthorne lives out the creation of a new style of masculinity – the "self-reliant manhood" that replaces the "bloodline hierarchy" of an aristocratic social model – he is able in his writing to show us the operation of that ideological system with disturbing clarity. Alienated from this cultural formation, even as he assents to some of its key values, Hawthorne writes into his texts its definitive features: its generational conflicts, its inner manifestations in self-division and emptiness, its projection of its own contradictions onto women and into the emotional life of marriage. Herbert's Hawthorne – victim, analyst, rebel – is at once deeply embedded in the interior history of his time and deeply useful to his present-day readers, inheritors of the gender system he excavates, as we "encounter, as though face to face . . . the patterning of our minds and hearts."

In the counterpart to Herbert's chapter, "Hawthorne and the question of women," Alison Easton surveys depictions of women in Hawthorne's fiction, from his earliest tales to the unfinished manuscripts that close his career. Easton begins by establishing the historical context within which American thinking about women emerges: as she sees it, ideas about women must be understood in relation to the making of a distinctive middle-class culture, and the assertions of ideology always fall short of the complexities of actual women's lives and the messiness of change. Within this unfolding history, Hawthorne operates ambivalently but insightfully, as his own explorations of the Woman Question track the conflicts and possibilities engendered by a rapidly changing culture. His earliest tales feature isolated female characters who exhibit or suffer in the plots of their lives the uneasiness of a culture in transition, while in crucial texts written after his own marriage ("The Birth-Mark," "Rappaccini's Daughter"), the couple becomes the site of struggles to define the nature and possibilities of women's lives. *The Scarlet Letter* obliquely handles the key questions of contemporary feminism, as they clustered around a new conception of marriage, built on a vision of emotional reciprocity that grounds new kinds of claims about the rights of women. In *The Blithedale Romance* and *The House of the Seven Gables*, Easton strikingly suggests, Hawthorne explores the economic vulnerabilities of middle-class women, as they play their role in the drama of class formation, while *The Marble Faun* seems to offer, via its depiction of Hilda and Miriam, a complex mix of unconvincing orthodoxies and muted possibilities. Like several of our contributors, Easton values Hawthorne's work for its inability or refusal to resolve the conflicts it so usefully exposes.

Three of our contributors give a new, historical force to what might be called questions of genre. In each case, a body of work – the sketch, the children's story – formerly under-interrogated or occluded from critical view, is shown to engage central Hawthornian issues or to perform significant cultural work. In "Hawthorne, modernity, and the literary sketch," Kristie Hamilton establishes the meaning and value of Hawthorne's "sketches" – those open form, loosely structured texts, neither story nor novel, which typically feature encounters between a wandering, observing, or imagining narrator and the fleeting phenomena of everyday life. Through Hamilton's readings, Hawthorne's sketches emerge not as minor texts that tediously or innocuously fill the spaces between the well-known stories but as one of the central interests and accomplishments of his work. Texts like "The Old Apple Dealer," "Foot-prints on the Sea-shore," and "The Old Manse" emerge as exemplary responses to and theorizations of the experience of modernity itself, and the values – aesthetic, experiential, ethical – of the sketch offer its readers a template for negotiating the anxieties and pleasures characteristic of a new, proto-urban American life.

Gillian Brown's chapter, "Hawthorne's American history," explores Hawthorne's sense of history and understanding of national identity – not, in the customary form, through Hawthorne's tales of colonial history, but primarily through his historical writing for children. Through Brown's readings of the historical narratives of *Grandfather's Chair* and her analysis of the sense of historical place generated in his works more generally, Hawthorne emerges as a pioneering theorist of children's literature, and the sponsor, through the imaginative interchanges he stages in such texts, of a distinctively open version of national affiliation. As Brown puts it, "In Hawthorne's seemingly paradoxical sense of national identity, you identify yourself as American by identifying with conventional markers whose artificiality you simultaneously recognize. To be an American is continually to feel a kinship that you can disown." The conjunction of history and childhood is addressed in a different way in Karen Sánchez-Eppler's chapter. Noting that Hawthorne wrote more pieces aimed at a juvenile audience than any other canonical male author of his time, she reads his life and work in relation to the transformation in thinking about child-rearing that marks the reconfiguration of the middle-class family in antebellum America. As the child changed from a potential sinner in need of a strict ruling hand to an idealized, innocent creature who required a strategically tender discipline by love, a market opened up for writing that would assist in that cultural project. Her "Hawthorne and the writing of childhood" argues that we find in his writing for and about children Hawthorne's most self-conscious attempt to enter, respond to, explore, and shape this ideological realm. Though Hawthorne's writings are part of a broad codification and calling into being of this view of childhood, in his texts childhood and its relationships emerge as no less permeable to complexity than adult life, and both his writing and his experience as a parent are marked by a sense of the uncanny mysteriousness and autonomy of children – an ungraspable quality that is both celebrated in his notebooks and figured forth in the character of Pearl. Indeed, Sánchez-Eppler proposes, for Hawthorne the child really *is* father to the man, for it is in his writing and thinking about children that Hawthorne discovers the model for the atmosphere and mix of emotions – "discomfort tinged with wonder and desire" – that distinguishes his practice of romance.

Like the chapters I have been describing, the next four pieces at once capture the present moment in Hawthorne scholarship and, by providing significant new readings of the novels, recast it. Brook Thomas's chapter begins with a question that has exercised many readers of Hawthorne's best-known novel. Why, in the famous forest scene, does Hawthorne generate so much sympathy for his transgressive lovers, but not allow them to begin a new life together? Thomas's answer to this question unfolds as a wide-ranging exploration of Hawthorne's political thought. "Love and politics, sympathy and justice in *The Scarlet Letter*" is a striking departure from previous political readings of the novel, which have ignored or occluded the relationship between questions of power and questions of love. Thomas instead describes the complex balance Hawthorne strikes between valuing the transgressive and the orderly, between espousing sympathy and honoring justice. Thomas's Hawthorne emerges not as conduit of liberal ideology, but as one of its sophisticated theorists.

Like Joel Pfister, Christopher Castiglia focuses on Hawthorne's understanding of the ideological processes that shape the inner self. "The marvelous queer interiors of *The House of the Seven Gables*" argues for the book's appealing sympathy with its "queer" characters – those, like Clifford and Hepzibah, made deviant by their excessive and inscrutable emotions, but whose deviance becomes a kind of hope, pressing back against the normative world as Hawthornian romance resists the conventions of the realistic novel. The defense of the "queer" mounted in the book takes the form of its disruption of two protocols of social control – the law and other manipulations of surface by figures of power, and internal forms of discipline associated with domesticity and reform – a disruption achieved by the tendency of both identities and emotions to exceed the categories thought to define them. Such resistances are at once costly – in the form of feelings of shame and abjection – to the "queer" characters who embody or enact them – and generative, forming the basis for an alternative sociability and ethics, an oblique but resilient happiness.

In "Sympathy and reform in *The Blithedale Romance*," Robert S. Levine reads the novel as a complex interrogation of the sympathy-based culture of reform so central to antebellum culture and its literary production. Though it has been customarily seen as an ironic, even cynical, send-up of the covert hypocrisy and arrogance of reformers and their notions, Levine shows us a book with a much more engaged, and productively critical, relation to the moral and emotional foundations of the wish to improve the lives of others – in short, a "re-radicalized" *Blithedale*. Levine achieves this recasting of the book through a strikingly new reading of Coverdale's narration, which argues that the novel is a later Coverdale's retrospective and comic critique of the limits of sympathy as that virtue was exercised by the sentimental reform culture of the 1850s – and exemplified by his younger self's outrageous shortcomings as both sympathizer and reformer. When read in this light, Coverdale's narrative implicitly urges its readers to ask much harder questions about the requirements of authentic social change and the relation between reformers and the objects of their solicitude. Indeed, the novel makes available, through its other characters, the possibility of imagining "a subaltern world of the poor and disenfranchised that eludes the appropriative gazes of reformers" and a correspondingly concrete sense of the social changes that might actually transform antebellum society.

In a sense, Emily Miller Budick's rich and nuanced chapter gives us the scholarly counterpart of the figure we glimpsed at the beginning of this Introduction, a Hawthorne whose texts become the occasion for a demanding, open-ended, and surprising kind of moral interrogation. In "Perplexity, sympathy, and the question of the human: a reading of *The Marble Faun*,"

Budick proposes that Hawthorne makes an argument about the nature of our responsibility to one another – and, by implication, an argument about the ethical value of art – by demonstrating the betrayal of that responsibility by the book's main characters. For Hawthorne, she claims, ethical action in the world must begin with an acknowledgment of the perplexity and mysteriousness of that world, and such an acknowledgment demands, from both people and forms of art, the apparently simple but almost unrealizable obligation to listen or witness, often uncomfortably and inactively, to the suffering of others. And because the characters of the novel represent not only a particular set of individual desires but also different systems of value and genres of art, the book offers a profound meditation on what the practice of sympathy might mean not only to individuals but to communities and cultures.

One might imagine Gordon Hutner's chapter as a kind of afterword to this volume, but readers might also use it as a point of entry, for it offers a much richer – and perhaps bleaker – account of the recent history of Hawthorne criticism than I have sketched above. "Whose Hawthorne?," riffing on the title of Lionel Trilling's classic 1964 essay "Our Hawthorne," unfolds as a comparison between the "liberal" Hawthorne belonging to an earlier generation of critics, and the "diminished" Hawthorne created by key studies of the eighties and nineties, which took Trilling's Hawthorne as the target and hence the enabler of their dismantling of a whole set of cultural pieties surrounding authorship. Hutner casts a dispassionate eye on both these Hawthornes (as well as a few in between), showing us how the cultural work done by these texts changes with our point of view, and reminding us that there are both losses and gains in the inevitable (but always contestable) "progress" of literary history. Hutner's chapter ends, in effect, with an open question: who will be the author we find in the work of those readers of this *Companion* who are encountering, composing, or teaching *their* Hawthorne even as I write?

Who, then, is this Hawthorne *Companion*'s Hawthorne? Happily, no single figure emerges from these pages, and the reader of this volume will encounter a writer with a striking range of interests, tactics, insights, and evasions – a writer so various, we might say, as to seem almost real. Still, while there is no unanimity in the conception of Hawthorne implicit in these chapters, there is, I think, a characteristic way of viewing the writer and his work that links many of these chapters together and gives us a revealing fix on the academic Hawthorne of the present moment. Again and again in this *Companion*, whether implicitly or explicitly, we encounter a Hawthorne positioned at a point of historical transformation, at the border that marks the emergence of a new configuration of emotional life, a new conception of civil society, a new sensibility attuned to a distinctively modern experience, a new understanding of men and women. The Hawthorne that continues to matter, and to matter so variously, many of these chapters seem to say, is neither a distant master nor an ideological vessel, but a writer made acute by the conflicts of meaning and value emerging all around him, whose articulate discomfort makes him – no less than the steadying Hawthorne spoken for by Carolyn from Boise – crucially of use.

NOTES

1. "College," *The Sopranos*, Season 1. Home Box Office. The information on Leon R. Kass is derived from Nicholas Wade, "Moralist of Science Ponders its Power," *New York Times*, 19 March 2002: C1–2. "The Scarlet Letter," *The Connection*. National Public Radio, WBUR, Boston, 16 June 2000.
2. See the fuller discussion of the recent history of Hawthorne criticism in Gordon Hutner's chapter in this volume. The two most powerful and influential "post-intentionalist" readings of Hawthorne are Sacvan Bercovitch's *The Office of "The Scarlet Letter"* and Lauren Berlant's *The Anatomy of National Fantasy*, both listed in this *Companion*'s Selected Bibliography.

I

LARRY J. REYNOLDS

Hawthorne's labors in Concord

Nathaniel Hawthorne spent three periods of his life in Concord, Massachusetts among a group of friends and neighbors called Transcendentalists. He and his wife Sophia first moved to Concord on 9 July 1842, the day of their wedding, and stayed more than three years at the Old Manse until October 1845, when they moved to Salem. These years are often described by biographers as idyllic, a long honeymoon in Paradise. Hawthorne cultivated this impression through his letters, notebooks, "The Old Manse" sketch, and stories such as "The New Adam and Eve." He left Concord in desperate financial straits, but after living in Salem, Lenox, and West Newton, Hawthorne returned to Concord as the famous author of *The Scarlet Letter* (1850) and *The House of the Seven Gables* (1851), and from May 1852 to July 1853, he lived in a house on the east side of town purchased from the Alcotts, which they called The Hillside and he renamed The Wayside. In 1860, after spending seven years abroad in England and Italy, Hawthorne returned to Concord and The Wayside once more, where he lived until his death in May 1864. He chose not to die there among his family, however, going instead on a trip with his friend Franklin Pierce, who was with him during his final hours in a New Hampshire inn where they had stopped for the night. In *The Blithedale Romance* (1852), Hawthorne, in the voice of his narrator Coverdale speaking of Hollingsworth, anticipated this end when he declared "Happy the man that has such a friend beside him, when he comes to die! . . . How many men, I wonder, does one meet with, in a lifetime, whom he would choose for his death-bed companions!" (III: 39).

The Blithedale Romance has often been read as a fictionalized account of Hawthorne's life at Brook Farm, the utopian community where he spent seven months in 1841, but it can also be seen as a response to his life in Concord during 1842–45. The tensions it treats and the issues it addresses first arose in Concord, where Hawthorne struggled to establish a family and a career surrounded by a group of thinkers, writers, and artists whose ideas, values, and activities challenged his own. Ralph Waldo Emerson, Margaret

Fuller, Henry David Thoreau, Ellery Channing, and Bronson Alcott were some of the would-be friends who disturbed him at the same time they fascinated him. Without apparent intent or malice, they exerted strong psychological pressure upon him, and he labored mightily to contend with their presence and influence. Throughout his life, he chose as his best friends men of limited originality and acuity, such as Horatio Bridge, Henry Wadsworth Longfellow, and Pierce. (Herman Melville, for two years, was the exception.) Though he came to regard Concord as his home, he never felt wholly at ease there. Abolitionism, which he termed "the mistiness of a philanthropic theory" (XXIII: 292), was but the last of a series of issues that put him at odds with his Transcendentalist neighbors. Sophia claimed that her husband was "without theories of any kind,"[1] which she intended as praise, yet the theoretical underpinnings of his conservatism were merely invisible to her and to him. Among the unexamined assumptions he regarded as self-evident truths were that there was a hierarchy of races, that African slaves were mentally and morally inferior to Anglo-European Americans, that men and women should occupy separate public and private "spheres," that a benevolent Providence was at work in the world improving the human condition, and that reform movements, such as utopianism, millennialism, vegetarianism, temperance, women's rights, and abolitionism, were misguided and futile at best, foolish and harmful at worst.

Two of the most prominent "theorists" of the day, persons whose ideas inspired much of the Newness, as it was called, were Emerson and Fuller. He met both at Brook Farm, but it was in Concord, beginning in 1842, that these figures became major influences in his life. The character of Zenobia in *The Blithedale Romance* quite obviously draws upon Fuller and her feminism but Hollingsworth constitutes a subtle partial portrait of Emerson, at least as he was perceived by Hawthorne. Hollingsworth proves the worst kind of friend to have – selfish and cold-hearted. He behaves as a spiritual vampire in his relations with Zenobia, Priscilla, and even Coverdale, and his magnetic attraction flows from his Christ-like image and seductive voice.[2] At Eliot's Pulpit, a huge rock in the woods, the narrator Coverdale has a vision of "the holy Apostle of the Indians, with the sunlight flickering down upon him through the leaves, and glorifying his figure as with the half-perceptible glow of a transfiguration." This vision then merges with the image of Hollingsworth, who ascends the rock and speaks "to us, his few disciples, in a strain that rose and fell as naturally as the wind's breath among the leaves of the birch-tree. No other speech of man has ever moved me like some of those discourses" (III: 119). Hollingsworth proves to be no holy apostle, however, but rather a cold, heartless, masquerader, willing to sacrifice others to his perfectionist schemes. Coverdale, from his "hermitage," sends a warning message to the fair Priscilla, telling her "that Hollingsworth's heart is on fire with his own purpose, but icy for all human affection, and that, if she has given him her love, it is like casting a flower into a sepulchre" (III: 100). In a number of ways, this warning stems from Hawthorne's "living for three years within the subtile influence of an intellect like Emerson's" (I: 25), as he puts it in "The Custom-House." The adjective "subtile," with its meanings of fine or keen on the one hand and sly or insidious on the other, captures the ambivalent feelings of attraction and repulsion with which Hawthorne regarded Concord's leading citizen. As this chapter will show, in Concord, he came to see Emerson as an angelic friend and a manipulative idealist, whose influence appeared chilling and often Satanic in its effects.

Hawthorne both identified with and tried to separate himself from this rival, especially in the realms of private affection and worldly regard. In "The Old Manse," his technique for dealing with Emerson is to place him and his followers a safe distance away. The sketch opens with the literal polarity of "two tall gate-posts" (X: 3) and ends with a reference to "my worst enemy" (X: 35), upon whom the author would not inflict his work. Though he expresses admiration for Emerson as a poet, he claims to seek "nothing from him as a philosopher" (X: 31) and emphasizes their geographical as well as intellectual separation. Emerson's house was "at the opposite extremity of our village" (X: 30) and thus marginal to "our magic circle" (X: 29) of repose Hawthorne attributes to the Manse. His writing style in the sketch – the apparently meandering structure, the slow-paced sentences, the images of peace and quiet – also serves to convey a political conservatism antithetical to the political activism at the other end of town. Using the concept of enchantment, Hawthorne strives to convey the superiority of his position gently and imperceptibly. "In one respect," he writes,

> our precincts were like the Enchanted Ground, through which the pilgrim travelled on his way to the Celestial City. The guests, each and all, felt a slumberous influence upon them; they fell asleep in chairs, or took a more deliberate siesta on the sofa, or were seen stretched among the shadows of the orchard, looking up dreamily through the boughs. (X: 28)

The "great want" of mankind is "sleep!," he declares, and this is his gift to his guests. There is a subtext to this creation that brings its benevolence into question, however, for, as Hawthorne was well aware, the Enchanted Ground of *Pilgrim's Progress* is the work of the devil, intended to lull pilgrims to sleep and thus prevent them from reaching heaven. In Part II, the guide explains that it is one of the last Refuges that the Enemy to Pilgrims has; wherefore it is as you see, placed almost at the end of the Way, and so it standeth against us with the more advantage. For when, thinks the Enemy, will these Fools be so desirous to sit down, as when they are weary; and when so like to be weary, as when almost at their Journeys end?[3]

Though enamored of Bunyan's allegorical narrative technique, Hawthorne thus seems willing to play the role of the devil as he borrows from it. His goal is to create a romantic imaginative space able to counter the theories, the activism, the frantic search for social reform, of the "hobgoblins of flesh and blood" (x: 30) at the other end of town.

The decision of the Hawthornes to move to Concord after their wedding in July 1842 owed much to Emerson himself, who had taken up residence in the village just before his wedding to his second wife Lidian in 1835. Once settled, Emerson sought to draw friends and admirers around him. "Here is a proposition for the formation of a good neighborhood," he wrote in his journal. "Hedge shall live at Concord, & Mr Hawthorne: George Bradford shall come then; & Mrs. Ripley afterward. Who knows but Margaret Fuller & Charles Newcomb would presently be added? These if added to our present kings & queens, would make a rare, an unrivalled company."[4] An obvious and benign goal of Emerson's project was to establish an ideal community that went beyond the boundaries of the isolated household yet avoided involvement with the "unrepentant" public. Though Emerson resisted the temptation to join the utopian community Brook Farm, because of its artificial design, he nevertheless believed that bringing likeminded friends to his village would allow each to meet and interact with one another "naturally," during walks in the woods or unannounced visits to one another's homes.[5] "Those of us who do not believe in Communities, believe in neighborhoods & that the kingdom of heaven may consist of such,"[6] he affirmed in May 1842.

Emerson was well aware that he displayed coldness in personal relations, including those with his wife. "A photometer cannot be a stove,"[7] he told her, implying she should not expect heat from a device meant to register light. Yet, despite his constitutional detachment, he sought to bring others near him because of the vitality they provided. Living with arrested consumption and always worried about dying young of lung failure like his brothers Edward and Charles, Emerson, after reading the Persian poet Hafez, declared, "expression is all we want: not knowledge, but vent: we know enough; but have not leaves and lungs enough for a healthy perspiration and growth."[8] The linking of leaves and lungs suggests a key insight into

Emerson's need for friends, for like leaves and lungs, friends provided him with inspiration and growth, feeding his spiritual body, keeping it vital. In his essay "Friendship" he elaborates upon the use of friends: "Is it not that the soul puts forth friends as the tree puts forth leaves, and presently, by the germination of new buds, extrudes the old leaf?"[9] What matters is not the life and death of the leaves, then, essential as they are, but rather the growth of the tree. Even in his essay "Experience," which treats the death of his young son Waldo in 1842, he calls the child "caducous,"[10] as if he were merely a leaf falling to the ground in the cadence of the seasons, having given the living ongoing tree (Emerson's soul) spiritual nourishment. In his poem "Saadi," published in the October 1842 *Dial*, Emerson offers a fascinating self-conception: "Most welcome, they who need him most, / They feed the spring which they exhaust."[11] In other words, he needs disciples as they need him. They revitalize him.

During the early 1840s as Emerson was attracting the Hawthornes and others to Concord, he drew upon a number of conceptual models to structure the kind of neighborhood he felt suitable to his needs; one was theological and involved Concord as an embattled cloud-land, out of which he, in the role of defiant archangel, supported by lesser lights, would utter truths that would send shudders through the "stern old war-gods"[12] of heaven (i.e., the Unitarian clergy of Boston and Harvard who attacked his "Divinity School Address"); a second model was educational and involved establishing an alternative open university in Concord, resembling the school of ancient Athens, where he and his friends would become peripatetic philosophers teaching young students and one another; the third was a utopian socialist community, an alternative to Brook Farm, located within Emerson's own home; and finally, the fourth was a version of the Mount of Transfiguration where Emerson would be a shining Christ on high, surrounded by awestruck disciples. (This fourth model at times transmogrified into a Golden Seraglio, with Emerson as a chaste Oriental prince surrounded by spiritual concubines.) Not surprisingly, each of these models had mixed success when Emerson tried to bring it to bear upon his actual circumstances; however, the fourth, featuring the Mount of Transfiguration, exerted considerable power within the Concord circle, and Hawthorne studied it closely, seeking to reverse its polarity.

Even before Emerson moved to Concord, he was looking for high ground upon which to see and be seen. "A year hence shall we not build a house on Grandfather's hill facing Washusett & Mondnoc & the setting sun?"[13] he asked his brother Charles. Such a plan satisfied his desire for the distant prospect and the opportunity to regulate social space much as a colonial authority would. Throughout the 1840s, Emerson colonized Concord with a number of his friends, and the most famous instance of his distribution and arrangement of differential space was his persuading Thoreau to build a cabin on Emerson's woodlot at Walden Pond, which practically made this Concord native into his tenant farmer; Thoreau, in exchange for use of the land, gave the Emersons a portion of the vegetables he grew there. In 1845 after Thoreau built his cabin, Emerson bought forty more acres across the pond and planned to put a house up on the cliffs there. He wrote Thomas Carlyle that "perhaps it will have two stories & be a petty tower, looking out to Monadnoc & other New Hampshire Mountains. There I hope to go with book & pen when good hours come."[14] He never followed through on this plan.

Thoughts of mountains, towers, and high ground, however, offered Emerson a sense of spiritual elevation and lent support to his conception of himself as the transfigured Christ. The biblical scene, as you may recall, appears in Matthew 17, which reads, "And after six days Jesus took with him Peter and James and John his brother, and led them up a high mountain apart. And he was transfigured before them, and his face shone like the sun, and his garments became white as light." When Emerson first saw Raphael's painting of this scene in Rome in 1833, he was deeply moved and recorded in his journal that "it seems to call you by name."[15] This painting, the most famous in the world at the time, depicts in its upper half a luminous Christ suspended above the mountain top within a region of brilliant white light. He looks upward with a serene gaze. As a young minister Emerson had identified with Christ, and his later self-representation as transfigured Christ structured his relations with members of his Concord circle. Wesley T. Mott has shown that Emerson, as an introspective young minister in 1826, regarded Jesus as his hero and "increasingly he came to discover traits in Jesus that he wished to emulate."[16] And as Joel Porte has shown, by 1836 in *Nature*, Emerson was actually identifying with the visionary voice of Christ.[17] One of the most telling signs that Emerson had made the transition from speaking about Jesus to speaking as Jesus appears in the following self-admonition in his journal:

> He that unites himself to the race separates himself from the Father but he who by love & contemplation dwells with the father, from him the Race always proceeds filially & new, and the actual race feel in his presence their degeneracy & his salutary redeeming force. Keep thyself pure from the race. Come to them only as savior, not as companion.[18]

Emerson's self-fashioning in these terms had amazing success with those Hawthorne knew well. In June 1839, Elizabeth Peabody visited the Emersons in Concord and wrote to her sister Sophia, saying, "Here I am on the Mount of Transfiguration, but very much in the condition of the disciples when they were prostrate in the dust." After describing her conversation with Emerson, she says that "Mr. Emerson is very luminous, and wiser than ever. Oh, he is beautiful, and good, and great!"[19] Thoreau, too, acquired this conception of Emerson, and in 1843 expressed in his journal his respect for his friend: "I have a friend, whom I heartily love, Whom I would always treat tenderly Who indeed is so transfigured to me that I dare not identify thy ideal with the actual."[20] And Sophia Peabody, before she married Hawthorne, subscribed to Emerson's Transcendental idealism and found him "the greatest man that ever lived . . . In all relations he is noble. He is a unit. His uncommon powers seem used for right purposes . . . He is indeed a 'Supernal Vision.' "[21] Sophia even tried to get Hawthorne to go with her to see and hear Emerson lecture, but he declined.

Emerson did not have to expend much energy to draw the Hawthornes to Concord, however, for they were predisposed to settle there. When Sophia visited the Emersons in May of 1840, she wrote Hawthorne describing the village, and he felt attracted at once. "Would that we could build our cottage this very now, this very summer, amid the scenes which thou describest. My heart thirsts and languishes to be there" (xv: 475). After the couple visited in May of 1842 and Emerson showed them around, they became even more convinced that it should be their first home. At the Manse and later at The Wayside, they hung on the walls a print of Raphael's *Transfiguration* which was a gift from Emerson himself. He gave it to Sophia ostensibly to thank her for a medallion she had made from a portrait of his brother Charles.

When Hawthorne moved to Concord he thus entered an Emersonian world, which inspired and challenged him. Emerson had preceded Hawthorne in his new house, the Manse, in the affections of his wife, Sophia, and in the natural setting he now found so appealing.[22] The Manse had been associated with the Emerson family for years: Emerson's grandfather had built the parsonage (in 1765); Emerson's father had been born there (in 1769); and Emerson himself had lived there (in 1834). Hawthorne's "little nook of a study," as he calls it in "The Old Manse," had been Emerson's own when he began *Nature*. "He was then," Hawthorne relates, "an inhabitant of the Manse, and used to watch the Assyrian dawn and the Paphian sunset and moonrise, from the summit of our eastern hill" (x: 5). Emerson had not built a house on this hill as he had planned – surely a relief to Hawthorne – but rather, this "great original Thinker" (x: 30), as Hawthorne calls him, lived at the other end of town. There his "wonderful magnetism" drew "young visionaries" to him, and from there he set out to conquer Hawthorne as a friend. As Sophia relates in one of her letters, "Mr. Emerson delights in him; he talks to him all the time, and Mr. Hawthorne looks answers. He seems to fascinate Mr. Emerson. Whenever he comes to see him, he takes him away, so that no one may interrupt him in his close and dead-set attack upon his ear."[23]

One result of Emerson's "attack," as Sophia calls it, was Hawthorne's decision to write about contemporary issues and contemporary figures, including Emerson. Whereas previously he had drawn upon New England history for the content of his tales, of the twenty-one pieces he wrote at the Manse for the collection *Mosses from an Old Manse* (1846), many include settings, issues, and characters impinging on his present life. In "The Old Manse," he subjects his more active neighbors to light satire: "Never was a poor little country village infested with such a variety of queer, strangely dressed, oddly behaved mortals, most of whom took upon themselves to be important agents of the world's destiny, yet were simply bores of a very intense water" (x: 31–32). When he turns to Emerson, himself, Hawthorne uses even more subtle satire, exaggerating the man's luminosity: "It was good," Hawthorne writes ". . . to meet him in the wood-paths, or sometimes in our avenue, with that pure, intellectual gleam diffused about his presence, like the garment of a shining-one . . . it was impossible to dwell in his vicinity, without inhaling, more or less, the mountain-atmosphere of his lofty thought" (x: 31). Before extending such praise, Hawthorne raises a question about the benevolence of this panoptic seer by describing his appeal to those "bats and owls and the whole host of night-birds, which flapped their dusky wings against the gazer's eyes, and sometimes were mistaken for fowls of angelic feather" (x: 31). The hellish features of the scene suggest that this figure may share some traits with Lucifer, the shining rebel angel who led his minions to hell.

In "The Celestial Rail-road," written in March 1843,[24] Hawthorne presents a sly caricature of Emerson in the character of Mr. Smooth-it-away, a gentlemanly stockholder of the railroad that supposedly takes modern pilgrims to the Celestial City with none of the difficulty faced by Christian in Bunyan's *Pilgrim's Progress*. Mr. Smooth-it-away explains how the famous "Slough of Despond" has been rendered no obstacle to modern pilgrims. "You observe this convenient bridge," he says. "We obtained a sufficient foundation for it by throwing into the slough some editions of books of morality, volumes of French philosophy and German rationalism, tracts, sermons, and essays of modern clergymen, extracts from Plato, Confucius, and various Hindoo sages, together with a few ingenious commentaries upon texts of Scripture." This constitutes a fair jab at Transcendental eclecticism, and despite Mr. Smooth-it-away's testimony that the bridge is solid, the narrator notices that it "vibrated and heaved up and down, in a very formidable manner" (x: 187). Later, the pilgrims encounter more explicit evidence of the "Newness" when they pass a cave that is home to the "Giant Transcendentalist." This beast "makes it his business to seize upon honest travelers, and fat them for his table with plentiful meals of smoke, mist, moonshine, raw potatoes, and saw-dust." As for his form, features, and substance, no one has been able to describe them, and as the travelers catch a hasty glimpse of him, he looks "like a heap of fog and duskiness" (x: 197). At the end of the story, the passengers must transfer to a steam ferry-boat and at this moment it becomes clear they are bound for hell rather than heaven. As Mr. Smooth-it-away waves farewell from the shore, he is revealed as the devil in disguise: "And then did my excellent friend, Mr. Smooth-it-away, laugh outright; in the midst of which cachinnation, a smoke-wreath issued from his mouth and nostrils; while a twinkle of lurid flame darted out of either eye, proving indubitably that his heart was all of a red blaze" (x: 206). Soon afterward, the narrator awakens from his dream.

Due to his own struggles to free himself and his wife from Emerson's influence, Hawthorne more than once satirized those held in Emerson's thrall. In his story "Hall of Fantasy," published in James Russell Lowell's *The Pioneer*, in February 1843, Hawthorne describes those who visit this imaginary place of dreams, fantasies, and visions, including a number of American authors, businessmen with wild commercial schemes, inventors of fantastic machines, noted reformers of the day, and religious fanatics. While observing the first group, the narrator relates that

> Mr. Emerson was likewise there, leaning against one of the pillars, and surrounded by an admiring crowd of writers and readers of the Dial, and all manner of Transcendentalists and disciples of the Newness, most of whom betrayed the power of his intellect by its modifying influence upon their own. He had come into the hall, in search, I suppose either of a fact or a real man; both of which he was as likely to find there as elsewhere. No more earnest seeker after truth than he, and few more successful finders of it; although, sometimes, the truth assumes a mystic unreality and shadowyness in his grasp. (x: 637–38)

This emphasis on Emerson's search for "a real man" apparently stemmed from Emerson's own approach to Hawthorne himself. In a letter to her mother dated 3 September 1843, Sophia praised Hawthorne's social graces by declaring

> Whatever he does, he does perfectly & like a man. And even Mr. Emerson who is ever searching after a *man*, used always to call him "The Man." Of me he asked "How is the *man* yonder?" when I met him. He had sense enough to see that it was all right, because he also as well as Mr. Hawthorne is *great*, but Mr. Emerson is not so whole sided as Mr. Hawthorne.[25]

Hawthorne successfully discredited Emerson in Sophia's eyes during their stay at the Manse, using techniques of satire and ridicule similar to those in his fiction; however, as he manipulated her views, he may have acquired guilt about doing so.[26] His fiction, beginning with his years at the Manse, highlights the victimization of women by men who possess mesmeric power. In *The House of the Seven Gables*, for example, he dramatizes Holgrave's hold over Phoebe, a character modeled on Sophia: "A veil was beginning to be muffled about her, in which she could behold only him, and live only in his thoughts and emotions." Later the narrator says, "There is no temptation so great as the opportunity of acquiring empire over the human spirit" (II: 212), and although Holgrave resists this temptation, Hawthorne seems to have wondered whether he himself had. When Sophia first met Hawthorne, she sensed the danger of his magnetism. "His presence," according to their son Julian, "from the very beginning, exercised so strong a magnetic attraction upon her that instinctively, and in self-defence as it were, she drew back and repelled him."[27] After their marriage, however, she came to trust him and told her mother, "He loves power as little as any mortal I ever knew; and it is never a question of private will between us, but of absolute right . . . His will is strong, but not to govern others."[28] Though Hawthorne's married life at the Old Manse appears on the surface to have been ideal, an undercurrent of dis-ease pervades the *American Notebooks*, as if Hawthorne knew some of his activities could not withstand moral scrutiny.

Some modern commentators on the marriage have blamed Sophia for the guilt Hawthorne displays. Walter Herbert, for one, has argued that

> Nathaniel could not expunge the self-assertion from Sophia's adulation, nor could he fail to recognize that her selflessness was managed so as to place pressure on his conscience. She treated him like a god, as believers generally do, with a prostration that embodied her hatred of the all-too-godlike power he exercised over her, and also expressed her determination to extract as many compensatory benefits as possible.[29]

Similarly, Brenda Wineapple has portrayed Sophia as a tyrannical, "mighty woman" able to use her poor health as "ample weaponry" against family members.[30] We have no direct evidence of Sophia's hatred or manipulation of Hawthorne, only her words expressing absolute devotion, and I would argue that Hawthorne himself cultivated this devotion and felt anxiety about his apparent success. Throughout his *American Notebooks*, one finds hints of his sense of his own corruption, and in his tales, the theme of the victimization of women predominates after his marriage. When he talks of the Concord River, in which he bathed daily and in which he learned to escape temporarily from the domestic scene within the Manse, a sense of identification emerges and ambivalence about its nature. He criticizes it for its muddiness and lethargy, and after bathing one day in Walden Pond, he confesses, "A good deal of mud and river-slime had accumulated on my soul" (VIII: 337). He discovers two kinds of water lilies growing in the river, a spotless white one, and a noisome, unclean yellow one, and in his notebook, he associates the first with his wife, the second with himself: "I possess such a human and heavenly lily, and wear it in my bosom. Heaven grant that I myself may not be symbolized by its yellow companion" (VIII: 319). When he imported this entry into "The Old Manse," he omitted the reference to himself.

Hawthorne's doubts about his own moral state as he labored to overcome Emerson's hold upon Sophia seem to have informed two of the most powerful stories he wrote at the Manse, "The Birth-Mark" and "Rappaccini's Daughter." Both explore the destructive effects upon a young woman of male dominance disguised as benign perfectionism. "The Birth-Mark" features the attempt by Alymer, the husband, to remove from the cheek of his new bride Georgianna a birthmark resembling a small hand, symbol of earthly imperfection, sexual desire, and prior possession by another. This mark provokes Alymer to use his knowledge and skill to remove it, which he does, killing his adoring wife in the process. As she dies, "a hoarse, chuckling laugh was heard again!" (x: 56) coming from the sooty Aminadab, mocking Alymer's impotence. Similarly, "Rappaccini's Daughter" features the death of an innocent young woman due to male rivalry and domination. Though well-intentioned, Dr. Rappaccini imprisons and slowly poisons his daughter to protect and perfect her; his rival Baglioni, through his protégé Giovanni, thwarts Rappaccini, killing Beatrice by means of the antidote he supplies. "To Beatrice . . . as poison had been life, so the powerful antidote was death." And as she dies, Baglioni calls out "in a tone of triumph mixed with horror," "Rappaccini! Rappaccini! And is *this* the upshot of your experiment?" (x: 28). Even in "The Artist of the Beautiful," as Owen Warland struggles to compete with the rough blacksmith, Robert Danforth, for the affections of Annie, the woman they both love, Owen ends up abusing her for her obtuseness. When she touches the minute machine he has made, "the artist seized her by the wrist with a force that made her scream aloud. She was affrighted at the convulsion of intense rage and anguish that writhed across his features" (x: 461). Though Owen by means of his artistry appears to rise above his rival at the end, the story leaves open the question of whether his creation of the Beautiful, in the form of the mechanical butterfly, compensates for the loss of the actual woman he once loved.

In these stories written at the Manse, it is the woman's recognition that she does not measure up to her would-be lover's ideal that hurts more than his physical treatment of her. Georgianna sees the disappointment in Alymer's eyes every time he looks at her and thus succumbs to his experiment. Beatrice sees hatred for her poisoned person in Giovanni's eyes, which is why she drinks the deadly antidote. And Annie turns to Danforth after Owen makes it clear she lacks the sensitivity he desires. Did Sophia ever feel such rejection and hurt? One entry in her journal, made in the winter of 1843, hints that she may have. Following a snowstorm, she writes,

> The earth was delicately white & the gold sunlight played on it like the glow of rubies upon pearl. My beloved was truly satisfied with the beauty (of its kind) & he is so seldom satisfied with any thing – weather, things or people that I am always glad to find him pleased. His demand is for perfection, & nothing short can content him. How can seraphs be contented with less.[31]

How indeed? Hawthorne, it seems, could be simultaneously angelic and as harsh as the devil. According to his sister-in-law Elizabeth, he used to say he inherited the "granite" that was in his father, Captain Hathorne, known as "the sternest man that ever walked a deck."[32]

During his years at the Manse, as he was taking Emerson's measure, seeing in him traits that he himself shared, Hawthorne gathered key information from their mutual friend, Margaret Fuller, who felt attracted to both men. During the summers of 1842 and 1844, Fuller went back and forth between the Manse and Emerson's house, where she was staying. Her friendship with Emerson had already peaked, but during these years, her friendship with Hawthorne deepened, spurred in part by Emerson's detachment. It would have been difficult for the two men to have remained unaware of the other's relations with Fuller. On 21 August 1842, she and Hawthorne spent an idyllic afternoon in Sleepy Hollow discussing all manner of topics. In his notebook, he records,

> Then we talked about Autumn – and about the pleasures of getting lost in the woods – and about the crows, whose voices Margaret had heard – and about the experiences of early childhood, whose influence remains upon the character after the recollection of them has passed away – and about the sight of mountains from a distance, and the view from their summits – and about other matters of high and low philosophy.   (VIII: 343)

Their intimacy is disrupted by an "intruder" who calls to Margaret and emerges "from the green shade; and behold, it was Mr. Emerson, who, in spite of his clerical consecration, had found no better way of spending the Sabbath than to ramble among the woods." This "intruder" takes Fuller away to his house while Hawthorne hurries home "where my little wife was very busy getting tea" (VIII: 343). This account, perhaps one source of the central forest scene of *The Scarlet Letter*,[33] suggests the unusual openness Hawthorne displayed in his relations with Fuller. In the summer of 1844, they became even closer as they went for moonlight walks and boat rides on the Concord and spent much time alone together. After one outing, Fuller confided in her journal,

> Last night in the boat I could not help thinking each has something – more all. With Waldo how impossible to enjoy this still companionship, this mutual visionary life. With William even . . . But then H[awthorne] has not the deep polished intellect of the one or the pure & passionate beauty of the other. He has his own powers: I seem to want them all.[34]

As Hawthorne surely discovered, the Fuller–Emerson relationship, though chaste, was emotionally charged. Fuller had initiated what Emerson called his "Summer Romance" in 1840, filling him with a desire to live with her and three new friends she had brought to him: Caroline Sturgis, Anna Barker, and Samuel Ward. Until Ward and Barker married, Emerson imagined that all of his friends, especially the beautiful Anna, the flirtatious Caroline, and the challenging Margaret, might live together with him, creating a multiple union of souls.[35] In a journal entry of 16 August 1840, he described the difficulties such spiritual polygamy faced, saying, nothing would

> be so grateful to me as to melt once for all these icy barriers, & unite with these lovers. But great is the law. I must do nothing to court their love, which would lose my own. Unless that which I do to build up myself, endears me to them, our covenant would be injurious. Yet how joyfully would I form permanent relations with the three or four wise & beautiful whom I hold so dear, and dwell under the same roof or in a strict neighborhood. That would at once ennoble life. And it is practicable.[36]

Emerson, it seems, persuaded himself that to establish such intimate relations posed no threat to his marriage. In fact, as Robert Richardson has pointed out, "in the early 1840s Emerson was living emotionally, though not physically, in what would now be called an open marriage . . . Nor were any of the new friendships clandestine. Lidian knew all about them, was herself often present, frequently copied Emerson's letters, and counted both Fuller and Sturgis among her own friends."[37] When marriage claimed his followers, though, Emerson reacted like a rejected suitor. Upon learning that Barker would marry Ward, he was crushed. In a letter to Sturgis, he confessed,

> The news which Anna told me at Cambridge affected me at first with a certain terror. I thought that the whole spirit of our intercourse at Concord implied another resolution. I thought she had looked the world through for a man as universal as herself & finding none, had said, "I will compensate myself for my great renunciation as a woman by establishing ideal relations."

In the letter Emerson goes on to assert that the poor world stands in "much need of shining examples of Denial,"[38] and he regrets that these two souls took a conventional path. Though married to Lidian, he sought from those he drew near a celibate intimacy that went beyond marriage in its elevation and importance. Whether this was fair to Lidian, he gave little thought, and neither did Fuller, but Hawthorne seems to have studied the situation. After a walk with Hawthorne through Sleepy Hollow in the summer of 1844, Fuller thus lamented her single state: "I shall never forget that my curse is nothing compared with that of those who have entered into those relations but not made them real: who only *seem* husbands, wives, & friends. H[awthorne] was saying as much the other evening."[39] Clearly it is the Emerson marriage he has in mind.

Hawthorne's engagement with the issues of marriage and ideal relations in Concord during the 1840s placed him within a larger national discussion about new experiments in living, including Fourier's "loves of harmony," the Shakers' radical celibacy, the Oneidans' "complex marriages," early Mormon polygamy, and the free love movement.[40] The new alternatives to traditional marriage, especially those proposed by Fourier, repelled Hawthorne, but others in Concord were willing to explore them, if only conceptually. Fuller, while trying to avoid becoming "intoxicated" with Emerson's presence, joined with him in reading the Persian Saadi's *The Desatir: or Sacred Writings of the Ancient Persian Prophets*, becoming entranced at times. After she took leave of him on 3 August 1844, she wrote in her journal of the form "half transfigured, of my Saadi so soft, so sweet to day! At parting I rose: he still sate with his eyes cast down. His hand I pressed to my heart: it was a gentle vow. He looked like the youngest child."[41] In this quotation, we catch glimpses of the sexual overlay that at times characterized Emerson's relations with his devout followers, and it is in this way that the image of the transfigured Christ becomes entwined with that of a Persian prince presiding over a virginal harem. An aroma of the erotic hangs over the conception, but Fuller in *Woman in the Nineteenth Century* (1845) speaks to the celibacy of such a living arrangement and points out that the Persian sacred books describe the great and holy prince Ky Khostrou, as being "an angel, and the son of an angel" . . . This Prince had in his Golden Seraglio three ladies of surpassing beauty, and all four, in the royal monastery, passed their lives, and left the world, as virgins. The Persian people had no skepticism when the history of such a mind was narrated.[42]

Why, she implies, should anyone object to such spiritual polygamy.

What Fuller disingenuously ignores, however, is the existence of another conception of the Orient at odds with her own. Whereas she, Emerson, and other Transcendentalists saw the Orient as a model for love in its highest, most pure form, Hawthorne and many of his contemporaries associated it with an exotic sensual world, where the harem suggested love slaves, imprisoned in a luxurious setting. As Luther S. Luedtke has shown, Hawthorne drew upon *The Arabian Nights* and the travel writings of European and American travelers to imbue his works with the exotic Otherness of this second conception, especially as he created his dark "Oriental" heroines: Beatrice Rappaccini, Hester Prynne, Zenobia, and Miriam Schaefer. "The intrigues between Hawthorne's bonded, passionate women and the male travelers who approach them with desire and fear," Luedtke points out, "were grounded in the many first-hand accounts Hawthorne had read of purdah, seraglios, and their captives in the East."[43] They were also grounded, I believe, in his knowledge of Emerson's magnetic hold upon a number of young persons, including Sophia and Fuller, during the late 1830s and early 1840s. In *The Blithedale Romance*, Hawthorne describes a luxuriant grapevine to convey his impression of Hollingsworth as a type. High in the white pine where Coverdale has his hermitage, "a wild grapevine, of unusual size and luxuriance, had twined and twisted itself up into the tree, and, after wreathing the entanglement of its tendrils around almost every bough, had caught hold of three or four neighboring trees, and married the whole clump with a perfectly inextricable knot of polygamy" (III: 98). Obviously, the snakelike behavior of this vine is meant to suggest its satanic qualities.

Hawthorne's observations of Emerson's polygamous propensities fed into his writings it seems, as did his own interactions with Fuller. She certainly shared the Oriental exoticism that Hawthorne attributed to a number of his dark female heroines, and she provided insight into the power and limitations of women within a patriarchal society. Thomas R. Mitchell has argued that the intense feelings aroused in Hawthorne by Fuller at this time found their way into "Rappaccini's Daughter" and all of the major romances, where Hawthorne struggled to exorcise Fuller's power over him. "Fuller posed a threat to him in a way that Emerson did not," Mitchell writes, "for by the example of her life, the insight of her texts, and the attraction she held for him, she called into question the very terms by which Hawthorne had defined his relationship with Sophia and challenged him to an intimacy that those very terms had served to deflect."[44] Hawthorne (in an infamous Italian notebook entry of 3 April 1858) writes about Fuller's "evil and defective nature" (XIV: 156), but the charge is baseless given her kindness to all who knew her well, and puzzling in light of Hawthorne's previous friendliness. It does make sense, though, if one sees it as motivated by guilt and anger about his attraction to her.[45] As for Sophia's whereabouts during Hawthorne's time spent with Fuller, she was occupied with the new baby Una, whom she was nursing, and she also went to Ellen Fuller Channing's house to nurse her new baby Greta. When Hawthorne was completing "Rappaccini's Daughter," in October 1844, several months after Fuller had departed Concord, Sophia asked him "Is Beatrice to be a demon or an angel?" and he responded "I have no idea!"[46]

Emerson's belief that chastity and celibacy were needed to establish the highest forms of human relations was shared by many in his circle, but the Hawthornes strongly disagreed. Thoreau's most explicit argument on behalf of purity through chastity appears in the "Higher Laws" chapter of *Walden*, where he asserts that "Chastity is the flowering of man; and what are called Genius, Heroism, Holiness, and the like, are but various fruits which succeed from it."[47] In Fuller's *Woman in the Nineteenth Century*, inspired in part by Anna and Sam's marriage, she explores the many barriers and injustices faced by women and urges them to stay single and chaste: "I have urged on woman independence of man, not that I do not think the sexes mutually needed by one another, but because in woman this fact has led to an excessive devotion, which has cooled love, degraded marriage, and prevented either sex from being what it should be to itself or the other."[48] The most enthusiastic praise of her argument came from Charles Lane, the English Transcendentalist who came to Concord in the fall of 1842, joined Alcott and his family at Fruit-lands, almost persuaded the Alcotts to forgo sexual relations, to Mrs. Alcott's dismay, and later joined the Shakers when Fruitlands failed. In his review, Lane declared, "The purity, we might almost say the existence of the species, depends more on continence, than on marriage. Self denial is the only hopeful means for any improvement, whether moral or physiological."[49]

The celebration of ideal relations, based on self-denial, continence, and chastity, expressed by the writers clustered around Emerson, challenged and provoked the Hawthornes, who were enjoying their new conjugal relations at the Manse. Sophia's erotic dances and willful voluptuous laziness brought them both much bliss, and following a visit of Charles Lane to the Manse, she wrote about the miraculous form that was her body. "Before our marriage," she declares, "I knew nothing of its capacities & the truly married alone can know what a wondrous instrument it is for the purposes of the heart . . . The profane never can taste the joys of Elysium – because it is a spiritual joy, & they cannot perceive it."[50] Her response to Fuller's book was that if Fuller "were married truly, she would no longer be puzzled about the rights of woman."[51] And as for Emerson's thoughts on friendship and love, Sophia spoke for her husband and herself when she told her mother in 1843 that "Waldo Emerson knows nothing of Love. He has never yet said any thing to show that he does. He is an isolation – He has never yet known what union meant with any Soul."[52] Herbert in *Dearest Beloved* has discussed the tensions and instability within the Hawthornes' marriage and has argued that they arose from mutual antagonism; however, my sense is that the tensions he locates within the marriage should be relocated between the Hawthornes and the rest of the Concord community. Hawthorne's portrayal of sexual repression in his works, then, does not signify misogynist loathing, but rather, his critique of the perverse purity of Emerson and his followers.

It is not sexuality that Hawthorne critiques as cold, twisted, and deadly in his writings, for he was less a Puritan than Emerson. "The Birth-Mark," "Rappaccini's Daughter," "The Artist of the Beautiful," and *The Scarlet Letter* respond, rather, to the sexual repression crucial to Emerson's conception of ideal human relations. In *The Scarlet Letter*, Hawthorne holds up for examination both the sacred, sexual love of Hester and Arthur and the loveless, sexless marriage of Hester and Roger, the latter a legal union imposed upon a beautiful young girl by a cold, selfish scholar. Hester claims that it is "a fouler offence committed by Roger Chillingworth, than any which had since been done him, that, in the time when her heart knew no better, he had persuaded her to fancy herself happy by his side." Hawthorne voices his accord by warning men not to impose upon a woman "the marble image of happiness" instead of "the warm reality" (1: 176). It is not adultery, then, that is the original sin of *The Scarlet Letter*, but rather a forced, loveless marriage, which Chillingworth sought "in order that the chill of so many lonely hours among his books might be taken off the scholar's heart" (1: 176). Like Hollingsworth, he has acted as a vampire, feeding off the innocence and vitality of his young wife, who turns elsewhere for love.[53]

Hawthorne completed his next study of unnatural unions, *The Blithedale Romance*, just before moving back to Concord in 1852. Ironically, the house and nine acres Hawthorne purchased from the Alcotts for $1,500 was at Emerson's end of town, less than a mile down the road. Emerson had recently completed his own fiction writing with Fuller's *Memoirs*, in which he sought to protect the image of this friend by downplaying her mystical side and claiming she had married the father of her child.[54] Hawthorne, on the other hand, had just portrayed her in the figure of Zenobia, a beautiful feminist, who drowns herself after being rejected by Hollingsworth. Emerson found *The Blithedale Romance* "ghastly and untrue,"[55] referring to its treatment of Brook Farm and Zenobia/Fuller, but one wonders if he saw himself in Hollingsworth. In any case, as Hawthorne and Emerson approached the age of fifty, their interests turned from personal relations to the current political scene, which was becoming more and more divisive due to the Fugitive Slave Act and the abolitionist movement. When Hawthorne moved to Concord, he found that Emerson and many of his followers, including Thoreau and Alcott, had become avid supporters of abolitionism, and this development further challenged his attempts to counter social realities with romance.[56]

During this stay of fourteen months, Hawthorne's success as romance writer allowed him to make a calculated effort to improve his financial lot by writing a campaign biography of his friend Franklin Pierce and a collection of children's stories entitled *Tanglewood Tales* (1853). Some sense of his tepid political enthusiasm can be seen in his response to the visit of the great Hungarian revolutionary Kossuth. In a letter to E. P. Whipple, Hawthorne asked "Are you a Kossuthian? I am about as enthusiastic as a lump of frozen mud, but am going to hear him at Charlestown, tomorrow, in hope of warming up a little" (XVI: 537). In *The Blithedale Romance* Hawthorne satirizes his own lack of political activism, when he has Coverdale say,

> Were there any cause, in this whole chaos of human struggle, worth a sane man's dying for, and which my death would benefit, then – provided, however, the effort did not involve an unreasonable amount of trouble – methinks I might be bold to offer up my life. If Kossuth, for example, would pitch the battle-field of Hungarian rights within an easy ride of my abode, and choose a mild, sunny morning, after breakfast, for the conflict, Miles Coverdale would gladly be his man, for one brave rush upon the leveled bayonets. Farther than that, I should be loth to pledge myself. (III: 246–47)

As Richard Brodhead has pointed out "typically, the quickening of Hawthorne's sense of involvement in the larger struggles of a society in conflict ends up producing not deepened commitment but deepened irony toward such commitment. The main source of this irony is Hawthorne's unregenerate fantasy."[57] The lethargy and repose Hawthorne cultivated in "The Old Manse" sketch persisted in his account of his own political interests, yet he displayed keen political instincts when his self-interest was involved. Soon after Pierce was nominated for President of the United States by the Democratic Party (the party most sympathetic at the time to the South and slavery), Hawthorne volunteered to assist him, claiming he sought nothing in return. In the Pierce biography, Hawthorne tried to diminish the importance of the anti-slavery cause by calling slavery "one of those evils which divine Providence does not leave to be remedied by human contrivances, but which, in its own good time, by some means impossible to be anticipated, but of the simplest and easiest operation, when all its uses shall have been fulfilled, it causes to vanish like a dream" (XXIII: 416–17). After Pierce's election to the presidency, he rewarded Hawthorne with the Liverpool consulate, reputedly the most lucrative office available.

After Hawthorne returned to Concord in 1860, he felt anew the need to protect himself from its more radical political currents (he had just had a running argument with his sister-in-law Elizabeth Peabody that hardened his opposition to abolitionism). During this period, he wrote a series of essays about England published as *Our Old Home* (1863) and tried to complete several romances treating the themes of the ancestral footstep and the elixir of life. These remained unfinished at his death and are now included in two volumes of his collected works, *The American Claimant Manuscripts* and *The Elixir of Life Manuscripts*. A sense of confusion and frustration characterizes Hawthorne during these years, and his letters indicate he felt homeless. "I have lost my home-feelings for the present, if not forever" (XVIII: 356), he wrote a friend in England. He tried to make The Wayside into a congenial setting through changes to the house, and like Emerson in the 1840s, he now sought high ground, building himself a towered study and spending hours in it and on the hilltop behind his house. Alcott, who tried unsuccessfully to befriend Hawthorne during these years, commented upon his "dodging about amongst the trees on his hilltop" (XVIII: 363) and hiding out in his "stolen castle" (XVIII: 364), secure from invasion. For a brief time, Hawthorne was excited by the Civil War, but his enthusiasm soon faded and he felt an "infinite weariness. I want the end to come, and the curtain to drop, and then to go to sleep" (XVIII: 543).

In his final years, Hawthorne found himself more and more at odds with his fellow Concordians. Emerson had defended John Brown and report-edly said his hanging would "make the gallows as glorious as the cross"[58]; Hawthorne publicly criticized Emerson in the essay "Chiefly About War Matters," and told Horatio Woodman, "I wish he would not say such things, and deem him less excusable than other men; for his apophthegms . . . do not so burn and sting his mouth that he is compelled to drop them out of it" (XVIII: 463). When Hawthorne dedicated *Our Old Home* (1863) to Pierce as an expression of loyalty at a time when the former president was being accused of treason during the Civil War, many in the North expressed out-rage. Emerson tore the dedication out of his complimentary copy and wrote in his journal that Hawthorne was "unlucky in having for a friend a man who cannot be befriended; whose miserable administration admits but one excuse, imbecility. Pierce was either the worst, or he was the weakest, of all our Presidents" (quoted in v: xxviii). Hawthorne justified the dedication by telling his sister-in-law Elizabeth that Pierce's "steadfastness and integrity" were "to me more sacred and valuable than the faculty of adapting one's self to new ideas, however true they may turn out to be" (xviii: 590). Though Hawthorne found slavery repugnant, he found violent political action, such as Brown's raid on Harpers Ferry and the Civil War itself, more so.

A number of explanations have been offered for Hawthorne's inability to complete his romances during his final years, including the shock of the Civil War, the disorientation caused by his years abroad, and the intimidation he felt about his own reputation, but more important than these was the debility caused by the means he had previously devised to contend with the activism of Concord's leading figures, that is, the Enchanted Ground of romance that no longer protected but, rather, enervated him. Wandering back and forth on the hill behind The Wayside, Hawthorne realized his refuge had become a prison, as he always feared it might. In one version of his last unfinished manuscript, he reveals how he has become the captive of the world he created. As the protagonist Septimus takes a walk to Boston, Hawthorne writes, "What a potency there is in change of place! . . . with every step that he took, it seemed as if he were coming out of a mist; out of an enchanted land, where things had seemed to him not as they really were." He passes "witch-like boundaries" and then feels "a great depression" fall upon him (xiii: 129). In the first person, Hawthorne's voice then intrudes in his narrative to declare, "I know well what his feeling was! I have had it oftentimes myself, when long brooding and busying myself on some idle tale . . . I have chanced to be drawn out of the precincts enchanted by my poor magic." At this point in the manuscript, Hawthorne inserts a note to himself: "(put the above in the third person)" (xiii: 130). When Septimus returns from Boston to Concord, the journey again conflates the Enchanted Land of "The Old Manse" with the Transcendentalism of the town as a whole: "with every step that he took, he found himself getting insensibly back again into the old enchanted land. The mist rose up about him; the pale mist bow of ghostly promise arched before him; and he trod back again, poor boy, out of the clime of real effort into the land of his dreams and shadowy enterprise" (xiii: 146).

In a later version of this unfinished story, Hawthorne makes the protagonist's home in Concord even more forbidding; it "seemed a more forlorn and wretched place than he could endure; a dismal dungeon, and his hillside, a growth of gloomy pines, among which he would gaze around seeking one on which to hang himself" (xiii: 447). As the protagonist, now named Hilliard, struggles to leave the village during the Revolutionary War period, he walks one or two miles down the road and feels as if he had come out of an Enchanted Land, where he had dwelt so long that his proper life and consciousness was in it, and his nature so much acclimated there that it had become his home; and now, by his sudden step out of that fantastic sphere upon the firm earth, all stable things seemed to whirl round, and made him dizzy.   (XIII: 445)

Several pages later, the manuscript breaks off as the protagonist contemplates "the readiest passage out of [his] existence" (XIII: 448). As Hawthorne thus fell victim to his own dream-work, the Civil War energized his neighbors. "Emerson is as merciless as a steel bayonet" (XVIII: 544), he wrote to a friend, and the image not only describes Emerson's commitment to the War, but also reveals the threat his activism posed to the writer of romance living down the road. The Transcendental sage of Concord had become a weapon-like foe, hurting Hawthorne severely at last without realizing it.

In an influential study, Richard Brodhead has speculated that "As Hawthorne acceded to the role of canonical author he himself began to find his work a bore," and apathy, lassitude, and ennui were the result.[59] Although this conclusion accords with Hawthorne's own self-criticism, it does not square with his actual labors. Hawthorne kept putting words on the page by the thousands.[60] Yet, like his protagonists, he had become a captive of his own Enchanted Ground. He thought for a time he wished to write about reclaiming a lost estate in England, and then about discovering the secret to immortal life, and finally a combination of the two, yet what lay behind these efforts was the question of how to contend with a world outside of his own imaginative creation, especially when no help was to be found there. Earlier he had cast Sophia in the role of his savior, the Dove who rescued him from "Castle Dismal," as he called the Manning house in which he spent his youth and the twelve years after graduation from Bowdoin College. In "The Custom House," it was the fabricated "A" of Hester Prynne that helped replace his toppled head, his emasculated self-image. Now, the towered Wayside was his, his Dove safely ensconced inside, yet the problem of imprisonment remained. Hawthorne's Wayside had become an unreal estate and its location in Concord was one reason why. There lived those who made him feel guilty about his conservative values and conventional friends. There lived those he had tried to marginalize but had successfully marginalized him. "Hawthorne lived afar from us," Emerson later recalled for a visitor. "He was always haunted by his ancestry . . . His gait and moods were of the sea. He had kinship to pirates and sailors."[61]

In "The Old Manse," Hawthorne claimed, after describing an enjoyable Transcendental experience on the river with Ellery Channing, that he found it sweet to return to the Manse, "not as to a dungeon and a chain, but as to a stately edifice, whence we could go forth at will into statelier simplicity!" The "gray, homely aspect" of the Manse, he says, rebuked "the speculative extravagances of the day! It had grown sacred, in connection with the artificial life against which we inveighed" (x: 25). At the end of his life, however, his second home in Concord was not only a stately edifice, thanks to the thousands of dollars spent on renovations, but "a dungeon and a chain" as well. He escaped from it at last, long enough to travel to Plymouth, New Hampshire and die with his friend Franklin Pierce at his side, but his body was brought back to Concord, where it was buried in the appropriately named "Sleepy Hollow."

NOTES

1. "Sophia Peabody Hawthorne's *American Notebooks*," ed. Patricia Dunlavy Valenti, in Joel Myerson, ed., *Studies in the American Renaissance, 1996* (Charlottesville: University Press of Virginia, 1996), p. 146.
2. Taylor Stoehr has discussed the free-love atmosphere in which *The Blithedale Romance* appeared and its relation to contemporary works such as Charles Wilkins Webber's *Spiritual Vampirism: The History of Etherial Softdown, and Her Friends of the New Light* (1853); see Stoehr's *Hawthorne's Mad Scientists: Pseudoscience and Social Science in Nineteenth-Century Life and Letters* (Hamden, CT: Archon Books, 1978), pp. 201–09.
3. John Bunyan, *The Pilgrim's Progress*, ed. N. H. Keeble (New York: Oxford University Press, 1984), p. 250.
4. *The Journals and Miscellaneous Notebooks of Ralph Waldo Emerson*, ed. William Gillman *et al.*, 16 vols. (Cambridge, MA: Belknap Press, Harvard University Press, 1960–82), VIII: 172–73. Hereafter abbreviated as *JMN*.
5. For an excellent discussion of Emerson's plans for a natural community in Concord, see Mary Kupiec Cayton, *Emerson's Emergence: Self and Society in the Transformation of New England, 1800–1845* (Chapel Hill: University of North Carolina Press, 1989), pp. 191–217.
6. *The Letters of Ralph Waldo Emerson*, ed. Ralph L. Rusk and Eleanor M. Tilton, 9 vols. (New York: Columbia University Press, 1939–94), III: 51.
7. *Ibid.*, IV: 33.
8. *JMN*, x: 68.
9. Ralph Waldo Emerson, *Essays: First and Second Series* (New York: The Library of America, 1990), p. 114.
10. *Ibid.*, p. 243.
11. See Ralph Waldo Emerson, *Collected Poems and Translations* (New York: The Library of America, 1994), p. 98–103, for the entire poem.
12. See "Uriel," in *ibid.*, pp. 15–16.
13. *Letters of Emerson*, I: 445.
14. *The Correspondence of Emerson and Carlyle*, ed. Joseph Slater (New York: Columbia University Press, 1964), p. 399. For a detailed account of Emerson's relations to various experiments in living, see Taylor Stoehr, "Transcendentalist

Attitudes Toward Communitism and Individualism," *ESQ: A Journal of the American Renaissance* 20 (2nd quarter, 1974): 65–90.

15. Emerson repeated this statement in his essay "Art," where he praises the painting's familiarity:

> A calm, benignant beauty shines over all this picture, and goes directly to the heart. It seems almost to call you by name. The sweet and sublime face of Jesus is beyond praise, yet how it disappoints all florid expectations! This familiar, simple, home-speaking countenance is as if one should meet a friend. The knowledge of picture-dealers has its value, but listen not to their criticism when your heart is touched by genius. It was not painted for them, it was painted for you; for such as had eyes capable of being touched by simplicity and lofty emotions.
>
> (*Essays: First and Second Series*, p. 207)

16. Wesley T. Mott, " 'Christ Crucified': Christology, Identity, and Emerson's Sermon No. 5," in Joel Myerson, ed., *Emerson Centenary Essays* (Carbondale: Southern Illinois University Press, 1982), p. 36.

17. Joel Porte, *Representative Man: Ralph Waldo Emerson in His Time* (New York: Oxford University Press, 1979), p. 76.

18. *JMN*, VIII: 186.

19. *Letters of Elizabeth Palmer Peabody*, ed. Bruce A. Rhonda (Middletown, CT: Wesleyan University Press, 1984), pp. 225, 226.

20. Henry D. Thoreau, *Journal, Volume 3: 1848–1851*, ed. John C. Broderick, *et al.* (Princeton, NJ: Princeton University Press, 1990), p. 18.

21. Julian Hawthorne, *Nathaniel Hawthorne and His Wife: A Biography*, 2 vols. (1884; rpt. New York: Archon Books, 1968), I: 186–87.

22. For analyses of the Hawthorne–Emerson relationship, see Gay Wilson Allen, "Emerson and Hawthorne, Neighbors," *Essex Institute Historical Collections* 118 (January 1982): 20–30; John McAleer, *Ralph Waldo Emerson: Days of Encounter* (Boston: Little, Brown, 1984), pp. 392–97, 411–21, and Larry J. Reynolds, "Hawthorne and Emerson in 'The Old Manse,' " *Studies in the Novel* 23 (Spring 1991): 60–81.

23. Hawthorne, *Nathaniel Hawthorne and His Wife*, I: 271.

24. Dates of composition for the Old Manse pieces are provided in John Joseph McDonald, "The Old Manse Period Canon," *Nathaniel Hawthorne Journal* 2 (1972): 13–39.

25. Henry W. and Albert A. Berg Collection, The New York Public Library, Astor, Lenox and Tilden Foundation.

26. See Reynolds, "Hawthorne and Emerson," 73–77.

27. Hawthorne, *Nathaniel Hawthorne and His Wife*, I: 180.

28. *Ibid.*, I: 271.

29. T. Walter Herbert, *Dearest Beloved: The Hawthornes and the Making of the Middle-Class Family* (Berkeley: University of California Press, 1993), p. 29.

30. Brenda Wineapple, "Nathaniel Hawthorne, 1804–1864: A Brief Biography," in Larry J. Reynolds, ed., *A Historical Guide to Nathaniel Hawthorne* (New York: Oxford University Press, 2001), p. 22.

31. "A Sophia Hawthorne Journal, 1843–44," edited by John J. McDonald, in C. E. Frazer Clark, Jr., ed., *The Nathaniel Hawthorne Journal 1974* (Englewood, CO: Microcard Edition Books, 1975), pp. 1–30; 8.

32. Hawthorne, *Nathaniel Hawthorne and His Wife*, I: 182.

33. See Thomas R. Mitchell, *Hawthorne's Fuller Mystery* (Amherst: University of Massachusetts Press, 1998), pp. 141–50.

34. " 'The Impulses of Human Nature': Margaret Fuller's Journal from June through October 1844," ed. Martha L. Berg and Alice de V. Perry, *Massachusetts Historical Society Proceedings* 102 (1990): 105. Berg and Perry identify "William" as William Hull Clark, with whom Fuller may have had an ill-fated love affair in 1843.

35. For an informative account of this "romance," see Dorothy Berkson, " 'Born and Bred in Different Nations': Margaret Fuller and Ralph Waldo Emerson," in Shirley Marchalonis, ed., *Patrons and Protégés: Gender, Friendship, and Writing in Nineteenth-Century America* (New Brunswick, NJ, and London: Rutgers University Press, 1988), pp. 3–30.

36. *JMN*, VII: 509–10.

37. Robert D. Richardson, Jr., *Emerson: The Mind on Fire* (Berkeley: University of California Press, 1995), p. 329.

38. *Letters of Emerson*, VII: 404.

39. " 'The Impulses of Human Nature,' " 92.

40. For specifics of this discussion, see Carl J. Guarneri, *The Utopian Alternative: Fourierism in Nineteenth-Century America* (Ithaca, NY: Cornell University Press, 1991), pp. 353–63.

41. " 'The Impulses of Human Nature,' " 109.

42. Margaret Fuller, *Woman in the Nineteenth Century*, ed. Larry J. Reynolds (New York: Norton, 1998), p. 83, n. 3.

43. Luther S. Luedtke, *Nathaniel Hawthorne and the Romance of the Orient* (Bloomington and Indianapolis: Indiana University Press, 1989), p. xxiv.

44. Mitchell, *Hawthorne's Fuller Mystery*, p. 120.

45. See Larry J. Reynolds, *European Revolutions and the American Literary Renaissance* (New Haven, CT: Yale University Press, 1988), p. 80.

46. Hawthorne, *Nathaniel Hawthorne and His Wife*, I: 360.

47. Henry David Thoreau, *The Illustrated Walden*, ed. J. Lyndon Shanley (Princeton, NJ: Princeton University Press, 1973), pp. 219–20.

48. Fuller, *Woman in the Nineteenth Century*, p. 103.

49. Quoted in *ibid.*, p. 228.

50. "Sophia Peabody Hawthorne's *American Notebooks*," p. 133.

51. Hawthorne, *Nathaniel Hawthorne and His Wife*, I: 257.

52. Henry W. and Albert A. Berg Collection, The New York Public Library, Astor, Lenox and Tilden Foundation.

53. For a discussion of the links between the Emersons' marriage and that of Hester and Chillingworth, see Herbert, *Dearest Beloved*, pp. 188–90.

54. For an account of the efforts of Emerson, William Henry Channing, and James Freeman Clark to create an acceptable image of Fuller in her *Memoirs*, which they edited, see Bell Gale Chevigny, "The Long Arm of Censorship: Mythmaking in Margaret Fuller's Time and Our Own," *Signs* 2 (1976): 450–60.

55. Quoted in McAleer, *Ralph Waldo Emerson*, p. 420.
56. For an overview of Hawthorne's attitudes toward the slavery controversy, see Jean Fagan Yellin, "Hawthorne and the Slavery Question," in *A Historical Guide to Nathaniel Hawthorne*, pp. 135–64.
57. Richard Brodhead, "Hawthorne and the Fate of Politics," *Essays in Literature* 11 (Spring 1984): 98.
58. *New York Daily Tribune*, quoted in Ralph L. Rusk, *The Life of Ralph Waldo Emerson* (New York: Columbia University Press, 1949), p. 402.
59. Richard H. Brodhead, *The School of Hawthorne* (New York: Oxford University Press, 1986), p. 79.
60. Nina Baym makes this point in her *The Shape of Hawthorne's Career* (Ithaca, NY and London: Cornell University Press, 1976), p. 252.
61. Quoted in McAleer, *Ralph Waldo Emerson*, p. 420.

2

JOEL PFISTER

Hawthorne as cultural theorist

Over the past couple of decades, many scholars have reread American authors and their literature as complicit carriers of capitalist, imperialist, nationalist, class, gender, ethnoracial, and sexual ideologies. This critical emphasis on literature's ideological relations to the reproduction of social contradictions has placed literary studies in a more provocative dialogue with cultural theory. In developing this dialogue, it is equally important to recognize that American authors have from the get-go been among America's most complex, self-reflexive, daring, and artful cultural theorists. When critics grant many of these authors and their fictions the credit they deserve, it is easier to see that their creative insights contribute much to modern understandings of the workings – and political possibilities – of culture.

I owe a special debt to Nathaniel Hawthorne for inspiring me to think about such matters, for my earliest readings of his work led me to value American literature as a theoretical resource.[1] In his "Custom House" preface to *The Scarlet Letter* (1850) Hawthorne punned on "customs" when he portrayed himself as a Surveyor of Customs. The term describes not only the government post he held in the Salem Custom House, but also a key aspect of his role as a writer who critically surveyed his culture's customs, habits of seeing and feeling, and patterns of making significance. Hawthorne learned – and unlearned – much through his narratives, allegories, and anti-allegories of culture, contradiction, and meaning production. To clarify my appreciation of Hawthorne's power as a cultural theorist, I offer here some brief analyses of his fictions. What I consider, however, is partial – by no means the whole story, or stories.

Social critic and cultural theorist

Hawthorne's fiction often addressed issues, themes, contradictions, and perspectives taken up by mid nineteenth-century social critics. In 1843 and 1844 alone his tales and sketches featured critical and sometimes satirical views of the demon of machinery, the ideology of technology-as-progress, destructive modes of labor, the exploitation of seamstresses in urban sweatshops, growing class division in cities, and money-mad American millionaires.[2] Even Hawthorne's retelling of Greek myths in *A Wonder-Book for Girls and Boys* (1851) engages in social criticism. "The Golden Touch," for instance, hints that nineteenth-century capitalist "love" and "value" can destroy rather than enrich family life: Midas turns to gold a daughter whom – he realizes too late – he loves much more than gold. The Hawthorne who was fired as Surveyor of Customs knew mid nineteenth-century New England not so much as the Puritans' "howling wilderness" that Young Goodman Brown allegorized as ruled by devils, but as the howling marketplace.[3] "In this republican country, amid the fluctuating waves of our social life," the narrator of *The House of Seven Gables* (1852) muses, "someone is always at the drowning point" (II: 38). Hawthorne was capable of being sexist, anti-Semitic, racist, and insufferably middle class – a purveyor of customs. More important, he had an admirable self-critical inclination to explore beyond his own ostensible ideological preferences. In writing fiction that shook up his own ideological tendencies, his social criticism often developed analytically as cultural theory.

Hawthorne's "Main-street" (1849), for example, gives a selective chronicle of Main Street from the era of Native-occupied "Salem" to the witch-hunts of the 1690s. This history is performed as a puppet show. The puppeteer-historian exhumes "Indians," dissenters, religious martyrs, and others ideologically immured beneath Main Street in his effort to restore historical memory. Pre-invasion Main Street is barely a path: "The white man's axe has never smitten a single tree; his footstep has never crumpled a single one of the withered leaves, which all the autumns since the flood have been harvesting beneath" (XI: 50). The puppeteer imagines how Squaw Sachem and her husband Wappacowet, a necromancer, would be horrified if they

> could see, as in a dream, the stone front of the stately hall, which [in the American future] will cast its shadow over this very spot; if he could be aware that the future edifice will contain a noble Museum, where, among countless curiosities of earth and sea, a few Indian arrowheads shall be treasured up as memories of a vanished race!
>
> (XI: 51)

As one twentieth-century critic wrote: "The Anglo-Saxon smashes the culture of any primitive people that gets in his way, and then, with loving care, places the pieces in a museum."[4] But in Hawthorne's "museum" the reader is encouraged to remember the smashing. Later the puppeteer relates how in the late seventeeth century the grandson of Squaw Sachem and Wappacowet sells his beaver skins in Salem only to obtain money to get drunk. The Christian marketplace lays "pavements" – like mendacious history books – "over the red man's grave" (XI: 55).

The Puritans' "Anglo-Saxon energy" (XI: 57) is a cocksure cultural and economic energy that uses religion as an imperialist alibi to persecute Natives and dissenters. It is like a collective version of the energy that drives Hawthorne's monomaniacs who chillingly insist: *it needs be done.* Hawthorne investigates how culture – made real through the built environment, categories of (racial, gender, class, religious) difference, and habits – can accustom its members to a set range of ways of producing and organizing life. Cultural structures – colonizing structures – take shape inside as well as outside minds and bodies. Puritan colonizers erect their buildings, and impose their customs, values, and ways of identifying in the hope of making it all seem like the only imaginable legitimate authority and reality. Dissenters are imprisoned, pilloried, burdened with halters, and whipped. The puppeteer even dramatizes the public whipping of a bare-breasted Quaker, Ann Coleman. Hawthorne, perhaps putting his own "soul" into every stroke of his pen, indicts his ancestor's perverse "spirit":

> A strong-armed fellow is that constable; and each time that he flourishes his lash in the air, you see a frown wrinkling and twisting his brow, and, at the same instant, a smile upon his lips. He loves his business, faithful officer that he is, and puts his soul into every stroke, zealous to fulfil the injunction of Major Hathorne's warrant, in the spirit and to the letter. (XI: 70)

In these ways Hawthorne uses fiction and history to unveil how certain fabrications of reality and "souls" were struggled over and made dominant – fabrications that did not always exist and that by implication can be changed. By the late seventeenth century the second-generation Puritans simply assumed that their Main Street – their familiar form of the Christian marketplace – had been "one of the perdurable things of our mortal state" (XI: 71). In 1940 Walter Benjamin, a great cultural theorist associated with the Frankfurt School, contemplated the largely unwritten history of the "anonymous forced labor" that has made so much wealth, culture, and systemic inequality possible, and asserted: "There has never been a document of culture which was not at one and the same time a document of barbarism."[5] Hawthorne, like Benjamin, wanted his readers to consider how barbarism took the form of "culture" – not only as cultural "documents," but as structures of daily life, customs, premises. His fiction attempts to see through, below, and beyond (some of) the cultural facades of Main Street America.

The industrial reorganization of intimacy

Hawthorne's "Fire Worship" (1843) is more than just a charming sketch about the increasing popularity of parlor stoves. Its analysis of the industrial transformation of domestic intimacy – like "Main-street" – is historically materialist in its explanation of the social making of consciousness.[6] The cast-iron stove, according to the narrator, has ignited a "great revolution in social and domestic life" (x: 138). It makes obsolete the open hearth, which is romanticized nostalgically as a symbol of the well-ordered, pre-industrial community wherein the warmth of faith and loyalty humanized public and private bonds: "While a man was true to his fireside, so long would he be true to country and law, to the God whom his father worshipped, to the wife of his youth, and to all things else which instinct or religion has taught us to consider sacred" (x: 140). The stove facilitates and symbolizes industrial America's colonization of the home.

Hawthorne's narrator personifies the stove's fire as an exploited laborer in iron confinement – reminiscent of the proletarians in New England's proliferating factories. "Alas! blindly inhospitable, grudging the food that kept him [fire] cheery and mercurial, we have thrust him into an iron prison, and compel him to smoulder away his life on a daily pittance which once would have been too scanty for breakfast!" (x: 139). The fire that propels the "steamboat" and "rail-car" languishes even at home as an air-tight "prisoner of his cage" (x: 139–40). While hearths frame visions of transcendence, stoves entomb the damned. "Voices talking almost articulately within the hollow chest of iron . . . my fire wood must have grown in that infernal forest of lamentable trees, which breathed their complaints to Dante." These gothic "sighs, burdened with unutterable grief" seemingly endanger the sentimental middle-class home: "We tremble, lest he should break forth amongst us" (x: 144). Here Hawthorne may have alluded to middle-class anxieties about widespread labor unrest and the formation of workers' unions in the late 1830s.

Hawthorne envisions the stove as an industrial agent of what can be termed "selfing." All selves are to some extent products of or responses to dominant material, cultural, and ideological processes of selfing.[7] The stove, the narrator suggests, helps produce a new form of air-tight domestic selfing characterized by mutual emotional privatization. "Domestic life, if it may still be termed domestic, will seek its separate corners, and never gather itself into groups." Air-tight intercourse will "contract the air of debate" (xi: 146).

Nonetheless, the narrator confesses that he has acquired several stoves – for their efficiency and economy.

"Fire Worship" contributes to what historian Philippe Ariès in 1960 nominated "the history of feelings." In the mid nineteenth century, Ariès argues, an "emotional revolution" accompanied the Industrial Revolution.[8] Hawthorne's sketch, like Ariès's history, situates industrial capitalism and homelife, factories and affections, the need for efficiency and sentiment, in the same analytical and explanatory framework, and imaginatively contributes to the theorizing and historicizing of material, cultural, and ideological machineries of selfing. The historical materialism of "Main-street" and "Fire Worship" affirms Antonio Gramsci's belief that the "starting point of critical elaboration is the consciousness of what one really is, and is 'knowing thyself' as a product of the historical process to date which has deposited in you an infinity of traces, without leaving an inventory."[9]

Cultural innerselfing

Hawthorne excelled as a cultural theorist of subjectivity formation. He conceptualized subjectivity in at least two ways that could be at odds. First, as in "Main-street" and "Fire Worship," he took account of the historical, material, and cultural "selfing" of the self. A clear example of Hawthorne's relational approach to the social selfing of selves is evident in Zenobia's remark about her more feminized half-sister Priscilla in *The Blithedale Romance* (1852): "She is the type of womanhood such as man has spent centuries in making" (III: 122). Zenobia perceives "womanhood" not as something natural or given upon which culture operates, but as an ideological invention of patriarchal culture that purveys an illusion of naturalness or psychological givenness. Hawthorne frequently foregrounded the idea that subjectivity is socially fabricated, not simply expressed.

Second, in other instances Hawthorne posited subjectivity as an expression of an "inner" *psychological self*. In *The Scarlet Letter* the agitated Dimmesdale emerges from his forest liaison with Hester usurped by his transgressive "inner man." Once his "man" is unrepressed, Dimmesdale's "interior kingdom" experiences "a total change of dynasty and moral code." The adulterous minister is seemingly overtaken by "a profounder self" than the self which he had felt constrained to present to the public. He desires to do "wicked thing[s]" that "would be at once involuntary and intentional, in spite of himself" (I: 217). In such passages Hawthorne reads subjectivity more categorically than relationally. The emphasis is more on the psychological force – rather than the cultural making – of Dimmesdale's "inner man."

Since the mid nineteenth century, middle-class readers have celebrated this second Hawthornian approach to subjectivity. In his 1851 review of Hawthorne, Henry Tuckerman gushed: "What the scientific use of lenses – the telescope and the microscope – does for us in relation to the external universe, the psychological writer achieves in regard to our own nature." Henry James lauded Hawthorne's "anatomizing" as "the deeper psychology." Numerous twentieth-century critics have compared Hawthorne and Sigmund Freud to suggest that it is Hawthorne's proto-psychoanalytic wisdom that makes his fiction "deep."[10]

While one might well value the psychological insights celebrated by these earlier critics, what may seem like Hawthorne's proto-psychoanalytic orientation should not be understood mainly as Yankee insight into a universal psychological self. Instead, that psychological discourse itself must be grasped as a historical, cultural, and ideological development integral to the production of class identity – an identity generally thought of as middle-class individuality. Hawthorne, along with some other antebellum psychological and sentimental authors, advice book writers, and book reviewers, was engaged in inventing a nascent – often compensatory – pop psychology for the middle class. This is a key ideological trend in the "emotional revolution" that was intertwined with the Industrial Revolution. This complex antebellum literature of the "emotional revolution," understood historically, made Freud's later psychoanalytic imaginings of the self and of the family predictable, in the sense that these fictions were, decades earlier, encoding and narrating – that is, helping to remake – the individual and the family *as* fundamentally psychological. Thus, Freud does not "explain" Hawthorne. Rather, nineteenth-century middle-class fiction like Hawthorne's, situated historically, helps to "explain" (the later emergence of) Freud and the popularity of psychoanalysis among the American bourgeoisie.

Hawthorne's two approaches to subjectivity – as product of cultural selfing or as psychological essence – have different political implications. His pop psychological fiction often conceived of "liberation" in highly individualized and socially narrow terms as the resistance of a desiring self to a culture reductively defined as systems of taboo (later articulated as the Freudian notion of culture-as-repression).[11] Hence Dimmesdale is tempted to mock Puritan taboos after his forest walk on the wild side with Hester. When Hawthorne's fictions advance more relational understandings of subjectivity, the struggle for liberation does not depend on giving expression to a middle-class inner self that society represses; it seems to rely more on identifying how the cultural selfing of subjectivity (usually labeled "individuality") is constituted by (transformable) social forces.

Of course, Hawthorne's two approaches to representing subjectivity some-times appear in the same fiction. In "Main-street," Hawthorne criticizes an "American" ideological self-perception shaped by structures – symbolized by Main Street's buildings and pavements – that promoted an historical amnesia which effaced the contradictions of Puritan imperialism. But Hawthorne's critique of the Puritans also deploys a repressed "inner man" model – note Sheriff Hathorne's constable's "smile" as he whips. This Puritan "inner man" makes an appearance in other tales, such as "Endicott and the Red Cross" (1838) and "The May-Pole of Merry Mount" (1836). Hawthorne uses these "inner men" to take psychosexual revenge on his Puritan forefathers by hint-ing that they projected impulses they denied in themselves onto others and then from these same tabooed impulses received substitutive satisfactions when persecuting the others. Consequently, the Puritans who persecute the pagan merrymounters for frolicking around the phallic maypole gain simi-lar – though displaced and disguised – satisfactions from lacerating them on their erect whipping post.

If it can be contended that the pop psychological slant of Hawthorne's fiction helped pave the way for a modern therapeutic narrowing of cul-tural theory (liberation defined as an individualized and psychologized battle against cultural repression and taboo), it can also be argued that Hawthorne's more social perceptions of how cultural selfing works expand our theoret-ical understanding of cultural and literary headmaking, heartmaking, and soulmaking. By engaging in the psychological and sentimental selfing of the middle class *and* by blowing the whistle on these ideological processes of class and gender selfing, Hawthorne gained remarkable insight into – and into his own participation in – the cultural emergence of American literature as a subjectivity industry. When the three (understudied) sketches to which I shall now turn are considered as a thematic cluster, it will be easier for me to suggest what was at stake in Hawthorne's contributions to and critiques of cultural and literary systems of what I will call "innerselfing."

In "A Book of Autographs" (1844) Hawthorne's narrator analyzes the handwriting of several of America's founding fathers as marks of character. (Early in the next century Freud – who inherited this romantic search for clues to "innerness" – would assign deep significance to psychopathological "parapraxes" such as slips of the tongue.)[12] Hawthorne's mid nineteenth-century interest in signs that might disclose the inner self was by no means unique, for rapid social, economic, and demographic change made the quest for precision in detecting motives and character seem exigent. Thus phre-nologists examined bumps on the head and physiognomists studied facial structure to decipher supposedly inborn character traits. Hawthorne, though intrigued by graphology, lampooned both phrenology and physiognomy. He may have been familiar with articles on handwriting featured in *Godey's Lady's Book* in the 1830s and 1840s. The authors analyzed the signatures of famous historical women, like Queen Elizabeth, in an attempt to gauge their femininity.[13] Hawthorne also may have read Edgar Allan Poe's three essays on autography (1836, 1841, 1842), which scrutinized the script of contemporary literati. Poe denounced the literary hacks he detested as having "clerky" writing. Because the systematized – or clerky "hand" – frustrated his attempt to measure depth of character, he claimed that such authors lacked individuality. Yet in his 1841 preface Poe acknowledged that his analyses were influenced more by his literary taste than his belief in handwriting as an index of character – he assigned psychological and literary capital only to authors he liked.[14]

Hawthorne's narrator, like the *Godey's* authors and Poe, endeavors to unmask the private self behind the public face – to glimpse in slips of the hand the unedited "deep" psychological individual that presumably drives the historical self. "An erasure, even a blot, a casual irregularity of hand, and all such imperfections of mechanical execution, bring us closer to the writer, and perhaps convey some of those subtle intimations for which language has no shape" (XI: 360). George Washington's gentlemanly, controlled hand denies the narrator access: it is too mechanical, too civil. His "command of hand" betrays "no physical symptom . . . of varying mood, of jets of emotion" (XI: 363). The narrator encodes this as a deficiency of individuality. "Is it, that his great nature . . . could not individualize itself in brotherhood to an individual?" (XI: 364). Generally, the narrator seems to devalue eighteenth-century personal life for its emphasis on ceremony, courtesy, civility, and formality. Rather than assign significance to Washington's achievement, persistence, and skill, the narrator ascribes interest to warmth, intimacy, sentiment, and psychological turmoil. Hawthorne is moving toward transforming the middle-class sentimental reader into a psychological reader. He is contributing to making the idea of the divided and introspective self a middle-class psychological value and fascination.

Aaron Burr's script titillates the narrator's curiosity. He depicts Burr – not unlike John Milton's Satan in *Paradise Lost* (1667) – as complex, contradictory, romantic, and interesting, as the possessor of individual and psychological capital. "How singular that a character, imperfect, ruined, blasted, as this man was, excites a stronger interest than if he had reached the highest earthly perfection of which its original element would admit!" (XI: 373). By implication, a concern with self-disclosure, slips, multiple meanings, and emotional conflict is what makes literature "deep" and "individual."

Both Poe and Hawthorne may well have been responding to the business orientation of new handwriting manuals. Eighteenth-century authors of these manuals emphasized that penmanship is an art to be mastered. But by the 1820s authors of chirography texts focused on training the business "hand" on a mass scale. Henry Dean's popular *Analytical Guide to the Art of Penmanship* (1807), for example, offers a system to "lessen the labour" of writing by decreasing the number of strokes. His standardized approach, he claims, is opposed to those "whose interest it is to envelop in mystery things the most plain and simple." Dean acknowledges that merchants and clerks shun "ornamental" writing.[15]

Although eighteenth-century handwriting guides equate character and penmanship, their ideological stress is not so much on disclosing or expressing character through writing, but on acquiring socially sanctioned "useful" character traits through the practice of writing. In a similar vein, Benjamin Franklin's *Autobiography* (Part One was published in 1791) frames writing as an activity that supports self-fashioning: the young Franklin learns his "individual" style by industriously imitating the essay style and wit of Joseph Addison and Richard Steele. Franklin encodes his slips in life with no deep, romantic significance as allegorical keys to his true, underlying individuality. He more playfully classifies his slips as "errata."[16]

Hawthorne's sketch participated in an emerging cultural debate about what counts as significant in evaluating selfhood. Mid nineteenth-century biographers of public figures had heated disagreements about whether they should only regard civic accomplishments as a "life," or probe private experience as the key that unlocks the meaning of public actions. "A Book of Autographs" sides with the latter group.[17]

Hawthorne's "Foot-prints on the Sea-shore" (1838) promotes a similar innerselfing. Here too Hawthorne inscribes involuntary disclosure – slips of the foot – as meaningful evidence of one's individual and psychological singularity. "By tracking our foot-prints in the sand we track our nature in its wayward course, and steal a glance upon it, when it never dreams of being so observed. Such glances always make us wiser" (IX: 454). The strand is like a psychological mirror that reflects moods and fantasies. It provides a compensatory therapeutic antidote to the standardizing world of marketplaces and work. Fascinated by the prospect of tracing his own footprints, the narrator predicts: "I shall think my own thoughts, and feel my own emotions, and possess my own individuality unviolated" (IX: 461). Perusing one's footprints seems tantamount to repossessing one's self – something perhaps also attempted through that other form of inscription called literary writing.

The "individuality" in this sketch – like the divided subjectivity that Hawthorne's narrator values in "A Book of Autographs" – is conceptualized according to the social logic of difference: not only does the individual imagine himself or herself as different from others, but more subtly as being constituted internally by differences. Hawthorne's narrator seeks to "possess" that depth of difference as a cultural sign of subjective potency (his never wholly fathomable "individuality"). Yet the emotionally reinvigorated narrator accumulates this psychological capital before returning to the crowded marketplace. If nineteenth-century domesticity performed this ideological function – with its sentimental power to funnel male workers, repaired by "angels in the house," back to the battleground of the marketplace – here a therapeutic preoccupation with one's (fantasies of) self performs a similar ideological recycling.

In "Monsieur du Miroir" (1837) Hawthorne complicates his reader's assumptions about his or her own individuality. Hawthorne is drawn less to a categorical understanding of individuality as an essence that can be repossessed than to a relational understanding of individuality as a class abstraction, a class identity, a class form of selfing. The narrator reflects on his reflection in the mirror and on the distortions of his reflections. He sees an unstable, fragmented self. But he begins to identify individuality not as an essence that is inherently different from itself, but as a cultural image ("monsieur"). It is "doubtful," the narrator concludes with literary self-reflexivity, "whether M. du Miroir have aught of humanity but the figure" (x: 159). "Figure" means body shape and literary trope. Hawthorne nudges his reader to reflect on how figures – literary figures – function in cultural selfing, and more specifically on how figures produced through culture, language, and vocabularies of selfhood shape notions of self-revelation. "Ah," the narrator confesses, "this M. du Miroir is a slippery fellow!" (x: 166). Slips of the hand or of the tongue are not self-evidently significant; rather these actions are culturally encoded to be read as meaningful reflections of "inner" individuality.

The "slippery" figure in the mirror does *not* yield intelligible truth – as an abstracted, contextless representation. Hawthorne does suggest that the psychological preoccupation with individual reflection is a characteristic of class identity. "The members of M. du Miroir's family have been accused, perhaps justly, of visiting their friends often in splendid halls, and seldom in darksome dungeons" (x: 166).

Hawthorne's self-reflexive emphasis on the figurative quality of identity is important in many of his *anti-allegorical allegories* (an ingenious formulation I borrow from Michael Davitt Bell).[18] If allegory posits an inner essence or meaning in a character – for instance, Edmund Spenser's Redcrosse Knight in *Faerie Queene* (1590) is an allegorical figure for Faith – an anti-allegorical method casts doubt on such clearcut internal definitions. Where an allegorist might represent a character whose characteristic of inner self seems palpable or natural, an anti-allegorist would be more interested in showing *how* the social assignment of cultural figures and allegories to characters may result in the shaping of their inner selves in particular ways.

"Egotism; Or, the Bosom Serpent" (1843) demonstrates the psychologizing self-definitional power that cultural figures can wield. In this tale Roderick Elliston seems to gestate a radar-like serpent in his bosom. It either detects or imaginatively allegorizes (encodes) serpents in the bosom of others. (The cause of Roderick's ailment – or singularity – is ambiguous, but it may be rooted in his obsessive jealousy about his estranged wife [x: 270–71].) Roderick's socially disruptive snake-charming grows intriguingly ridiculous until it becomes obvious that Hawthorne wishes his readers to read it not in any reductive way as a psychological allegory or a case study of compulsion based on the premise of a universal snake-infested inner self, but more complexly as a self-critical and parodic anti-allegorical allegory of a psychological allegorist run amok (x: 277). Hawthorne motivates readers to consider his culture's dominant range of figures or stereotypes that shape self-imagining (here the religious-based idea of woman-as-bosomy-serpent [x: 268]). He hints that subjectivity can become pathologically psychologized by the ideologically limited cultural allegories, symbols, and images made available to represent it. Read in this theoretical light the tale may be more about cultural obsession production than obsession and more about the process of cultural innerselfing (the self popularly conceptualized as snakepit) than the public exposure of humanity's reptilian interiority. To rework Zenobia's comment about Priscilla, readers may wonder: is Roderick the type of obsessional snakes-on-the-brain manhood such as Judeo-Christian culture has spent centuries making it?

"The Birth-Mark" (1843) is another self-reflexive, anti-allegorical allegory about the allegorizing operations of culture. Aylmer, a rather literary monomaniacal alchemist, plots his experiments in a library stocked with pseudo-scientific lore. He allegorizes the birthmark of Georgiana, his beautiful newlywed, not just as her sole aesthetic flaw, but as her "liability to sin, sorrow, decay, and death" (x: 39). As the tale unfolds Aylmer induces his bride to re-encode her birthmark – in the shape of a crimson hand on her left cheek – in his categories and thus to reread herself and her inner significance. Hawthorne exhibits the power of culture not only to compel its subjects to read and reread themselves along certain lines, but to produce obsession and pathologize bodies. Georgiana is thus culturally and allegorically innerselfed as she compulsively embraces Aylmer's – and, in a more encompassing sense, her culture's – pathological allegory of flawed womanhood. Culture is efficacious as a socializing force – as a sleight of hand – when it persuades its subjects that the identities and norms it applies to them originate deep within their nature. Indeed, the tale suggests that culture can give women the psychological incentive to pathologize themselves – a byproduct of the intense ideological pressure to perform as "angels in the house."

Some mid-century women, however, as Hawthorne knew, identified and rejected feminized heartmaking, headmaking, and bodymaking – cultural angelmaking. Contemporary *Godey's Lady's Book* critics dissented from feminized innerselfing. They objected that patriarchal culture's pathologizing of women's bodies relied on convincing women to read themselves and their putatively "feminine" essences in insidious ways.[19] Georgiana's cosmetic surgery transmutes her into a feminized "angel" in the house expurgated not of sin, sorrow, decay, and death, but of life.

One dimension of the historicity of Aylmer's and Georgiana's lethal allegorical experiment in angel stereotyping is that they experience the ideological pressure to carry it out not historically but psychologically. Hawthorne also complexly situates this seemingly "psychological" tension between husband and wife in history through the multivalent figure of the "bloody" (x: 38) hand-under-erasure. Georgiana's pathologized "hand" in marriage links her to an emerging industrial world (often figured in contemporary writings as an alchemy that transmutes nature) in which deskilled workers increasingly were being called and controlled as "hands." Hawthorne-the-theorist bonds the social predicament of the angel-in-training with that of alienated workers who had less of a hand in determining the conditions of their labor. As I have argued in detail elsewhere, Hawthorne's rich cultural symbolism challenges readers of this tale to retheorize the more-than-psychological gender relations he depicts as being connected to larger social, industrial, and class relations that produced compensatory middle-class ideological and emotional needs for clearly ordered sex roles.[20]

Hawthorne's theoretical scope is as expansive in *The Scarlet Letter*. In just a few sentences Hawthorne makes Hester Prynne his most far-reaching cultural theorist. As I noted, in *Blithedale* Zenobia asserts that men have long attempted to "make" women – a concise articulation of the social construction of gender theme earlier allegorized in "The Birth-Mark." Hester's fleeting revolutionary vision goes beyond Zenobia's constructionism to wonder about what purposes the establishment of sexual difference serve in the production of society at large. Through Hester Hawthorne intimated – as he did more symbolically and less explicitly in "The Birth-Mark" – that gender innerselfing of a certain kind was structurally requisite because it helped make the social fabrication of systemic power and emotional life possible. Hester predicts that for women to "assume a fair and suitable position," three reconstructions must occur: first, "the whole system of society is to be torn down, and built up anew"; second, men must modify the "hereditary habit" – conventional notions of masculinity – that has come to seem like "their nature" but which is not; and third, women must undergo "a still mightier change" in their role, self-images, expectations, and feelings than men (1: 165–66). Hester grasps that the binary classification of sex roles is locked into the economic, political, religious, and cultural operation of the whole social system, and that any tinkering with these seemingly "opposite" gender roles (that challenges the naturalness of this "opposition") may threaten the reproductive powers of the system.

Hawthorne goes only so far in his momentary theoretical empowerment of Hester. Her perception that seemingly discrete sectors of social power are interdependent remains vague. This vagueness helps make the vast project of social and gender change seem, if not quite inconceivable, then hopeless. Hawthorne punishes Hester for her unfeminine ability to theorize in two ways. All that brainwork, Hawthorne decides, must make her unlovely, less of a woman. More damning, she sacrifices what Hawthorne maintains is the regular feminine throb of her heart (1: 166). Even Hester's vision warns that the woman who tries to "undergo a mightier change" risks evaporating "the ethereal essence, wherein she has her truest life" (1: 165–66). Hawthorne here tries to regain control of Hester by innerselfing her – by defining the female "essence" she has compromised. Although Hester herself recognizes that gender selfing is one important way in which social power reproduces its complex structure of expectation, incentive, normality, and need, Hawthorne would have his readers believe that it is Hester's determinative emotional attachment to therapeutic angelhood and motherhood that restrains her from further revolutionary theorizing and action. Hawthorne lets Hester blow the whistle on cultural innerselfing (the systemic feminization of females) as a theoretical prelude to redefining and containing her as an emotional product of this innerselfing.

The cultural job of industrial-era soulmaking

"The Artist of the Beautiful" (1844) is one of Hawthorne's most complex contributions to the cultural theory of subjectivity formation. Owen Warland, the aspiring romantic artist, repudiates his trade as a mender of mechanical signs of the time – timepieces – to invent what he construes as a sign of the timeless – a minute mechanical butterfly made of modified watch parts. The tale, a mix of ideological crosscurrents, at turns both affirms and criticizes the romantic urge for aesthetic and subjective autonomy and transcendence. It prompts readers to consider some of the historical motives and needs of romantics who try to use culture to fabricate what they imagine to be "spirit."

Aylmer aspires to be not just an alchemical spiritualizer but a soulmaker in whose "grasp the veriest clod of earth assumed a soul" (x: 49). Warland, another monomaniac, is likewise obsessed "with the notion of putting spirit into machinery" (x: 459) – an objective akin to the American literary author's cultural challenge to put "soul" or "individuality" into what Thomas Carlyle in "Signs of the Times" (1829) called the "Age of Machinery." In this famous essay Carlyle, more than Hawthorne, shows some concern for the plight of the "living artisan [who] is driven from his workshop to make room for a speedier and inanimate one." Hawthorne's artisanal artist seems to regard individualist alienation more than class exploitation as the pressing problem in an industrial America that worships industrial utility, conformity, and time-discipline. Carlyle, who like Hawthorne in "Fire Worship" is attentive to the effects of industrialization on subjectivity, articulates this cultural and spiritual alienation as the fear that industrial culture has made "men mechanical in head and heart, as well as in hand."[21] Hawthorne's story, however, goes beyond Carlyle's critique in its analytical consideration of the romantic invention of subjective potency, not oversimply as a spiritual protest against industrial capitalism, but as a reproductive mechanism of industrial capitalism and as a strategic device to demarcate class difference.

As Warland labors at animating his butterfly machinery, he rather conventionally believes that he has been inspired by his former master's daughter, Annie Hovenden. But Annie's artisanal class identification with "iron" men and utilitarian values shatters Warland (and his butterfly machine-in-progress). Annie falls for the town blacksmith, whose vision and values are more grounded and commonsensical than the artist's. Hence artisanal Annie fails Warland as a middle-class symbol of "true womanhood" – a potential "angel of his life." The artist imagines his erstwhile muse "fad[ing] from angel into ordinary woman" as she rejects him and displays her artisanal sympathies. Of course, Annie does not know she is failing the artist's test because she is unaware that she is supposed to behave like a middle-class angel. In his imposition of conventional gender expectations on the artisanal maid, the artist makes her "as much a creation of his own, as the mysterious piece of mechanism" (x: 464).

Warland's beautiful, artfully made mechanical butterfly can be read as his miniature technological winged substitute for a shrunken angel in the house. His flying machine lacks angel's wings but possesses butterfly wings and even emits a "halo" (x: 474). This well-oiled butterfly-with-a-halo features some stereotypical feminine characteristics: it is charmingly vulnerable (crushable), functions as a decorative object of display, never talks back, sparkles (no dangerous, illuminating, or high-flying fireworks), and it responds sensitively and immediately to its beholder's emotional state. In 1838 women's rights pioneer Sarah Grimké recounted how she refused to accept her lot among the ornamental "butterflies of the fashionable world." Three decades later Fanny Fern, another feisty advocate of wingless women, exhorted her readers not to allow themselves to be made into "a butterfly . . . [or a] machine, which, once wound up by the marriage ceremony, is expected to click with undeviating monotony until Death stops the hands."[22] The butterflies that Grimké and Fern have in mind are the opposite of the unfeminized, "impenetrable," iron-bodied, golden-winged gorgons Hawthorne describes in his reworking of the Medusa myth, "The Gorgon's Head" (1851). The militant gorgons – not unlike women's rights supporters, often termed "monsters" in antebellum America – literally petrify frightened males and females who behold their flight (VII: 12–13, 28–29). Hawthorne's tale of butterflymaking implies with self-irony that the male artist who cannot find a compliant angel of flesh and blood might opt to construct his own version to ideal, insect-scale specifications.

Because the unangelic Annie, according to the narrator, is not "enlightened by the deep intelligence of love" (X: 460) and is "incapable of any deep response" (X: 464), she cannot interpret the supposedly deep spiritual significance of the artist's dainty butterfly, which appears to her and other members of her class as useless. Thus it behooves the artist to spell out his butterfly's symbolic depth for the seemingly shallow Annie. In it, he announces, "is represented the intellect, the imagination, the sensibility, the soul, of an Artist of the Beautiful!" (X: 471). But the butterfly's glittering fragments and wheels within wheels have no inherent meaning. It is the artist who assigns its fragments and wheels deep cultural meaning, significance, and value: his cultural imagination makes its motor and gears advertise what he calls the (male artist's) "soul."

Warland's intricate invention also operates as a mechanism of class distinction. The butterfly's alleged symbolic interiority – the soul or individuality of the artist – makes the uncomprehending (or perhaps just uninterested) artisanal class seem superficial. According to the tale's scheme of representation, the blacksmiths and watchmakers of this "iron" class appreciate only signs of the time, not what romantic members of the middle class prefer to read as signs of the timeless. Warland's very name suggests warfare. Even though Warland himself is a member of the artisanal class, he is much more like an alienated middle-class artist in disguise. On one level, his butterfly is his class project, class mobility, class flight. The former watchmender's romantic spiritualized reading of his text-with-wings elevates him, at least in his own eyes, high above the merely mechanical, seemingly non-individual, soulless "lower" orders. His visionless former master, Peter Hovenden, is in fact going blind from having practiced his trade (X: 449).

Hawthorne's symbolic tale climaxes as the infant of Annie and her black-smith crushes the unique butterfly. Warland, rather than being upset or shocked, derives immense artistic and even retributive satisfaction from witnessing this destruction of his mechanical winged "soul," as if by demolishing his butterfly the "iron" people have destroyed their own souls. For Warland this is further evidence of the war in which his ostensible aesthetic transcendence is a sort of weapon and strategy. He knows that his fellow myopic class members will interpret his aesthetic yet mechanical invention as a merely decorative plaything, a waste of time in a culture dedicated to the Franklinian maxim "time is money." The butterfly's sophisticated machinery cannot be mass produced and is not for sale as a commodity. So the smug artist, with a calm, self-assured vindictiveness, emerges from the final scene with a symbolic victory in his pulverized butterfly. The laboring class, he is convinced, has shown its hand – even its children (bereft of Wordsworthian innocence) are made of iron and spiritually damned. Whereas the artist, still in possession of a higher vision of himself and his spiritual worth, experiences himself as an aristocrat of subjectivity – an artful prince among artisans.

Hawthorne's artist's romantic middle-class understanding of art differs from the way many mechanics' institutes of the 1820s and 1830s sought to utilize art and culture. Addresses delivered before the Massachusetts Charitable Mechanics Association, for instance, stress that the artisan's education in science and drawing is his pathway to self-making, self-respect, self-control, and the fulfillment of his civic and national responsibility. Speakers at the association aimed to elevate the cultural distinction of the practical and the useful.[23]

Timothy Claxton's *Memoir of a Mechanic* (1839) also has this agenda. Claxton, who began his career as a mechanic (a whitesmith) in England, eventually helped found the Boston Mechanics' Institution (1826), the Boston Lyceum (1829), and the Boston Mechanics' Lyceum (1831). His career reads like an inversion of Warland's. As a boy, he gleefully built a clock and learned the usefulness of mechanical drawing. Although Claxton celebrates the inventive "mind [that] marks out tracks that have never been trodden before," he derides efforts to invent a "perpetual motion machine" and praises Paris' Academy of Sciences for denouncing all such experiments as "a mere waste of time." In his youth Claxton himself had labored under the delusion that he could invent a perpetual motion machine, but he abandoned this pursuit to invent a better mousetrap (literally). In 1832 he established a periodical in Boston titled *The Young Mechanic*, which "sprung from the noble desire to elevate the character of his class."[24] Claxton is the ideal young mechanic that Hawthorne's watchmaker refuses to emulate. Rejecting the artisanal ideology of self-making, Warland reinvents upward mobility as middle-class butterflymaking.

Intriguingly, while Hawthorne's tale sometimes seems to subscribe to the notion of an essential or universal selfhood (here signified as the nonconformist "soul" of the true artist), his story also stimulates readers to imagine, or visualize, gender, individuality, and interiority as cultural products of class-identity machinery. By this I mean a cultural or class machinery of individuality, of aesthetic, spiritual, or psychological depth that is designed by one class in part to hoist itself above a class encoded as a "lower" class whose "iron," mechanical members are presumed to be insufficiently deep, individual, universal, literary, and human. The romantic artist therefore carries out a crucial class program: he not only puts his soul into his work, he puts his idea of a soul into his middle-class readers. His soul machinery puts a class-specific soul and a class-specific individuality (disguised and aestheticized as universal individuality) into readers who also are workers – mainly middle-class workers. The romantic artist's ideological class assignment is to decorate this middle-class idea of individuality – to make it seem interior, spiritual, aesthetic, and elevating, and even, by implication, psychologically rebellious and thus subjectively potent. Ideally, the romantic soul will not seem like a product of industrial machinery or industrial times – the soul's great ideological utility will be that it seems like it has nothing to do with utility.

Yet I cannot stress enough that Hawthorne roots the "transcendence" of this class project in several ways. Hawthorne's representation of Warland's obsession with working on his butterfly, for example, brings to mind contemporary advice manuals' warnings against the sin of "solitary vice" – masturbation.[25] The artist became "more absorbed in a secret occupation, which drew all his science and manual dexterity into itself." His labors to spiritualize his "machinery" required the "delicate power of his fingers" (x: 452).

Operating in tension with the narrator's (sometimes ironic) sympathy for the artist's tactile butterfly labors is the telling fact that this winged soul is a mechanical product of the industrial revolution. Warland uses his soul machine both to launch a dubious and easily crushed flight from the capitalist world and to legitimate his feeling of human and spiritual superiority – class superiority – over his fellow "iron" artisans. The artist's seemingly defiant language of romantic individuality, Hawthorne suggests, is also the *spiritualized language of class*. Warland's imaginary "liberation" into spiritual autonomy is individualized rather than expansively politicized. Left behind in this "liberation" is the artisanal and shopkeeping class who – far from being seen as occupying a lower rung in an unfair power structure – are simply depicted (by Warland and sometimes by Hawthorne's narrator) as too obtuse to appreciate the intricate, mechanical flapping of the (middle-class) soul.

Hawthorne's romantic middle-class individualizing of the artist, his interests, and his "genius" is more apparent when compared with Pueblo and Navajo concepts of artistry. "There was always some kind of artistic endeavor that people set themselves to, although they did not necessarily articulate it as 'art' in the sense of western civilization," observes the Acoma author Simon Ortiz. "One lived and expressed an artful life, whether it was in ceremonial singing and dancing, architecture, painting, speaking, or in the way one's social-cultural life was structured." As the anthropologist Gary Witherspoon notes, in Navajo culture just about everyone is an artist. One stands out if one does *not* practice the arts. The Navajos' collective commitment to beautifying the world through art differs from Warland's more individualist concerns. They do not conceive of art as a practice through which one cultivates a sense of oneself as aesthetically, psychologically, or spiritually autonomous from society.[26] In the end Warland's spiritual and subjective potency seems to come from cynical social disengagement – writing off the possibility of changing society through art and perhaps writing off society altogether.

But read more contextually the romantic artist's apparent disengagement is also a peculiar form of engagement. Warland's understanding of his rebelliousness has relevance even today as a romantic manifesto for American artists, authors, and dissidents. The American author or artist, like the butterflymaker, must often demonstrate that it is possible to refashion and reassemble not only the tools and products, but the values and perceptions of an industrial world that too frequently categorizes and dismisses certain types of "art" as useless, meaningless, unprofitable. If industrial capitalism at times tries not only to crush the author's or artist's work, but to mock and demolish the alternative constructions of values and meaningfulness that informed its creation, Hawthorne's tale suggests that this destruction will fail if the creator develops and exercises the cultural power to resignify the worth not just of the creation but of the endeavor. However disengaged Hawthorne's artist may want to be, his "spirit" is constituted not just by imagined autonomy but by relationship and struggle – adversarial engagement. "[T]he ideal artist . . . must keep his faith in himself . . . he must stand up against mankind and be his own sole disciple, both as respects his genius, and the objects to which it is directed" (x: 454). The story clarifies that creating "beauty" in the structure of meaning, value, incentive, motive, and fascination termed "America" is never solely a diversion; it is unavoidably an engagement with what is, and – given what "America" is – it is in some cases an intense engagement with reimagining what "America" can be.

Although the artist's romantic rebellion retains its utopian (and individualistic) appeal in modern America, it must not obfuscate the class engagement of the artist's rebellion that I have sought to clarify – a class engagement that may have yet another dimension than that of the middle class versus artisanal class conflict. In the 1930s William Charvat noted that most American romantic authors seemed "indifferent" to the "distress of the worker" in the depression of 1837, and that the class tension that did absorb them was "the struggle . . . between their own homogeneous patrician society and a rising materialistic middle class without education and tradition." Hawthorne may have transposed this "intramural" middle-class antagonism onto the conflict between artist and artisans.[27]

Yet the tale also suggests that the middle class as a whole had begun to put individualistic soul rebellion to tactical use in forming its ideologically diverse spectrum of subjectivities. If on one level the tale promotes the ideological oppositions individual versus society, or artist versus philistines, on another level it foregrounds romantic individuality as an industrial-era product and a compensatory class need. True, Warland's romanticism rebels against Franklinian values essential to the economic elevation of the middle class. Still, for all of the differences between Franklin's work-ethic literature and the romantic artist's aesthetic of transcendence, Franklin equipped workers with secular incentive while the romantic artist outfitted them with compensatory secular souls to help mitigate their alienation (even better, to transmute their acknowledgment of their experience of alienation into a sign of their subjective depth). Franklin and the romantic artist both developed technologies of selfing that individualized motives and aspirations – developments unlikely to trigger collective rebellion. Hawthorne portrays a subtle social-emotional system: to operate as a flexible machinery of individualistic motive production, capitalism required not just Franklinian entrepreneurs, inventors, and proletarians who would encode self-sacrifice and competition as necessary for character-building and success, it also, more riskily, needed authors and artists to expand the cultural range of incentives, self-images, and permissible (individualized) rebellions – it needed them to serve as designers and advertisers of cultural-spiritual breathing space, as soulmakers. Mid-century capitalism was "iron" *and* romantic: it required subjectivity – "individuality" – to emotionally grease its gears and to serve as a relatively containable focus of discontent.

In 1840 Hawthorne worked as a weigher and gauger of coal and salt at the Boston Custom House – an alienating venture that, like his later experience in Salem's Custom House, made him all the more keen to return to the financial gamble of writing. On 7 April, he recorded that he was "plagued" by two sets of coal-shovelers whose simultaneous labors he had to tally in icy weather. "Any sort of bodily and earthly torment," he complained about the (supervisory) work, "may serve to make us sensible that we have a soul that is not within the jurisdiction of such shabby demons, – it separates the immortal within us from the mortal." The next moment, less secure in his self-evident, autonomous "soul," and blasted by mortal necessity, he confessed: "the wind has blown my brains into such confusion that I cannot philosophize now."[28] Hawthorne knew that American romantic literature, paradoxically, as an expanding industry of cultural selfing, helped put soul back into American work(ers) even when it despised the work.

Coda

There are at least three reasons why I keep turning to Hawthorne to better theorize the powers and workings of culture. First, many critics and readers have long praised Hawthorne for his historical knowledge and understanding. But his subtle historical thinking focused on more than eras, movements, material transformations, or famous political figures. In much of his work Hawthorne demonstrated a theoretically expansive grasp of the historicity of "personal" relations, emotions, and bodies. Like some modern historians and theorists of subjective forms, he frequently concentrated on how social power was reproduced through the constitution of subjectivities – what I have termed cultural processes of selfing and innerselfing. Hawthorne certainly contributed to the ideological making of the nineteenth-century middle-class psychological self. Yet he also repeatedly made the cultural fabrication of feelings, self-reflection, self-monitoring, and identity his theme, and often saw hyper-psychological relations as the strained effect of these fabrications. Furthermore, he probed connections between these fabrications and the creation of gender, class, and individual difference in America.

Although Hawthorne wrote during the period of forced "Indian" removal from East to West (the "Trail of Tears"), the imperialist war against Mexico, and mounting abolitionist protests against slavery, his fiction was not especially concerned with the production of racial difference and race relations. When his fiction did attend to race matters, it tended to survey the situation of Natives (evident in "Main-street") more than that of African Americans. Some of Hawthorne's fictions, however, resonantly register symbolic links between the constructions of emotions, self-images, and social power that did preoccupy him and the making of whiteness. Curiously, in "The Birth-Mark" Georgiana's whitewashed, "removed" red hand is a miniature version of red hands that Natives painted on their faces – represented vividly in several of George Catlin's much-exhibited and popular "Indian" portraits of the 1830s and 1840s.[29] And in "The Minister's Black Veil" (1836) Reverend Hooper's black veil induces widespread feelings of guilt in his New England Puritan parishioners – just when, in Hawthorne's own time, abolitionists were indicting New England for its complicity with slavery. Both tales exhibit charged white anxieties about acknowledging color – red, black – as a public issue.

Second, I appreciate Hawthorne-the-whistleblower – the artist who used fiction to challenge some of his own ostensible ideological preferences and limits. The Hawthorne who defended conventional domesticity and gender roles in his journals, letters, and fiction also created Hester, Zenobia, and Miriam in *The Marble Faun* (1860). Even when Hawthorne plots to contain the critical and dissenting forces he unleashes, he often invests these forces with the power to fascinate and to question prevalent middle-class assumptions. If at one point Hawthorne laments that Hester-the-radical-theorist has not learned her lessons from the scarlet letter (1: 166), through much of the novel he complicates – unfixes – what the letter (adulteress, author, ambiguity, the first letter of the alphabet, allegory, angel, America, and so on) means. Hawthorne was not only a surveyor of customs, he was a surveyor of premises and of meaning production. Notwithstanding his occasional uneasiness in doing so, he often saw culture not as an authoritative given, but as potentially alterable processes, practices, performances, structures of significance, and systems of identification.

Third, when I contemplate Richard Ohmann's sagacious observation that "Human activity [is] always political, if not *only* political," I think of Hawthorne's cautionary parodies, anti-allegories, and parables of theoretical monomania.[30] If in "The Hall of Fantasy" (1843) Hawthorne, despite his skepticism, acknowledged that even "the heart of the staunchest conservative . . . could hardly have helped throbbing in sympathy with the spirit that pervaded these innumerable theorists . . . [who sought] a better and purer life than had yet been realized on earth" (x: 180–81), in "Earth's Holocaust" (1844) he more resolutely recoiled from fierce theorist-reformers who cast the objects of their consuming hatred into a mammoth bonfire. Perhaps no tale illustrates Hawthorne's wariness of ideological single-vision as visually and in some instances as compassionately as "The Minister's Black Veil." The story begins one Sunday in the late seventeenth century when Reverend Hooper for ever dons a black veil and – as I mentioned above – startles his congregation. Hooper's funereal fig leaf has myriad effects. On the one hand, his preaching becomes more moving. Hooper's visual emblem – which, like Roderick's serpent, Georgiana's birthmark, and Warland's butterfly, has no intrinsic significance – serves as a screen upon which the cultural and

religious meanings that Puritans associate with blackness and veils are projected. It constantly reminds his flock that they deny their sinfulness and
mortality as they live their daily life. More parishioners than ever become
converted when seeing themselves and their Puritanized souls in Hooper's
inky mirror. On the other hand, they become nervous about mingling with
their minister, who perceives everyone, including himself, only in one light –
or lack of light. More like a prince of darkness than a white-veiled bride of
Christ, Hooper reads Holy Scripture through the obscuring lens of his veil.

The minister's "faint smile" that shows below the veil – perhaps not so
unlike Sheriff Hawthorne's constable's smile – may signal both the spiritual
and egotistical pleasure he gets from making public the invisible black veils
that he believes drape his fellow sinners. His in-your-face reformism blurs
the boundary between his righteousness and self-righteousness (the sin of
pride). Hawthorne seems to suggest that when *every* relation in life is seen
allegorically through one filter, there are distortions as well as illuminations.
Cultural theorists would do well to remember this. Sin is real, Hawthorne
realizes, if one accepts dominant definitions of "sin." Yet he questions how
much significance should be placed on one's preoccupation with sin and
complicity with sin. To be sure, Hawthorne is not prescribing evasiveness,
forgetfulness, and denial as culturally salutary – though the opening scene,
before Hooper makes his veiled debut, is graced with Sunday sunshine, frisky
romance, and "lusty" church bell ringing. However, he does suggest that
monomaniacally scenting out sin can itself become a sinful pathologizing
of others. What Ohmann and Hawthorne, taken together, seem to say is
that there is even more at stake in thinking critically about culture than
unveiling its relations to the reproduction of systemic social contradiction
and complicity – a crucial and sometimes hazardous task, and that the ability
to imagine a culturally vital reorganization of life, value, and feeling depends
partly on recognizing the life-enhancing and playful as well as mystifying and
damaging powers of culture, and partly on maintaining critical humility.

NOTES

1. I owe a special debt to Fumio Ano, President of the Hawthorne Society of Japan,
   for inviting me to deliver the earliest version of this chapter as a "special lecture"
   at the society's annual meeting in Nihon University in Tokyo, May 2000. My
   many conversations with him and with Keisuke Kawakubo, Vice-president of
   the society, yielded great insights into my subject, especially when we compared
   nineteenth-century Japan and America.
2. See "The Procession of Life" (1843), "The Celestial Railroad" (1843), "The New
   Adam and Eve" (1843), "The Intelligence Office" (1844), "The Christmas Ban-
   quet" (1844).

3. See Joel Pfister, "Afterword," in Hawthorne, *A Wonder-Book for Girls and Boys*, illustrations by Walter Crane, Introduction by Ola D'Aulaire, Afterword by Joel Pfister (New York: Oxford University Press, 1996), pp. 243–54, especially p. 247.

4. Oscar B. Jacobson, *Kiowa Indian Art* (1929), quoted in Oliver LaFarge et al., *Introduction to American Indian Art* (1931) (Glorieta, NM: Rio Grande Press, 1970), p. 109.

5. From Walter Benjamin, "Theses on the Philosophy of History," translated by Fredric Jameson in Jameson's *The Political Unconscious: Narrative as a Socially Symbolic Act* (Ithaca, NY: Cornell University Press, 1981), p. 281.

6. For a reading of this sketch in historical relation to an interpretation of a parlor stove, see Joel Pfister, "A Garden in the Machine: Reading a Mid-Nineteenth-Century Two-Cylinder Parlor Stove as Cultural Text," in Jules David Prown and Kenneth Haltman, eds., *American Artifacts: Essays in Material Culture* (East Lansing: Michigan State University Press, 2000), pp. 149–66.

7. See Joel Pfister, "On Conceptualizing the Cultural History of Emotional and Psychological Life in America," in Joel Pfister and Nancy Schnog, eds., *Inventing the Psychological: Toward a Cultural History of Emotional Life in America* (New Haven, CT: Yale University Press, 1997), pp. 17–59, see p. 21.

8. On these matters see Philippe Ariès, *Centuries of Childhood: A Social History of Family Life,* trans. Robert Baldick (New York: Vintage, 1962), pp. 40, 386, 413, and Ariès, "The Family and the City," in Virginia Tufte and Barbara Myerhoff, eds., *Changing Images of the Family* (New Haven, CT: Yale University Press, 1979), p. 32.

9. Antonio Gramsci, *Selections from the Prison Notebooks of Antonio Gramsci,* ed. and trans. Quintin Hoare and Geoffrey Nowell Smith (New York: International Publishers, 1971), p. 324.

10. On nineteenth-century readings of Hawthorne as "deep," see the anonymous review of Hawthorne's *Twice-Told Tales* in *Boston Miscellany of Literature* 1 (February 1842): 92; anonymous review of Hawthorne's *The Scarlet Letter* in *Graham's Magazine* 36 (May 1850): 346; Mr. Duyckinck, "Nathaniel Hawthorne," *The Literary World* 6 (March 1850): 323–25; Charles Hale, "Nathaniel Hawthorne," *To-Day: A Boston Literary Journal* 38 (September 1852): 177–81, see p. 179; Anne C. Lynch Botta, *Hand-book of Universal Literature* (New York: Derby & Jackson, 1860), p. 537; Henry T. Tuckerman, "Nathaniel Hawthorne," *Southern Literary Messenger* 17 (June 1851): 344–49. Also see Joel Pfister, *The Production of Personal Life: Class, Gender, and the Psychological in Hawthorne's Fiction* (Stanford, CA: Stanford University Press, 1991), p. 27 (James) and pp. 1–2, 5, 9, 17, 27–28, 50–52, 140–41 (Freud and Freudian approaches to Hawthorne).

11. Here Hawthorne theorizes in ways that Michel Foucault would develop in his work, particularly *The History of Sexuality, Volume 1: An Introduction*, trans. Robert Hurley (New York: Vintage, 1980).

12. Freud, *The Psychopathology of Everyday Life* (1901), ed. James Strachey, trans. Alan Tyson (New York: Norton, 1966).

13. See Hawthorne, "Phrenology," *The American Magazine of Useful and Entertaining Knowledge* 2 (March 1836): 337; Hawthorne, "The Science of Noses," *The American Magazine of Useful and Entertaining Knowledge* (March 1836):

268; Sarah J. Hale, "An Evening's Conversation About Autographs," *Godey's* 22 (April 1841): 146–49, see p. 146.

14. Poe, "Autography" (*Southern Literary Messenger*, February 1836), "A Chapter on Autography" (*Graham's Magazine*, December 1841), "An Appendix on Autography" (*Graham's Magazine*, January 1842); republished in *The Complete Works of Edgar Allan Poe*, vol. xv, ed. James A. Harrison (New York: AMS Press, 1965), pp. 139–261.

15. See Henry Dean's second edition, *Analytical Guide to the Art of Penmanship* (Baltimore: S. Jeffries, 1808). Also consult Tamara Plakins Thornton, *Handwriting in America: A Cultural History* (New Haven, CT: Yale University Press, 1996).

16. Benjamin Franklin, *The Autobiography of Benjamin Franklin* (New Haven, CT: Yale University Press, 1964), pp. 43, 70, 86, 96, 99, 122, 129.

17. See Scott E. Casper, *Constructing American Lives: Biography and Culture in Nineteenth-Century America* (Chapel Hill: University of North Carolina Press, 1999).

18. Michael Davitt Bell, *The Development of the American Romance: The Sacrifice of Relation* (Chicago: University of Chicago Press, 1980).

19. See Harriet Beecher Stowe's letter to the editor, "Editor's Table," *Godey's* 26 (January 1843): 58 and Sarah J. Hale, "Editor's Table," *Godey's* 26 (May 1843): 249–50. For a recent example of how dominant social forces can stigmatize women with birthmarks, see Steven Greenhouse, "Lifetime Affliction Leads to a US Bias Suit," *New York Times* (30 March 2003): A14. When Samantha Robichaud, of Northport, Alabama, was considered for a promotion to manage a McDonald's fast-food restaurant, her supervisor informed her that her birthmark would forever hold her back. The author of the article is not wholly clear as to whether he reads Robichaud's birthmark or the social encoding and stigmatizing of her birthmark as her "lifetime affliction." Hawthorne was clearer about such matters.

20. Pfister, *Production of Personal Life*, pp. 13–58, and on Herman Melville's industrial versions of this tale – "The Bell-Tower" (1854) and "The Tartarus of Maids" (1855) – pp. 104–21.

21. Thomas Carlyle, "Signs of the Times," *Critical and Miscellaneous Essays*, vol. II (New York: Hurd and Houghton, 1876), p. 138.

22. See Sarah Grimké, *Letters on the Equality of the Sexes and the Conditions of Women* (New York: Burt Franklin, 1970 [1838]), pp. 46–47 and Fanny Fern [Sara Payson Parton], "The Women of 1867," in her *Ruth Hall and Other Writings*, ed. Joyce W. Warren (New Brunswick, NJ: Rutgers University Press, 1986), pp. 343–44.

23. See *Annals of the Massachusetts Charitable Mechanics Association, 1795–1892* (Boston: Press of Rockwell and Churchill, 1892). I thank David Zonderman for recommending that I peruse this journal and Timothy Claxton's autobiography.

24. Timothy Claxton, *Memoir of a Mechanic: Being a Sketch of the Life of Timothy Claxton* (Boston: G. W. Light, 1839).

25. On the relevance of mid-century fears about solitary vice to Hawthorne's fiction, see Pfister, *Production of Personal Life*, pp. 23–24, 139–40.

26. Simon Ortiz, quoted in Patricia Penn Hilden, *When Nickels Were Indians: An Urban, Mixed-Blood Story* (Washington D.C.: Smithsonian Institution Press,

1995), p. 45. Gary Witherspoon, *Language and Art in the Navajo Universe* (Ann Arbor: University of Michigan Press, 1977), pp. 152–53.

27. William Charvat, "American Romanticism and the Depression of 1837" (1937), in Matthew J. Bruccoli, ed., *The Profession of Authorship in America, 1800–1870: The Papers of William Charvat* (Columbus: Ohio State University Press, 1968), pp. 49–67, see pp. 64, 66.

28. Hawthorne, *American Note-Books*, in *The Works of Nathaniel Hawthorne*, vol. VI (Boston: Houghton Mifflin, 1882), pp. 221–22.

29. See Pfister, *Production of Personal Life*, p. 192 n. 36.

30. See Richard Ohmann's new introduction to the republication of his classic, *English in America: A Radical View of the Profession* (Hanover, NH: Wesleyan University Press, 1996), p. xviii. For an analysis of some of the implications of Ohmann's insight, see Joel Pfister, "Complicity Critiques," *American Literary History* 12 (Fall 2000): 610–32.

3

T. WALTER HERBERT

Hawthorne and American masculinity

The governing paradox

Hawthorne lived out the classic story of masculine success in America, overcoming early hardship to achieve wealth and fame. Orphaned by the death of his father when he was four years old, he was reared in the household of his mother's family, and lived in near-poverty for most of his life: only at age forty-eight was he able to afford a home of his own. College life at Bowdoin gave Hawthorne friendships with some of the most prominent men of his time, notably Franklin Pierce and Henry Wadsworth Longfellow, but did not prepare him for the profession he chose. Becoming a writer was a long struggle, requiring Hawthorne to surmount recurrent frustration and periods of acute self-doubt, as well as severe financial hardship. But at the end of his life, in 1864, Hawthorne was well-to-do and his writings were counted among the masterpieces of world literature. Hawthorne's intimate friends and relations hailed him as an exemplar of true manliness, distinguished by the "military self-command" that had seen him through the hardships and yielded so spectacular a triumph.[1]

Yet a desolating sense of unreality plagued Hawthorne throughout this classic American success-story: "If you know anything of me," he wrote in his last years, "you know how I sprang out of mystery, akin to none, a thing concocted out of the elements, without visible agency – how, all through my boyhood, I was alone; how I grew up without a root, yet continually longing for one – longing to be connected with somebody – and never feeling myself so" (XII: 257).

Hawthorne looked upon his fierce professional strivings as compensatory, an unavailing effort to dispel his abiding misery. "I have tried to keep down this yearning," he writes, "to stifle it, annihilate it, with making a position for myself, with being my own past, but I cannot overcome this natural horror of being a creature floating in the air, attached to nothing; nor this feeling that there is no reality in the life and fortunes, good or bad, of a being so unconnected" (XII: 258).

Consider the paradox: Hawthorne had established an imposing record of manly achievement, but was haunted by the horror of an unreal life. This conjunction of fulfillment and misery belongs to the style of masculinity that Hawthorne lived out, which took form as a dominant American style between Hawthorne's birth in 1804 and his death in 1864, as an emerging political and economic order radically transformed American society. During this era, American men enjoyed amazing new opportunities for self-fulfillment; but also suffered new forms of oppression and distress. The compound of triumph and despair in Hawthorne's life illuminates a paradox inherent to the masculine existence that men of his class perforce lived out, under the new social conditions that governed their lives in the first half of the nineteenth century, conditions that have survived in altered form into our own time.

Colonial America had been composed of small-scale communities that were governed by face-to-face networks of familial connection, through which young men were guided to maturity through apprenticeships managed by their fathers, or foster-fathers. A man's eventual place in society was pretty much determined at birth. This life-pattern was displaced during the early nineteenth century, as the expanding capitalist and industrial economy of the new republic created opportunities on the western edge of the former colonies and in rapidly growing urban centers. To individual men, this unstructured and anonymous new environment seemed like a turbulent and unpredictable ocean, as full of danger as of promise. In *Advice to Youth*, one of many popular guidebooks for young men trying to make their way in this world, David Magie declared that "You must be a law to yourselves, in the mart of trade, the cabin of the steamboat, and the crowded inn, or you will soon make shipwreck of faith and good conscience."[2]

Instead of depending on family connections, a young man was now compelled to "make a name for himself" through his own unaided efforts. The instant popularity of Ralph Waldo Emerson's writing rests on the astuteness with which he promotes this emerging "self-reliant" style of manhood.

Masculinity is not a fixed bundle of traits dictated by male genes. On the contrary, styles of manhood vary from place to place and from time to time, as demonstrated by anthropological researches into cultures around the world, historical researches into earlier epochs of Western (and other) societies, and sociological studies that explore the diverse styles of manliness that flourish within contemporary cultures. To be sure, masculinities are not socially constructed out of nothing. Gender theorists who attempt to force a choice between "nature" and "nurture" are fundamentally mistaken: traditions of manhood are formed by the interplay between genetic endowment and social conditioning. Both "nature" and "nurture" are always involved, and they produce a variety of results.[3]

This process was unknown in Hawthorne's time, even unthinkable. Hawthorne believed that the genders – manhood and womanhood – were securely founded in nature. For him, they were universal timeless structures from which individual women and men might deviate only at substantial cost. He believed that a woman could become a writer, for example, only by violating the womanhood ordained for her by nature, and he warned against "a false liberality that mistakes the strong division lines of Nature for mere arbitrary distinctions."[4] As he labored at the Salem Custom House, likewise, Hawthorne worried that his own manhood might be impaired, since receiving government wages could sap his "sturdy force" and "self-reliance." How long could he keep such a job, he wondered, "and yet go forth a man?" (1: 39–40).

The theory that manhood and womanhood are established by nature was enshrined as an article of faith in the middle-class white society that inherited the American Revolution. Heroes of the revolution like Washington and Jefferson were aristocrats. They fought for the principle that all men are created equal, but their lives were fundamentally shaped by the opposite belief. They were both slaveholders, and the whole pattern of their social experience taught them that aristocrats are born to a place in society that gives them the right to rule over common men, and that common men are required by their place to obey their betters.

Benjamin Franklin, by contrast, was not given a distinguished name at birth. Franklin moved from Boston to Philadelphia in order to free himself from the network of family and apprentice relationships into which he was born, and to seize the opportunities for personal advancement offered by the new urban society. The expression "self-made man" became current during this era, to describe those who found the way to wealth through their own intelligence and self-discipline, and Franklin celebrated his own life as an exemplar of this new ideal.[5] His *Autobiography* still serves as a parable of masculine fulfillment in America, vindicating the claim that every man possesses a natural manhood equal to that of any other man.

Champions of manhood equality, who fought against the aristocratic ideal, invoked a mythical "state of nature" where men lived solitary self-sustaining lives, and then brought societies and governments into being by agreeing to a "social contract" through which they voluntarily yielded certain natural rights to the collective order. Our knowledge of human prehistory, and of primates generally, demonstrates the falsehood of this myth; but it was overwhelmingly plausible to men of Hawthorne's time, because it served as an ideological weapon in the battle against the continuing prestige of bloodline hierarchy. The terms of this battle are echoed in the distinction Hawthorne draws between "mere arbitrary distinctions" that mark aristocratic status and the "strong division lines of Nature" that separate women from men.

The ideology of natural genders also served to defend traditional male dominance against the claim that the doctrines of democratic equality required that women should enjoy the same rights as men. In 1792, Mary Wollstonecraft's *Vindication of the Rights of Women* was published in England, sounding themes that had long been discussed informally in America. When John Adams was attending the Constitutional Convention in 1776, Abigail Adams wrote to inform him that unless their rights were respected, women were "determined to foment a Rebellion, and will not hold ourselves bound by any Laws in which we have no voice, or Representation."[6] Defenders of male privilege answered that the bodily differences between men and women demand a social arrangement in which women are subservient.

Hawthorne shared this anti-feminist sentiment, but his commitment to the new standard of self-sufficient manhood was anything but wholehearted. The brisk optimism of Franklin and Emerson was alien to Hawthorne's temperament, and he discerned the systematic cruelties at work in a world of self-reliant self-seeking. The economic opportunities of the newly emerging capitalist society were available only to white men; and white men who pursued those opportunities were compelled to lead a life of unceasing competition against other men. The "man's world" of incessant self-reliant self-seeking forced individual men into anxious solitude, cutting them off from the emotional support other men could provide, and cutting them off from their own capacity for nurture and compassion. Hawthorne called it "the agony of the universal struggle to wrest the means of existence from a host of greedy competitors" (VIII: 332). At the end of his life Hawthorne was himself agonized by the eerie sense of unreality that results from such alienation, and self-alienation.

Yet Hawthorne could not repudiate the ideal of self-reliant masculinity, despite its harsh demands. When his college friend George Hillard raised a fund to rescue the family from poverty, Hawthorne accepted the money with gratitude, but not without condemning himself. "Ill success in life is really and justly a matter of shame," he wrote to Hillard. "I am ashamed of it, and I ought to be. The fault of a failure is attributable – in a great degree, at least – to the man who fails. I should apply this truth in judging of other men; and it behooves me not to shun its point or edge in taking it home to my own heart. Nobody has a right to live in this world, unless he be strong and able, and applies his ability to good purpose" (XVI: 166).

Hawthorne's effort to live a life of self-reliant masculinity brought him life-long consternation, the sense of unreality that pursued him even in the midst of success; and he was aware that the two sides of this paradox were con-nected to each other. Hawthorne's intuition looks forward to the twentieth-century awareness that gender roles are social products, and may be scripted in terms that are internally contradictory, or at odds with individual tem-peraments and gifts. Joseph Pleck has defined this as "gender role strain," the misery produced by liabilities built into the construction of manhood (or womanhood) that an individual has internalized.[7] Yet Hawthorne did not pursue his psycho-social insights from the stance of a detached observer, but amid his guilt-stricken rebellion against the demands of "natural manhood," and his lifelong fascination for women who were correspondingly oppressed by the emerging conventions of "true womanhood."

Henry James noted Hawthorne's "catlike faculty of seeing in the dark,"[8] his genius for gauging and depicting tragic dilemmas that were invisible to those who endured them. The theory of natural genders – like other powerful ideological constructions – blinded its adherents to the cruelties they suffered and inflicted in its name. Committed to the rising capitalist and democratic order, Hawthorne pledged his allegiance to self-reliant manly self-making; but he was uncannily attuned to the unmaking of such manliness, and to the injustices that it systematically inflicted on women.

The enduring power of Hawthorne's art rests in good measure upon the acuity with which his literary creations explore these painful complexities. Ideologues and social critics in his time (as in our own) offer illuminating analyses, but Hawthorne's literary power offers the reader an imaginative engagement with the stress-laden structures of self-reliant American mas-culinity. Hawthorne creates stories about things that imagined characters say and do; he creates sentences and paragraphs that are nuanced word by word under the cross-pressures that they work to body forth; he draws us into a transaction that provides an encounter, as though face to face, with the patterning of our own minds and hearts.

Transition to the new order

In *The House of the Seven Gables*, Hawthorne celebrates the rising order of self-reliant manhood as it displaces the society of bloodline hierarchy. Holgrave, his protagonist, is a young man "self-dependent" from boyhood, and possessing a "natural force of will." Holgrave has made his living as a schoolmaster, then as a salesman in a country store, then as a political editor, a pedler, a dentist, a public lecturer, and now as a daguerreotypist. But he has not floundered down this path irresolute and self-divided. On the contrary, his ad-hoc pursuits bear witness to Holgrave's firm and consistent identity, what Hawthorne terms his "innermost man" (II: 176–77).

Holgrave is descended from the Maule family of Salem, who were cheated out of a choice piece of real estate by the Pyncheons, members of the pre-Revolutionary landed gentry whose descendants still occupy the great house (of seven gables) that the Pyncheons had erected on the property. In colonial times the Maules were carpenters, representatives of the artisan class that gave rise to the culture of manly self-making, and Hawthorne foretells the future victory of natural manhood by staging a contest between colonial aristocrat and commoner. Maule appears in a woolen jacket and leather breeches, faced off against Gervayse Pyncheon with his flowered waistcoat, lace-embroidered blue velvet coat, and powdered wig. This regalia of aristocratic privilege is ludicrously discomposed as Pyncheon goes down to defeat. "How the man of conventionalities shook the powder out of his periwig," Hawthorne jeers, "how the reserved and stately gentleman forgot his dignity" (II: 205–06).

Hawthorne declares that descent from a distinguished family is a liability in the new economic and political order that favors self-made men. The Pyncheons cling to "an absurd delusion of family importance" that has bred inhuman ruthlessness in certain descendants and "a liability to sluggishness and dependence" in others (II: 19). "Once in every half-century," Holgrave remarks, "a family should be merged into the great obscure mass of humanity, and forget all about its ancestors. Human blood, in order to keep its freshness, should run in hidden streams" (II: 185). The Pyncheons are fated to lead a self-confounded existence, strangling on the contradictions that follow from trying to lead an aristocratic life in a society now defined by the culture of manly, self-reliant men. This complex of meanings is captured in the curse uttered against the Pyncheons in colonial times, when they had used their social position to cheat the Maules: "God will give you blood to drink!" (II: 8).

But Hawthorne's narrative also dramatizes the afflictions of men in the new social order. He was aware that the transition from a traditional to a modern society was not clean and decisive, and that the invulnerable "innermost man" of the self-reliant individual is chronically riddled with conflict.

In his classic study of democratic social forms in America, Alexis de Toqueville notes that the new American system does not abolish hierarchy: certain men continue to govern, while others obey. "When the transition from one social condition to another is going on," he observes, "there is almost always a time when men's minds fluctuate between the aristocratic notion of subjection and the democratic notion of obedience." In a frankly hierarchical society, a man in a subservient position merges his identity into that of his master, and thus "assumes an imaginary personality." When the new order asserts itself, these men are haunted "by a confused and imperfect phantom of equality" which leads them to look upon any man more powerful than themselves "as an unjust usurper of their rights."[9]

Writing two decades later, Hawthorne recognized that the fluctuating consciousness that Tocqueville discerned in the transition to a democratic society actually survived that transition, to become typical of the new order. Because hierarchy continues in the tumult of self-guided individual competition, the identities of actual men stand vacant, haunted by the specters that inhabit the two discrepant worlds: the "imaginary personality" instilled by habits of deference and the "phantom of equality" that whispers to every subordinated man that he is a sovereign.

"My Kinsman, Major Molineux" portrays the quandary of a young man who carries the social habits of deferential hierarchy into the era of their revolutionary overthrow. Robin Molineux comes to town expecting that his distinguished kinsman will provide him an "establishment in life" (XI: 224), as befits his aristocratic entitlements, only to discover that the townspeople are preparing to tar-and-feather the Major because they resent the royal authority he serves. Faced with this dilemma, Robin undergoes a psychological revolution; he is compelled internally to repudiate, as by an inborn natural force, the deferential social habits that had been bred into him.

Groggy and disoriented at having to retract the "imaginary personality" he had projected into his kinsman, and spurred on by the "phantom of equality" that has aroused the townspeople, Robin finds relief by joining in the gleeful abuse that is showered upon his kinsman. Hawthorne emphasizes the cruelty of the lynch-mob, even as he depicts Robin's ardent participation in it: "On they went, in counterfeited pomp, in senseless uproar, in frenzied merriment, trampling all on an old man's heart" (XI: 230).

Yet this degrading ritual serves Robin as an initiation into the world of self-made men, and instills the psychic disposition required to succeed in it. Pale with a guilt that he cannot afford to recognize, Robin accepts the guidance of a townsman, who points toward the future he must now accept: "as you are a shrewd youth, you may rise in the world without the help of your kinsman, Major Molineux" (XI: 230).

In *The House of the Seven Gables* Holgrave confronts an embodiment of the old patriarchal order in the form of Judge Pyncheon. But Pyncheon also embodies the evils and unrealities that menace Holgrave because they are inherent to the psychic anatomy of his self-making. Judge Pyncheon is identified with the corruptions that were intrinsic to the bygone aristocratic society, but he simultaneously dramatizes the moral liabilities of the new urban and industrial regime. In the anonymous new cities, power drains out of face-to-face networks of personal knowledge, to be concentrated in the hands of men who are skilled at managing superficial encounters, so as to win friends and influence people. Pyncheon, with his practiced outward show of benevolence, is just such a confidence man; and he has also mastered the arts of political manipulation that emerged as local communities were subsumed into the national systems of patronage and publicity. Organizing a mass electorate, like exploiting anonymous interpersonal encounters, depends on employing new forms of deceit.

We meet Pyncheon on the threshold of becoming Governor of Massachusetts, yet the election is months away, and is virtually irrelevant. Pyncheon will obtain the office because he has gained the support of men who are "skilled to adjust those preliminary measures which steal from the people, without its knowledge, the power of choosing its own rulers" (II: 274). He has insinuated himself into the favor of these political operatives through large financial contributions, which he can afford because of "his real estate in town and country, his railroad, bank, and insurance shares, his United States stock" (II: 98). Pyncheon's investments actually produce nothing of social value, and he himself does no useful work. Instead, he increases the money value of his holdings by exploiting his insider knowledge of the new financial systems. He makes it a custom to visit the Insurance Office so as to hear and appraise the current gossip, and to drop "some deeply designed chance-word, which will be certain to become the gossip of tomorrow" (II: 270), sending prices up or down, depending on what will bring him a profit. He is also well practiced in creating pseudonymous bank accounts, both foreign and domestic, and uses other arcane methods, "familiar enough to capitalists" (II: 234), by which the bewildering maze of financial institutions may be arranged to conceal the character and extent of his possessions.

Jaffrey Pyncheon represents not only aristocratic privilege, descending from a corrupt past to block democratic progress, but anti-democratic arrangements that are native to the new economic and political order. He is a figure of the irony according to which a presumptively republican America sponsored the formation of a capitalist oligarchy.

Pyncheon enjoys formidable advantages of family and position, but he is nonetheless a self-made man. He does not rest on his privileges, to say nothing of parading them; on the contrary, he has parleyed his ancestral possessions into an imposing accumulation of new wealth. Hawthorne portrays Pyncheon as the opposite of Holgrave, but also as Holgrave's secret twin. We learn in due course that Holgrave likewise pursues his financial interest through stealth, concealing the fact that he is a descendant of the Pyncheon's ancestral enemies, the Maules.

Holgrave is fascinated and horrified by the fate of Jaffrey Pyncheon, who dies in keeping with the curse, blood bursting from his mouth as he sits alone in the parlor of the great house. Pyncheon embodies the spiritual empti-ness – ultimately the metaphysical horror – of a man made of masks in an anonymous modern society. Holgrave is shaken to his foundations when he confronts the Judge's fate: it "threw a great black shadow over everything; he made the universe, so far as my perception could reach, a scene of guilt, and of retribution more dreadful than the guilt" (II: 306).

Why is not Holgrave jubilant, given the age-long injustice done against his family? Why should he be frightened or depressed at this triumphant vindi-cation of the Maules? Yet Pyncheon's death represents the nemesis peculiar to the masculine existence Holgrave is seeking to live out. Holgrave rec-ognizes that so long as his undertakings are self-produced, self-made, and self-ratified, they are connected to nothing that can give them human value. "My past life, so lonesome and dreary; my future, a shapeless gloom, which I must mould into gloomy shapes" (II: 306).

Hawthorne supplies Holgrave with the antidote to this spiritual ailment that became conventional in antebellum America, namely a divinely pure woman. In the emerging domestic ideal, "true womanhood" matches "self-made manhood," and the household is now defined as "woman's sphere," a place uniquely attuned to the spiritual needs of self-made men. The "true woman" creates "the home," which offers a redemptive solace that counter-acts the corruption and spiritual desolation of "the world."

Holgrave is rescued by Phoebe Pyncheon, a country cousin of the Salem family who has escaped the family curse, and she fills the old house with sunshine. Wherever she goes, she radiates a magic that answers the yearning of unconnected men.

> Phoebe's presence made a home about her – that very sphere which the outcast, the prisoner, the potentate, the wretch beneath mankind, the wretch aside from it, or the wretch above it, instinctively pines after – a home! She was real! Holding her hand, you felt something; a tender something; a substance, and a warm one; and so long as you should feel its grasp, soft as it was, you might be certain that your place was good in the whole sympathetic chain of human nature. The world was no longer a delusion. (II: 140–41)

Within the domestic sphere, so the convention taught, a wife lives out the essence of her natural womanhood by bearing and rearing children, and by cultivating an atmosphere of selfless devotion to which the husband can return from the soul-destroying competition that he must wage in the public world of business and politics. Phoebe's purity of soul offers a redemption exactly suited to Holgrave's spiritual needs, and the two become engaged to marry at the conclusion of the narrative.

The House of the Seven Gables does not describe the married life of Phoebe and Holgrave, or the advent of children, and it exempts Holgrave from the requirements of gaining the financial capacity to support such a household. It turns out that Phoebe is the only heir of Jaffrey Pyncheon, which means that upon marriage the great fortune comes under Holgrave's control. Since Holgrave is descended from the Maule family, this conclusion serves Hawthorne's desire to represent the emergence of the middle-class family as correcting the wrongs inherent to the ancestral order of bloodline hierarchy. But it leaves urgent questions unanswered. How will Phoebe respond to the realization that her husband kept secret his relation to the Maule family in seeking the marriage that made him rich? How will the corrupt business arrangements required to manage Jaffrey's fortune affect their life together?

Hawthorne does not pursue these questions. *The House of the Seven Gables* dramatizes the social changes that produced the domestic ideal, but it does not explore the interior of that presumptive paradise, or the politics that unfold when "natural manhood" and "true womanhood" enter the intimacies of married life, and the economic forces that belong to "the world" bear in upon "the home."

Hellfire in the domestic paradise

Exponents of the domestic ideal hailed the sexual union of husband and wife as an enactment of the sacred intimacy between them. Families defined by lineage during the colonial era often joined husband to wife by parental agreement, because marriage involved the merging of financial establishments. But in the expanding economy of the early republic, the financial prospects of a couple depended upon the teamwork between them, more than on the acquisition of a patrimony. It became conventional for a man and woman to marry by mutual consent. Marriage itself was conceived as an intimate communion of souls, and the word "intercourse" was detached from commercial relations and applied to coition, signifying its central place in the communication between husband and wife.

The sexual life of a married couple lay at the heart of the domestic paradise that provided a refuge from the heartless world of male competition, yet it was defined nonetheless by economic forces. The manhood that was required for survival in the soulless combat of the capitalist economy could not be laid aside when a man escaped his disconcerting relations to other men, and came home to his wife. Within marriage his sexuality was perforce self-policed, because failure to exercise the manly virtue of stoical self-containment could destroy the family's prospect of entering the middle class, or of remaining within it.

In the colonial order, households were centers of economic production, and children could be put to work at farming or shoemaking or carpentry, and help provide for the support of the family. In the new urban and industrial economy, by contrast, large families became a liability. Men now left the home to make a living, and middle-class couples became "prudent procreators," in Mary Ryan's memorable phrase.[10] Having too many children could overwhelm a family's finances, and since reliable means of contraception did not exist, sexual abstinence was the only sure means of controlling the number of offspring. Thus the pressures of the marketplace bore directly on the sexual relations of husband and wife.

The result was a new sexual order, signaled by an extensive advice literature aimed at promoting "male purity." As the studies of G. J. Barker-Benfield and Stephen Nissenbaum have illustrated, sexual anxieties became commonplace among middle-class men during this era, inspiring an anti-masturbation mania that warned against sexual "pollution." Sylvester Graham's program of diet and hygiene acquired many adherents, who hoped to escape the dreaded consequences of "excessive lasciviousness" within marriage as well as without.[11]

An ideal of purity became a defining virtue of the domestic angel, and assigned women the task of allaying male sexual anxiety. Before the early nineteenth century women were generally believed to possess more powerful sexual desires than men, and to govern them less easily. But the new sexual order reversed this. "Pure" women were expected to display a radiant nun-like innocence, which aided men in retaining self-control by transmuting their lust into reverent admiration. Since a virtuous wife prompted her man to pay her adoring attentions that would not get her pregnant, her purity was a form of psychic birth-control, necessary to the limitation of family size on which the maintenance of middle-class status depended.

Early in their marriage, Hawthorne praised his wife Sophia for possessing exactly such purity. He likened her to a "pond-lily," of the sort that he found rooted in a disgusting slime at the bottom of the Concord River, which he saw as an emblem of sexual contamination. The river bottom is the resort of eels, frogs, and mud-turtles, Hawthorne tells us, that he could scarcely bear to touch. Unlike the yellow lily, whose foul odor and stained petals give evidence of its nasty rootage, the pond-lily is transcendently pure. "It is a marvel," Hawthorne remarks, "how the pond-lily derives its loveliness and perfume, sprouting as it does from the black mud over which the river sleeps, and from which, likewise, the yellow lily draws its unclean life." Transmuting sexual filth into stainless innocence, the pond-lily becomes an icon of woman's purity. "I possess such a human and heavenly lily," Hawthorne concludes, "and wear it in my bosom" (VIII: 318–19).

The need to place marital sex under rigorous voluntary control created a middle-class sexual culture that was structured by pairs of opposing categories, the most notorious being the whore/angel dichotomy. For women aspiring to be domestic angels, a single deviance from absolute purity was "ruin," since the line separating pure women from their fallen sisters could only be crossed once, and only in one direction. Dramas of lost purity, both personal and literary, became a cultural obsession.

Together with the male purity movement, and the anti-masturbation campaign, there emerged a new genre of pornography during this era, which featured endless repetitions of a single narrative, in which innocent damsels are despoiled by worldly rakes. Unlike the illicit writing of the pre-revolutionary era, this new genre does not invite the reader to laugh at sexual vices, but to enter a gothic realm in which he shares the guilt that follows from the corrupting of innocence. Men reading the new porn were sexually aroused by the contamination of innocent damsels, even as they were horrified.[12]

The angel/whore dichotomy aided males in coping with their chronic sexual anxiety. The angel sustains the man as he wishes to imagine himself, his existence – including his sexuality – regulated by the imperatives of self-reliance. The "whore" embodies the man exhilarated but guilt-stricken by a sexual arousal that defies voluntary control. The chronic sexual conflict afflicting men was thus projected onto women, under the theory that nature ordains for women a purity that is fatally contaminated by lust. Imagining that this paradox of male sexuality was inherent to the essence of womanhood had the advantage (for men) of concealing its source in the core dilemmas of self-reliant masculinity. For men to acknowledge such dilemmas as their own would provide an additional confounding instance of male abjection – the lack of self-command that bedevils self-commanding manhood.

Set against his fellows by the folkways of competition, the self-sufficient man is set against himself by the whole range of his human vulnerabilities. His need for companionship, his subjection to the contingencies of a market economy, his exposure to illness, to accident and misfortune, to the tumults of his sexuality: the whole burden of what men suffer lies in a zone of experience that such a man can ill afford to acknowledge, since it refutes the ideal of manhood he is compelled to uphold. Every self-reliant man is haunted by a specter of "not-manhood," imposed by his tacit awareness that meeting the demands of self-sufficient manhood is impossible. The male-dominant culture of Hawthorne's time created ideals of womanhood, in particular of womanly sexuality, that were organized by the internal contradictions of the male role, as the new social order defined that role.

Hawthorne was fascinated lifelong by the male psychodynamics of feminine purity, and treats them in such early tales as "Young Goodman Brown" and "The Minister's Black Veil." The anxiety deepens in the works he produced following his marriage, as does the intensity of his vision of contaminated womanhood. As Nina Baym observes, "The Birth-Mark" and "Rappaccini's Daughter" express a male imagination for which sexual attraction is virtually indistinguishable from revulsion.[13]

In *The Scarlet Letter* Hawthorne explores the intramale conflicts that are produced by the ideal of masculine self-command, and the sexual consternations that result. The characters of Arthur Dimmesdale and Roger Chillingworth depict the fragments into which men's souls are broken by this convention, and he explores the complex fabric of their interaction. Roger and Arthur spend more time with each other than either spends with Hester Prynne, and as the narrative unfolds they are more intimately involved with each other's lives than with hers. These inseparable opposites decide to live together, and in the end they die together.

Roger Chillingworth, with his cold scientific composure, dramatizes a self-control that has itself become compulsive, as the opening scene indicates. He sees his wife on the scaffold, with another man's child in her arms; and this spectacle triggers an involuntary effort of self-command.

> A writhing horror twisted itself across his features, like a snake gliding swiftly over them, and making one little pause, with all its wreathed intervolutions in open sight. His face darkened with some powerful emotion, which, nevertheless, he so instantaneously controlled by an effort of his will, that, save at a single moment, its expression might have passed for calmness. After a brief space, the convulsion grew almost imperceptible, and finally subsided into the depths of his nature. (1: 61)

Roger masters this passion by exercising his "will," but so "instantaneously" that the effort itself is marked as automatic. Momentarily visible is a snake-like writhing, which intimates the erotic energy that is invested both in the hidden feelings and in the compulsion to keep them concealed. The "penetrative" glance that precedes this "convulsion" likewise bespeaks the sexual passion that Chillingworth has incorporated into his commitment to a rational self-possessed masculinity.

From the outset of his researches into the identity of Hester's lover, Roger looks forward to the crescendo of sexual excitement that will mark his progress. "There is a sympathy that will make me conscious of him. I shall see him tremble. I shall feel myself shudder, suddenly and unawares. Sooner or later, he must needs be mine!" (1: 75). His desire for such moments of delicious tremor is Roger's chief motive for pursuing Arthur. Hawthorne describes nothing in the way of a real investigation: no other suspects are even considered, and Roger makes no effort to dig up tangible evidence. Instead, Hawthorne notes, Roger falls victim to "a terrible fascination, a kind of fierce, though still calm, necessity seized the old man within its gripe, and never set him free again, until he had done all its bidding" (1: 129).

As sexual self-containment governs Roger's craving, so it defines the self-loathing that consumes Arthur Dimmesdale. Because of his adultery with Hester Prynne, Arthur experiences himself as contaminated, his existence "utterly a pollution and a lie" (1: 143). The passions that lie hidden behind Roger's calm face ravage the surface of Dimmesdale's life, making the tortures of failed masculine virtue visible to everyone in the community. The success of Arthur's ministry depends, in fact, on his skill at offering the public a chance to participate vicariously in the torment of his inner life. His listeners are moved by his "tremulously sweet, rich, deep, and broken" voice (1: 67); they are attuned to a "cry of pain" that softens their hearts, no matter what his ostensible topic may be (1: 243).

The manliness Arthur has polluted through yielding is the same that Chillingworth has demonized through unconscious denial and the quest for vicarious fulfillment. This specific form of pollution – the vice correlative to just such a manliness – makes Arthur "intimate with the sinful brotherhood of mankind; so that his heart vibrated in unison with theirs" (1: 142).

The interplay of opposites portrayed by Chillingworth and Dimmesdale reflects the notions of manhood and womanhood that we have outlined. Chillingworth's obsessive self-containment and self-reliance are gendered "manly," while Dimmesdale's submission to emotional tumult is "womanly." Only when these two figures are taken together does the formation of American masculinity itself come clear: what the conventional ideal of manhood calls "manly" is only one side of a two-sided reality.

Fascinated by the liabilities that followed from this ideological denial, Hawthorne explores them in his fiction through paired figures that are analogous to Roger/Arthur. The blacksmith and the watchmaker are counterpoised in "The Artist of the Beautiful," like Jaffrey and Clifford Pyncheon in *The House of the Seven Gables*, Hollingsworth/Coverdale in *The Blithedale Romance*, and Robert Hagburn/Septimius Felton in the manuscripts that he left unfinished at the end of his life. Pursuing the restive tensions and secret affinities between these figures permits Hawthorne to brood over the tragic dilemmas that came to afflict masculine experience during his era, which produce their continuing harvest of misery in our own time.

The disgust at "non-manliness" persists not only as a blight upon the relations of American women and men, but also as a systematic injustice against gay men. Homophobia imagines that men animated by same-sex desire are themselves not "real men," but embody an opposite of manhood all the more loathsome because secretly alluring.[14] Hawthorne himself was prominently characterized by such "non-manly" traits. His notable shyness and preference for solitude resulted in good measure from the fact that his emotional life, like that of Arthur Dimmesdale, was exceptionally turbulent, so that he found routine social interactions difficult. Talking to Hawthorne, said his college friend Henry Wadsworth Longfellow, was "like talking to a woman."[15]

Hawthorne was also a man of extraordinary physical beauty, who was well aware – and uneasily aware – of awakening sexual desire, both in women and in men. Even if Hawthorne had not been artistically inclined, to say nothing of leading the life of a writer, his familiar social relations would have made his "manhood" suspect. The factors that converged to give Hawthorne a "feminine" identity had a paradoxical result: they led him to insist all the more compulsively on his commitment to the conventional ideal of masculine self-direction.

There is good reason to believe that a sexual bond took form between Hawthorne and Herman Melville, as their friendship blossomed in the 1850s. Melville, likewise tormented by self-doubts over his artistic vocation, found "ineffable socialities" in the encouragement and comradeship that Hawthorne offered him.[16] The ardent fraternal feeling that pervades Melville's early letters to Hawthorne gave way to an uneasy estrangement that troubled Melville long after Hawthorne himself was dead. Little documentary evidence survives to indicate Hawthorne's response to Melville's overtures, and what remains is characteristically enigmatic and self-contained.

Hawthorne never challenged outright the ideal of self-reliant masculinity that made his own existence suspect, but he poured his distresses into a procession of womanly characters who recur in his fiction as frequently as the paired males. Hester Prynne, Zenobia in *The Blithedale Romance*, and Miriam in *The Marble Faun* share a bitter resentment at the lot of women, and imagine a transformation of society in which the systematic injustice that they suffer will be abolished. Hawthorne condemns all these characters for violating their womanly "nature," yet they are among his most powerfully realized and enduring creations. Hawthorne judges Hester Prynne against the standards of the gender system against which he found himself wanting, yet readers have come to judge that gender system itself against the figure of Hester Prynne.[17]

Toward democratic masculinities

It may seem strange to say that Hawthorne offers a vision of masculinity through Hester Prynne. She does, of course, bear a child; and she is confined to needlework as her means of support because other avenues of gainful effort are closed to her. Yet as many critics have noted, the depiction of Hester's womanly plight is governed by Hawthorne's masculine concerns. Hawthorne's ambivalence appears not only in the way he condemns Hester's rebellion, but also in his portrayal of that rebellion, where his own resistance to the ruling gender system finds the freedom to declare itself.

Hester bitterly resents the thwarted life that her society has compelled her to accept, and sees her plight as bearing on "the whole race of womanhood. Was existence worth accepting, even to the happiest among them?" She gauges the social changes that are necessary to remove the injustices women suffer:

> As a first step, the whole system of society is to be torn down, and built up anew. Then, the very nature of the opposite sex, or its long hereditary habit, which has become like nature, is to be essentially modified, before woman can be allowed to assume what seems a fair and suitable position. Finally, all other difficulties being obviated, woman cannot take advantage of these preliminary reforms, until she herself shall have undergone a still mightier change; in which, perhaps, the ethereal essence, wherein she has her truest life, will be found to have evaporated. (1: 165–66)

Thus Hawthorne restates his creed, that manhood and womanhood are gender identities ordained by nature and nature's God, universal essences at once biological and ethereal. Yet this avowal is undermined by shrewdly framed expressions of skepticism. Is it the "nature" of the male sex that must be changed, or merely its "long hereditary habit"? Is it *necessary* for the "truest life" of woman to be sacrificed, or is that only a danger? Is the psycho-social revolution Hester contemplates a perversion, or is it simply very difficult?

Hester exercises a "freedom of speculation" dramatically at odds with the conventions that govern the social arrangements that enmesh her. "In her lonesome cottage thoughts visited her, such as dared to enter no other dwelling in New England." Hester possesses an emancipated intellect, native to the revolutionary politics racking the English homeland during this era: "Men of the sword had overthrown nobles and kings. Men bolder than these had overthrown and rearranged – not actually, but within the sphere of theory, which was their most real abode – the whole system of ancient prejudice, wherewith was linked much of ancient principle" (1: 164).

Thus Hawthorne evokes the struggle taking place in his own time concerning democratic standards of equality. In speaking of "ancient prejudice" he alludes to the doctrines of bloodline hierarchy and manhood inequality, while "ancient principle" refers to the belief that nature ordains the subservience of women to men. Hawthorne ostensibly claims here that male dominance should be preserved.

Hester's rebellion asserts the reverse, and speaks for the feminist movement afoot in Hawthorne's time. Two years before *The Scarlet Letter* was published, the Seneca Falls Convention of 1848 issued a "Declaration of Sentiments," which echoes the Declaration of Independence, stating that "all men and women are created equal."[18] Hawthorne modeled the character of Hester Prynne on that of Margaret Fuller, a longstanding friend who had published *Woman in the Nineteenth Century* in 1846 where she likewise insisted that the charter of democratic equality demands equal rights for women.

Hawthorne gives Hester feminist convictions that challenge the validity of the masculine role that Hawthorne found it so hard to live out. As Hester imagines the advent of a new society grounded on gender equality, she recognizes that changing social arrangements must be accompanied by changes in the emotional anatomy of women and men. The "very nature" of men must be "essentially modified," while women must undergo a change that reorganizes the "ethereal essence" that seems at present to define "her truest life." Hester is herself a harbinger of just such a reconstruction; she recognizes that intellectual boldness, despite its traditional association with manhood, is native to her character.

Hester creates a frontier selfhood, beyond the boundaries that map conventional differences between manhood and womanhood, and her courage in doing so may provide inspiration to men in our own time who, like Hawthorne, feel themselves stigmatized as "effeminate" or "queer" by the masculine code that became conventional in Hawthorne's era. Such a frontier selfhood also beckons men who are haunted, as Hawthorne was haunted, by the horror that accompanies relentless, self-reliant self-seeking, the realization that "there is no reality in the life and fortunes, good or bad, of a being so unconnected" (XII: 258).

Hawthorne was present at the creation of an American masculinity that is now being challenged across a broad front, in the name of egalitarian relations between women and men.[19] Hawthorne was sharply aware that the reigning model of manhood, defined by unceasing self-reliant competition, violated his own native temperament. He stubbornly insisted on the right to fulfill that temperament in defiance of conventional prohibitions, and portrayed that defiance in Hester. He recognized implicitly that any single model of manhood, made compulsory for all males, alienates men from themselves and one another, just as unitary doctrines of "true womanhood" stunt the lives of women. The democratic masculinities being fashioned in our own time promise a greater measure of justice and fulfillment not only for women, but also for men, and the visionary courage that Hawthorne projects into Hester Prynne animates the effort to realize those prospects.

Hawthorne's art lives, and will continue to live, not because it codified or subverted the gender system that came to dominance in the early nineteenth century, but because it captures the atmosphere of cultural creation itself, the transitional state in which no convention altogether rules, and new possibilities become visible.

NOTES

1. Rose Hawthorne Lathrop, *Memories of Hawthorne* (Boston: Houghton Mifflin, 1897), p. 480.
2. Quoted in Karen Halttunen, *Confidence Men and Painted Women: A Study of Middle-Class Culture in America, 1830-1870* (New Haven, CT: Yale University Press, 1982), p. 25.
3. For an intercultural study, see David Gilmore, *Manhood in the Making: Cultural Concepts of Masculinity* (New Haven, CT: Yale University Press, 1990). For historical studies see Michael Kimmel, *Manhood in America: a Cultural History* (New York: Free Press, 1996), and Anthony Rotundo, *American Manhood: Transformations in Masculinity From the Revolution to the Modern Era* (New York: Basic Books, 1993). For multiple masculinities within our own culture see R. W. Connell, *Masculinities* (Berkeley: University of California Press, 1995). For a discussion of the nature/nurture issue see Richard Wrangham and Dale Peterson, *Demonic Males: Apes and the Origins of Human Violence* (Boston: Houghton Mifflin, 1996), pp. 94–96.
4. Nathaniel Hawthorne, "Mrs. Hutchinson," in *Fanshawe and Other Pieces* (Boston: np, 1876), pp. 168–69.
5. See Irvin G. Wyllie, *The Self-Made Man in America: The Myth of Rags to Riches* (New Brunswick, NJ: Rutgers University Press, 1954).
6. *The Book of Abigail and John: Selected Letters of the Adams Family, 1762–1783*, ed. with an Introduction by L. H. Butterfield (Cambridge, MA: Harvard University Press, 1975), p. 121.
7. See Joseph Pleck, *The Myth of Masculinity* (Cambridge, MA: MIT Press, 1981), and "The Gender Role Strain Paradigm: An Update," in Ronald F. Levant and William S. Pollack, eds., *A New Psychology of Men* (New York: Basic Books, 1995).
8. Henry James, "Hawthorne," 1897. Reprinted in *The Shock of Recognition*, ed. Edmund Wilson (New York: Modern Library, 1943), pp. 425–565, p. 502.
9. Alexis de Tocqueville, *Democracy in America*, 2 vols. (New York: Alfred A. Knopf, 1976), II: 180–81.
10. Mary Ryan, *Cradle of the Middle Class: The Family in Oneida County, New York, 1790–1865* (Cambridge: Cambridge University Press, 1981), p. 180.

11. G. J. Barker-Benfield, *The Horrors of the Half-Known Life: Male Attitudes toward Women and Sexuality in Nineteenth-Century America*, 2nd edn. (New York: Routledge, 2000). Stephen Nissenbaum, *Sex, Diet and Debility in Jacksonian America: Sylvester Graham and Health Reform* (Westport, CT: Greenwood Press 1980), pp. 106–10.

12. See David Reynolds, *Beneath the American Renaissance: The Subversive Imagination in the Age of Emerson and Melville* (New York: Alfred A. Knopf, 1988), pp. 211–24. See also T. Walter Herbert, *Sexual Violence and American Manhood* (Cambridge, MA: Harvard University Press, 2002).

13. Nina Baym, "Thwarted Nature: Nathaniel Hawthorne as Feminist," in Fritz Fleischmann, ed., *American Novelists Revisited: Essays in Feminist Criticism* (Boston: G. K. Hall, 1982), pp. 63–66.

14. Michael Kimmel, "Masculinity as Homophobia: Fear, Shame and Silence in the Construction of Gender Identity," in Mary M. Gergen and Sara N. Davis, eds., *Toward a New Psychology of Gender* (New York: Routledge, 1997), pp. 22–47.

15. George Parsons Lathrop, "Biographical Sketch," *Tales, Sketches, and Other Papers by Nathaniel Hawthorne with a Biographical Sketch by George Parsons Lathrop* 1883 (Freeport: Books for Libraries, 1972), pp. 441–559.

16. Merrell R. Davis and William H. Gilman (eds.), *The Letters of Herman Melville* (New Haven: Yale University Press, 1960), p. 142. For a discussion of the relationship between Hawthorne and Melville, see Edwin Haviland Miller, *Salem is my Dwelling Place: A Life of Nathaniel Hawthorne* (Iowa City: University of Iowa Press, 1991), pp. 353–65.

17. See Carolyn G. Heilbrun, *Toward a Recognition of Androgyny* (New York: Knopf, 1972).

18. Aileen S. Kraditor, *Up from the Pedestal: Selected Writings in the History of American Feminism* (Chicago: Quadrangle Books, 1968), p. 184.

19. For a summary, see T. Walter Herbert, "Democratic Masculinities," chapter 7 of *Sexual Violence and American Manhood* (Cambridge, MA: Harvard University Press, 2002).

4

ALISON EASTON

Hawthorne and the question of women

In 1802, less than thirty-one weeks after her wedding, Elizabeth Manning Hathorne gave birth to her first child, Elizabeth. Nathaniel Hawthorne the writer, her second child, was born two years later. Interestingly, there are only two things we can say with certainty about this bridal pregnancy. First, we do not know how Hawthorne's parents, their families or indeed Hawthorne himself regarded it. Second, the reason that we cannot infer their responses is that, while one in three brides were pregnant in the last third of the eighteenth century, by 1850 when Hawthorne published *The Scarlet Letter* bridal pregnancies had become infrequent and completely unacceptable.[1]

When sexual codes alter thus much and so quickly, something much wider is happening in society. This late eighteenth-century incidence of premarital sex was "a product of profound social disequilibrium,"[2] and disappeared once familial, social, and economic situations changed yet again. Hawthorne's lifetime (1804–64) spans a period of great and rapid change when, in little over half a century, America transformed itself politically, economically, and in its social arrangements. Hawthorne grew up surrounded by family and townspeople born around or before the Revolution. As he reached adulthood, the Early Republic was metamorphosing into Jacksonian America as the onset of industrial capitalism reinforced an ethos of individualism. He married in 1842 at a time when the so-called middling classes were consolidating, not without difficulty, into a new bourgeoisie in an urbanizing and industrializing northeast. Spending much of the troubled 1850s in Europe, he nonetheless returned to America in time for the Civil War. Furthermore, these enormous changes were contested and uneven in spread.

Increasingly, in the Northern states, key points of disturbance in this evolution were slavery, the new urban/industrial working class, and, particularly for the emergent middle class, the condition of women. Profound ambivalences about women lay at the center of both middle-class emotional life and the republic's idea of itself as a nation of liberty and equality. Even though the

Revolution had excluded women politically from its democratic promises, it nonetheless initiated a persistent debate about female roles, while ushering in new economic structures that would simultaneously constrain women and encourage their social questioning.[3]

This is one of those historical moments that remind us that patriarchal structures do not remain constant, and the sites of tension change. Class formation too is a crucial factor. Post-Revolution family structures and values gradually but significantly altered, placing new emphasis on a love-relationship between husband and wife and on nurturing self-governance in children, and rather less on wider kin and community relations. There was an accompanying shift away from traditional categorizing of women in terms of subservience, weakness, and inferiority toward a notion of the tender female "heart"; women's social dependency was reconstructed as a female concern for others. So, while women might want the same increased opportunities as men and indeed some did paid work in the burgeoning capitalist economy until the late 1830s, new sex role distinctions were firmly in place by the end of the eighteenth century that would eventually pin most married white women and unmarried middle-class women to the home. In the late 1830s the middle-class home emerged, re-imagined as a private sanctuary from the world of money-making.

So, powerful ideological images came to dominate bourgeois women's lives and thinking about women mid-century. Nonetheless, Hawthorne was in his thirties before this view of marriage became dominant, and even when well established, it was never a wholly shared, coherent, or simple vision socially. There was bound to be a gap between lived experiences, and the bourgeois ideology of "True Womanhood," that is to say a pious, asexual, submissive, domestic femininity. Women also knew the importance of self-reliance, hard work, orderliness, and practical skills. Nor were they "passionless"; rather, the evidence is that sexual experience was highly valued but extremely private. While fervid attempts were made to close the gap between ideology and experience, Hawthorne was to explore the multiple implications of this socially constructed doubleness.

This duality of image and actuality was not resolved by the simple rejection of "True Womanhood." There is a curious ambivalence about this apparently conservative notion of femininity. Despite appearances of coherence and authority, ideologies always contain the seeds of contradiction, dissension, and change; middle-class womanhood, turned another way, revealed radical potential. Paradoxically, middle-class women used these feminine values creatively and dynamically to critique the republican and capitalist world that gave these values existence. The first feminist and reformist interventions in the 1830s, 1840s, and 1850s were not just historically concurrent with the establishment of middle-class domesticity; certain forms of feminism existed in symbiotic relationship with it. Whereas present-day feminists might see domesticity in conflict with opportunities outside the home or espouse a radically oppositional stance, their mid nineteenth-century predecessors deployed the utopian elements of women's "nature" and domestic ideology (the home as a morally better world), together with the politics of equal rights, to work for improved models of marriage, family, and hence society.

Although ideological efforts were made to contain the question of women through the concept of separate gendered "spheres" of existence, men's and women's lives were, of course, inextricably intertwined; only in ideology were women and domesticity totally aligned to the exclusion of the public. Margaret Fuller, the greatest feminist thinker of mid-century America, based her analysis, *Woman in the Nineteenth Century* (1845), on this understanding that women were not insulated from the public realm, nor were men detached from the domestic, but that all inhabited a common world, albeit differently. There was no way that Hawthorne could have been unaffected.

Hawthorne's personal position, too, involved some fascinatingly unstable gender and class boundaries. As his college contemporaries settled down, he seems to have continued to resist the worlds to which he was expected to belong, remaining half inside, half outside. The more he became implicated in a middle-class world from the late 1840s, the more it had the power to disturb him. Hawthorne's situation has to be construed in terms of class and gender together. An impoverished patrician male facing with distaste the competitive, commercialized world though relishing the individualism at its base, he came to know from personal experience the fragility of middle-class life and, most importantly, understood that life as a construction.[4] This does not mean that Hawthorne always rejected the middle-class world (obviously it was preferable to poverty), but he had a different understanding of it from many of his contemporaries.

Even before these 1850s understandings, there is much to encourage views at a tangent. From the age of four, the fatherless Hawthorne was raised in an extended family that included several generations of women, in a town with powerful women and a state that included many independent-minded, unmarried women, including his sister, Ebe, and his sister-in-law, the educationalist and associate of the Transcendentalists, Elizabeth Palmer Peabody. Indeed, Sophia Peabody, equally intelligent and independent-minded, wed Nathaniel in the house in which Margaret Fuller held her ground-breaking "Conversations" on feminist topics (that Sophia herself had attended).[5] Hawthorne's skepticism about reformers does not mean that he did not share their questions.

Moreover, Hawthorne, as an author with only limited periods of paid public employment, demonstrated in his own person the fallacy of that economic and ideological separation of home and work, writing as he did at home and thus in more continuous contact with what was deemed the female sphere. His position, however, was distinct from women's, and while a striking number of his contemporaries commented on his "feminine" qualities, this certainly did not mean that he identified with women. Authorship was one of the few kinds of work that brought men directly into competition with women. It might, nonetheless, suggest that acquaintances had spotted in him something unconventional that had to be construed as "feminine" in such a dualistic gender culture. His relationships with women were a confused mixture of the supportive and the competitive, but readerly connections with women were undoubtedly important.[6] So, the "Woman Question," as the nineteenth century liked to call it, becomes a double one for Hawthorne's critics. There is evidence of both feminist and misogynist views in his imaginative and non-fictional writings which have been hotly debated, but there simply is no certainty about what he believed, and we should be wary when his texts make apparently definitive pronouncements. The inconsistencies and shifts in attitudes are hardly surprising given how much he wrote over a long, disturbed period. There is, too, the matter of readers' complicities and resistances, our inevitable historical blinkers. It is undeniably tempting for twenty-first century critics to construct Hawthorne in our own image, but to read his works as simply feminist or misogynist – as presently defined – we would have to ignore a great deal.

So, rather than pursue a primarily biographical and/or psychoanalytical approach to Hawthorne on the question of women (compelling though such approaches can be), this chapter aims to see what his texts look like in the context of these shifting, contradictory gender/class patterns. These are unresolved and often turbulent texts whose attractions lie in their instabilities. The texts embody his society's contradictions concerning women, yet troubled though the narrator of "The Haunted Mind" is by dreams, he is also "wide-awake in that realm of illusions" (IX: 304). Likewise, Hawthorne's modern readers will find him ahead of us in the work of identifying his society's dreams and contradictions about women. He thematizes its problems, quotes its formulations so that we hear them freshly, and dramatizes its conflicts, while his sense of historical change in the way men and women live modifies his own and his culture's attachment to the idea of an unchanging female "nature."[7]

In one of Hawthorne's earliest stories, "The Wives of the Dead" (1832), two women, married to brothers and sharing one household, have heard on successive days of their husbands' deaths at sea and on the frontier. During the ensuing night each woman, separately while the other sleeps, learns (or perhaps, only dreams that she learns) that her husband is alive after all. The tale exquisitely suggests through setting and action how, even alone and in loss, their subjectivity is persistently bound up not only with their husbands but also with sister-in-law, neighbours, ex-suitors and other townspeople. This pre-Revolutionary world of wide interconnections is different from the highly privatized, middle-class family structure that was to establish itself in 1830s America. Its loss is prefigured here: for all the attractive images of sharing and affectionate caring (the open bed-curtains and window), each woman's thoughts are hidden even from the person whose situation directly mirrors hers, and the tale's promise of wholeness may be imaginary. This introversion is reinforced by the way that events are presented as real, yet could be, we reluctantly realize, only the baffled incredulity of the very recently bereaved.

Hawthorne's work in the 1820s and 1830s has many disastrous "wives of the dead" whose lives, even if their husband still lives, are hollowed out by his actions or, alternatively, by the woman's own desires, and yet retain the shape of their original relationships: Faith in "Young Goodman Brown," Dorcas in "Roger Malvin's Burial," Catharine in "The Gentle Boy," and Mrs. Wakefield in "Wakefield," to name the most familiar. These female "haunted minds" differ from their bewildered, divided male counterparts in retaining a stronger sense of the connections that, even when fractured, still define them as daughters, wives, and mothers. Thus, the adulteress's story in "The Hollow of the Three Hills," Hawthorne's earliest extant tale, is presented entirely through hyper-vivid scenes of her family filling her mind. This relational female subject is characteristic of the period's ideas about women, although "The Wives of the Dead" suggests interconnectedness throughout that community. This tale's unusually extended treatment of female subjectivity is facilitated by the centrality of the women's friendship, the only relationship offering equality in this world.

In other tales of this period, female intersubjectivity means that "widows" are profoundly affected when the male protagonist repeatedly rejects, abandons, or destroys his home. Given the traditional location of women within a household, this raises a key question: who or what are women when "unhoused"? In some cases, the catastrophe that overwhelms the husband, severing him emotionally from the world of which he nonetheless remains a part, leaves the narrative trapped inside his head. In "Roger Malvin's Burial," when Reuben's imagined guilt compulsively takes the family journeying ever closer to Dorcas's father's long unburied body, she is absorbed in a pretty family "day-dream" (x: 352). Her retention of household rituals in the wilderness (white tablecloth, and song about the hearth) proves as delusional as her original settlement-bred expectations that unwittingly triggered Reuben's disastrous lie to "her whom he most loved and trusted" (x: 349). At the terrifying denouement she wakes from that dream to the violent obliteration of her family and lapses into unconsciousness. Wakefield, on the other hand, has a more complicated investment in his wife as a guarantor of his identity in the anonymous city: his impulsive move to live for twenty years secretly in an adjacent street, is predicated on his desire to see how his "exemplary wife will endure her widowhood, of a week" (IX: 134) and longer. While she "sometimes doubts whether she is a widow" (IX: 133) and remains in the family house, her husband's continued absence eventually reduces her to a mere shadow thrown by the hearth and glimpsed from the street. The tale deliberately turns from her: "our business is with the husband" (IX: 133) who is and is not a husband.

Such "unhousings," even when set back historically, reflect fears and desires of a transitional early nineteenth-century America, moving away from older forms of social, economic, and intimate relationships, but before a bourgeois family structure emerged to impose some imagined order. This unease gets focused on ideas of "home" and the women who inhabit it. One story, "The Ambitious Guest," sees a traditional, extended family living beside a busy commercial highway leave their home, its security threatened by landslides, only to flee "right into the pathway of destruction" (IX: 333). Faith in "Young Goodman Brown" is a subtler exploration of the same doomed desire to find a refuge. Events are precipitated by Brown's rejection of his wife's appeal to stay home: because he imagines that "'twould kill her to think" (x: 75) of the witches' Sabbath, he fails at this point to heed her remark, "A lone woman is troubled by such dreams and such thoughts that she's afeard of herself, sometimes" (x: 74). Later middle-class ideology created the image of pure, selfless women to help stabilize a shifting society, but Faith cannot be thus simplified, and Brown's refusal consciously to acknowledge this turns her out into the forest (either in actuality or in his imagination). Because of the cunningly irresolvable narrative indeterminacies, the tale demands that the reader live with a double view of her whereas Brown can see only warring incompatibles: her desires outside common moral codes, and her loving care for her husband.

Tales dealing centrally with a woman made literally homeless by her sexuality or activism show signs of struggle between alarm at female autonomy and understanding that as wife, mother, or daughter she cannot simply be rejected. "The Gentle Boy" shifts uneasily before the spectacle of Catharine, a proselytizing Quaker challenging patriarchal authority. Hawthorne's contemporary sketch about another challenger of the seventeenth-century Puritan state, Ann Hutchinson, makes the explicit connection with some early nineteenth-century women moving into the public realm: "there are portentous indications, changes gradually taking place in the habits and feelings of the gentle sex" (XXIII: 66). But whereas the narrator of the sketch, "Mrs. Hutchinson," clings to the idea of a "natural" domestic femininity, the extended fictional form of "The Gentle Boy" works to expose dramatically the incoherent violence, ambivalent responses, and multiple ironies that such female protagonists unleash. Quakerism is not only an image of civil disturbance; it is also the means of suggesting a complex femininity, apparently conventional in its stress on pacifism and the promptings of the "heart" that can make the men "tender" or "gentle," and yet giving strikingly eloquent, angry public voice to anti-patriarchal dissent and "mighty passion" (IX: 81).

"The Gentle Boy" does not, however, validate female rebellion. Something complicated is enacted that may be less satisfying to some twenty-first-century feminist readers looking for a narrative of liberation and autonomy, but also rather more interesting. First, whatever the political rights in the dispute, the tale is interested in the violent feelings both sides provoke in each other. Second, these reactions become muffled and confused when dealing with women. Catharine's sackcloth and ash-strewn hair (a deliberately un-beautiful undress) dramatize distraught widowhood, yet this is less important than her faltering but persistent maternal identity, most movingly in her physical memory of holding her newborn child. She evokes in the narrator and spectators pity and condemnation in equal part. If her assertion of spiritual autonomy is a trope for early radical feminist dissent, the child presents the irreducible problem.

While the tale momentarily offers a "practical allegory" (IX: 85) that contrasts Catharine with the other bereaved mother – calm, domestic Dorothy – the tale's interest lies elsewhere in its exposure of mixed motives and complex ironies. Dorothy is one of a cluster of female characters in Hawthorne's work at this time, whose "simplicity" (the key word) fends off the threat of duplicity, hidden depths, or, most threateningly, a combination of overt sexuality and lack of democratic attachments. But other sentimental and comic versions of these simple women reveal them to be props in a lonely masculine fantasy, fables of idealized home-making in settings remote from urban modernity.

The immature Robin in "My Kinsman, Major Molineux" (1832), faced with revolutionary riot, concedes that a man may have "several voices," but adds, "Heaven forbid that a woman should!" (XI: 226). "The Gentle Boy" with its unreconciled voices may appeal to modern readers' appreciation of irony, but its sentimental force made it Hawthorne's single most popular work until *The Scarlet Letter*. Admiring readers included the feminist Fuller, who assumed the tale's then anonymous author was female, and Sophia Peabody, who during her subsequent engagement to Hawthorne illustrated a third reprint. In the tale its first readers recognized powerful, central elements of their formulation of the "Woman Question": issues of liberty and power (the woman unhoused), but also issues of distinct female family responsibilities ("duties") and women's place (a "home") within a community.

In comparison, the enclosure and subjection of women in two major short fictions written in the next decade are shocking. Georgiana in "The Birth-Mark" (1843) makes the move from "my mother's side" (x: 37) to hearth and marriage bed, and then to a closeted boudoir in her husband's laboratory. Beatrice in "Rappaccini's Daughter" never leaves the walled garden where her botanizing father practices his experimental medicine. In these tales men and women inhabit the same sphere, but this is a murderous intimacy. Both men subject these women's bodies to radical physical change in violent pursuit of a masculine dream of physical perfection and absolute power. Both women protest impotently – Beatrice asserts that she is more than poisonous flesh, while Georgiana, without claiming even that degree of autonomy, would rather be dead than continue to disgust her husband with her birthmark. Both women die, sacrificing themselves for men demonstrably undeserving of such inordinate devotion.

These tales reflect significant change. Hawthorne's marriage in 1842 coincided with the major shift in social and emotional structures in urban America as a new, well-to-do middle-class existence assumed its distinctive shape in the developing industrial capitalist economy, with men out at work and women at home. By placing love at the center of marriage, a peculiarly intimate relationship was being constructed in which men and women, defined as if belonging to two different planets, were enclosed together in inescapable intimacy. For women, the choice of partner could be frighteningly important. These tales register a newly explicit and coercive ideology with its confusing demands that men were to worship their wives as their moral superiors even while remaining heads of household. So, marriage, rather than political power, was the key site for the "Woman Question": Fuller's *Woman in the Nineteenth Century*, sold out within a week of publication, was read as a kind of marriage manual.

Hawthorne's position is harder to define. The Hawthornes' precarious finances in the first ten years of marriage demystified the bourgeois illusion, while their initial residence at Concord among Transcendentalists and other dissenting figures signaled their desire to distance themselves somewhat from the new moneyed class and its dominant ideologies. More than half the tales written at Concord, including "Rappaccini's Daughter," were published in the *Democratic Review*, a journal committed to women's issues. Sophia and then Nathaniel Hawthorne were good friends with Margaret Fuller during this important period – a time also central in Fuller's life while she was evolving her feminist analysis of women's position. While this association did not make Hawthorne a feminist in the Fuller mold, it seems that Fuller helped open up the debate on marriage and gender roles that had first become pressing for Sophia and Nathaniel during their long engagement: they had wanted to get their marriage right. Fuller too had high hopes of them as an exemplary marriage, and admired Hawthorne's independence and writings.[8]

One of the first stories written after Hawthorne's marriage imagines a second Adam and Eve wandering decorously and judiciously through a nineteenth-century Boston whose inhabitants have vanished but whose artefacts, such as dress shop, prison, legislature, and wealthy mansion, remain freshly intact. While this millennial fable proceeds with a light touch, its stated task of distinguishing between what is "natural" and what is socially constructed ("the world's artificial system") (x: 247) identifies the issue central to the "Woman Question." Whereas a twenty-first century feminist analysis would concentrate mostly on the social construction of gender identities and be wary of the "feminine," concepts of an innately female nature were used in the nineteenth century as part of reformist as well as conservative arguments about the position of women. So, Fuller envisages both masculine and feminine in each sex, while Hawthorne combines an awareness of the social constructedness of much that is customarily called "natural" with a continuing sense that there are qualities distinctive to the female sex.[9] When Beatrice Rappaccini is described as "poor victim of man's ingenuity and of thwarted nature" (x: 128) the tale indicates its interest in both elements.

This combined concern with "nature" and "social construction" makes for a certain instability and mystery in Hawthorne's texts. The fantastic in "The Birth-Mark" and "Rappaccini's Daughter" is the necessary means by which we are helped to "see what prisoners we are" mentally ("The New Adam and Eve," x: 247), and to reveal the latent absurdity of these powerful constructions. In these two tales female interconnectedness now takes a sinister form: Beatrice and Georgiana, as young women wooed or very recently wed, are particularly subjected to masculine prescription (the father, the suitor, the older husband). Here, female dissent, whether in dreams, adultery, or preaching, becomes muted, fruitless reproach, or metamorphoses into a self-sacrifice that, particularly in Georgiana's case, sounds like a desperate quotation from a manual on wifely submission. Neither woman is naïve: Georgiana encourages an experiment whose disastrous result she can guess, and Beatrice lies to Giovanni about the poisonous flower the first time she meets him.

Both Georgiana's and Beatrice's bodies are patently "unnatural," literally man-made, processed to meet two of the commonest requirements of patriarchal femininity: Beatrice's sexual purity must be defended at all costs, and Georgiana's attraction to her husband is dependent on beauty. In pursuit of women who are unflawed, unconflicted, unassailable, and hence unthreatening to masculine intactness, these men create doubleness. Georgiana, looking in the mirror, sees a finally unmarked face but knows she is dying, while Beatrice has been given a lethal body which has nothing to do with her apparently "simple, natural, most affectionate" ("Rappaccini's Daughter," x: 120) nature. Fuller diagnosed contemporary masculinity in terms of Orpheus in the Underworld, that is to say, men in hell wretchedly seeking but losing their wives.[10] Whereas Fuller thought it was time for Euridice (Orpheus' wife) to call to her husband, Hawthorne's tales are despairing: here "holy love" ("The Birth-Mark," x: 52) is impotent or delusory (as Fuller understood, male devotion to women imprisons them), and restrictive roles are non-negotiable. These are marriages of the doomed or the damned.

At the end of *The Scarlet Letter*, "Women, more especially, – in the continually recurring trials of wounded, wasted, wronged, misplaced, or erring and sinful passion, – or with the dreary burden of a heart unyielded, because unvalued and unsought, – came to Hester's cottage, demanding why they were so wretched, and what the remedy!" (1: 263). The red A's original religious and judicial "office" (1: 166) (that is, function) has startlingly metamorphosed into a feminist conversation. Paradoxically, in this post-adultery novel, marriage is central, as indeed it was for most nineteenth-century women's lives (nearly 90 percent married). While the novel of adultery is one standard way to explore marriage, *The Scarlet Letter*'s unusual concern exclusively with the deed's denouement gives sustained attention to a figure encountered earlier, the "unhoused" woman; the once married woman reveals female subjectivity more fully in separation. In addition, as Fuller had noted in *Woman in the Nineteenth Century*, it is the unattached woman who tests many common gender assumptions.

In "The Custom-House" Hawthorne imagines the kind of novel he had tried to write (a "romance") as a middle-class sitting room at night, littered with the family's doings but defamiliarized by moonlight. But *The Scarlet Letter* turned out differently: true, its repeated use of the word "intimacy" signals Hawthorne's continued preoccupation with the new closeness of nineteenth-century married relations, but its seventeenth-century setting, precluding direct consideration of middle-class domesticity or contemporary class relations, opens up a more hypothetical examination of the question of women. Boston's experimentalism, policing sexuality in the attempt to create a just society, parallels the utopian community in which Hawthorne lived briefly prior to his marriage: Brook Farm had sought to create perfectionist (rather than political) alternatives to the new capitalist workplaces and privatized domestic arrangement but, despite its founders' feminist credentials, was traditional in male/female relationships and experienced sexual scandal.[11] Indeed, the dismissal of Hester's story in "The Custom-House" as "proving of no public concern" (1: 30) invites the opposite judgment. Strikingly, the novel touches on so much of nineteenth-century female experience highlighted by contemporary feminist analyses as requiring public recognition and social reform: marriage, domestic abuse, divorce, child-rearing, and child custody, working women (including seamstresses), political exclusion, and, crucially for our purposes, "fallen" women condemned for their sexual history (a highly public topic).[12]

The novel returns to "The Gentle Boy" topic of a woman publicly at odds with the state; this time, the initiating concern is with sexuality, intimacy, and secrecy, the mother does not abandon her child, nor is the child "gentle." With a "dead woman's features" (1: 226) in public, Hester is one of Hawthorne's wives of the dead, but with redoubled complexity. Three extraordinary conversations open up a dissenting discussion on marriage: with Chillingworth in prison and again seven years later on the seashore, and the forest meeting with Dimmesdale. Notably, Hawthorne's first audiences found this material disquieting in ways that most twenty-first century readers, in Western society grown accustomed to divorce, are unlikely to do. Whereas "highly respectable" (1: 259) spectators of the final scaffold scene subsequently censor their memories, these explicit conversations are impossible for the reader to ignore.

With profound subversion the early prison encounter perversely enacts a domestic, family scene – sick child tended in the doctor's arms, intimate conversation of husband and wife. Whereas on the theocratic scaffold Hester is unambiguously guilty, the private discussion redefines the rights and wrongs of marriage in emotional and sexual terms that condemn both parties to that loveless contract. The betrayed husband startlingly announces, "We have wronged each other" (1: 74). The novel is still taking marriage very seriously, but here its "intimate and sacred" quality (1: 118) makes demands irrelevant to the Mosaic code. By the time Hester continues this conversation seven years later at the settlement's edge, she has evolved an even more radical position that swings from agonized responsibility for Chillingworth's psychological destruction to revulsion (triggered by ugly sexual memories) at his "fouler offence" (1: 176).

Despite *The Scarlet Letter*'s historical sense in other matters, these two scenes anachronistically dramatize nineteenth-century issues which were the inevitable outcome of the shift toward a concept of marriage based on love choice, intimacy, and mutual consideration. Whereas bridal pregnancies, such as Hawthorne's mother's, had been an earlier, benign aspect of this change, now the inevitable gap between new expectations and actualities produced, on the one hand, a conservative gender ideology touting wifely submissiveness to keep the lid on the ideas Hester expresses, and, on the other hand, feminist attempts to conceptualize a good marriage (Fuller, for example, lists different kinds of marriage in *Woman in the Nineteenth Century*). This new view of marriage also disturbingly underlies Hester's avowal to Dimmesdale that, "What we did had a consecration of its own. We felt it so! We said so to each other!" (1: 195).

Simultaneously, in the face of troubling outcomes of past decisions, Hester finds herself evolving an additional, and eventually alternative, discourse of responsibility to her former lover which, again, would have been disturbing to the novel's earliest readers since she is "connected in a union . . . unrecognized on earth" (1: 80): to admit Chillingworth's continued existence with, "'he *was* my husband'" (1: 194, my emphasis), must seem immensely challenging. The phrase, "wives of the dead," here takes on immense complexities. It is not a simple matter of substituting one set of obligations for another; indeed, although Hester finally works out a morality that justifies doing this, the novel's climax suggests its impossibility.

So, the novel cannot be read in approving sympathy for doomed lovers (nor, for that matter, disapproval). The novel stays open, pushing the reader simultaneously or sequentially toward seemingly opposing views, or rather toward the recognition that it cannot be a matter of one view or another but rather an inextricable web of relationships that creates complex subjects. This is achieved partly by means of a narrator who struggles with confusion even while censuring Hester's dissidence. Slippery syntax also keeps the reader uncertain about narrative focalization – that is, whether we are being shown a character's subjective view or whether these statements have some kind of external authority.

Nor can the novel be read in terms of a stark opposition of individual conscience and the state (as in the dispute concerning Anne Hutchinson or the Quakers). Hester is not simply, to use Fuller's terms for unconventional women, the "outlaw."[13] She exists in relation to others, including the town (for example, teaching Pearl the catechism). She is clearly not "simple." We know her not only as wife and lover, but as daughter, nurse, public employee making ceremonial garments, counselor, and crucially mother. Like marriage, motherhood is a "sacred" relationship (see 1: 114) in this novel. At the Governor's Hall, even estranged husband, lost lover, established cleric, and state leader, each with different agendas, are corralled into concurring with Hester's right to raise her child. But this is no sentimentalized mother/daughter dyad flourishing ex-patriarchally. What is also going on is the matter of Pearl's fatherless state – the need "to show a father's kindness towards the poor, deserted babe" (1: 116). There is huge anxiety around Pearl and parenting, and it emerges most insistently at the very moment when Hester and Dimmesdale reunite: her mother looking for advice, her father unpleasantly expressing fear of public connection and impatience at her rage.

In the role of wild child, Pearl evinces an innocent curiosity about meeting the "Black Man": she is gentle in the forest, but like the animals there reacts fiercely in defence. Thus she complicates the question of women's "nature" in a novel that repeatedly assumes knowledge of, or speculates upon, supposedly innate female qualities. The novel asks, "That unsunned snow in the matron's bosom, and the burning shame on Hester Prynne's, – what had the two in common?" (1: 87), and in answer suggests a "sisterhood" (1: 87) – not a co-operative relationship since the townswomen are patently hostile at first, but the possibility that the common distinction between "virgin" and the "fallen" occludes elements in common. On this basis Hester is exemplary of other women's potential, and her final role as counselor is therefore comprehensible and powerful. Moreover, her speculation on the question of women brilliantly blurs the distinction between nature and culture: "As a first step, the whole system of society is to be torn down, and built up anew. Then, the very nature of the opposite sex, or its long hereditary habit, which has become like nature, is to be essentially modified, before woman can be allowed to assume what seems a fair and suitable position" (1: 165).

Most significantly, the equation of "wild" with "fallen" is disrupted in Pearl whose green seaweed letter mirrors her mother's A (she must after all engage with social signification), yet promises uncensored passion, creative growth, and a fresh start (Pearl disappears finally into some "unknown region" [1: 262]). In the wonderful seaweed letter scene Pearl's insistent questioning of the scarlet letter's meaning (plus imagining her mother's questioning of the green A) further opens possibilities, and suggests more than child's play. The adult "noble woman" that Hester then glimpses in the child offers an image of apparently innate femininity very different from mid nineteenth-century gender conventions, but nonetheless conversant with other qualities recognizable from women's actual lives and indeed celebrated by Fuller: "the stedfast principles of an unflinching courage, – an uncontrollable will, – a sturdy pride, which might be disciplined into self-respect, – and a bitter scorn of many things, which, when examined, might be found to have the taint of falsehood in them" (1: 180). Not knowing how this new femininity will be expressed, Hester is scared into a harsh and surprisingly conservative response: she censors Pearl's discussion, substitutes a stereotypical image of feminine vanity for the letter's meaning and threatens the "naughty" daughter punitively with a "dark closet" (1: 181). Hester's subversion and submission turn out to be fearsomely interconnected, but Pearl suggests true difference.

One must then ask whether this aborted moment of sympathy between mother and daughter is recuperated in the final scaffold scene which "developed all [Pearl's] sympathies" (1: 256). "Tenderness," a recurring term in the novel, is central here. It is deemed particularly "feminine," and associated with natural impressionableness, ready sensitivity, demonstrative affection, considerate compassion, ready forgiveness, and support. It is not mere softness; it involves strength and passion, including the erotic, and the loving male is capable of it too. The longing for such tenderness started that seaweed letter exchange; indeed, from a nineteenth-century viewpoint the emotional structure of tenderness derives primarily from the mother/child relationship (something on which Dimmesdale himself relies as he finally totters, childlike, to the scaffold).[14] As Fuller remarked, "All the secret powers are 'Mothers.' There is but one paternal power."[15] So while the narrator, with decidedly conservative views on women, fixes Pearl's tears into a "softened and subdued" (1: 262) womanhood, the qualities that they signal suggest a more passionate and transformative femininity. However, although Fuller envisaged a feminist revolution – "And will not she soon appear? The woman who shall vindicate their birthright for all women; who shall teach them what to claim, and how to use what they obtain"[16] – Hawthorne's novel severely qualifies this in suggesting that "the angel and apostle of the coming revelation" (1: 263) can only be a happy woman. But Pearl leaves Boston and there are only unhappy women at Hester's door.

Class issues are given direct, substantive attention in Hawthorne's next two novels, *The House of the Seven Gables* and *The Blithedale Romance*. They reflect a deep, fearful interest in class generally in the 1850s, a time of social crisis when, as Hawthorne himself experienced, bourgeois existence became dominant ideologically, yet remained highly vulnerable to economic uncertainty.

Women are a focal point in Hawthorne's deconstruction of these class formations. In an economy where only 30 percent of women (mainly unmarried and seldom middle class) did paid work, middle-class women's material dependency on male family members demonstrated their social ascendancy. But this also contained the threat of destitution and the loss of the fiercely promoted feminine "decency" that distinguished their middle-class existence in moral terms while veiling its actual financial base. So the event most likely to dismantle the bourgeois illusion is the woman going out to work, or in the case of *House of the Seven Gables*, the private home shockingly opened up to commerce when unsupported gentlewoman Hepzibah starts her shop. Historically, separation of money-making work premises from the home was fundamental in the new capitalist order; here the shop is tellingly part of the house. Hawthorne's earlier motif of the "unhoused" woman now takes a new form and an economic meaning.

The tale of Alice Pyncheon, embedded in the novel and written by Holgrave for middle-class magazines, also highlights the centrality of women to a narrative of social change that heralds democratic, commercial opportunity. Maule's violation of Alice is both classed and gendered. Alice, whose home is tended so beautifully by servants, ends up sexually and socially humiliated in serving Maule's bride, and like a poor working woman walks home shivering to her death. Maule's action is triggered by the *classed* expression of her sexual attraction for Maule (he becomes the "brute"[II: 201] object of her gaze). Her "purity," that is sexual status rather than sexual feelings, proves not to be guaranteed, as she confidently believed, by her gentlewoman's position. The story, then, anachronistically gives Holgrave his needed class triumph, but implicitly deconstructs female "decency" to show its purely economic basis in *any* class.

Hepzibah, belonging to a pre-bourgeois genteel generation, acknowledges her "companionship" (II: 241) with the seamstress across the road only when she is utterly unsupported; mostly, she prefers to construct Phoebe's skills in the shop and school as unladylike. But Phoebe has a "little air of ladylike assumption" (II: 117) in making clear to Judge Pyncheon that she is not a waged shop-assistant, and thus, though she declares that, "I mean to earn my bread" (II: 74), she doubles as a mid-century middle-class home-maker. While Phoebe, the worker, is transformed into a bourgeois gentlewoman, the novel critiques this social movement by a self-conscious use of pretty discourses of the domestic feminine that clearly exposes the fragility and narrowness of Phoebe's feminine world which middle-class ideology mystified.[17] With her looks affected by the working world and her weakness acknowledged, she will only preserve her charm by inherited money, and her integrity by compromises negotiated in an oddly unromantic final scene with her future husband.

The flip-side of middle-class "decency" is duplicity and hypocrisy – what Hawthorne calls "humbug," embodied in Judge Pyncheon, the account of whose death becomes a brilliantly ironized picture of masculine public success. *The Blithedale Romance* continues this examination. From his temporary hotel accommodation in the city and with the perspective of dis-integrating utopian aspirations, Coverdale looks across to the substitute domesticity of a boarding-house in a row of "fashionable residences" (III: 149), and notes the "artificial" and "veil"-like "humbug" of showy but uniform house-fronts compared to the greater "truth to native and character-istic tendencies" (III: 149) of their back view – an observation confirmed by the revelation of the expensively dressed Zenobia at one of its stage-curtained windows, and later by Moodie's slum dwelling, housing seamstresses and the poorest racial group, the Irish.

Similarly, Blithedale is the "back view"; it remains inside the "boundaries of the ordinary life" (III: 18) even though it imagines itself beyond them. Blithedale makes the deep structures of class and gender evident precisely because it attempts an alternative to the industrial capitalist order: Coverdale acutely notes that the well-to-do communards are under no financial com-pulsion, the relations between them and the supposedly equal farm workers are uncertain, and their involvement with capitalist "competition" (III: 19) inescapable. Priscilla and Zenobia as half-sisters underscore the differences that economic status makes: the wealthy heiress Zenobia readily identifies Priscilla as seamstress, that icon of female working-class poverty, and places her socially below her dressmaker.

Class obliterates gender loyalties, including Zenobia's version of feminism (a problem historically addressed by the contemporary activist journal, *The Una*, which reviewed Fuller's *Woman in the Nineteenth Century* in the person of a seamstress begging Fuller to take cognizance of working women's very different situation). Zenobia mocks Coverdale with the common assump-tion that an upper-class man would never marry Priscilla (III: 170); whether Hollingsworth marries her for her newly wealthy family or her ingrained subservience, she is formed by her environment rather than by some inher-ent "nature." Riches, education, and concomitant health endow Zenobia with a glamor that excites Moodie into leaving her in undisputed possession of his wealth.

Nonetheless, Blithedale's "back view" on 1850s society permits an unveil-ing of the question of women that is not purely ironic in its understandings. We are encouraged to see a touching and apparently typical female ado-lescent wildness in Priscilla, "more untameable, and regardless of rule and limit" than boys (III: 73), even though she is to become an almost parodic epitome of mid-century "true womanhood" – conventionally pious, sub-missive, asexual, a "gentle parasite" (III: 123). Zenobia embodies another version of the adult feminine: the terms repeatedly used are "generous," "noble," "frank," "passionate," "liberal," and, gentlewoman though she is, she is "unveiled" as attractively sexual. But what she calls society's "secret tribunal" (III: 215) condemns her, ostensibly for abusing Priscilla, covertly for her sexual assertiveness. The emotional structures of traditional romance are her undoing, and, underlying these, the failure of men to find a responsive "womanhood" in themselves (III: 103) – despite the fleeting "tenderness" (III: 55) which Hollingsworth once showed that recalls the femininity that Fuller believes natural in men. Coverdale fully appreciates her feminist politics but cannot help simply ogling her body while craving the delicacy in the despised Priscilla.[18]

Zenobia is not one of Hawthorne's wives of the dead; true, we never quite know if she has been married (though she seems sexually experienced), but her presence at Blithedale suggests a desire for a personal fresh start, and her explicitly feminist eloquence at Eliot's Pulpit signals needed freedoms for all women (the novel's composition coincided with the beginnings of concerted public agitation for women's civil rights). Hawthorne's final published novel, *The Marble Faun*, continues the exploration of creative women who work alone in their own premises, and walk busy streets, enter public buildings, and talk to strangers by themselves. Though events disprove her, Miriam speaks of many "distinguished" women who are alone, employed, satisfied, creative, and like Hilda "utterly sufficient to herself": "When women have other objects in life, they are not apt to fall in love" (IV: 121). As if Hester Prynne had actually fled as she planned, Miriam established herself in Rome "without introduction" where her "ambiguity . . . did not necessarily imply anything wrong" (IV: 20). True, this disturbs – Kenyon asks anxiously, "Are you sure of her?" (IV: 108) – but Rome's foreignness provides Hawthorne with a licensed setting for female autonomy.

A considerable amount of the novel's action takes place in often crowded public places (indeed, it feels intrusive finally to enter Hilda's apartment). With the ideological confining of an essentialist "femininity" to the middle-class home in mid-century America, women's actual presence on the streets disturbed gender and class boundaries, bringing many forms of threatening difference together into a kind of intimacy.[19] Hawthorne himself in his *English Notebooks* records his fascination at the private life, particularly of women, spilling onto Liverpool slum streets.

But carnival on Rome streets is policed by soldiers of a "despotic government" (IV: 456) who have had the supposedly free Miriam under surveillance. The men, even Donatello who is "outside the rules" (IV: 14), cannot protect the women from harassment or detention. The price of Hilda's intactness in Rome is an insulating asexuality and, when assailed by seeing others' violence, the espousal of a moral universe where there should be no challenging interchange between good and evil and where the act of confession is simply a purging of alien knowledge. For all her physical mobility, Hilda is in thrall to patriarchal "Old Masters" (IV: 334), her exemplary "dove"-like femininity patently criticized.

But, most interestingly, the novel begins to dismantle the culturally conventional binary of pure woman/fallen woman. Some of Miriam's paintings are "things that haunt me" (IV: 45), but others depicting more conventional feminine subjects, nonetheless, include the artist herself looking on. In a rare scene in a private dwelling, the marble saloon at Donatello's Monte Beni, Miriam's conversation with Kenyon movingly explores forms of femininity that recall Pearl's promise. Hilda's rejection of Miriam has set Miriam "free" of the customary "reserves and decorums of my sex" (IV: 287), and Kenyon both acknowledges this as shocking and yet accepts this "indecorous" (IV: 286) behavior. He has identified an "intimate equality" (IV: 283) between Donatello and Miriam despite huge differences, and sees a beauty that is linked, in terms we have met before, with a "tender gladness" (IV: 286) – here defined as the "intimate help" (IV: 285) a woman, unlike a man, can give.

But this is help *in extremis*. The novel offers no reassurance; we do not see Hilda bring Kenyon "home" (IV: 461) to America. In a strange scene, dropped late into the novel, an ancient statue of Venus is found by Donatello and Miriam. The "poor, fragmentary woman" is assembled by Kenyon into a "Womanhood" that is "perfect to the mind" (IV: 423). Hawthorne in his Notebooks describes seeing the actual classical statue, the Venus de Medici, as "all womanhood in one": "I felt a kind of tenderness for her" (XIV: 298). In the novel, however, the statue falls apart into "a heap of worthless fragments" (IV: 424).

In Hawthorne's last, unfinished novel, *Septimius Felton*, the hero is given advice in his pursuit of earthly immortality: "On the whole, shun woman, for she is apt to be a disturbing influence" (XIII: 105). Hawthorne had not, of course, followed this passionless counsel. Septimius's dying aunt Kezia reflects, "a white woman's life is so dull" (XIII: 122) with its "tame" decencies and housework; she imagines, with echoes of Goodman Brown's Faith, flying above the town and living in the woods. Hawthorne seems to have seen both the worlds of house and woods as parts of one female subjectivity. Dismantling that simple binary of "good" and "wicked" women, he struggled to redefine "womanhood." In his life misogyny fought, at times very unpleasantly, with some kinds of feminist understandings. But his writings performed their cultural work differently. Starting his exploration with the figure of the widow (or quasi-widow) rather than with the figure of the maiden (young, sexually attractive, unmarried) took him by a different route, giving him a sense of a subjectivity both intricately connected personally and socially, and yet in excess of those connections. To go on then to read his works in terms of nineteenth-century feminism, more particularly the forms of feminism he was most likely to have contact with, is to see, first, that his formulations of the feminine in his fictions may be less conservative than they may first appear to many twenty-first century readers, but, second, that his fiction does not speak from any unambiguously feminist position even while it poses many of that feminism's key questions.

NOTES

1. Daniel Scott Smith and Michael Hindus, "Premarital Pregnancy in America 1640–1971: An Overview and Interpretation," *Journal of Interdisciplinary History* 5 (1975): 537–70. See also Nina Baym, "Hawthorne and His Mother: A Biographical Speculation," *American Literature* 54 (1982): 1–27.
2. Smith and Hindus, "Premarital Pregnancy," p. 557.
3. The historical account of women's experience that follows is based on: Nancy F. Cott, *The Bonds of Womanhood: "Women's Sphere" in New England, 1780–1835* (New Haven, CT: Yale University Press, 1977); Stephanie Coontz, *The Social Origins of Private Life: A History of American Families, 1600–1900* (London: Verso, 1988); Steven Mintz and Susan Kellogg, *Domestic Revolutions: A Social History of American Family Life* (New York: Free Press, 1988); Jeanne Boyston, *Home and Work: Housework, Wages, and the Ideology of Labor in the Early Republic* (New York: Oxford University Press, 1990); John D'Emilio and Estelle B. Freedman, *Intimate Matters: A History of Sexuality in America*, second edn. (Chicago: University of Chicago Press, 1988); Karen Lystra, *Searching the Heart: Women, Men, and Romantic Love in Nineteenth-Century America* (New York: Oxford University Press, 1989); Barbara Welter, *Dimity Convictions: The American Woman in the Nineteenth Century* (Athens: Ohio University Press, 1976); Lee Virginia Chambers-Schiller, *Liberty, A Better Husband: Single Women in America: The Generations of 1780–1840* (New Haven, CT: Yale University Press, 1984); Carroll Smith-Rosenberg, *Disorderly Conduct: Visions of Gender in Victorian America* (New York: Knopf, 1985); Nancy A. Hewitt, *Women's Activism and Social Change: Rochester, New York, 1822–1872* (Ithaca, NY: Cornell University Press, 1984); Stuart M. Blumin, *The Emergence of the Middle Class: Social Experience in the American City, 1760–1900* (Cambridge: Cambridge University Press, 1989); Alice Kessler-Harris, *Out to Work: A History of Wage-Earning Women in the United States* (New York: Oxford University Press, 1982); Christine Stansell, *City of Women: Sex and Class in New York, 1789–1860* (New York: Knopf, 1986).
4. See Michael T. Gilmore, "Hawthorne and the Making of the Middle Class," in Wai Chee Dimock and Michael T. Gilmore, eds., *Rethinking Class: Literary Studies and Social Formation* (New York: Columbia University Press, 1994), pp. 215–38; David Leverenz, *Manhood and the American Renaissance* (Ithaca, NY: Cornell University Press, 1989).
5. See Margaret Moore, *The Salem World of Nathaniel Hawthorne* (Columbia: University of Missouri Press, 1998); Edwin Haviland Miller, *Salem is My Dwelling Place: A Life of Nathaniel Hawthorne* (Iowa City: University of Iowa Press, 1991);

and T. Walter Herbert, *Dearest Beloved: The Hawthornes and the Making of the Middle-Class Family* (Berkeley: University of California Press, 1993).

6. John L. Idol, Jr., and Melinda M. Ponder, *Hawthorne and Women: Engendering and Expanding the Hawthorne Tradition* (Amherst: University of Massachusetts Press, 1999); for issues of authorship and sexual identity for Hawthorne, see Evan Carton, *"The Marble Faun": Hawthorne's Transformations* (New York: Twayne, 1992).

7. For Hawthorne as cultural analyst, see Richard H. Millington, *Practicing Romance: Narrative Form and Cultural Engagement in Hawthorne's Fiction* (Princeton, NJ: Princeton University Press, 1992).

8. See Thomas R. Mitchell, *Hawthorne's Fuller Mystery* (Amherst: University of Massachusetts Press, 1998) for details of the Hawthorne/Fuller connection.

9. Margaret Fuller, *The Essential Margaret Fuller*, ed. Jeffrey Steele (New Brunswick, NJ: Rutgers University Press, 1992).

10. See *ibid.*, p. 252.

11. See Anne C. Rose, *Transcendentalism as a Social Movement, 1830–1850* (New Haven, CT: Yale University Press, 1981).

12. On female moral reform, see Smith-Rosenberg, *Disorderly Conduct*, pp. 109–28. Poverty, a key women's issue not present in *The Scarlet Letter*, is taken up in Hawthorne's next novel.

13. See *The Essential Margaret Fuller*, p. 284. Fuller, however, offers a complex argument that society should continue outlaw until the "law" is changed by those who resist in a law-abiding way (p. 286). Jamie Barlowe, *The Scarlet Mob of Scribblers: Rereading Hester Prynne* (Carbondale: Southern Illinois University Press, 2000), is the most recent in a line of interpretation that finds a radical otherness in Hester. For studies offering a different subject position and a different sense of resistance and negotiation, see Lora Romero, *Home Fronts: Domesticity and Its Critics in Antebellum United States* (Durham, NC: Duke University Press, 1997); Millington, *Practicing Romance*, chapter 4; Leverenz, *Manhood*, pp. 259–78.

14. See Ian D. Suttie, *The Origins of Love and Hate* (1935; Harmondsworth: Penguin, 1963), for a psychoanalytic exploration of tenderness and modernity's taboo on it.

15. *The Essential Margaret Fuller*, p. 48.

16. *Ibid.*, p. 347. For other understandings of these elements, see Joel Pfister, *The Production of Personal Life: Class, Gender, and the Psychological in Hawthorne's Fiction* (Stanford, CA: Stanford University Press, 1991); and Amy Schrager Lang, *Prophetic Woman: Anne Hutchinson and the Problem of Dissent in the Literature of New England* (Berkeley: University of California Press, 1987), pp. 161–92.

17. See Millington, *Practicing Romance*, pp. 115–22.

18. See further, in relation to both *House* and *Blithedale*, Alison Easton, "My Banker and I Can Afford to Laugh!: Class and Gender in Fanny Fern and Nathaniel Hawthorne," in Karen L. Kilcup, ed., *Soft Canons: American Women Writers and Masculine Tradition* (Iowa City: University of Iowa Press, 1999), pp. 219–36.

19. See Mary P. Ryan, *Women in Public: Between Banners and Ballots, 1825–1880* (Baltimore, MD: Johns Hopkins University Press, 1990); see also Hawthorne, *The French and Italian Notebooks, Centenary Edition*, XIV: 298.

5

KRISTIE HAMILTON

Hawthorne, modernity, and the literary sketch

In "Hawthorne and the Twilight of Romance," Roy Harvey Pearce claims that "in *The Marble Faun* . . . the sketch becomes the structural core of the novel itself and dominates its form."[1] This is not, however, a felicitous development in Pearce's view, for he has just described the author as having been subject throughout his career to the "danger" of falling prey to the genre that "so charmed Hawthorne's age." For Pearce, this seduction story represents the ruin of an author who succumbs in Italy to what he has long flirted with – the "easy way": the "semi-melodramatic," "quasi-philosophical" form in which "the writer takes no definite stand." Since it was first published in 1948, Pearce's essay has remained one of the most influential standard interpretations of *The Marble Faun* and, though garnering less attention, one of the more fully developed discussions of a constitutive relationship between Hawthorne's literary sketches and his romances. The literary-historical narrative Pearce fashions emerges from his effort to pinpoint the difference between what he perceives to be the successful projects of the first three romances and the "inadequacy and failure" of *The Marble Faun*. Unlike the earlier romances and "great tales," in which "form, materials, and meaning cohere, each implicating and demanding the other," *The Marble Faun* ends "with 'half-developed hints' – apparently the more desirable because half-developed." Throughout his reading of the book, Pearce repeatedly demonstrates the lack of "wholeness" and expresses disappointment that "meaningfulness exists only in the largest, almost scattered details of the story . . . Such meaningfulness, thus is seldom felt wholly, for it is not worked out systematically." Finally Pearce regrets Hawthorne's substitution of this "mysterious, half-known, deliciously felt content" for clear, internally coherent meaning. This is "romantic twilight," writes Pearce, not only for Hawthorne but for "the American romance itself."[2]

While my chapter will not share Roy Harvey Pearce's elegiac estimate, itself melodramatic, of the import of Hawthorne's full-fledged embrace of the sketch in his last published romance, I am in agreement with him that the

99

sketch had always been on Hawthorne's mind. Indeed, the sketch was profoundly interesting to Hawthorne not as a seductively easy form of writing
but rather as a genre that was inherently useful and responsive to the needs of
American writers and readers of the first half of the nineteenth century and
beyond. In his sketches, Hawthorne developed a consistent and increasingly
assured line of thought that it was in the ephemeral – in the evanescence that
would characterize the "new reality" of the mid nineteenth century – that
meaningfulness now resided, an uneasy recognition for Hawthorne that cul-
minated in *The Marble Faun*'s espousal of the modern.[3] That espousal finds
arresting expression in this passage from the novel about the very medium
of the sketch, whether pictorial or literary:

> There is an effluence of divinity in the first sketch, and there, if anywhere
> you find the pure light of inspiration, which the subsequent toil of the artist
> serves to bring out in stronger lustre, indeed, but likewise adulterates with
> what belongs to an inferiour mood. The aroma and fragrance of new thought
> were perceptible in these designs, after three centuries of wear and tear. The
> charm lay partly in their very imperfection; for this is suggestive, and sets
> the imagination to work; whereas the finished picture, if a good one, leaves
> the spectator nothing to do and if bad, confuses, stupefies, disenchants, and
> disheartens him.
> (IV: 183)

These words, in the chapter entitled "An Aesthetic Company," are spoken by
the narrator, who elaborates upon the effects of the contents of a portfolio of
old drawings. The passage is fascinating in the context of nineteenth-century
sketch writing because it ascribes a specific sort of aesthetic force to sketches:
in the sketch, "new thought" may be perceived not rationally but sensuously,
as if it bore "aroma and fragrance." The narrator had earlier explained that
"hasty rudeness made the sketches only the more valuable; because the artist
seemed to have bestirred himself at the pinch of the moment, snatching up
whatever material was nearest, so as to seize the first glimpse of an idea that
might vanish in the twinkling of an eye" (IV: 137). Thus, the very imperfection
of the sketch, created by its inception in haste, places its mode of expression
in the arena of suggestion. Suggestion is described here as the manifestation
of a brand-new idea at the moment of its conception, captured and rendered
perceptible even after three centuries, but, in the first instance, sketched only
to forestall its imminent loss. The reception of artistic work that was made
meaningful by its very incompletion would need to be of the inferential kind
that Hilda later describes just before she is presented with the unfinished bust
of Donatello: "[T]here is a class of spectators whose sympathy will help them
to see the Perfect, through a mist of imperfection. Nobody, I think, ought
to read poetry, or look at pictures or statues, who cannot find a great deal

more in them than the poet or artist has actually expressed. Their highest merit is suggestiveness" (IV: 379).

In what follows, I will outline, more particularly, what brought Nathaniel Hawthorne to value the sketch in such certain terms, endowing it as he did with a sensuous sort of permanence that so improbably resisted wear and tear and that called forth imaginative sympathy in readers. In order to do so, I will examine briefly the cultural and literary context within which Hawthorne wrote sketches and then offer readings of a number of sketches that help to unpack the import of his recurrent, one would almost say compulsive, probing of the new, of the ephemeral, and, of the sketch. What will become clear is that Hawthorne's conceptualization of the sketch is intertwined with his interest in the modern problem of evanescence – the character of modern existence that seemed to him and others to saturate psychic and social life. Embedded within the very concept of the modern was the threat of its own obsolescence,[4] and the new sense that rapid change was at the core of human experience underwrote broad cultural narratives of the self as constantly on the verge of its own dissolution. In many of his sketches, Hawthorne not only scrutinizes the phenomenon of evanescence as it shapes new literary forms but also as it constitutes modern subjectivity. He repeatedly explores strategies by which the modern (usually male) subject may revitalize himself in rhythm with the times and may gain a new kind of enduring presence. Indeed, Hawthorne's thinking about genres such as the sketch and, though not my subject here, new modes of evaluative narration such as his multivalent version of romance, offers moderns the means for achieving a permanence of recorded life and thought – even after their inevitable passing. These aesthetic methods and forms rival the monuments of earlier eras while being made of more fittingly buoyant materials. To emphasize Hawthorne's recurrent concern with modernity and what was recognized as "the new," as I do, is not to characterize him as unconcerned with the past or with history. Far from it. Rather I mean to call attention to his ongoing project of assessing the capacities of the current literary and social developments of his day for providing dynamic engagement with both the past and the present and to highlight his efforts to formulate solutions to problems that had not seemed so pressing before.

Throughout Hawthorne's lifetime, the sketch played a prominent role in the formation of American literature and culture because it took shape within and made visible and debatable the many changes and multiple sites of social transformation emerging in the early nineteenth century. Most broadly, these changes included more widely disseminated literacy, technological advancements enabling the production and distribution of newspapers, magazines, and books, the growth throughout the US of urban centers, geographic expansion of the nation's boundaries, the process of consolidation of a dominant middle class, increased physical and social mobility enhanced by technologies that built railroads, canals, and factories, and the concomitant intensification of a commercial economy in which literature circulated as a favored leisure commodity. Sketch writers proliferated in this environment from the 1820s through the 1860s. *The Sketch-Book* (1819–1820) by Washington Irving had established generic legitimacy for a purposely fluid literary form that evoked but was not limited in reference to the practice of visually rendering "scenes, characters, and incidents" that struck a sketcher's "sauntering gaze" during travel.[5] Englishwoman Mary Russell Mitford, widely read in the US, had set a precedent for proximate, participatory observation of communal habits closer to home in *Our Village: Sketches of Rural Life, Character, and Scenery* (1824–32).[6] The stature and commercial viability won for the sketch by Irving and Mitford, combined with its brevity and informality, made it appealing and accessible to the widest range of writers and readers.

The sketch created and met appetites for mass market intimacy, for first-hand documentary observation, for the mapping of social types and regional specificities, for quick access to packaged leisure, and, ultimately, for linguistically mediated modeling of new modes of perception.[7] Irving had given currency to the unmarried, leisured detachment of his persona Geoffrey Crayon. Ik Marvel's and Herman Melville's nightmares and daydreams of domestic heterosexual encounters and bachelor utopias followed or questioned Irving's lead.[8] Harriet Beecher Stowe, Augustus Baldwin Longstreet, Caroline Kirkland, and Alice Cary peopled villages and towns with regionally identified characters who complicated the already mythologized picturesque timelessness associated with rural places. Harriet Jacobs and Harriet E. Wilson, Sarah Bagley and Harriet Farley rendered the sketch's association with documentary evidence the foundation for polemics against, respectively, African American enslavement, racism and indentured servitude, exploitation of industrial workers, and class prejudice. Fanny Fern, Lydia Maria Child, N. P. Willis, Solon Robinson, and Edgar Allan Poe created personae who traveled the urban sidewalks of the *flâneur*, "botanizing" urban life (as Benjamin puts it) with an eye toward critique, reform, desire, and alienation.[9] Together the vast numbers of varied antebellum sketches map local and national culture and debate the meanings and practices that inhered in daily life with the onset of modernization. In 1843, Child wrote, with unsuppressed exasperation, in her *Letters from New York* of the "perpetual changes" that characterized the nineteenth century: finally, she asks: "Do you want an appropriate emblem of this country, and this age? Then stand on the side-walks of New-York, and watch the universal transit on the first of May."[10] If we would look for an appropriate trace of the experience of perpetual change in the period, we need only read the sketches that seemed everywhere its substantiation.

Hawthorne's sketch writing emerged in the thick of this literary dialogue about modern life. "The Old Apple-Dealer" (1843), published in the middle of Hawthorne's career, articulates many of the related conditions and concepts that made the sketch, as a form, one of his major preoccupations. Having tried to capture the character of a "hueless" old man selling apples and gingerbread daily in a railway depot, Hawthorne's observer turns finally to a contrast as the clearest way of distilling the profound impression the old man has made, one that has set him apart from the other "citizens" of the observer's "inner world." The subjects with whom the aged vendor is most dramatically compared are a train and its passengers:

> I look at him in the very moment of intensest bustle, on the arrival of the cars. The shriek of the engine, as it rushes into the car-house, is the utterance of the steam-fiend . . . He has skimmed rivers in his headlong rush, dashed through forests, plunged into the hearts of mountains, and glanced from the city to the desert-place, and again to a far-off city, with a meteoric progress, seen, and out of sight, while his reverberating roar still fills the ear. The travellers swarm forth from the cars. All are full of the momentum which they have caught from their mode of conveyance. It seems as if the whole world, both morally and physically, were detached from its old standfasts, and set in rapid motion . . . He and the steam-fiend are each other's antipodes; the latter is the type of all that go ahead. (*Tales and Sketches*, p. 719)[11]

Nathaniel Hawthorne's sketch of the old apple-dealer is a glimpse of modernity made visible by the juxtaposition of apparent opposites elevated to the status of types, the before and after of the modern. The train, endowed here with sentience and capable of "utterance," has been "compell[ed] to serve as a beast of burden" (p. 719); however, the disposition of this beast, now diabolic or at least starving for steam, is contagious. His habits – skimming, rushing, dashing, plunging, glancing – are "caught" by his live cargo, the travelers who "swarm" in "rapid motion." In this narrative of speed, vision can be global ("from the city to the desert-place and again to a far-off city") and the globe or, at least, the nation, is perceived at a glance, but in no more than glances. Objects of observation, like the cars and the observers they carry, are "seen, and out of sight." It might seem, in this sketch, that modernity is being pitted against that which still withstands it, an "old standfast" in the person of a man who remains immune to motion and to whom observers/readers could anchor themselves.

Yet, in the final paragraph of Hawthorne's sketch, the narrator – a "student of life" who has wanted to make more of the old man than the already conventional "needy man who has seen better days" (p. 717) – tellingly collapses the contrast he has built. On the one hand, the narrator asserts the difference the old man's "soundless" soul would represent were its depths audible or accessible to the "stranger's eye" (p. 719). But in this sketch, the subjunctive case marks what may be desired but not what may be known, for the "student of life" cannot see beneath the old man's surface, and instead pictures the apple-dealer on the verge of flitting away, as well.[12] At sketch's end, all human being, both in death and in life, is characterized by a state of evanescence: "[T]he present shapes of human existence are not cast in iron, nor hewn in everlasting adamant, but moulded of the vapors that vanish away while the essence flits upward to the infinite. There is a spiritual essence in this gray and lean old shape that shall flit upward too" (p. 720). It is the ephemeral quality of existence then, communicated through but not contained by its modern conveyances, that permeates "the whole world" – including "[o]ur old man of gingerbread and apples" (p. 717). The narrator himself, though attempting to slow down and make subtle his own and his readers' interpretation of the old man, seems caught in the discourse of speed, of vanishing, and of continuous change. His self-conscious narration of his role as a sketcher who would "individualize a character . . . [with] the most delicate pencil" interpolates the form itself in the phenomenon with which he grapples. In a world of flitting images, a genre predicated on fleeting suggestiveness and by definition unfinished may most fittingly instantiate the vaporous essence of a figure whose description is "too negative . . . to be seized upon, and represented . . . by word-painting" (p. 714). Inwoven in the self-conscious monologue of the observer in "The Old Apple-Dealer" is an assertion of the phenomenological significance of sketching and the sketch, both elementally invaluable to perceiving and conveying a world imbued with momentum.

In this 1843 sketch, it is apparent that Nathaniel Hawthorne was not only a writer of sketches but a theorizer of the form, as sketching was entangled in his mind and practice with the ongoing transformation of the perceiving subject, of the role of the author, of national culture, and of literature itself in modernity. Central to these changes was the development of new technologies such as those studied by Wolfgang Schivelbusch and Jonathan Crary.[13] In a contextually dense account of the impact of the emergence of the "railway journey" as a common experience, for example, Schivelbusch argues not only that individual subjects were reconstructed as "moderns" through a newly constituted panoramic mode of perception brought about by train travel, but also that a new aesthetic was articulated in the first half of the nineteenth century. He writes: "[I]t was velocity that made the objects of the world attractive . . . The traveler who gazed through the compartment window at such successive scenes, acquired a novel ability . . . the synthetic philosophy of the glance." Schivelbusch concludes convincingly that, in the course of one generation, "[t]his vision no longer experienced evanescence: evanescence had become the new reality."[14] The links between sketch writing and modernity as Hawthorne conceived them in his early sketches are numerous: the perception of ephemerality and speed as fundamental to modern experience, an imposing sense of the new and the present, the necessity and functionality of fleeting leisure, a dangerous but potent privacy, panoramic or mobile vision, and the fragmentation of everyday experience and its aesthetic consequences. But it is his articulation and scrutiny of evanescence as constitutive of psychic and social experience that most strikingly informs his understanding of the sketch's powers.

Residual traces of the new

The relative lack of association in Hawthorne criticism of his early writings with questions of modernity may be understood in part as a result of the focus on the metropolis in accounts of the modern from Walter Benjamin to Georg Simmel to Henri Lefebvre.[15] Since Hawthorne's direct experience of major urban centers was limited in the 1820s and 1830s, it has seemed far from obvious that he would have had reason to be engaged in a project of cultural analysis that centered on changes thought to be distant from his home in Salem. As Dana Brand has argued, however, Hawthorne was absorbed from the 1820s in a course of reading that included a number of British periodicals and authors engaged in literary and journalistic debates about the modern metropolis – *The Spectator, The Rambler, Gentleman's Magazine,* Dickens, Hazlitt, and Lamb, to name but a few.[16] Hawthorne was writing, furthermore, within the milieu described above of other American writers already busily sketching Americans on the move in cities, between regions and towns, on stagecoaches, canals, and, by the 1830s, on trains. Unsurprisingly, therefore, his earliest formulation of an understanding of temporality as located and most clearly perceptible in the new and the always already passing occurs in sketches that stage the reading of materials and genres identified with immediacy and ephemerality – specifically, the reading of newspapers and handwritten letters.[17] The conclusion he draws is that the assumed opposition between evanescence and permanence is actually an outdated misconception. In the forms and situations he examines, the evanescent paradoxically endures and preserves traces of the new as it emerges, thereby enabling later access to original instances already passed.

"Old News," a three-part sketch published in 1835, implies with its title a distillation of the experience of temporality within modernity. Combining a play on the common phrase, "that's old news," with a rendering of the quality of newness in the plural, not the singular (as in, there can be more than one "new"), Hawthorne evokes from the outset a conception of time in which what has just emerged is already in the process of becoming obsolete. The narrator of the triptych has been reading newspapers from three different periods of American history, separated by twenty years, and has set as his task the re-presentation not only of the contents of these periodicals but also, significantly, the very experience of their reading. The first sketch opens with a characterization of the generative powers contained in newspapers:

> Here is a volume of what were once newspapers – each on a small half-sheet, yellow and time-stained, of a coarse fabric, and imprinted with a rude old type. Their aspect conveys a singular impression of antiquity, in a species of literature which we are accustomed to consider as connected only with the present moment. Ephemeral as they were intended and supposed to be, they have long outlived the printer and his whole subscription list, and have proved more durable, as to their physical existence, than most of the timber, bricks, and stone, of the town where they were issued. These are but the least of their triumphs.
> (*Tales and Sketches*, p. 251)

Hawthorne's close description of the look and feel of colonial newspapers emphasizes the sensory experience inhering in the reading process: the unusual size, the color, and stains on the page engage the narrator's vision, the paper made of fabric is distinctive for its texture, and even the typography is visually "rude" and "old" from the perspective of an early nineteenth-century reader used to the size and shape of the lettering of newer print technologies. The immediate sensate experience of what had heretofore been the past, "magically" (p. 262) made possible through a medium fashioned to be "ephemeral" and for the "present moment," is key to the overall project of Hawthorne's narrator. It is by "tak[ing] one of the little dingy half-sheets between thumb and finger" that the narrator can "picture forth" a colonial reader, imagining him as he holds the pages "wet from the press, and steaming" (p. 251). Here the traces of "antiquity['s]" prior status as literally hot off the presses are available for imaginative reinvigoration via the material experience of holding what has visibly been handled before by people now at rest under a "grave-stone" (p. 258).

The motif of material access to a past generation's immediately sensuous experience is reiterated in the second sketch, "The Old French War," when first the narrator describes the pages of a twenty-years-newer newspaper as "discolored, here and there, with the deeper stains of some liquid, as if the contents of a wine-glass had long since been splashed upon the page" (p. 259). Once again the narrator elaborates from the physical residue of the first moment of reception to a street scene of the arrival of the news: "[W]e may fancy ourselves in the circle of listeners, all with necks stretched out towards an old gentleman in the centre, who deliberately puts on his spectacles, unfolds the wet newspaper, and gives us the details of the broken and contradictory reports . . . flying from mouth to mouth" (p. 262). In this passage, the frame of the triptych is doubled within the content of the sketch itself. Our narrator, who has read and will report on the "broken and contradictory" accounts found in an old periodical, begins by calling to his readers' imagination the experience of standing side by side with another now vanished circle, then craning their necks in high anticipation, as a now also absent other narrator proceeds to recount news so new that the ink recording it is not yet dry.

In the first sketch of "Old News," the narrator had dramatized as arrogance a different perception of the relationship between the living and the dead. Having evoked the colonial major pondering "paragraph[s] of provincial politics . . . ship news, and commercial advertisements," the speaker preemptively asserts: "Observe and smile! He may have been a wise man in his day; but, to us, the wisdom of the politician appears like folly because we compare its prognostics with actual results" (p. 252). Thus, the narrator tempts "us," ninety years later, with a superior attitude because "we" know which ships sank, which businesses failed, and what the major should and should not have been worried about. What immediately follows, though, is the thesis that propels the triptych: "Yet, [the major's] avocations were not so vain as our philosophic moralizing. In this world we are things of a moment, and are made to pursue momentary things, with here and there a thought that stretches mistily towards eternity, and . . . may endure as long. All philosophy, that would abstract mankind from the present, is no more than words" (p. 252). The "durable" quality and "triumph" asserted in the triptych's opening paragraph of a "species of literature," intentionally "ephemeral," is its ability to revivify predecessors as fellows caught in the act of being utterly absorbed in the heat of the moment and current concerns. Those who have already passed are cast as exempla for nineteenth-century readers of their own state of being "things of a moment." The aim of the triptych is not, therefore, or not merely, to invest the past with overlooked significance but rather to instigate a ponderable self-consciousness in readers of their own circumscription within a present that is, at once, all and all, and on the verge of vanishing, and, paradoxically, still capable of being retraced.

In the third sketch of "Old News," the narrator changes his strategy for evoking a past fully preoccupied, as are his readers, with a "pursuit of momentary things" (p. 252). The last newspaper to be described, from the time of the American Revolution, shows fewer "traces" of "antique fashions" and reveals manners so close to a "modern cast" that the narrator "doubt[s]" whether his sketch has produced the effect of finding "the life of a past age preserved between the leaves" (p. 275). Yet this doubt articulates the aim of the third sketch. In order to expose assumptions with a "modern cast" as ephemeral and not the pinnacle of human progress, the narrator reads the Revolution's news from the point of view of an old Tory who has outlived his generation and who, understandably, "mistake[s] the temporary evils of a change, for permanent diseases of the system which that change was to establish" (p. 274). Readers are asked to consider the centrality of change itself and the inherent transience of its "evils" or its good in the unfolding of a culture's shared presumptions. Hawthorne writes: "Such an old man among new things are we, who now hold, at arm's length, the rebel newspaper of the day" (p. 270). He might have said and certainly means to imply that nineteenth-century readers are also fast becoming "old men" holding at arm's length future newspapers the contents of which will seem troublingly strange.

Readers are made aware, via "The Old Tory," of their having been blinded by or ensnared in their own moment and as having forgotten how much their post-Revolutionary presuppositions are "new things" that will also pass. Again, it is tempting to understand "Old News" as making a Hawthornean move to engage readers in recognizing their place within an evolving history from which they cannot, even if they would, fully separate themselves. However, in this triptych, Hawthorne places his emphasis on how utterly and understandably four different generations are absorbed by their present moment while remaining in the thrall of change. That an age can emerge reinvigorated through a few pages of a newspaper and then be brought to a close in the length of a brief sketch only reinforces the profound rapidity – and is meant by Hawthorne to do so – with which the new becomes old. "Old News" becomes, then, a banner headline for the emergence of the narratives of speed and vanishing that were already imagined by some both to characterize reality in the 1830s and to imbue the conception of even history itself. A lost sense of obvious cause and effect or clear-cut resolutions – the kinds of omissions and half-developed provisions with which *The Marble Faun*'s narrator almost taunts readers twenty-five years later – is made frightening and fathomable in a world where evanescence is the bottom line, the source of both terror and pleasure and the shape of new knowledge. Only through such resilient forms as newspapers and sketches, it seems, can the old or young now hope to be remembered.

In other sketches of the 1830s, Hawthorne addresses explicitly, often with humor or irony, the phenomenon of change as saturating daily and epochal life, including two pieces spoken in the voice of an entrepreneurial newspaper carrier ("Time's Portraiture," "The Sister Years") who seeks to reap a lit-tle extra profit from his particularly close relationship with Time. The light satire "A Rill from the Town-Pump," published the same year as "Old News" (1835), combines a historical rendering of Salem with a narrative of modern-ization as the town's water pump recounts the fate of succeeding generations interconnected with the changes in a watering-place from fountain to mud-puddle to the new apparatus that bubbles over with enthusiasm for himself – the Town-Pump. Beginning with "Indian sagamores," according to the speaker, "[O]ne generation after another . . . cast their waxing and wan-ing shadows in [the fountain's] glassy bosom, and vanished from the earth, as if mortal life were but a flitting image in a fountain. Finally, the fountain vanished also . . . [I]n the course of time a Town-Pump was sunk . . . and when the first decayed, another took its place – and then another, and still another" (*Tales and Sketches*, pp. 310–11). This self-styled champion of the contemporary temperance movement, envisioning his own inevitable obso-lescence, hopes that "when I shall have decayed . . . if you revere my mem-ory, let a marble fountain, richly sculptured take my place upon this spot" (p. 313). The wish for memorialization is depicted as a reaction, not unique to the Town-Pump, in the face of the very rapidity with which one may be replaced and forgotten – "Such monuments should be erected everywhere" (p. 313). The cultural anxiety invoked by Hawthorne's use of humor to voice a desire to be permanently remembered is causally linked in the sketch to a heightened apprehension of a world shadowed by successive vanishings. In such a world, durable notice would be at a premium because it was so unlikely. Since monuments of marble cannot be everywhere, it falls to more mobile forms capable of outliving "timber, bricks, and stone" (p. 251), to document fleeting lives. How good of the author, then, and how telling, to remember the Town-Pump at the close of his other now more well-known sketch "The Custom-House"!

In 1843, Hawthorne returned to his earlier formulation of an explicit relationship between ephemeral forms of writing and the articulation of an intensified perception of human life as evanescent. When he does so, in "The Old Manse," it is something of a surprise to see just how consistent is his thinking on the question. At the close of the preface to his third volume of tales and sketches, he writes in the tone of apology, cataloguing what he has not been able to accomplish during his stay at the Manse: "No profound treatise of ethics – no philosophic history – no novel, even that could stand, unsupported, on its edges. All that I had to show, as a man of letters, were these few tales and essays, which had blossomed out like flowers . . . These fitful sketches, with so little of external life about them, yet claiming no profundity of purpose" (*Tales and Sketches*, p. 1149). Such language from

Hawthorne's prefaces to his sketchbooks has been taken by some to be a genuine expression of anxiety, humility, or chagrin at his own frequent recurrence to sketch writing, and it may certainly be the case that Hawthorne's feelings were mixed about the form through which he had long attempted to realize his ambition as a man of letters. Yet such an anxiety in Hawthorne would have been much less intense and much more commingled with pleasure and commitment than we might now imagine, not only because sketch writing was a dominant and critically accredited mode of literary production, but also because Hawthorne himself had developed reasons, as we have seen, for valuing the sketch.

After welcoming readers into "The Old Manse," Hawthorne as narrator begins by comparing himself to his immediate predecessor in the house, a pastor whom he imagines to have written many sermons under its roof. As he would later similarly seem to fret in "The Custom-House," Hawthorne asserts that he finds himself lacking when contrasted with an earlier generation's accomplishments, "I took shame to myself for having so long been a writer of idle stories" (*Tales and Sketches*, p. 1124) and resolved "at least to achieve a novel, that should evolve some deep lesson, and should possess physical substance enough to stand alone" (p. 1124). In the opening and in the closing passages, then, Hawthorne specifically invokes the presumption that the size of the text (it can "stand alone" or "stand . . . on its edges") corresponds to its depth and force. In both places, he admits that he has failed to meet such combined criteria. It is in the middle portion of the sketch and in the role of a reader rather than writer, however, that Hawthorne departs from his framing gestures toward the superior value of lengthier and supposedly more profound literary works. During his visit to the old Manse's garret library on a rainy day, he pages through the "venerable books" stored there and finds them "all . . . dead alike" (p. 1136):

> Nothing, strange to say, retained any sap, except what had been written for the passing day and year, without the remotest pretension or idea of permanence. There were a few old newspapers, and still older almanacs, which reproduced, to my mental eye, the epochs when they had issued from the press . . . It was as if I had found bits of magic looking-glass among the books, with the images of a vanished century in them. (p. 1137)

Here, as in "Old News," it is ephemeral forms that endure, that "retain sap," that memorialize as they reinvigorate – all the more enlivened because they are not in one piece. The pastor and "his brethren," Hawthorne goes on to say, produced "nothing half so real, as these newspaper scribblers and almanac-makers had thrown off, in the effervescence of a moment . . . It is the Age itself that writes newspapers and almanacs" (p. 1137). In the context of such a reexamination, "fitful sketches" and "trifles" are invested by effervescent association with the newspaper's "kind of intelligible truth" (p. 1137), unavailable from the treatise, the history, or perhaps even the novel. Hawthorne's concluding remarks in "The Old Manse" may also take on a broader significance in light of this commentary on ephemeral composition: "For myself, the book will always retain one charm, as reminding me of the river, with its delightful solitudes, and of the avenue, the garden, and the orchard, and especially the dear old Manse . . . and the sunshine glimmering through the willow-branches while I wrote" (p. 1149). Having just provided a detailed, anecdotal tour of the very places here named, Hawthorne's seemingly personal valuing of "fitful sketches" as reminders of passing pleasures and flickering sunlight may now also recall to readers' mental eye, like "bits of magic looking-glass," these places they have never actually seen, gratification and worries they have not had first-hand, and the acts of writing that pictured them forth.

Leisure, potent brevity, and memorials in bits and pieces

In "The Old Manse," Hawthorne disavowed for his tales and sketches any "profundity of purpose" and admitted that they contained "little of external life." In so doing, he placed his work apart from the informational realm of newspapers and within the discourse of leisure that surrounded antebellum sketch writing. From Washington Irving's angling and Ik Marvel's reveries about dream-girls, to Harriet Farley's imagined escapes from the Lowell mill loom, to Caroline Kirkland's ironic pencilings on gossip and Lydia Maria Child's strolls through New York City, sketch writers carved out leisure as their territory and often fashioned their sketches as private moments of shared relaxation, conversation, or reflection with readers. If this seems somehow at odds with the hustle and bustle that sketches also invoked, Hawthorne's sketches among others offer clear, explicit illustration that leisure and a life imbued with momentum, time off and time on, are part and parcel of the same system.[18] It was the new role of the author in emerging modernity to provide both the occasion and the materials for a respite from labor. Sketches in particular offered leisure in brief, keeping pace with the times by supplying quick remedies for anxiousness or ennui. The conventional persona of the sketch writer, male or female, foregrounded his or her character as an idler, thereby becoming the very embodiment of what readers could wish, for a short time, to be.[19] As Richard Millington has argued, likening the "geography of leisure" to the "place" of romance, Hawthorne himself had designs on this new "cultural space" in his early writing as an arena for a complicated version of rest: "Hawthorne invariably evokes romance as a distinctive location, a place that, by virtue of its nearness to but difference from the environs of customary life, permits a deepened version of the kind of restoration – intellectual, imaginative, psychological – that leisure's advocates had in mind for the wearied middle-class brain-worker."[20] Hawthorne's deepening of the space of leisure in sketches is, of course, often absorbed with, in more and less direct ways, the modern problem of evanescence: the threatened disappearance of the self, strategies for thwarting it, and the dangers involved in the attempt.

Hawthorne's sketches "with so little of external life" in them focus frequently on those times and places of between-ness, when "life" can be felt as internal, where a pause is possible, at least in imagination, and when the self has time to look into itself. In "The Haunted Mind," such a time is 2:00 a.m., when "Yesterday has already vanished among the shadows of the past; tomorrow has not yet emerged from the future. You have found an intermediate space, where the business of life does not intrude; where the passing moment lingers, and becomes truly the present" (*Tales and Sketches*, p. 200). Hawthorne's intermediate spaces are not always preserves of pleasure but do enable a heightened, undistracted consciousness that prolongs "passing moments." In such moments, as "The Haunted Mind" depicts them, the figures of emotion, presumably repressed when one is consumed with the "business of life," can emerge – passion and feeling, sorrow and hope, shame, guilt and fear – and be experienced as what the narrator calls "human life" in the space of an hour. Other instances of such enhanced awareness occur in Hawthorne on Thanksgiving night in "The Village Uncle," in a chance stroll with a child in "Little Annie's Ramble," on the beach in "Foot-prints on the Sea-shore," during an actual vacation in "My Visit to Niagara" and "Sketches from Memory," and through the altered perspective effected by one too many glasses of Madeira in "Fancy's Show Box."[21] In all of these cases, it is the sketch itself, of course, that opens such intermediate spaces for the reader and provides the material that enables self-contemplation. These in-between times are figured as occasions of the utmost privacy, and privacy can be, in Hawthorne, either the site of imaginative engagement and assertion for the individual self or the location of the greatest risk of solipsism or narcissism, but is usually both.

In "Foot-prints on the Sea-shore" (1838), Hawthorne fashions two classes of evanescence. The first is evanescence as the effective annihilation of the self, brought on by the crowds and momentum of modernity, in which the individual is rendered invisible to others and incapable of self-recognition. The competing (and compensatory) conception of evanescence proffered in the sketch is as a natural state of being in which the individual infers the substance and value of his own fleeting existence in the infinite signs of transient predecessors on, in this case, the beach. In this latter version, evanescence itself is cast as the source of self-knowledge with leisure as the vehicle to a wider, more sustaining awareness. Nature as leisure space becomes the site of the small epiphanies and pleasures that are the footprints of the individual self.

The title of the sketch is another of Hawthorne's doubled images, invoking both the moment of inscription (footprints) and its vanishing (in the sand). Like old newspapers that link the reader to the people of bygone ages through material traces like wine-stains on a page, this sketch invokes sensuous connection to the narrator's person via the tracks marking his prior bodily presence in the place where he has walked when "the yearning for seclusion becomes a necessity" (*Tales and Sketches*, p. 561). At one remove from solitude itself, the occasion of this narrator's sketching is the retracing of his own footsteps on previous excursions and his re-creating of past activities, sights, feelings, and thoughts along the way – all for the reader's recreation. Taking the "reader's fancy arm in arm with mine," the narrator bids "Farewell, then, [to the] busy world!" and sets off on a sea-shore ramble where the "spirit . . . enlarge[s] its sense of being" (p. 561). This self-enlarging process shared by the narrator with his reader is cast as necessary to the "health and vigor" diminished by remaining too long in the fray (p. 561). Near the conclusion of the sketch, the narrator reveals what has been at stake in a day full of rock-skipping, bird-watching, treasure-hunting, girl-spying, daydreaming ephemeral pleasures: "[W]hen, at noontide, I tread the crowded streets, the influence of this day will still be felt; so that I shall walk among men kindly and as a brother, with affection and sympathy, but yet shall not melt into the indistinguishable mass of human kind. I shall think my own thoughts, and feel my own emotions, and possess my individuality unviolated" (pp. 569–70). The fending off of annihilation – the violence to individuality threatened by "crowded streets" – and the recuperation of a capacity for social emotion and thought may seem accomplished as if by magic by the sheer inutility of a day devoted to leisure. But Hawthorne's leisure works harder than that – it explains what looks like magic.

When Hawthorne's narrator, a "peaceful outlaw," goes looking for a reprieve from the melting crowd, what he finds is more evanescence but with a difference. Glimpses of three girls on the beach who vanish in the distance are replaced by the contemplation of "beach-birds" looking for food. "With a philosophy that mankind would do well to imitate, they drew continual pleasure from their toil for a subsistence. The sea was each little bird's great playmate . . . [T]hey floated as lightly as one of their own feathers on the breaking crest. In their airy flutterings, they seemed to rest on the evanescent spray . . . they took wing over the ocean, and were

gone . . . [I]t is really worth a sigh, to find no memorial of them save their mul-
titudinous little tracks in the sand" (pp. 562–63). The cue is overt in this passage to find an analogy between feathered laborers and the human kind, all
of whom ride lightly the waves of toil and rest. The passing acknowledgment
of seemingly inadequate little memorials leads the narrator to retrace ["o]ur
tracks" which "will guide us with an observing consciousness" to remember
what "we" have seen, touched, and felt (p. 563). "Thus, by tracking our
foot-prints in the sand, we track our own nature in its wayward course,
and steal a glance upon it, when it never dreams of being so observed. Such
glances always make us wiser" (p. 563). Here, in the intermediate space and
time of leisure where the "passing moment lingers" ("The Haunted Mind,"
Tales and Sketches, p. 200), the narrator and his "arm in arm" reader can
recuperate and dwell upon their very own "little tracks" deep with suggested
living and comprehended in a glance.

From footprints in the sand to their other obvious analogue – writing – is
but a short step for Hawthorne's narrator. The passage described above is
immediately followed by a frenzy of imagined compositions in the sand, the
pleasure of which lies partially in the act of self-inscription and partially in
the assurance of their content's near immediate erasure, since they last only
for the few moments between waves: "love verses . . . may be inscribed"
along with "thoughts, feelings, desires, warm outgushings from the heart's
secret places" (p. 564). Even the gigantic letters of one's name written in the
sand will be "swept over" by time's "effacing waves" just as has happened
already to "the names of statesmen, and warriors, and poets" (p. 564). This
rendering of the felt certainty of ephemerality as also the achievement of
utter expressive freedom is left unqualified in the sketch and marks a new
aesthetic sensation born of cultural haste. Outgushings, and glimpses, and
airy flutterings are made precious by the very brevity of their character.

What is refashioned here are not, then, the properties of evanescence but
rather its association with absolute obliteration. For this beach is full of the
traces of others who have come and gone away, memorials in bits and pieces.
"[O]ur idle pastime" (p. 563) has included collecting feathers, finding whale
bones, and launching boats made of driftwood. Significantly, all are "discov-
eries" that inspire remembrance of passing life and former inhabitants whom
this speaker can imagine alive again: veins in rocks look like "inscriptions"
that he fancies are "forgotten characters of an antediluvian race," the bodies
of a dead seal, shark, and seabird seem, at first, animate and respectively
frightened, terrifying, and lovely in repose. A jawbone ten feet long recalls
the "leviathan of former ages" to which it had belonged (p. 565). Armed
with these proofs against utter erasure, now the materials of present enjoyment, but also evidence of inevitable obsolescence, this narrator fashions

uneasy but sensuous consolation. Such solace, it goes without saying, is also inscribed and embodied for the reader – and the writer – in the literary sketch itself.

Within the space Hawthorne has created for the mutual articulation of leisure and selfhood is a hidden recess of even deeper privacy, where the narrator has spent "many a secret hour" (p. 567). It is in this nook surrounded by the walls of a high cliff that Hawthorne dramatizes the tension between the risks and rewards of leisured solitude. Having chanced upon three girls of "flesh and blood" whom he peeped at as they "lav[ed] their snowy feet in the sunny water," he admits that there is "something in the encounter that makes the heart flutter with a strangely pleasant sensation" (p. 566). Upon feeling so pleasantly, he immediately scrambles for his nook where so often his "musings melted into its rocky walls and sandy floor" (p. 567). While lunching with appetite, the narrator describes this recess as his private place for active fantasy, beginning then to dream first of two lovers who leave "no foot-prints" (pp. 167–68) and then of "a single shade" for whom he will "be myself her lover" (p. 568). Hawthorne evokes in these titillating passages the dual antebellum discourses of bachelor reverie and masturbation, made both thrilling and threatening for readers in anti-onanism advice manuals of the day.[22] The danger of daydreaming and self-pleasuring for single men in particular but one generalizable to the broader reading public as well, was that energy and passion could be all used up when spent un(re)productively. Though taken quite literally as a physiological pathology, the bachelor's succumbing to masturbatory fantasy was also a figure in antebellum culture, therefore, for the self-induced dissolution of the self. Thus, in his seaside cave, Hawthorne's narrator is flirting with another sort of melting brought on not by the crowd but by too much solitude. Just in the nick of time, however, the author reintroduces the "flesh and blood" girls who now peep over the precipice at the narrator. Their laughter recalls him to notice the late hour and to turn from "cold" fancies to warm sights of white feet.

In this way, Hawthorne's outlaw is drawn from the verge of solipsism. His proximity to excessive autonomy is signaled by his too exultant encapsulation of the day: "Climb we, therefore, the precipice, and pause a moment on the brink, gazing down into that hollow chamber where we have been, what few can be, sufficient to our own pastime – yes, say the word outright! – sufficient to our own happiness" (p. 569). Yet, while Hawthorne sketches a thin line between egotism/onanism and self-possessed individualism, this narrator so full of recognized self-sufficient desire rediscovers his emotional, imaginative, and physical relish for the society of women and men and for the home of which he had been, for a time, quite without need (pp. 569–70). Such a taut connection between brief, leisured self-articulation and full social participation is similarly dramatized in "The Old Manse" when the narrator Hawthorne and Ellery Channing go fishing on the Assabeth river, limiting their self-deliverance from "straight-laced habitudes" to the length of "one bright semi-circle of the sun" (p. 1138). Likening himself and his friend to "Indians or any less conventional race," the narrator tells of their achieving, in the "recess" where they ate and laughed and in the boat in which "up-gushed our talk," a "profit . . . not in any definite idea – not in any angular or rounded truth . . . but in the freedom which we thereby won from all custom and conventionalism" (pp. 1140–41). This liberty, delicious because it is known in advance to be temporary, is manifested in free expression, fantasy, and appetite – now homosocial instead of autoerotic: "[t]he evanescent spray was Ellery's; and his, too, the lumps of golden thought" (p. 1141). After such an outing, it is once again "sweet" for the narrator to make a confident return to "the system of human society" in which it would be "impossible to be slaves again tomorrow" (p. 1141) precisely because of the "wild days" now concretely memorialized in the ephemeral "heap of ashes and half-consumed brands" that remain behind on the sketched riverbank.[23]

So, similarly, Hawthorne had concluded in "Little Annie's Ramble," a sketch in which another such "intermediate space" of experience had been enabled by the presence and perspective of a literalized figure of the new and of unworldliness – the child Annie. Here the older narrator concludes with an explanation of the value of childlike, non-utilitarian leisure:

> Say not that it has been a waste of precious moments, an idle matter, a babble of childish talk, and a reverie of childish imaginations . . . unworthy of a grown man's notice . . . Not so; not so . . . As the pure breath of children revives the life of aged men, so is our moral nature revived by their free and simple thoughts, their native feeling, their airy mirth, for little cause or none, their grief, soon roused and soon allayed . . . After drinking from those fountains of still fresh existence, we shall return into the crowd, as I do now, to struggle onward and do our part in life . . . but, for a time, with a kinder and purer heart.
>
> (*Tales and Sketches*, pp. 234–35)

In "Little Annie's Ramble," the adult male not only enjoys but requires periodic forays into unburdened and ephemerally emotion-filled experience in order to act as a moral, feeling citizen rather than a blank integer in the crowd. Again and again, in Hawthorne's sketches, evanescence – the division of time into mere moments that pass hastily away – carries its own logic, its own consolations and remedies, and its own forms and modes of expression. In no uncertain terms, he makes clear that what is at stake is more than a reprieve from fast-paced change. The objective of the new leisure, as imagined by Hawthorne, is the active fending off by the individual, and, by implication, by the modern age itself, of premature obsolescence. To this end, the realm of non-utilitarian privacy carries the social value of renewing participatory energy for the here and now. The long-term effect of the pursuit of temporary pleasures, of excursions, daydreams, and sketches, is the leaving of legible footprints that will be sensuously discernible to oneself and to those who will follow. When Hawthorne locates the source of revitalization outside the struggle of the crowd and in "fresh existence," he writes from within the effects of emergent modernity. There are new needs and, thus, new gratifications and perils in a world of increased momentum. It follows, then, that Hawthorne's "intermediate spaces" haunt as much as they satisfy and are meant to do so. Such fleeting, tightrope-walking escapes from the discipline of social systems (and even from closely managed narratives of full disclosure) are made more exhilarating and self-consolidating by their protocols of return.[24] Through the force of their suggestiveness and by their forays into regions "half-known [and] deliciously felt," to borrow Pearce's apt phrase,[25] Hawthorne fashioned his sketches to be crucial provisions for sustaining modernity and its subjects.

NOTES

1. Roy Harvey Pearce, "Hawthorne and the Twilight of Romance," in *Historicism Once More: Problems and Occasions for the American Scholar* (Princeton, NJ: Princeton University Press, 1969), p. 195. For excellent recent work on Hawthorne's sketches as a body of work within the context of modernity and in relation to his romances, see Dana Brand, *The Spectator and the City in Nineteenth-Century American Literature* (Cambridge: Cambridge University Press, 1991), especially chs. 4, 6, and 7. Although Brand's tight focus on the figure of the *flâneur* as the basis for his assessment of Hawthorne's sketches leads him to draw broad conclusions about these short works that differ from mine, his thickly contextualized readings contribute in crucial ways to our understanding of the significance of emergent modernity not only in the works of Hawthorne but of other male American sketch writers as well.
2. Pearce, "Hawthorne and the Twilight of Romance," pp. 191, 195, 175, 176, 191, 186, 189, 181, 191, 176.
3. For a fuller discussion of modernity in *The Marble Faun*, see Kristie Hamilton, "Fauns and Mohicans: Narratives of Extinction and Hawthorne's Aesthetic of Modernity," in Robert K. Martin and Leland S. Person, eds., *Roman Holidays: American Writers and Artists in Nineteenth-Century Italy* (Iowa City: University of Iowa Press, 2002), pp. 41–59.
4. For an evocative account of this facet of modernity from the nineteenth century to the present, see W. J. T. Mitchell, *The Last Dinosaur Book: The Life and Times of a Cultural Icon* (Chicago: University of Chicago Press, 1998), especially chs. 11, 12, 13, 18, and Coda.
5. Washington Irving, "The Author's Account of Himself," *The Sketch Book of Geoffrey Crayon, Gent.*, ed. Haskell Springer (Boston: Twayne, 1979), p. 9.

6. Of Mitford's popularity in the US in the early nineteenth century, James T. Fields writes: "The recognition which America, very early in the career of Miss Mitford, awarded her, she never forgot, and she used to say, 'It takes ten years to make a literary reputation in England, but America is wiser and bolder, and dares say at once, 'This is fine,'" in *Yesterdays with Authors*, 1871 (Boston: Houghton Mifflin, 1883), p. 276.

7. For a more complete version of this account of the sketch in American literary and cultural history, see Kristie Hamilton, *America's Sketchbook: The Cultural Life of a Nineteenth-Century Literary Genre* (Athens: Ohio University Press, 1998). For other significant discussions of the sketch in antebellum literary culture, see Brand, *The Spectator and the City*, especially chs. 4, 5, 6, 8; Judith Fetterley, "Introduction," *Provisions: A Reader from 19ᵗʰ-Century American Women* (Bloomington: Indiana University Press, 1985), pp. 1–38; Sandra Zagarell, "The Narrative of Community: The Identification of a Genre," *Signs: Journal of Women in Culture and Society* 13 (1988): 498–527; Gregory R. Wegner, "Hawthorne's 'Ethan Brand' and the Structure of the Literary Sketch," *The Journal of Narrative Technique* 17 (1987): 56–66; Jeffrey Rubin-Dorsky, "Washington Irving and the Genesis of the Fictional Sketch," *Early American Literature* 21 (1986/87): 226–47; Ann Douglas, *The Feminization of American Culture* (New York: Knopf, 1977; Anchor-Doubleday, 1988), especially pp. 237–40; Thomas H. Pauly, "The Literary Sketch in Nineteenth-Century America," *Texas Studies in Literature and Language* 17 (1975): 489–503; Fred Lewis Pattee, *The Development of the American Short Story: A Historical Survey* (New York: Harper and Brothers, 1923).

8. For an illuminating reading of Marvel's and Melville's bachelor sketches as articulating the conflict between normative heterosexual masculinity in the antebellum period and emergent oppositional male sexuality and plural masculinities, see Vincent J. Bertolini, "Fireside Chastity: The Erotics of Sentimental Bachelorhood in the 1850s," in Mary Chapman and Glenn Hendler, eds., *Sentimental Men: Masculinity and the Politics of Affect in American Culture* (Berkeley: University of California Press, 1999), pp. 19–42.

9. Walter Benjamin, *Charles Baudelaire: A Lyric Poet in the Era of High Capitalism*, trans. Harry Zohn (London: Verso, 1983), pp. 36–37.

10. Lydia Maria Child, "Letters from New York," in Judith Fetterley, ed., *Provisions: A Reader from Nineteenth-Century American Women* (Bloomington: Indiana University Press, 1985), p. 201.

11. Citations from all of Hawthorne's sketches are taken from the Library of America edition of *Hawthorne: Tales and Sketches* (New York: Library of America, 1982), which reproduces the text of the Centenary Edition.

12. Brand argues that the narrator foregrounds his failure to see beneath the old man's surface and to describe his history and asserts that, in this way, Hawthorne "reaffirms the opacity of the world by showing how little an honest *flâneur* or panoramic spectator would actually accomplish," in *The Spectator and the City*, pp. 111–13.

13. Wolfgang Schivelbusch, *The Railway Journey: The Industrialization of Time and Space in the Nineteenth Century* (Berkeley: University of California Press, 1986); Jonathan Crary, *Techniques of the Observer: On Vision and Modernity in the Nineteenth Century* (Cambridge, MA: MIT Press, 1990). Crary argues that a

new model of vision and a new observer were produced in the early rather than the late nineteenth century as the result of the invention of optical devices such as the phenakistiscope and the stereoscope and of new visual forms such as the panorama and diorama along with the emergence of empirical studies of the physiology of vision. Together these innovations brought about changes now associated with the onset of modernity and the eventual dominance of visual culture. For an articulate overview of the major components of modernity and of its theorists' work, see Mike Featherstone, "Postmodernism and the Aestheticization of Everyday Life," in Scott Lash and Jonathan Friedman, eds., *Modernity and Identity* (Oxford: Blackwell, 1992), pp. 265–90.

14. Schivelbusch, *The Railway Journey*, pp. 60, 64.

15. Walter Benjamin, *Charles Baudelaire: A Lyric Poet in the Era of High Capitalism*, trans. Harry Zohn (London: Verso, 1983); Georg Simmel, "The Metropolis and Mental Life," trans. H. H. Gerth and C. Wright Mills, in Kurt Wolff, ed., *The Sociology of Georg Simmel* (Glencoe, IL: Free Press, 1950); Henri Lefebvre, *Everyday Life in the Modern World*, trans. Sacha Rabinovitch (New York: Harper & Row, 1971).

16. Brand, *The Spectator and the City*, pp. 106–07.

17. Hawthorne's aspiration for ephemeral forms – that they memorialize in a sensuously dynamic rather than a static, "dead" way, in keeping with more hurried times – would seem to pose the conceptual and physical problem of how to achieve something akin to the tactile and visual immediacy of the trace of life figured as coarse fabric pages and wine-stains in "Old News," this, when newer ephemera were so neatly printed and reprinted on the new pages of magazines and books. Staging this problem becomes the premise of the 1844 sketch "A Book of Autographs" (1844), where Hawthorne thinks about the limits of print media, when compared with an even less modern form than newspapers, the handwritten letter. The vividness with which the letters under examination are evoked makes the argument that his sketch can work the magic of imagined sensation through self-conscious, descriptive immediacy.

18. For an excellent discussion of middle-class leisure, the newly invented vacation, and Hawthorne's work, see Richard Millington, "Where is Hawthorne's Rome? *The Marble Faun* and the Cultural Space of Middle-Class Leisure," in Martin and Person, eds., *Roman Holidays*, pp. 9–27. For a discussion of the broad cultural identification of literature in general and the sketch in particular with leisure as a central component of middle-class identity, see Hamilton, *America's Sketchbook*, especially ch. 2.

19. It is, however, important to note, contra Ann Douglas, that there were wide variations on this theme emerging from gender, class, race, and other social positionings and innumerable agendas embedded in the broad category of leisure. See Douglas, *The Feminization of American Culture*, pp. 237–40.

20. Millington, "Where is Hawthorne's Rome?," pp. 14, 9, 14.

21. Millington has pointed to a similar phenomenon in the long romances, *ibid*.

22. Three recent studies that draw compelling conclusions about the relationship between antebellum sexuality and identity formation based in part upon studies of anti-onanism advice literature are: Bertolini, "Fireside Chastity," pp. 19–42; G. M. Goshgarian, *To Kiss the Chastening Rod: Domestic Fiction and Sexual Ideology in the American Renaissance* (Ithaca, NY: Cornell University Press, 1992);

T. Walter Herbert, Jr., *Dearest Beloved: The Hawthornes and the Making of the Middle-Class Family* (Berkeley: University of California Press, 1993). All three cite fascinating material from the cultural history by G. J. Barker-Benfield, *The Horrors of the Half-Known Life: Male Attitudes toward Women and Sexuality in Nineteenth-Century America* (New York: Harper, 1976).

23. See Millington, "Where is Hawthorne's Rome?," pp. 14–17, for an acute discussion of Hawthorne's aspirations in "The Old Manse" as a giver of "rest, in a life of trouble" (Hawthorne, *Tales and Sketches*, p. 1144).

24. "Egotism; Or, the Bosom Serpent" and "Wakefield" are both stories of self-imposed seclusion gone wrong, in which Hawthorne aggressively pesters the delicacy of his own recurrent formulation of restorative self-scrutiny in solitude combined with the protocol of return. Roderick's obnoxious hyper-visibility upon his return to commune with his fellows in the crowd is not at all of the kind and pure-hearted sort imagined by the narrator of "Little Annie's Ramble," and, inversely, Wakefield's inadvertent and intoxicating self-imposed invisibility is quite immune to even a good, solid bump from Mrs. Wakefield.

25. Pearce, "Hawthorne and the Twilight of Romance," p. 181.

6

GILLIAN BROWN

Hawthorne's American history

Every one who has considered the subject, knows full well that a nation without fancy, without some romance, never did, never can, never will, hold a great place under the sun.[1]

In this 1853 proclamation, Charles Dickens articulates the nineteenth-century belief in the importance of fancy in books for children that has remained a guiding assumption about children's literature ever since. "The fairy literature of our childhood," according to Dickens, significantly affords a "precious old escape" from the world which "is too much with us, early and late."[2] This is why he objects to his friend George Cruikshank writing temperance messages into fairy tales; Dickens would keep social and political agendas outside the realm of fancy. It might seem odd, then, that he expressly associates fancy and romance with the very worldly institution of national-ism. But the Dickensian defense of fancy astutely recognizes the imaginative character of nationalism: like fairy tales, nations seem to exist independently of the local concerns and interests of their citizens. Nations garner fealty from their inhabitants by convincing them to believe in and find refuge in realms beyond themselves, realms apart from immediate experience.

The fairy stories that Dickens and his contemporaries were writing for juvenile readers thus schooled them in the imaginative dynamics of nationalism. One of those contemporaries in the United States – Nathaniel Hawthorne, who had just published *A Wonder-Book for Girls and Boys* (1852) – had already identified the crucial role of fancy in nationalism in such 1830s stories as "The Gray Champion" and "Legends of the Province-House."[3] But Hawthorne from the start saw nationalism not merely as a realization of fancy in which a powerful sense of nation and the practices that strengthen, expand, and perpetuate a nation emanate from a fanciful sensibility. For Hawthorne, any investment that persons develop in places and pasts, in specific countries and histories, proceeds imaginatively. Since nationalism, like other human formations, owes its existence to the imagi-native faculty, it registers rather than rationalizes (either positively or nega-tively) the function of imagination.

Thus fiction does not require confirmation in the sphere of history where the record of nations gets written. Instead, as Hawthorne's prefaces repeatedly stress in their famous insistences on the values of romance, the inevitably fanciful enterprise of writing history generates narratives that readers must be careful not to confuse with actual events. Because all accounts of reality operate through mental processes, romance, with its range for speculation, seems to Hawthorne the best literary register of the human relations that compose history. Acknowledging the romantic character of history in no way dispels its very real force. On the contrary, romance prompts Hawthorne and his readers to explore the literary techniques by which national stories achieve and maintain their power.[4]

Hawthorne began his professional career as a writer of history for children, and in these writings delineated the imaginative basis upon which persons build a patriotic sense – both how Americans in the nineteenth century made up the story of their nation and how they might make up other stories. In Hawthorne's account of American history, we see not just the romantic composition of nationalism but also the imaginative configurations whereby children, fancy, and nation become so firmly linked that ever after this association has seemed a natural fact. As Hawthorne employs and engages just emerging styles of juvenile literature, he illuminates the imaginative processes of identification entailed in nationalism. His study of the diverse and sometimes strange movements comprising identification does not produce an imitable model of American identity, as we might expect. Hawthorne instead develops an account of American nationalism in which national identification continually operates in tandem with resistances to it.

The importance of Arbella Johnson

American history, according to Hawthorne, begins with the story of the Lady Arbella Johnson. She is the first historical personage to appear in *Grandfather's Chair*, the series of sketches of colonial American life that Hawthorne wrote "to make a lively and entertaining narrative for children."[5] Arbella was a sister of the British Earl of Lincoln; she married Isaac Johnson, a wealthy member and benefactor of the Puritan company who founded the Massachusetts Bay Colony in 1630, a decade after the first Puritan settlement at Plymouth Rock. After sailing to North America with her husband on the ship named after herself, the Lady Arbella soon died from an illness that began during the voyage. Other than these few facts, no other information about Arbella Johnson exists. From Hawthorne's reading in John Winthrop's letters and diaries about the colony and in George Bancroft's monumental *A History of the United States from the Discovery of the American Continent*, he would have found Arbella briefly mentioned as an example of the many suffering emigrants who died "weekly, yea, almost daily" from the "unforeseen hardships" of the settlement. "The virtues of the lady Arbella Johnson could not break through the gloom," Bancroft writes, "and as she had been ill before her arrival, grief hurried her to the grave."[6]

By 1841, when Hawthorne's *Grandfather's Chair*, and its sequels *Famous Old People* and *Liberty Tree*, first appeared, children in the United States were accustomed to learning that their nation began with Columbus's discovery of the West Indies and the subsequent British settlement of North America. Since the revolution, schoolbooks for American children celebrated these voyages of exploration and immigration as key moments in the making of the nation. The portrait of the past promoted through popular juvenile histories by Noah Webster, John Frost, Emma Willard, and the brothers Charles and Samuel Goodrich, simplified the various enterprises and experiences of different peoples over more than three centuries into a chain of events culminating in the formation of the United States.[7] This teleological portrait gained greater force through Bancroft's cultural and intellectual treatment of American history as the progress of "freedom and liberty of conscience" following from the successful migrations of Europeans fleeing tyranny.[8] While Hawthorne follows contemporary historical practice in representing the American experience as an "unbroken thread" of events (*Grandfather's Chair*, VI: 8), he curiously chooses to begin his history of the United States with a character who plays no role in the advance of the settlement, indeed, who dies one month after her arrival in New England. His history records the losses incurred in the course of progress, and thus, along with the sad story of Arbella, recalls the sufferings of American Indians, French Acadian exiles, persecuted Quakers, and British loyalists, all who lose for ever their accustomed ways of life as the British colonies grow and attain independence.

By remembering some of the victims of and losers in American progress, Hawthorne demonstrates that history is a much more disparate and disquieting experience than the official chronology of significant actors and deeds suggests. The Lady Arbella might figure in a feminist narrative of what George Eliot called the lives of the obscure, or in a revisionist account of the Puritan settlement. While Hawthorne opens the door to these possibilities that later cultural historians and novelists have explored, his own interest in the Lady Arbella is primarily fanciful rather than polemical. Rather than signifying the costs entailed in the geographical movements of the Puritans, this obscure woman marks for Hawthorne the mental processes of transport and transformation that historians and their readers practice. Writing history for a child audience clarifies the imaginative activity that characterizes all relations to history, whether the historical narrative recounts actual or imaginary events.

In imagining the experiences of past persons, present persons develop an affective as well as cognitive connection to their predecessors. The sympathy Hawthorne evokes for Arbella's sad fate displays the psychological investments that history regularly elicits. That this investment emerges from an imaginary sense of the past in no way diminishes the reality of previous events or the real force of people's commitments to their countries. By beginning his American history with "this true story of the gentle lady, who had come so far to die so soon" (VI: 18), Hawthorne both acknowledges and marshals the vital function of fancy in forming national feeling and the allegiances and acts that follow from it. His remembrance of the victims and losers in American history alongside its victors and luminaries bespeaks his recognition that imagination and affection can be narrow and must be, for reasons of time and space, selective. Though unusually broad and varied, the selection of historical personages and experiences that Hawthorne includes in *Grandfather's Chair* notably omits African Americans, leaving them outside the circuit of representation and affinity linking the American people. Like historical happenings, the imagination of history can be both inclusive and exclusive.

The function of fantasy and feeling in the always selective presentation and reception of history is, of course, now so familiar to us as to seem unworthy of comment. A long line of modern expositions of history, from the diverse perspectives of Marx, Nietzsche, Freud, Benjamin, and Fanon, to mention only a few, has recognized the powerful affective dynamics of history for both personal and national identity. Contemporary elementary history books, with such titles as *How Would You Survive as an American Indian?* and . . . *If You Were There When They Signed the Constitution*, acknowledge and employ a now traditional historiographical tactic of establishing an identity between the readers and subjects of history.[9] This writing tactic has its own history, inextricable from the changing history of childhood and books in which Hawthorne participated. Hawthorne helped establish the standard mode of writing and conveying American history when he began *Grandfather's Chair* with the fanciful sketch of Arbella, who like all of us, did not survive life in the land of the American Indians and was not there when the descendants of the surviving settlers signed the Constitution.

The importance of being imaginative

Once fancy and feeling become central to the project of teaching children history, the child emerges as a reader and critic whom writers must please with "a lively and entertaining narrative" (*Grandfather's Chair*, VI: 6). In order that children will want to read about historical figures and events,

Hawthorne tries in *Grandfather's Chair* to write a narrative that conveys a sense of the "private and familiar existence" led by historical personages rather than "that cold array of outward action, which we are compelled to receive as the adequate representations of their lives" (VI: 5–6). No evidence of outward action even exists in Arbella's case. The absence of conventional historical data here prompts Hawthorne's fictional sketch of Arbella's state of mind. One can only imagine how Arbella registered the hardships that her company experienced, and Hawthorne accordingly urges his young readers to "suppose" her "thinking mournfully of far-off England" and wondering "whereabouts in the wilderness her friends will dig her grave" (VI: 16, 17). For Hawthorne, the very vagueness of facts about Arbella's life inspires fancy and speculation; from these processes, Arbella's life gains a substantiality denied her by the historical record. His account of Arbella, inviting readers to imagine themselves privy to her thought and feelings, thus epitomizes the exercise of imagination required to get any sense at all of a personage's "private and familiar existence" (VI: 5). Writing an imaginative history for children, Hawthorne writes a brief for the psychological realism that he later so effectively employed in *The Scarlet Letter*, his full-scale romance about a similarly obscure woman in American history whose traces are supposedly discovered in a forgotten manuscript. Hawthorne's portrait of Hester Prynne has so deeply affected readers that generations of Americans have taken (and continue to take) the novel's representation of Puritan life in the colonies as an authoritative reference work on the New England Puritans.[10]

Grandfather's Chair is, as Hawthorne announces in the preface to the book, an imaginative narrative about both well-known and unknown figures from the past. But even though he "has assumed the license of filling up the outline of history with details, for which he has none but imaginative authority," Hawthorne believes that his literary method does not "violate nor give a false coloring to the truth." Indeed, he asserts, "there is certainly no method, by which the shadowy outlines of departed men and women can be made to assume the hues of life more effectually, than by connecting their images with the substantial and homely reality of a fireside chair" (VI: 5). Describing historical personages through "the adventures of a chair," Hawthorne uses a favorite device of eighteenth-century novels, the narrative link and perspective of a non-human narrator – an animal or object which has witnessed events over time and space, often over limits humans cannot pass. Readers might follow events over vast distances or time spans through the experiences of a mobile mouse or flea or a well-traveled coach or an often exchanged coin or a long-lived piece of furniture like the chair. *The Whole History of Grandfather's Chair* thus follows in the wake of novels such as *The Secret History of an Old Shoe* (1734), *The Genuine and Most Surprizing*

Adventures of a Very Unfortunate Goose-Quill (1734), *The Memoirs and Interesting Adventures of an Embroidered Waistcoat* (1751), *The Adventures of a Guinea* (1760), *The Adventures of a Corkscrew* (1775), *The Adventures of a Watch* (1788), and *The Adventures of a Pin* (1790). Tobias Smollett furnished perhaps the most unique narrative figure in this genre with his *The History and Adventures of an Atom* (1769). Titles by the sisters-in-law Mary Ann Kilner and Dorothy Kilner, such as *The Memoirs of a Peg-Top* (1785) and *The Adventures of a Hackney Coach* (1781), regularly appeared in early nineteenth-century American publishing advertisements.

The advantages of the non-human narrator are of course the advantages of the fiction writer: omniscience, mobility, invisibility, and immunity with respect to the characters and actions presented in the narrative. The novelist obviously holds a privileged perspective on a person or event that he or she invents – the intelligence of an insider unhampered by the interests and limitations of insiders. By making this special knowledge strikingly figural – embodied in an animal or materialized in an object – the novelist emphasizes the superiority of literary technique to human cognizance. From the perspective of Grandfather's chair, Hawthorne can show scenes from American history that neither Grandfather nor his grandchildren ever could see.

At the same time that non-human narrators dramatize the limits of human faculties, they display the imaginative techniques through which humans can sometimes overcome or alter these limits. In their perspectival superiority, non-human narrators epitomize human mental capabilities. Indeed, such figures can be intelligible to readers only because they are personifications. To accept the old oaken chair as a historian, Grandfather and his grandchildren must ascribe consciousness to it, the capacity to perceive, remember, and characterize occurrences. Hawthorne accordingly endows his chair with not only consciousness, but the ability to walk and the qualities of diligence and alacrity. "On its sturdy legs, it trudges diligently from one scene to another, and seems always to thrust itself in the way, with most benign complacency, whenever a historical personage happens to be looking for a seat" (VI: 5). At the end of the three-volume history, the chair even speaks. Thus the technique of personification, one of the oldest of representational conventions, registers a continual effort to widen the scope of human consciousness, to know histories other than those available through one's own experience.[11]

Like all narrators, the chair embodies its own history in addition to the history it tells. As Hawthorne introduces Arbella's story and subsequent stories of seventeenth- and eighteenth-century American colonial life, he fashions a tale of this chair which accompanies and conveys his version of history. To the sparse known details of Lady Arbella's birth, marriage, emigration, and death, Hawthorne adds his own invention: the story that Arbella's father gave on the occasion of her marriage an elegant oak chair; that Arbella took this chair with her on the voyage west; and that after her death the chair passed into the possession of a series of significant actors in colonial and revolutionary history, ranging from Roger Williams and Anne Hutchinson to the successive governors Winthrop, Dudley, Bellingham, and Endicott, to Cotton Mather to George Washington and Samuel Adams. At the beginning of the nineteenth century, Adams sells the chair to its present owner, who teaches his four grandchildren their national history by telling them about the many events supposedly witnessed by the chair.

The old man narrator who imparts historical, geographical, practical, and moral information is a familiar figure in nineteenth-century children's books. Recalling seers and ancient storytellers, the figure possesses and represents the voice of authority and wisdom. The longevity of this old man also signifies linkages between the past and present; he stands as witness to times children themselves cannot know, or even sense. Children thus learn to accept knowledge beyond their own empirical experience. As the old man's reminiscences introduce children to times beyond their compass, his stories initiate children in the narrative practice of remembrance. Keyed to a wider span than reminiscence, remembrance can register what even the old storyteller never knew firsthand.[12] Peter Parley, the most popular of these narrators, furnished lessons to generations of American children through the series of books named after him which Samuel G. Goodrich published from the 1820s to the 1850s. Parley is a gouty old man who has "seen a great many things, and had a great many adventures" which he loves to relate.[13] Hawthorne himself had written one of the books for Goodrich's series, *Peter Parley's Universal History on the Basis of Geography* (1837).[14] When he imagined the narrator figure for his own histories, Hawthorne intensified the authoritative stature and intimate appeal of the storyteller by refining the gouty, garrulous, prosy Peter Parley into the quiet, kindly, loving, and beloved Grandfather.

Though Goodrich designed these books primarily to inform children (although the information in the books is usually speculative and often erroneous), Hawthorne was more interested in gaining "the attention of my pupil by every available art." He therefore explained in his preface to the *Universal History* that he had "spiced" "the dryer parts of the work" with "tales and legends" and had "dealt pretty largely in anecdotes and sketches" (XXIII: 265). Even as he emphasizes geography in this book (with descriptions, maps, and engravings), Hawthorne regards it not as material to be learned but as a way of giving each country "a local habitation and a name" in the mind of the child reader, before telling the country's "story" (XXIII: 265). Like poetry, geography provides a vivid point of reference, a physical and linguistic landmark for mental travels. So for Hawthorne, the task of presenting children information about the world is primarily literary.

Hawthorne teaches history to children through an interactive reader response model, the frame story of Grandfather relating his tales to his four grandchildren, Laurence, Clara, Charley, and Alice, who variously respond to and comment on what they hear. Thus the child audience, both inside and outside the book, enter the world of narrative conventions: into conscious- ness of their acceptance of fictive devices such as all-knowing patriarchal storytellers and talking chairs, and into comparisons between the narratives they encounter, such as the Peter Parley histories and the Grandfather's Chair chronicles. In the four grandchildren and their comments, child readers can find counterparts of themselves, and hence another point of connection and comparison with their own experience. Hawthorne thereby familiarizes chil- dren with literary techniques as well as historical information. As children follow the personifications and perspectives presented in a narrative, and engage with the unknown or remote phenomena to which these narrative techniques provide access, they must use the same imaginative procedures that they find in Hawthorne's writing. *Grandfather's Chair* provides literary encounters through which children can realize their own critical faculties.

The importance of children's minds

Hawthorne can insist upon the identificatory and imaginative activities entailed in learning history – what we might call the affective experience of history – because he assumes the fundamental role of these activities in childlife. Now so long a demonstrated scientific fact that it seems an ancient and eternal verity, child psychology was just becoming a cultural article of belief in nineteenth-century America. The American revolution, by estab- lishing political respect for the rights and desires of each generation, had elevated the status of children. If children represented the nation's future, it was in the nation's interest to find and implement the best methods for their upbringing. A national educational mission began with the formation of public schools and increased production of American schoolbooks, in keeping with the features and aims of United States culture as well as with contemporary conceptions of children's capacities and tastes.

In tandem with the political focus on children, religion also promoted the study of children and their states of mind. As Protestant theology and practice replaced the Calvinist tenet of infant depravity with the notion of infant innocence, children appeared to be more complex beings than the definition of them as objects of care and potential conversion suggested. The longstanding religious imperative to educate and reform sinful children already acknowledged the independence of the child's soul and mind; with the new religious respect for the child's affinity to God and goodness, children seemed not just different but better beings. Thus, in Horace Bushnell's words, "the aim, effort, and expectation" should be "not that the child is to grow up in sin, to be converted after he comes to a mature age" but that he has "loved what is good from his earliest years."[15] The idea that children knew and valued goodness from their earliest years followed from Frederick Froebel's belief that children were born with aesthetic sense – that each child is "an infinite sensibility already." Froebel, who formulated and instituted the first kindergartens in Europe, recommended that educators take hints "from the spontaneous play of children fresh from the hands of the Creator."[16] Hawthorne's sisters-in-law Elizabeth Peabody and Mary Peabody Mann (sisters of his wife Sophia Peabody) introduced the United States to kindergartens patterned after Froebel's model.[17]

Following Froebel's conception of the child as "a harp of a thousand strings,"[18] requiring sensitive handling to bring out its harmonies, the study and practice of all stages of childlife and child-rearing became a priority, propelling the new professions of education and psychology. Hawthorne therefore wrote his history books for a young audience whose intelligence and individuality were just beginning to be appreciated. Bronson Alcott, who structured his experimental school in Boston upon conversations with children (ranging from the ages three to twelve) about philosophical and theological subjects, firmly believed that "we greatly underrate the genius of childhood," rarely "giving them credit" for "thoughts of their own."[19] *Grandfather's Chair* endorses and intensifies Alcott's respect for children's cognitive abilities by including children in the frankly fantastic exercises of historical identification. To extend the franchise of fantasy to children might seem either redundant or regressive: children are already imaginative and their growth into adulthood entails coping with reality. But the fantastic activity to which Hawthorne invites children is not merely playful; on the contrary, Hawthorne admits children to the fundamentally imaginative nature of experience – even and especially, of the experience so seemingly exempt from fancy, the official record of experience called history.

Hawthorne follows Froebel and Peabody in believing fancy a "peculiarly human faculty" that operates in concert with understanding. Both fancy and understanding act upon the sensuous impressions from which the child builds knowledge of the world. Both faculties, Peabody explains, are activities of the human will: fancy is "the will, acting among these impressions in a wild and sovereign way" whereas understanding is "the will arranging impressions according to the order of nature."[20] Froebel accordingly advises that the education of young children allow for both exercises of will, for the pursuit of individual interests as well as the promotion of general order. The best way to do this is to design lessons after the fashions of children's play; to institute this pedagogical philosophy, Froebel renamed lessons plays.[21] Indeed, Peabody stresses, children can practice understanding, ordering their impressions to standards, only in conjunction with fancy, treating their impressions as their desires and tastes dictate. Children's fancy represents and manifests "their own motive" for knowledge, which must undergird any project of education. Though fancy may be a "kind of thinking" that "delights" in transcending the facts of nature in its creations, and sometimes sets the laws of nature at defiance, it is nonetheless conducive and indispensable to "the soundness of the understanding."[22] As Peabody urged teachers to cherish the child's faculty of fancy, Hawthorne likewise saw the pedagogic power of fancy, or what we nowadays call fantasy. Fantasy as Hawthorne uses it is not aimless or unconstrained play but an often painful moral and intellectual activity. Arbella's story asks children to feel her pain, a request that can be met only if children can suppose themselves in circumstances far outside their ken. Hawthorne's project of teaching American history proceeds according to the modern pedagogical protocols popularized by Peabody, respecting and using children's imaginative and sympathetic range.

Within that range, children could variously develop knowledge of the world, often by seemingly strange or mistaken paths. Like children in our own time, most children in Hawthorne's time knew nothing about the Lady Arbella but readily recognized the story of the Plymouth Rock settlement. Peabody vividly recalled her own first impression upon hearing about this historical event, which she related to her students at Alcott's school:

> I thought I saw a dark sea, and a cloudy, stormy sky, which looked gloomy. And I saw a ship on the horizon, which came on very fast, faster and smoother than any other ship ever sailed, in a beautiful curved line. As it came near, there was a company of women standing on the deck, two and two, taking hold of hands, and each one had white robes on, which fell over her feet, and every eye was looking up, as if she saw God sitting above the clouds; and their faces were full of joy and love. At last the vessel stopped near a large rock on the shore. I did not see a single sailor, or any anchor, I never had heard of an anchor, but it seemed to me these women walked off the deck upon the rock; and walked over the rock carefully, looking at their feet, and holding up their robes; and they glided over the frozen snow into a high, dark, deep evergreen forest; and under the trees they knelt down and worshipped God, though there were no meeting-houses, and not a single dwelling-house; and then they went into the bushes, and took broken pieces of trees, and made little huts, like Indian wigwams, which they went into. This was the picture that rose up in my mind, as I was told . . .[23]

At this point, Peabody's students interrupt, finishing her sentence with the words "the story of the Pilgrim Fathers!" Peabody recounts this memory to demonstrate how imaginative responses to stories can operate in tandem with an understanding of the intended meaning of a story. Her fanciful sense of the Pilgrims did not exclude her basic understanding of their historical importance. Even though Peabody as a child misunderstood a word about the Pilgrims, thus misconceiving them as an all-female group, she still gets the crucial point that this was a pious company. Since she knew nothing about the process of landing a ship – "I never had heard of an anchor" – she sees not the actual difficult search for a safe landing point reported by the Pilgrims but a swift dreamlike gliding procession from deck to rock to snow to forest. Yet "had I seen the thing as it really was outwardly – the Pilgrim Fathers in seamen's clothes, and looking just like any other men," Peabody stresses, "I should not have taken the idea of how different their minds were from those of common people . . . so the very mistakes which I had made, helped me to see more of the truth, than I should have seen, had my real eyes been there, looking at their real bodies."[24] The advantage of imagination is that it does not require real bodies as evidence of reality; it instead can summon images of bodies or objects which exist outside the temporal and spatial limits of the imaginer. Peabody's lesson here is that "a story sometimes changed its outward form when it went into the mind; and yet carried all the important truth into the mind." Thus fancy facilitates learning.

In valuing the special access afforded by imagination, Peabody and Alcott helped advance the educational uses of the imagination. This pedagogical enterprise not surprisingly generated a publishing boom in books for children keyed to their newly credited cognitive status. When Peabody undertook the publication of new schoolbooks in line with her pedagogical theories, she decided fiction writers would be the most suitable authors for her series. Her brother-in-law, the education reformer Horace Mann, had previously turned down Hawthorne as an author for a series of juvenile books that he was preparing because Mann wanted "something nearer to duty & Business."[25] For the very reason that Mann found Hawthorne unsuitable for his publishing project – his authorship of *Twice-told Tales* (1837), which included such supernatural and fantastic stories as "The Legends of the Province House," "The Grey Champion," and "Dr. Heidegger's Experiment" – Peabody thought Hawthorne a perfect writer for the books she envisioned. Hawthorne already had been thinking of collaborating with his college friend Longfellow on "a book for the young" that might "entirely revolutionize the whole system of juvenile literature."[26] After Longfellow dropped out of the project, Hawthorne undertook the *Grandfather's Chair* series for Peabody.

Grandfather's Chair met Peabody's expectations for an imaginative history and implemented her respect for child intelligence by representing the varieties of readerly experience that children might have. Just as the child Peabody developed her own picture of the Pilgrims, the four children in Hawthorne's book display different tastes in stories and different responses to the historical stories they hear. Laurence pursues spiritual and intellectual explanations, Charley delights in martial matters, Clara focuses on domestic and realist interests, and Alice fastens on emotional connections. Thus, when Grandfather finishes telling the story of Arbella, Hawthorne relates that "Charley, almost at the commencement of the foregoing narrative, had galloped away, with a prodigious clatter, upon Grandfather's stick, and was not yet returned" (VI: 18). While "bold, brisk, restless" Charley has been busy with his own fantasy (VI: 11), the other children have "listened attentively" to "this true story of the gentle lady, who had come so far to die so soon" (VI: 18). The story causes the youngest child, Alice, both to cry and to convert her sense of grief into sympathetic joy: "Oh, the lady must have been so glad to get to heaven!" (VI: 18). Clara wonders about the subsequent fate of Arbella's husband and observes the sadness of the fact "that one of the first things which the settlers had to do, when they came to the new world, was to set apart a burial ground" (VI: 19). Laurence, "a boy of twelve, a bright scholar, in whom an early thoughtfulness and sensibility began to show themselves" (VI: 11), suggests another way to think about this first burial ground. "Perhaps," Laurence muses, "if they had found no need of burial grounds here, they would have been glad, after a few years, to go back to England" (VI: 19).

All these responses testify to the considerable cognitive and critical abilities of children. Hawthorne notes even the inattentive response of Charley, the child who chooses to attend to some other imaginative narrative. By depicting the range of children's readerly activities, Hawthorne foregrounds the affective aims of the writer who would establish ties between children and the stories that compose a national history. To link children to history – to make them believe the past is a crucial part of themselves – requires psychological tact and imaginative skill. Grandfather contents himself with getting Charley to listen to accounts of battles while obliging Clara with details about balls and clothes. He so successfully engages the other children in his chair's history that "Laurence would sometimes sit a whole hour, especially at twilight, gazing at the chair, and, by the spell of his imagination, summoning up its ancient occupants to appear in it again" and Alice, likewise engrossed, would talk "with the gentle lady Arbella, as if she were still sitting in the chair" (VI: 31). To engage all the children to his stories, Grandfather speaks to their different interests. The children thus come to identify with historical personages and events – to value them because they experience them as aspects of their own lives. In the "wild and sovereign" movements of children's individual fancies, Hawthorne finds the best ground upon which to build affiliations. Love for and loyalty to the nation thus begins with the imaginative narratives of the past that children absorb in tandem with their own fancies.[27]

The importance of place

An initial sense of a lineage with the past comes to children from their parents and grandparents, living witnesses to prior times. The timeline can extend further backward once children accept the notion of stories coming from even earlier ancestors. Family ties forge and sustain a relation to the past, a relation to both the dead and the places they inhabited. When Laurence suggests that the building of burial grounds gave the New England settlers a reason to stay in America, he expresses Hawthorne's own strong sense of the bonds formed by the mixing of bodies with soil. Hawthorne was living in his birthplace and working in the Salem Custom House while writing *Grandfather's Chair*. In "The Custom House" preface to *The Scarlet Letter*, he presents a more extensive and bleaker view of the attachment between persons and places. Whereas Laurence sees the burial of bodies in New England as the foundational moment of new affiliation for the British emigrants and thus for a new nation, Hawthorne expresses strong reservations about how, over time, these affiliations forcibly bind descendants to the place of their ancestors. "This long connection of a family with one spot, as its place of birth and burial, creates a kindred sentiment between the human being and the locality, quite independent of any charm in the scenery or moral circumstances that surround him. It is not love, but instinct" (*The Scarlet Letter*, I: 11). Propelled by a "sentiment" so strong it seems like an "instinct," the native cannot dispel kinship with his or her place of birth. There is no willful understanding or fancy involved in this sentiment; it supersedes all other feelings and cognitions. Thus, "though invariably happiest elsewhere," Hawthorne cannot deny that Salem's "spell survives" (I: 8, 11). The memory of his first ancestor – "the earliest emigrant of my name" – "still haunts me, and induces a sort of home-feeling with the past" (I: 8, 9). This feeling is coercive instead of congenial, inducing Hawthorne to settle in Salem, to follow his ancestors in a successive "sentry-march along the Main Street" (I: 11). Such a sense of subjection makes the tie to one's native town an "unhealthy connection" that "should at last be severed" (I: 11).

In Hawthorne's view, ancestral grounds simply cannot nurture and sustain the individual. "Human nature will not flourish, any more than a potato, if it be planted and replanted, for too long a series of generations, in the same worn-out soil" (1: 11–12). As different generations mark the passage of time, the standing relation between persons and places becomes unfruitful. Hawthorne therefore commits himself to transplantation: "my own children have had other birthplaces, and so far as their fortunes may be within my control, shall strike their roots in unaccustomed earth" (1: 12).

Hawthorne would disenthrall new generations from the influence of the past by moving them to different places. Rooted "in unaccustomed earth," his children can be free of the haunting sense of obligation to follow familial patterns. Rather than identifying with ancestral places, children should remember the example of ancestral emigration. In mobility lies the possibility of democratic life, a life based on self-determination.[28] The power of places does not at all diminish in Hawthorne's revision of the kinship between persons and places. Instead, individuals learn to use the affective power of places as an imaginative engine to take them to different situations, to enlarge and enliven their social connections.

Geography, as Hawthorne stresses in *Peter Parley's Universal History on the Basis of Geography*, gives the child reader an entry into history. By giving a country "a local habitation and a name," geography orients the reader, providing a point of departure for mental transports into historical narratives. The specification of place, by name and local habitation, which is to say, by linguistic materialization, reflects the representational nature of the relations between persons and places, whether the places be near or far, familiar or exotic. Applying Shakespeare's immemorial description of poetic efficacy to geography, Hawthorne implies that countries are among the imagined objects – part of "the airy nothing" – that words make solid and present. By including countries in the inventory of the imaginary, Hawthorne redirects the affective power of place so that it flows from human minds instead of over them. He thereby reconceives the influence of place as an imaginative opportunity. Though readers of history are embedded in their immediate world, this condition, instead of confining them, can enable them to view worlds elsewhere in space or time.

Geographical orientation thus affirms as it employs the "wild and sovereign" ways of fancy that Peabody and Hawthorne so value. Reference to locale ideally operates not to compel a certain affective relation to history, as in the connection Hawthorne felt to Salem, but to encourage any and all imaginative relations to history. This vision of place serving rather than dictating individual experience pervades Hawthorne's accounts of the sources of his own literary fancies. Throughout his career, he cites places as the inspiration if not the content of his fiction. An old home in Salem called the House of the Seven Gables inspired Hawthorne to write the novel of the same name. Memories of Brook Farm, the experimental community which Hawthorne joined for a short period, generate *The Blithedale Romance*. From other locales in which Hawthorne lived – the Old Manse in Concord, a house in the Berkshire Mountains, and Rome – come the stories that form *Mosses from an Old Manse*, *A Wonder-Book*, *Tanglewood Tales*, and *The Marble Faun*. Hawthorne's habit of describing his fiction as emanating from familiar places roots imaginative activity in immediate life, but, tellingly, in a transient life so that the conditions of imagining frequently vary.[29]

  Once exorcised of dictates from the past, places might become healthy and fruitful for their residents. As a locale provides a fertile ground for fancy, both conventional and unconventional lines of thought can emerge. As Hawthorne is the first to insist, places summon associations peculiar to each individual. When he lived in the Old Manse in Concord, he saw "many strangers come in the summer-time, to view the battle-ground" where American revolutionaries famously fought British soldiers (*Mosses from an Old Manse*, x: 10). What interests Hawthorne is not the granite monument erected at this historic site to commemorate "an epoch of national history," but "the grave – marked by a small, moss-grown fragment of stone at the head, and another at the foot – the grave of two British soldiers, who were slain in the skirmish" (x: 8–9). Hawthorne is deeply impressed by a long-standing local story that he heard from the poet James Russell Lowell about how one of these men died:

> A youth, in the service of the clergy man, happened to be chopping wood, that April morning, at the back of the Manse; and when the noise of battle rang from side to side of the bridge, he hastened across the intervening field to see what might be going forward. It is rather strange, by the way, that this lad should have been so diligently at work, when the whole population of town and country were startled out of their customary business by the advance of British troops. Be that as it might, the tradition says that the lad now left his task, and hurried to the battle-field, with the axe still in his hand. The British had by this time retreated – the Americans were in pursuit – and the late scene of strife was thus deserted by both parties. Two soldiers lay on the ground; one was a corpse; but, as the young New Englander drew nigh, the other Briton raised himself painfully upon his hands and knees, and gave a ghastly stare into his face. The boy – it must have been a nervous impulse, without purpose, without thought, and betokening a sensitive and impressible nature, rather than a hardened one – the boy uplifted his axe, and dealt the wounded soldier a fierce and fatal blow upon the head. (x: 9–10)

To Hawthorne, this image of the boy has overshadowed "all that history tells us of the fight." Often, "as an intellectual and moral exercise," he has "sought to follow that poor youth through his subsequent career, and observe how his soul was tortured by the blood-stain, contracted, as it had been, before the long custom of war had robbed human life of its sanctity, and while it still seemed murderous to slay a brother man" (x: 10). From the graves of these two British men on the Concord battleground, Hawthorne gets no patriotic remembrance, nor even the correlative to patriotic celebration of the dead, respect for the slain enemy. He follows, instead, his own fancies about the guilt felt by the imagined youth.

These musings, off the patriotic track of remembrance that Concord customarily generates, then move to the previous history of the site where "in some unknown age, before the white man came, stood an Indian Village" (x: 11). Long before the revolutionary war, long before receiving the name Concord, this place was inhabited by people whose ancient connection to American lands goes unmarked and unremarked. Excavating this earlier layer of history, Hawthorne imagines the place called Concord in images other than the revolutionary war imagery which nineteenth-century American exercises of imagination had established as one of the preeminent landmarks of national history. Hawthorne finds on the Concord battleground relics of Indian life: "the spear and arrow heads, the chisels, and other implements of war, labor, and the chase" (x: 9). By picking up "an arrowhead that was dropt centuries ago, and has never been handled since," he seems to receive it "directly from the hand of the red hunter" (x: 11). This imagined personal contact then "recalls to life the painted chiefs and warriors, the squaws at their household toil, and the children sporting among the wigwams" as "the little wind-rocked papoose swings from the branch of a tree" (x: 11). The character of this place as it was for the Indians thus remains palpable to nineteenth-century people who pick up from the ground upon which they walk and work ancient artefacts through which they can see a distant civilization.

Hawthorne's archaeological perspective on Concord registers both the insistent materiality and perpetual malleability of places. As Indian artefacts bear witness to their inhabitation of the land, these objects also mark the evanescence of Indian life. Walking through Concord in 1843, Hawthorne notices not only Indian relics but also "stone fences, white houses, potato fields, and men doggedly hoeing, in their shirt-sleeves and homespun pantaloons" (x: 11). Subject to time, places change and bear the marks of different inhabitants. Places, as Hawthorne describes them, are always furnished, and thus inhabited. To observe the details of Concord life, whether in the imagined scene of the Indian village or the actual sight of nineteenth-century farmers, is to validate the existence of persons in this place, whatever the temporal and spatial location of the observer. Moreover, the details themselves – chisels, spears, wigwams, fences, houses, hoed fields – vividly conjure the activities by which humans make places their own. Concord is thus continuous with its inhabitants, and also with everyone else who comes into contact with it, whether by visit, conversation, picture, or book. Once understood as resources for the range of human pursuits, places facilitate innumerable projects, of which nationalism is just one.

Hawthorne's account of Concord operates to reconceptualize the conventional sense of place; in his description, the solidity of places continually dissolve, to then solidify again in a different form. Places function not just as reference points, but as points of departure. Hawthorne's New England landscape operates like the painting in Hans Christian Andersen's story of "The Sandman." Hanging on the wall of a boy's bedroom, this painting depicts a landscape in which a river winds through a forest past castles, "on its way to the open sea."[30] At night, when the Sandman comes to tell stories to children, it becomes possible to enter the painting and follow the path of the river, to yet other scenes. This notion of a familiar landscape or landmark affording a window onto other places and times has inspired the literary travels of generations of readers to Wonderland and the world beyond the Looking-Glass, to Neverland and Oz, to Narnia and the Hogwarts Express from Platform 9 and $\frac{3}{4}$. Hawthorne's mining of American sites for their imaginative possibilities helped establish this now standard image of immediate surroundings becoming conveyances to elsewhere. The metamorphic properties of places are key to modern children's literature, producing a transnationality of experience in which children everywhere on the globe become familiar with the same fictive realms.

Thus the human faculty of dreaming, in which everyone can readily pass through the usual spatial and temporal limits, figures quite prominently in nineteenth-century children's fiction. Alice dreams Wonderland; like the Sandman, Peter Pan comes to children at bedtime. One night when the Sandman comes to the little boy in Andersen's story, he shows the boy his brother, who "is also called the Sandman, but he only visits you once and then he carries you away on his horse. He tells you a story, but he knows only two. One is the loveliest story ever told, so beautiful you cannot imagine it; the other is so ugly and terrifying that it, too, is indescribable." This other Sandman is called Death. The end of consciousness, the state where imagination cannot reach, appears here as a perpetual ride. Even when the body comes to its final resting place, stories continue to carry it away. This vision of Death makes the boy think "Death is a nice Sandman."[31] Andersen's fairy tale about children and dreams celebrates the fantastic mobility of the human mind by which even the grave becomes a magic carpet.

Hawthorne likewise casts death as a storyteller: the Concord burial ground relates tales of Indians, colonists, and revolutionaries; the Lady Arbella's grave imparts a narrative of Puritan suffering. And just as the Sandman who brings dreams introduces children to the stories of death, Grandfather's stories familiarize his grandchildren with the lives of the departed, and thus with the evanescence of persons. Grandfather's stories come from his dreams as he dozes in his chair. At the close of Hawthorne's series, the children no longer beg Grandfather to tell another story, but to "dream a new dream every night" (VI: 210). Because dreams operate according to their own shifting narrative principles, they epitomize the untold tales upon which persons can embark.

What children learn in *Grandfather's Chair* is not so much the importance of American history as the value of dreams – of the fancies that make up both the content and reception of history. Hence the stature of any national history rests within each generation. The stories people compose and tell are most often, as the chair tells Grandfather, about the injustice, deceit, and hatred exercised "in the dealings of man with man, and nation with nation" (VI: 209). Teaching children history, Hawthorne sadly notes, entails exposing them to "dark pictures" of mankind "from age to age engaged in constant strife, battle and bloodshed" ("Introduction" to *Peter Parley's Universal History*, XXIII: 266). The fanciful American history of *Grandfather's Chair* suggests that we need to understand Dickens's identification of national greatness with fancy as one of the highly select modern stories that has been told about nationalism. Fancy affords views of the negative as well as positive acts that form nations.

This is not to say that Hawthorne's critical use of fancy denies or eliminates the constructive role of romance in nationalism. Both critical and celebratory perspectives emanate from fancy, which itself emanates from human minds. While fancy may carry us away from our living conditions, it arises from a variety of responses to those conditions. These responses may be incoherent or ambivalent. Even as Hawthorne's fanciful account of American history stresses the unnaturalness of connections between persons and places, it offers its own vision of American ties. Of all the stories Grandfather tells, the children find most memorable the account of John Eliot, who translated the Bible into the Indian language (the particular language is never specified). Alice wishes "to kiss good Mr. Eliot" who "realized that an Indian possesses a mind, and a heart, and an immortal soul" (VI: 49, 43). Laurence reports seeing Eliot's Bible in the Boston Athenaeum and laments that "there were no Indians left to read it" (VI: 44). But Laurence laments unnecessarily, as Grandfather explains, because the disappearance of the Indians does not alter the significance of Eliot's labor. Eliot believed that "the red men were descendants of those lost tribes of Israel of whom history has been able to tell us nothing . . . He hoped that God had sent the English across the ocean,

Gentiles as they were, to enlighten this benighted portion of his once chosen race" (VI: 48). Grandfather links Eliot with "the prophets of ancient days" and "those earliest apostles and evangelists" in bringing God's word to "the new world of the West. Since the first days of Christianity, there has been no man more worthy to be numbered in the brotherhood of the apostles, than Eliot" (VI: 48–49). For Grandfather, Eliot represents the link between America and Israel, modern and ancient moments.

Placing Eliot and the American Indians in the teleology of Christian history, Grandfather situates American identity in eternity, offering a longer genealogy to Americans than that found in the chronicles of Puritan settlement. Though not rooted in the American continent, this situating of Americans connects them to all places in the world at all times. Grandfather's historical portrait therefore gives nationalism an even stronger narrative than the nativist stories it replaces, as is attested by the fact that such myths about American Indians often worked in the United States to forward white supremacist nationalism.[32] Though *Grandfather's Chair* here may seem to contradict Hawthorne's cautionary view of the traditional claims shaping American history, the storytelling framework of the book reminds us that Grandfather's Christian narrative of America is yet another fantasy which can be embraced or replaced. As children learn their national identities by inhabiting faraway times and places, they become as entangled with their imaginary affiliations as with their biological and geographical ones. But they can disentangle themselves and establish other affiliations, committing themselves to different stories.

Writing his juvenile history with the understanding that children's literature clearly functions to produce national identity, Hawthorne unsettles the geographical and nativist foundations of national affiliation. By showing identifications with land and ancestry to be imaginative and hence variable, he underscores the artificiality of national identification. Recognizing the artificiality of geographical and biological affiliations, however, never extinguishes these identifications. Children still learn and get shaped by American traditions even as they encounter or develop diverse views of these traditions. In Hawthorne's seemingly paradoxical sense of national identity, you identify yourself as American by identifying with conventional markers whose artificiality you simultaneously recognize. To be an American is continually to feel a kinship that you can disown.[33]

This state of being never resolves into a simple univocal position. The dynamic bipolarity Hawthorne discerns in the experience of American identification involves a perpetual negotiation between susceptibility to and skepticism of convention. Children, in their ongoing elective relations to stories, easily perform this feat as they absorb what all the Sandmen show and tell.

The problem is, they, and the adults they become, which is to say, we, are the Sandmen.

NOTES

1. Charles Dickens, "Frauds on Fairies," *Household Words* 1853; rpt. in *A Peculiar Gift: Nineteenth-Century Writings on Books for Children*, ed. Lance Salway (Harmondsworth, Middlesex: Kestrel Books, 1976), p. 111.
2. *Ibid.*, pp. 111, 118.
3. Nathaniel Hawthorne, *A Wonder-Book for Girls and Boys* (Boston: Ticknor, Reed, and Fields, 1852); "The Gray Champion" and "Legends of the Province-House" appeared in the collection *Twice-told Tales* (Boston, 1837).
4. Hawthorne's work has generated an ongoing critical preoccupation with the significance of romance, a bibliography far too extensive to list here. In my chapter, "romance" simply refers to the imaginative form through which Hawthorne relayed and investigated a variety of views about American experience.
5. Nathaniel Hawthorne, *Grandfather's Chair: A History for Youth* (Boston: E. P. Peabody, 1841), p. 6; rptd. as *True Stories* in *The Centenary Edition of Nathaniel Hawthorne*, vol. VI.
6. George Bancroft, *A History of the United States from the Discovery of the American Continent*, vol. 1 (Boston: Little, Brown, and Company, 1834), p. 357.
7. For informative descriptions of the first American history schoolbooks, see Charles Carpenter, *History of American Schoolbooks* (Philadelphia: University of Pennsylvania Press, 1963), pp. 196–211 and Clifton Johnson, *Old-Time Schools and School-books* (New York: Dover, 1963), pp. 318–81.
8. Bancroft, *History of the United States*, p. 225.
9. Scott Steedman, *How Would you Survive as an American Indian?* (New York: Franklin Watts, 1995); Elizabeth Levy, *. . . If You Were There When They Signed the Constitution* (New York: Scholastic, 1987). Each of these titles belongs to series stuctured on the principle of personal connection announced by the titles.
10. High-school teachers, calling in to the C-Span American Authors television show in the spring of 2001, reported that their students often thought the novel a history book.
11. For a more detailed account of personification and its pedagogical uses, see my "Fables and the Forming of Americans," in *The Consent of the Governed: The Lockean Legacy in Early American Culture* (Cambridge: Harvard University Press, 2001), pp. 57–82. See also Steven Knapp, *Personification and the Sublime: Milton to Coleridge* (Cambridge, MA: Harvard University Press, 1985).
12. Walter Benjamin, noting that historiography is "the record kept by memory," identifies two forms of memory operating in narratives: shortlived reminiscence and perpetuating remembrance. Walter Benjamin, "The Storyteller," in *Illuminations*, ed. Hannah Arendt (New York: Schocken Books, 1969), pp. 97–98. I thus here follow Benjamin's recognition of the integral relation between history and memory, and of the role of stories in enlarging the scope of memory beyond individual experience.
13. Gillian Avery, *Behold the Child: American Children and Their Books 1621–1922* (Baltimore, MD: Johns Hopkins University Press, 1994), p. 78.

14. Nathaniel Hawthorne, *Peter Parley's Universal History on the Basis of Geography* (Boston: Samuel E. Goodrich, 1837). Hawthorne's preface to this volume is reprinted in *Miscellaneous Prose and Verse* in *The Centenary Edition of the Works of Nathaniel Hawthorne*, XXIII: 263–66.
15. Horace Bushnell, *Christian Nurture* (1847; rptd. Grand Rapids, MI: Baker Book House, 1979), p. 10. On the influence of Protestantism on American child-rearing attitudes, see also Philip Greven, *The Protestant Temperament: Patterns of Childrearing, Religious Experience. and the Self in Early America* (New York: Alfred A. Knopf, 1977); Barbara Welter, "The Feminization of American Religion," *Dimity Convictions: The American Woman in the Nineteenth Century* (Athens: Ohio University Press, 1976), pp. 83–102; Bernard Wishy, *The Child and the Republic: The Dawn of Modern American Child Nurture* (Philadelphia: University of Pennsylvania Press, 1968).
16. Elizabeth Palmer Peabody, *Lectures in the Training Schools for Kindergartners* (Boston: D. C. Heath & Company, 1886), pp. 2, 197.
17. Mary Mann and Elizabeth P. Peabody wrote about Froebel's kindergarten philosophy and their own implementations of it in *Moral Culture of Infancy and Kindergarten Guide* (New York: J. W. Schemerhorn & Co., 1869). Following the popularity of Peabody's public lectures on kindergartens, Froebel's influential book *The Paradise of Children*, translated by Edward Wiebe, was first published in the United States in 1869. Hawthorne used Froebel's title for the title of his retelling of the Pandora story in *A Wonder-Book for Girls and Boys*.
18. Quoted in Peabody, *Lectures for Kindergartners*, p. 210.
19. A. Bronson Alcott, *Conversations with Children on the Gospels* (Boston: James Munroe & Co., 1836), pp. xvi–xvii.
20. Quoted in Peabody, *Lectures for Kindergartners*, p. 208.
21. Froebel thus extends John Locke's well-known liberal pedagogical recommendation that "learning might be made a play and recreation to children." John Locke, *Some Thoughts Concerning Education* (1693), ed. Ruth W. Grant and Nathan Tarcov (Indianapolis, IN: Hacket Publishing Company, 1996), p. 114.
22. Peabody, *Lectures for Kindergartners*, pp. 209, 210.
23. Elizabeth Palmer Peabody, *Record of a School: Exemplifying the General Principles of Spiritual Culture* (Boston: Russell, Shattuck & Company, 1836), pp. 60–61.
24. *Ibid.*, pp. 62, 61.
25. Quoted in "Historical Introduction" to *Grandfather's Chair*, VI: 291.
26. Quoted in *ibid.*, p. 298. Hawthorne began making notebook entries on this project. He later developed these into his revision of mythology for American children in *A Wonder-Book for Girls and Boys* (1852) and its companion volume *Tanglewood Tales* (1853).
27. This is to differ from Lauren Berlant's formulation that, for Hawthorne, "nations provoke fantasy." *The Anatomy of National Fantasy: Hawthorne, Utopia, and Everyday Life* (Chicago: University of Chicago Press, 1991), p. 1. While the nation certainly affects its citizens, and especially seems to preoccupy Hawthorne in *The Scarlet Letter*, Hawthorne significantly presents the nation – and critical accounts of it – as part of people's imaginative and actual lives, not as the determinant of them. Since Hawthorne asserts that the sense of nation can exist only through and by fantasy, any form of national fantasy (a fantasy that American

citizens share) functions variably as it exists in tandem with an array of diverse relations to predominant ideas and with an array of untold other mental processes.

28. The forced emigration of African Americans obviously stands outside Hawthorne's democratic vision of migration, which may explain why his history does not include the fact of slavery which counters the narratives of self-determination he imagines.

29. Thus, it is important that as Hawthorne's prefaces repeatedly present briefs for romance, they also detail the places from which his romances take off.

30. Hans Christian Andersen, "The Sandman," *The Complete Fairy Tales and Stories*, trans. Erik Christian Haugaard (New York: Anchor, 1983), pp. 177–87. This story is sometimes translated as "Little Shuteye."

31. *Ibid.*, pp. 186–87.

32. See, for example, Walter Benn Michaels, "Race into Culture: A Critical Genealogy of Cultural Identity," *Critical Inquiry* 18. 4 (Summer 1992): 667. For other important treatments of the temporal logics of national identity, see Benedict Anderson, *Imagined Communities: Reflections of the Origin and Spread of Nationalism* (London: Verso, 1983); Homi Bhabha, "Anxious Nations, Nervous States," in John Copjec, ed., *Supposing the Subject* (London and New York: Verso, 1994).

33. For a different but congruent formulation of Hawthorne's account of identity, see Stacey Margolis, "Blithedale and Other Associations," in *The Public Life of Privacy in Nineteenth-Century American Literature*. In this forthcoming book, Margolis argues that Hawthorne perceives and portrays personal relations in terms of political (specifically, party) affiliations, thus developing a profoundly social account of the self.

7

KAREN SÁNCHEZ-EPPLER

Hawthorne and the writing of childhood

> If I pride myself on anything, it is because I have a smile that children love; and
> on the other hand, there are few grown ladies that could entice me from the
> side of little Annie; for I delight to let my mind go hand in hand with the mind
> of a sinless child. So, come, Annie; but if I moralize as we go, do not listen to
> me; only look about you, and be merry!
>
> "Little Annie's Ramble," IX: 122.

This scene of a grown man entering the public sphere hand in hand with
a young child is repeated throughout Nathaniel Hawthorne's fiction. Most
often it serves as an introductory scene, as in the evening stroll of Peter
Hovenden and his daughter Annie that begins "The Artist of the Beautiful,"
but sometimes too, as when Dimmesdale takes Pearl's hand in the marketplace, it can suggest a kind of resolution. Hawthorne's self-presentation as
a writer who wishes to make public on the streets of the town or the pages
of a book his connection with childhood, provides important insights into
his conception of authorship: much of Hawthorne's authorial persona and
cultural legacy are rooted in the "pride" and "delight" with which he claims
for himself a mind that goes "hand in hand with the mind of a sinless child."
This chapter is concerned with how for Hawthorne childhood enables not
only publicity but authorship itself.

Hawthorne wrote more pieces directly aimed at a juvenile audience than
any other canonical male author of the antebellum period. In this way,
as in so many others, his literary work is strikingly similar to that of the
"scribbling women" he so famously damned. Thus his role as a writer of
children's books does much to illuminate the gender politics of his authorship. As many scholars have argued, Hawthorne's preeminence in American literary studies (how he fell into the American canon from the beginning and stayed, until *The Scarlet Letter* became the most ubiquitous of
American schoolbooks) derives in large part from the intimate and uncanny
power with which his romances express and enforce new national norms.
Hawthorne's fictions work to articulate middle-class domesticity, revealing the complex interdependence of class and gender in family formation;[1]
they serve to define the social and intellectual status of authorship;[2] and
they help to express the nature of citizenship.[3] One powerful and largely

overlooked way Hawthorne's fiction does all this is through the writing of childhood.

"The whole system of juvenile literature"

Before the war of 1812 America largely imported or reprinted child-rearing manuals and didactic children's literature from the parental British press. But during the 1820s these books were supplemented, and by the 1830s largely replaced, by a literature for and about children that would celebrate and inculcate American values. To write and use such books responded both to patriotic feeling and nation-building needs. Even as antebellum American adults continued to read Scott or Dickens more avidly than any American author, they increasingly purchased American storybooks, magazines, and schoolbooks for their children. In these early decades there was very little space or desire for delight in this fiction: the education of the young was a serious moral, spiritual, and political undertaking. Juvenile fiction taught honesty, charity, piety, industry, and self-control mostly through stories of good children who learned to curb wild or selfish whims under the guidance of wise adults, or alternatively through the example of naughty children naturally punished by the consequences of their wrongheaded ways. Hawthorne's story "Little Daffydowndilly" allegorically adopts both formulas in the "rambles" of a boy who runs away from school to evade Mr. Toil and instead finds him everywhere, finally recognizing Toil even in the face of his grave wandering companion. "Daffydowndilly," Hawthorne writes, "had learned a lesson" (XI: 207). The heart of that lesson, as in most children's stories of the period, was the internalization of social values: "when he became better acquainted with Mr. Toil, he began to think that his ways were not so very disagreeable, and that the old school master's smile of approbation made his face almost as pleasant as even that of Daffydowndilly's mother" (XI: 207). There are signs of discomfort with the reign of toil in Hawthorne's story: a certain sympathy with Daffydowndilly's dislike of school at the story's beginning, and a whimsical suggestion at the end that "old Mr. Toil was a magician" (XI: 207). We know, too, that the young Hawthorne shared the boy's pain at the way schooling separated him from his mother: "The happiest days of my life are gone. Why was I not a girl that I might be pinned all my life to my Mother's apron" (XV: 117). But despite this chaffing against convention, and despite the temptation to read this story as a parody, "Little Daffydowndilly" fits quite comfortably within even the most traditional expectations for didactic juvenile fiction, as attested by its initial publication in *Boys and Girls' Magazine* of 1843. In particular, Daffydowndilly's capacity to internalize this lesson – to love toil rather than simply fearing the task-master – articulates the essential transformation required throughout juvenile fiction: the cultivation of a self-regulating conscience.

During the first half of the nineteenth century, attitudes toward child-rearing gradually underwent a similar transformation, replacing the "awful birch rod" (XI: 200) that Daffydowndilly sees in his schoolmaster's hand at the story's beginning, with the "smile of approbation" that proves at the story's end to be the more effective incentive to industrious and virtuous toil. America's Calvinist traditions rooted child-rearing in the concept of "infantile depravity" – the belief that all children were born steeped in original sin. Such depraved children needed to be wrenched from Satan, their will broken, before they could learn to choose right. Already sinful at birth, salvation was a matter of conversion, so that for example the Reverend Francis Weyland could publish in *The American Baptist Magazine* (1831), as an aide and incentive to other parents, an account of how he starved his fifteen-month-old son into submission.[4] But if this grim and punitive attitude toward childhood persisted in evangelical families, the tendency throughout the century – following Locke's notion of childhood as a blank slate and Rousseau's portrait of Emile as naturally innocent and receptive – was toward ever more Romantic and idealized images of childhood, such as the "sinless child" Hawthorne produces with little Annie. Horace Bushnell's 1847 treatise on *Christian Nurture* is the most famous and fully articulated account of how children, born innocent, might require not conversion but merely a gentle and constant nurture to be true Christians from birth. "Infancy and childhood," Bushnell claimed, "are the ages most pliant to good."[5] This goal of nurturing the good in children, rather than subduing the bad, is a harbinger not only of changing attitudes toward children, but also of gradual shifts in the whole structure of the middle-class family.

"The only right way to govern any one is by giving them confidence in your kindly feelings towards them – by love"[6] and this new mode of discipline by love is tied, as many scholars have shown, to the new prominence of mother, rather than father, as the source of domestic order – initiating as Mary Ryan put it, "the empire of the mother."[7] Thus the decades of the 1830s–50s, the years in which Hawthorne wrote his juvenile fiction and formed his own domestic household, were a period of extensive change in the ideals and functioning of the middle-class family. From our historical vantage it is easy to see the direction of historical change, but such developments are always uneven in practice; sinfulness and sinlessness, punishment and affection, paternal and maternal governance coexist not merely as alternative modes of understanding within the nation, but often in flux within a single family, or even within an ambivalent self.

The increasing value placed on domestic influence is linked in complex ways to the rise of female authorship. When Hawthorne complained to his publisher in 1854 over the prominence of "D—d scribbling women" and their novelistic "trash" (XVII: 304), fiction by women did in fact account for nearly half of the books on American best-seller lists, including a large proportion of the most popularly successful novels.[8] But this was a strikingly new phenomenon. When in the 1830s Hawthorne began publishing his tales in Massachusetts's periodicals and gift books, the literary marketplace was much smaller, more precarious, and more male. In these earlier decades, when there was more resistance to female authorship in general, children's literature appeared to many women as a profitable and less compromising entry into a literary career. The very strictures that enforced and idealized feminine domesticity also served to mark women as experts on hearth and home: so that Lydia Maria Child could assert that the advice in *The Mother's Book* derived from both "standard works on education" (largely written by men), and "an intelligent and judicious mother."[9] Thus it is not surprising that many of the most important and successful antebellum American women authors wrote for children. Besides Lydia Maria Child (whose *Juvenile Miscellany* published pieces by many of these women), Fanny Fern, Grace Greenwood, Sarah Josepha Hale, Lydia Sigourney, Catherine Sedgwick, Harriet Beecher Stowe, and Susan Warner all included in their literary labors the goal, as Child put it in a letter to Sedgwick, of "expanding young and ductile minds to the influence of truth."[10] Thus while children's literature and advice books helped to enable female authorship, the increasing prominence of these women made domestic behavior and the emotional life of families into a fruitful literary domain. In seeking to publish in the gift book and juvenile markets Hawthorne was placing himself and his literary success very much in the company of women, his audience more buoyed than threatened by the increasing prominence of feminine authorship.[11] For example, the Christmas annual *Youth's Keepsake*, where Hawthorne first published "Little Annie's Ramble," included many anonymous pieces, but most of the named authors were women – Miss Gould, Mrs. Sigourney, Mrs. S. J. Hale, or the pseudonymous "Florence" – and the only identified male authors in this collection were J. G. Whittier and Hawthorne, still himself publishing pseudonymously as "the author of 'The Gentle Boy.'"[12] But juvenile fiction was never a purely female sphere, and indeed the most successful and numerous books for children of the 1830s and 1840s were John Abbott's *Rollo* books and the *Peter Parley* stories of Samuel Griswold Goodrich.

Goodrich is a particularly relevant figure both because his career exemplifies the burgeoning market for children's literature, and because in his success he provided a publishing platform for the young Hawthorne. Many of Hawthorne's early tales were published in Goodrich's literary annual *The Token*, but Goodrich's publications for the family market also drew upon Hawthorne's talents: Goodrich hired him in 1836 as editor of the shortlived *American Magazine of Useful and Entertaining Knowledge* and as a ghost-writer of one of the Peter Parley books, *Peter Parley's Universal History on the Basis of Geography, for the Use of Families.* Samuel Goodrich began his publishing career in 1816 producing British reprints. By 1823 he had begun to court American works and, as he reminisces, he included among his ambitions "a reform – or at least an improvement – in books for youth." When in 1827 he published the first Peter Parley book, he kept his authorship secret since "nursery literature had not then acquired the respect in the eyes of the world it now enjoys." Thirty years later Goodrich felt free to crow about his relation to Peter Parley: "I am the author and editor of about one hundred and seventy volumes, and of these seven million have been sold!"[13] The Peter Parley books reveal an odd mix of morals, information, and entertainment: the volumes in the series ranging from compendia of scientific information, history, or even comparative religion, to collections of folk tales – everything, that is, that a democratic nation would wish to pass on to its fledgling citizens. In such compendia, as in Goodrich's *American Magazine*, the yoking of the "useful" to the "entertaining" displays some uncertainty about the value of pedagogical wares in this expanding market. Utility may be what families need, but is it what they want? Goodrich's success as a children's author and publisher derived from his capacity to respond to these conflicting cultural desires, to blend as it were toil and smile. The character of Peter Parley, an old man with a gouty leg, is the main source of pleasure in these books and Goodrich's chief innovation in the genre of pedagogical literature. Thus the books, instead of merely providing a lesson in history or botany, offer this information through the framing device of this garrulous old teacher and storyteller. Still Goodrich keeps his priorities clear: what matters is not the pleasure to be derived from this fictional character but the moral precepts he offers: "when I tell you stories of things that never happened," Parley assures his young readers, "my real design is to give you lessons of importance."[14] Perhaps one can trace to Peter Parley Hawthorne's penchant for framing his stories for children through the narrations of old men – Grandfather in *Grandfather's Chair*, or Mr. Temple in *Biographical Stories for Children*, or even the narrators of "Little Daffydowndilly" and "Little Annie's Ramble" – after all little Annie "is deeply read in Peter Parley's tomes" (IX: 124). But the differences between them are far stronger, since a prime impetus of all Hawthorne's writing lies in dissolving any such rigid distinction between "stories" and "lessons."

Hawthorne's letters reveal his own sense of writing for children as a lucrative and useful means of supporting a literary career. As Elizabeth Freeman and Meredith McGill have shown children often serve in Hawthorne's fiction to figure the avidity of consumer desires – Annie's "pleasure in looking at the shop windows" (IX: 123) or the consumptive feats of the little "cannibal" who frequents Hepzibah's shop in *The House of the Seven Gables* – suggesting how closely Hawthorne associates the market with children.[15] In fact this assessment of the literary marketplace proved reasonably true. Hawthorne's combined lifetime earnings from his juvenile fiction of $2,460, plus £50 in British royalties, exceeded the sales of even his most successful adult novel, his lifetime earnings on *The Scarlet Letter* amounting to only $1,500.[16] Hawthorne tried to make an institutionally supported income from his writing for children, initially composing his juvenile histories – *Grandfather's Chair*, *Famous Old People*, and *The Liberty Tree* – in the hope that Horace Mann could be convinced to adopt them as schoolbooks for the state of Massachusetts.[17] Showing a similar attitude toward the juvenile market, Ticknor and Fields were quick to prop and profit off the critical success of *The Scarlet Letter* not only by reissuing *Twice-told Tales*, but also by reprinting these failed attempts at schoolbooks in a single volume intended for family reading: *True Stories from History and Biography* (1851). Hawthorne's real financial success as a children's author only comes, however, in the next few years when Ticknor and Fields urge him to produce and swiftly publish his retelling of Greek myths for children: *The Wonder-Book* (1852) and *Tanglewood Tales* (1853).

Hawthorne was often dismissive of these juvenile efforts: noting with humorous sarcasm to his sister Elizabeth "our pay as Historians of the Universe will be 100 dollars" or explaining to his college classmate Henry Wadsworth Longfellow that though he "must scribble for a living, but this troubles me much less than you would suppose. I can turn my pen to all sorts of drudgery, such as children's books etc." (XV: 247, 252). There is a peculiarly feminine and domestic taint to this literary "drudgery" as Hawthorne shared with his sister in the production of most of the juvenile work he sold to Goodrich during these years. While editor of the *American Magazine of Useful and Entertaining Knowledge* Hawthorne's letters from Boston to his home in Salem mingle demands that his sisters take care of his laundry and that Elizabeth write for the magazine: "I have but two clean shirts left. Where is that stock? Ebe should have sent me some original poetry – and other concoctions." Many of his letters to Salem during these months end not with a signature but with the injunction "concoct – concoct – concoct" (XV: 239, 230, 240).

However one assesses the literary merits of the compendia of anecdotes and information that Nathaniel and Ebe Hawthorne compile for the *Magazine* or the *Universal History*, there is something in this idea of concocting a literature for children that truly appeals to Hawthorne. He had, after all, published "Little Annie's Ramble" a year before Goodrich offered him the editorship, and the preface to the *Universal History* describes the project with remarkable nuance, complexity, and pride:

> A work which gives in detail the history of mankind, must necessarily be voluminous . . . the young reader . . . looks upon the formidable row of octavos, in which such a wilderness of lore is collected, as a maze in which he is sure to get lost, and he therefore prudently resolves to keep clear of it.
>
> Abridgements of general history have been usually liable to still greater objections. They are little more than dry lists of dates, presenting no pictures to the imagination, exciting no sympathies in the heart, and imparting few ideas to the understanding. To steer clear of bewildering difficulties on the one hand, and repulsive chronological brevity on the other – the Scylla and Charybdis which beset the adventurer in this attempt – and at the same time to weave into a few pages a clear, vivid and continuous tale of the great human family . . . demands a nicer understanding of the youthful heart and intellect, and more art in the adaptation of language to simple minds, than can often be at the command of any man.[18]

Here is not "drudgery" but adventure as fraught with dangers as Greek epics or the American wilderness. Hawthorne's aversion to "dry lists" and "repulsive chronologies," his celebration of imagination, sympathy, and understanding intimate the aesthetic project that he would later call "romance." Stretched between adventure and emotion, the preface's ideas about genre prove to be just as much about gender. Does this book require "a nicer understanding of the youthful heart and intellect . . . than can often be at the command of any man" because the niceties of child-rearing are not really of manly concern? Or is Hawthorne claiming here a "command" that exceeds that of other men? Hawthorne clearly wishes in this preface to mark the difficulty of his task and to celebrate his success in fulfilling it, even if he equivocates on the gendered terms of that success. His description of the uses he foresees for this history puts even more pressure on the concept of "command":

> I have written for the *Young*, but as I desire that these volumes may not be forced upon anybody as a monitor or master, I say in the title page that it is designed for families. I wish it to be permitted to enter the family circle, and

take its chance to make its way. If it is placed, not as a task-book, but rather as a storyteller, on the table, perhaps the children may patronize it; perhaps the parents may deign to look into it.[19]

For both children's literature and for the structure of the family, Hawthorne prefers desire to force. The new ideal of a home governed by affection requires, to Hawthorne's mind, a new kind of literature for children, one that resists hierarchies and control, and that celebrates storytelling as the most effective means of knowing.

A year later, Hawthorne wrote to Longfellow about the possibility of collaborating on a collection of fairy tales for children. His motives are primarily monetary, but he imagines that the project could "revolutionize the whole system of juvenile literature." "I think that a very pleasant and peculiar kind of reputation may be acquired in this way – we will twine for ourselves a wreath of tender shoots and dewy buds, instead of such withered and dusty leaves as other people crown themselves with" (xv: 266–67). The family circle becomes a laurel wreath in this fantasy, changing the basis of what counts as reputation, and who can confer it. Hawthorne stresses the financial rewards of such a collection – money was a worry to him, and it is obvious that he feels keenly the difference between his position and that of Longfellow teaching at Harvard – but his excitement stems from something else. What becomes clear in reviewing Hawthorne's early musings on children's literature is how much new images of the family structured by love, rather than authority, and epitomized by the ideal "dewy" child, become conflated with new ideas about the power of storytelling. Hawthorne does indeed see himself as revolutionizing a "whole system."

"Father are you going to write all this?"

"A domestic career has been begun; there is a wife to be loved and to love, and there are children to be born and raise," Julian Hawthorne explains in his memoir of his parents' marriage. The "History of Happiness" that he finds in the couple's letters and journal notebooks has been read more ambivalently by later critics, who have found something ominous and destructive in the intensity with which Nathaniel and Sophia constructed and idealized their domestic bliss. T. Walter Herbert has seen in the nervous breakdown of the couple's first child, Una, at the age of fourteen, the psychic costs of the Hawthornes' insistence that their "home is paradise" (VIII: 316).[20] Critics have long noted the gap between the idyllic domesticity the Hawthornes claimed and the perverse, destructive form that familial relations take in so much of Hawthorne's fiction – finding in this tension one source of the psychological nuance of his writing as well as the power of that writing to forge the emotional values of middle-class domestic life.[21] Hawthorne's pieces for children, rarely discussed by these scholars, are the most self-conscious instance of this process, since with these tales Hawthorne expressly seeks "to enter the family circle" or, as he called it in his preface to *Mosses from an Old Manse*, "our magic circle" (x: 29).

"Little Annie's Ramble" was first published in the annual *Youth's Keep-sake, a Christmas and New Year's Gift for Young People* in 1835, almost a decade before Hawthorne had children of his own, and a few years before his courtship of Sophia. It is a fantasy of communion with a child which simultaneously remains oddly anti-domestic, telling as it does of Annie's ramble away from home. The *Youth's Keepsake* clearly intended its stories as holiday gifts for children and the copy at Smith College suggests that the volumes were indeed used in this way: the first page is inscribed "Eliza P. Humphrey, from her father Jan 1st 1835." Hawthorne both addresses and speaks past such young readers; his story is as much for Eliza's father, suggesting the pleasure that grown men should or could take in little girls, as it is for Eliza herself. Ultimately the story would be reprinted in *Twice-told Tales* – the shift in audience reflecting on the disturbing shifts of tone in the piece itself.

> What would Annie think if, in the book which I mean to send her, on New Year's day, she should find her sweet little self, bound up in silk or morocco with gilt edges, there to remain till she become a woman grown, with children of her own to read about their mother's childhood! That would be very queer.
>
> (IX: 124)

Such confusions of outside and inside, author and narrator, reader and character, world and book are the principal charm of this story, but also the principal source of threat. The editors of *Youth's Keepsake* were particularly pleased by this conceit and used a picture labeled "Little Annie" as the frontispiece of the entire volume. Then, on page 151, immediately below this passage with its playful conflation of child and book lies a note, "Does not our Frontispiece resemble your 'Little Annie'? EDITOR" calling the author's attention to the press's fine treatment of his story, calling the readers' attention to the gift book's expensive plates, but even more offering to make true Hawthorne's whimsical fantasy in the suggestion that Eliza Humphrey and all the daughters of all the fathers that purchased this book could find themselves "bound up" in it. The relation between book, man, and child is, as Hawthorne puts it, "very queer."

In the didactic tradition of early nineteenth-century children's literature the tale of a child who "strayed from her home" (IX: 128) is a familiar conceit, one that reveals the dangers of town and affirms that children should be obedient and at home. In such accounts a hearth-side pastime like reading would keep a child safe. Hawthorne's story appears to reject such traditional didacticism; the narrator insists that this ramble into the world is a harmless pleasure that leaves Annie "untainted" (IX: 129). The story proclaims itself similarly detached from monitory responsibilities: to "be merry" is better than to "moralize." But the conclusion of the sketch makes clear that the narrator's version of this afternoon ramble is not the only perspective. The bell of the town crier that opened the story, that clang of communal order and public knowledge, ends it as well, this time announcing not circuses but "the loss of a little girl who has not once let go of my hand!" (IX: 129).

In the nonchalance with which the narrator discounts the mother's fear of losing Annie, in the worldly cynicism with which he describes all that they see as they roam the streets of the town, and most of all in his obsessive fascination with Annie's "pure, instinctive delicacy of taste" (IX: 127), the narrator himself appears as the source of taint. He does not admit that their grasping of hands could be compatible with loss, could indeed be the very sign of loss. "Here we see the very same wolf – do not go near him, Annie! – the self same wolf that devoured little Red Riding Hood and her grandmother" (IX: 127), he warns as they tour the caravan, dissolving the bounds between fairy tale and real. To the extent that we hear a strain of wolf in the narrator's cajoling tones, the act of storytelling itself appears suspect. In presenting himself as a writer of children's stories, then, Hawthorne suggests the perverse as well as the innocent possibilities of that role. To "go hand in hand with the mind of a sinless child" intrudes hands into minds in a manner that will echo as horror throughout Hawthorne's mature fiction, as "the Unpardonable Sin" of "Ethan Brand," or as the torture Chillingsworth dispenses to Dimmesdale who "knew that no friendly hand was pulling at his heart-strings" (*The Scarlet Letter*, I: 171).

Presenting itself as an innocent children's story, "Little Annie's Ramble" thus also tells a story of adult lechery and disillusionment: "I have gone too far astray for the town crier to call me back!" the narrator moans (IX: 129). Yet even this layered understanding of the story is too simple, for if it distrusts the narrator's self-presentation it still endorses the image of Annie as a "sinless child." One of the most destabilizing things about this story, however, is how Annie is cast as initiating this "strange couple": at least as the narrator sees and describes it, Annie is the one who feels "that impulse to go strolling away" and "comes bouncing on tiptoe across the street" to take a stranger's hand (IX: 121), and it is she who "has not once let go" of that hand. One of the most seductive things about this story, in other words, is how it presents the little girl as herself the source of seduction.[22]

The narrator insists at the story's end that it is not a story at all, that nothing has happened in it, and that Annie can return home "with an untainted and unwearied heart, and be a happy child again" (IX: 129). Yet perhaps nothing has happened for the quite different reason that Annie never was such a "happy child" in the first place. The stroll began, after all, because the narrator could "see that the pretty child is weary of this wide and pleasant street" (IX: 121). The adult life weariness that he claims at the end can be alleviated by contact with the "still fresh existence" and "sweet magic" of "an hour or two with children" (IX: 129) proves part of childhood itself since Annie too is weary.

The shifting character of innocence and taint in this story comes to haunt Hawthorne's experience of parenting. A similar idealization of childhood innocence prompts Nathaniel and Sophia to name their first daughter "Una" – much against the advice of family and friends – as "the symbol of the one true union in the world" as Nathaniel put it in a letter to Sophia (XVI: 37),[23] and as a harbinger "of a most delicate spirit, impatient of wrong & ugliness – demanding beauty of all things & persons – & like the 'heavenly Una' of Spenser" as Sophia noted in the family journal that she and Nathaniel both wrote in sporadically until 1852. Though she is careful to counter these beatific predictions for her daughter with the assurance that "At the same time she will recognize the Real."[24] Sophia began this notebook on 3 April 1844, exactly a month after Una's birth; Nathaniel did not write in it until 20 June 1847 when he recorded some of Una's words:

> "I'm tired of all sings, and want to slip into God. I'm tired of little Una Hawsorne." "Are you tired of Mama?" "No." "But are you tired of Papa?" "No." "I am tired of Dora, and tired of little Julian, and tired of little Una Hawsorne."
>
> (VIII: 398)

Tired of nurse and brother and self, here is a world-weariness greater even than "Little Annie's." Sophia records this scene as well in her different style, Nathaniel's detached quotation tempered in her version by sympathetic explanation: "Rain & cold. Una had a day of infinite ennui, like a bird with wings tied to its side. . . . 'I am tired of all ↑th↓ sings'."[25] It is easy to imagine "I am tired of all sings" becoming a kind of family code. What are these parents doing when they fondly and critically write these remembrances of Una, the world-weary, self-weary child, moping in the Hawthorne parlor? The family notebook is full of such observations. There is clearly a pleasure for both parents in recording childish oddities and badness at least as great as that offered by accounts of the children's goodness. As Sophia puts it, "In short there never were such divine children, far diviner than if more spotless of blame – I cannot explain this remark now."[26] What Sophia cannot explain is the way that she is charmed by her child, how affection transmutes moral categories and evades ideology.

Though critics are right to note the idealizing and gendering pressures that the Hawthornes put on their children, and most forcefully on their first child Una, the predominant feeling in these notebook entries is one of wonder, of the uncanny mysteriousness of children.

> But to return to Una, there is something that almost frightens me about the child – I know not whether elfin or angelic, but, at all events, supernatural . . . I now and then catch an aspect of her, in which I cannot believe her to be my own human child, but a spirit strangely mingled with good and evil, haunting the house where I dwell. The little boy is always the same child, and never varies in his relation to me. (VIII: 431)

Hawthorne writes these notes in the days awaiting his mother's death, discomfitted in part by Una's fascination with her grandmother's sickroom. Critics often quote this passage because it is so closely echoed in the phrases Hawthorne will use to describe Pearl in *The Scarlet Letter*. But its portrait of Una's startling changeability is one that both parents repeat throughout these pages. Here is Sophia:

> I never knew such a combination of the highest refinement & rudest boorishness – one lies at the door of the other – When she was a little infant, in one position as she lay asleep, she reminded <me> us of Pan – almost Caliban – & in another the most sweet, angelical etherial – spiritual aspect beamed forth.[27]

Sophia's correction from "me" to "us" marks the pressure of family unity – to parent as one – but in so doing it emphasizes the shared sense of this evaluation, how since infancy the couple have been telling stories, assigning symbolic, mythic, literary names to make sense of this life that they have produced but that they cannot contain or predict. Child-rearing manuals stressed the parental duty to mold the moral being of children, yet what the Hawthornes record most powerfully in this notebook is the autonomy of these beings, the impossibility of control or authorship over what should be "my own human child." That Julian seems less troubling in these terms may be a mark of gender difference (there apparently being less need to explain aggression or wildness in a boy), or even a matter of character. But there is also the difference made by Una's position as first child – how in the parenting of Una the Hawthornes define for themselves what the mysterious relations between parent and child may be. The questions the notebook raises as questions about Una, are thus also questions about childhood itself, about how infantile lives come to take a recognizable human form, to be inscribed within moral and social codes, and what role parents might occupy in that process. In this family record charm and ideology collide.

Pearl has long fascinated and confused readers of *The Scarlet Letter*. As Barbara Garlitz first noted, the responses of early reviewers described her either as "an imbodied angel from the skies" or as "a void little demon" and such polarities have continued to characterize critical response.[28] Garlitz's efforts to make sense of this duality, like those more recently of Franny Nudelman, convincingly show how Pearl conforms to nineteenth-century child-rearing doctrine: naturally innocent – "worthy to have been brought forth in Eden" (*The Scarlet Letter*, 1: 90) – Pearl had nevertheless imbibed from her mother the passion and sinfulness of the act that conceived her. In *The Mother's Book*, Lydia Maria Child had warned "it is not possible to indulge anger, or any other wrong feeling, and conceal it entirely. If not expressed in words, a child *feels* the baneful influence. Evil enters into his soul as the imperceptible atmosphere he breathes enters his lungs."[29] Hawthorne describes Pearl's moral inheritance precisely in terms of such atmospheric transmission.

> The mother's impassioned state had been the medium through which were transmitted to the unborn infant the rays of its moral life; and, however white and clear originally, they had taken the deep stains of crimson and gold, the fiery luster, the black shadow, and the untempered light, of the intervening substance. Above all the warfare of Hester's spirit at that epoch was perpetuated in Pearl.
>
> (1: 91)

Drawing on *The Mother's Book* and similar manuals, Nudelman explains that the "intersubjectivity" of mother and child reveals the circular nature of familial authority: in such a system "a mother's efforts to discipline her child cannot be easily distinguished from her efforts to discipline herself."[30] Or as Lydia Maria Child expressed it, "the first rule, and most important of all, in education, is, that a mother govern her own feelings, and keep her heart and conscience pure."[31] Such mutual effects had been apparent to Hawthorne as early as "Little Annie," whose narrator concludes of children "Their influence on us is at least reciprocal with ours on them" (IX: 129). These readings make sense of the doubleness of Pearl, how her spirit, like Una's is "strangely mingled with good and evil." They suggest as well, why it is that Pearl who "could not be made amenable to rules" (1: 91) nevertheless serves to forestall her parents' flight into lawlessness. Why it is she who issues the command "Come thou and take it up!" (1: 210), restoring the scarlet letter and the punitive power of communal judgment to her mother's breast.

In the chapter "The Child at the Brook-Side" Hawthorne stresses the multiple and reflective nature of the child's power. As Pearl reiterates her demand until her mother complies, the narrative voice focuses on the repetition of Pearl's gestures and emotions in the reflecting water of the brook. "At length, assuming a singular air of authority, Pearl stretched out her hand, with the small forefinger extended, and pointing evidently towards her mother's breast. And beneath in the mirror of the brook, there was the flower-girded and sunny image of little Pearl, pointing her small forefinger too" (I: 209). As many scholars have noted, Pearl's authority here is communal authority, emphasizing the bonds of relationship and responsibility against Hester's antinomian vision of personal freedom and escape.[32] The multiplication of Pearls in her reflected image and echoing cries, makes her many, "a hidden multitude" (I: 210). But if this doubling serves to conjure communal disapproval, allowing Pearl to express societal claims and enforce Puritan law, it simultaneously manages to mark the mysteriousness of relationship and identity: "This image so nearly identical with the living Pearl, seemed to communicate somewhat of its own shadowy and intangible quality to the child herself . . . In the brook beneath stood another child, – another and the same" (I: 208). This play of separation and oneness, "another and the same" – how one's own human child can be nevertheless so alien – is mirrored in Hawthorne's writing about his own parenting. Alongside the understanding of the family circle as the source of reciprocal, circular, social discipline runs a sense of the family as "shadowy and intangible," and of childhood as ungraspable as a reflection in a forest pool.

The imagery of "haunting" provides one of Hawthorne's most potent tools for romance. In the Custom-House introduction to *The Scarlet Letter*, "moonlight in a familiar room" works this transformation, making "the domestic scenery" of the middle-class parlor into "spiritualized" "things of intellect."

> Nothing is too small or too trifling to undergo this change and acquire dignity thereby. A child's shoe; the doll seated in her little wicker carriage; the hobbyhorse; – whatever, in a word, has been used or played with, during the day, is now invested with a quality of strangeness and remoteness, though still almost as vividly present as by daylight. Thus, therefore, the floor of our familiar room has become a neutral territory, somewhere between the real world and fairy-land, where the Actual and the Imaginary may meet and each imbue itself with the nature of the other. Ghosts might enter here without affrighting us.
>
> (I: 36)

It seems only fitting that Hawthorne should first work this magic on childhood toys, things which he chooses precisely because "trifling" and yet which were always in their daily usage subject to just the sort of transformation he describes. The normal, expected, purpose of doll or hobby-horse is to become real in a child's imagination, to cry or gallop. Thus the production of this neutral territory, the work of romance, not only transforms the domestic scene, but is modeled on it and particularly on the play of children. His mother stands as the specific ghost Hawthorne alludes to here, the "beloved" newly lost at the time of this writing.[33] To imagine her return then is to cast himself as child. Hawthorne may be disquieted by his daughter's way of "haunting the house where I dwell," but it is a discomfort tinged with wonder and desire, and it is, moreover, a practice that he seeks to emulate in his writing of romance.

The *Wonder-Book*, Hawthorne's most successful of children's books, largely imagines the idealization of childhood and the expectations of culture as seamlessly united. Written in Lenox during the summer of 1851, in the light of the critical success of *The Scarlet Letter* and *The House of the Seven Gables*, it marks Hawthorne's most sanguine domestic and literary period, a moment when he feels most confident that his creative vision and public taste might indeed coincide.[34] Here the innocence of children, the felicity of literary production, and the clarity of authorial control all appear certain. In this book the college student Eustace Bright tells six stories based on Greek mythology to a group of loosely related children with such simultaneously prosaic and blossomy names as "Milkweed," "Squash-Blossom," or "Dandelion." The frame narrative of Eustace and the flower-children is lively and detailed, presenting a year's worth of storytelling on hillside walks and by a winter fire and providing one of Hawthorne's fullest literary portraits of affluent and pleasurable domesticity. It is a domesticity clearly propped by this storytelling, suggesting how much literary enjoyment and the kind of shared cultural norms carried by Greek mythology inform the ideal middle-class household. Sophia writes in the notebook about acting out such myths with the children, Una playing Pandora, and Julian in "a jaunty cap" as Mercury.[35] Eustace Bright titles his narration of the myth of Pandora "A Paradise of Children":

"... when the world was as new as Sweet Fern's bran-new humming-top. There was then but one season of the year, and that was the delightful summer; and but one age for mortals, and that was childhood."

"I never heard of that before," said Primrose.

"Of course, you never did," answered Eustace. "It shall be a story of what nobody but myself ever dreamed of, – a Paradise of children, – and how by the naughtiness of just such a little imp as Primrose here, it all came to nothing."

(*Wonder-Book*, VII: 63)

It tells of how "troubles" come into the world together with aging, so that childhood appears anterior to pain. Still, of course, Pandora's "vexation" at the mystery of the box, her "naughtiness," precedes and prompts the act of opening it. It arises moreover from domestic unhappiness, from Pandora's inability to play happily with little Epimetheus and the other children. The Paradise of childhood thus rests upon obedience and domestic accord. It is worth noting that Primrose is chastised – the "little imp" – for questioning the authority of the storyteller. At the end of the volume Hawthorne himself figures as a character, "That silent man, who lives in the old red house near Tanglewood avenue, and whom we sometimes meet, with two children at his side," and Eustace makes clear that his authority is not to be doubted:

> If our babble were to reach his ears and happen not to please him, he has but to fling a quire or two of paper into the stove and you, Primrose, and I, and Periwinkle, Sweet Fern, Squash-Blossom, Blue Eye, Huckleberry, Clover . . . would all turn to smoke, and go whisking up the funnel! Our neighbor in the red house is a harmless sort of person enough, for aught I know, as concerns the rest of the world; but something whispers to me that he has a terrible power over ourselves, extending to nothing short of annihilation.   (VII: 169–70)

In a sense *A Wonder-Book*, though perhaps the most "sunny and happy" of Hawthorne's books,[36] is also the most deluded since it wins that sunniness through a dual simplification that imagines both parenting and writing as acts of simple fiat. Here childhood appears truly as a parental paradise, Locke's tabula rasa offered literally as a blank page on which the father-author can write.

The notebooks suggest that however happy these months may have been in the Hawthorne household, their happiness was not of this controlled or controlling variety. Hawthorne mailed the manuscript for *A Wonder-Book* to his publisher Ticknor and Fields on 15 July 1851, and on 28 July Hawthorne records in the notebook "at seven o'clock, A.M. Wife, E. P. P. [Sophia's sister Elizabeth Palmer Peabody], Una, and Rosebud, took their departure, leaving Julian and me in possession of the Red Shanty" (VIII: 436). The notebook account "Twenty Days with Julian & Little Bunny, By Papa" is full of the glee of domestic inversions – Julian shrieking because he can with "baby gone" (VIII: 436), or Nathaniel smoking and taking "the little man" on a picnic with Melville and the Duycknicks where Julian eats only gingerbread (VIII: 464). There are some domestic trials as well: "The little man woke me with his exclamation between two and three o'clock; and I found him, wonderful to say, in a perfectly soppy state. There had been a deluge in his bed and nowhere else" (VIII: 452). But there is no sense of authorial omnipotence, rather if anyone is the wielder of words it is Julian:

Either I have less patience to-day than ordinary, or the little man makes larger demands upon it; but it really does seem as if he had bated me with more questions, references, and observations, than mortal father ought to be expected to endure. He does put me almost beside my propriety; never quitting me, and continually thrusting in his word between the clauses of every sentence of all my reading, and smashing every attempt at reflection into a thousand fragments. (VIII: 454)

The Hawthorne children do scribble in the pages of this notebook, their own words, drawings, and wildly wielded pens erupting around their parent's words, insisting on being part of this writing thing that their parents do. Clearly they know that one way that they matter for their father is as a subject of writing.

Enter Una – "Where is little Julian?" "He has gone out to walk." "No; but I mean where is the place of little Julian that you've been writing about him." So I point to the page, at which she looks with all possible satisfaction; and stands watching the pen as it hurries forward. "I'll put the ink nearer to you," says she. "Father are you going to write all this?" . . . I tell her that I am now writing about herself – "that's nice writing," says she. (VIII: 403)

Una, with narcissistic satisfaction, finds the writing that is her, "nice writing" indeed. Pearl seems herself "the scarlet letter in another form; the scarlet letter endowed with life!" (I: 102) and in her fascination with the A it appears "as if the one only thing for which she had been sent into the world was to make out its hidden import" (I: 178). Such ties to the letter, to literacy, as pleasure, as discipline, as disruption, even as self proves one of the central subjects of *The Scarlet Letter*, and no doubt one reason why it has become such a powerful pedagogical force – a kind of American primer.[37] Ultimately it is in this mirroring of child and writing that Hawthorne stakes the nature and meaning of authorship, both for the family and for the romance.

NOTES

1. See for example Michael T. Gilmore, "Hawthorne and the Making of the Middle Class," in Wai Chee Dimock and Michael T. Gilmore, eds., *Rethinking Class: Literary Studies and Social Formation* (New York: Columbia University Press, 1994), pp. 215–38; and T. Walter Herbert, *Dearest Beloved: The Hawthornes and the Making of the Middle-Class Family* (Berkeley: University of California Press, 1993).
2. See Richard H. Brodhead, *The School of Hawthorne* (New York: Oxford University Press, 1986).
3. See for example Sacvan Bercovitch, *The Office of "The Scarlet Letter"* (Baltimore, MD: Johns Hopkins University Press, 1991); and Lauren Berlant, *The Anatomy*

of National Fantasy: Hawthorne, Utopia, and Everyday Life (Chicago: University of Chicago Press, 1991).

4. William G. McLoughlin, "Evangelical Child Rearing in the Age of Jackson: Francis Weyland's Views on When and How to Subdue the Willfulness of Children," *Journal of Social History* 9.1 (Fall 1975): 20–43.

5. Horace Bushnell, *Christian Nurture* (rpt. New Haven, CT: Yale University Press, 1947), p. 14.

6. Maria J. McIntosh, *Ellen Leslie* (New York: Dayton and Newman, 1842), p. 84.

7. Mary P. Ryan, *The Empire of the Mother: American Writing about Domesticity, 1830 to 1860* (New York: Haworth Press, 1982).

8. Susan Coultrap-McQuin, *Doing Literary Business: American Women Writers in the Nineteenth Century* (Chapel Hill: University of North Carolina Press, 1990), p. 2.

9. Lydia Maria Child, *The Mother's Book* (Boston: Carter and Hendee, 1831), p. vi.

10. Carolyn L. Karcher, ed., *A Lydia Maria Child Reader* (Durham, NC: Duke University Press, 1997), p. 97.

11. See Nina Baym, "Again and Again, the Scribbling Women," in John L. Idol and Melinda M. Ponder, eds., *Hawthorne and Women: Engendering and Expanding the Hawthorne Tradition* (Amherst: University of Massachusetts Press, 1999), pp. 20–35.

12. *Youth's Keepsake, a Christmas and New Year's Gift for Young People* (Boston: E. R. Broaders, 1835).

13. Samuel G. Goodrich, *Recollections of a Lifetime, Or Men and Things I Have Seen in a Series of Familiar Letters to a Friend*, 2 vols. (New York: Miller, Ortoal and Mulligan, 1856), II: 167, 279, and 284.

14. Samuel G. Goodrich, *Parley's Book of Fables* (Hartford, CT: White, Dwier, 1836), p. 6.

15. Elizabeth Freeman, "Honeymoon with a Stranger: Pedophiliac Picaresque from Poe to Nabokov," *American Literature* 70.4 (December 1998): 863–97; and Meredith McGill, *American Literature and the Culture of Reprinting. 1834–1853* (Philadelphia: University of Pennsylvania Press, 2003), pp. 248–52.

16. Laura Laffrado, *Hawthorne's Literature for Children* (Athens: University of Georgia Press, 1992), p. 135.

17. See *The Letters, 1813–1843*, XV: 21–26.

18. *Peter Parley's Universal History on the Basis of Geography, for the Use of Families* (1837), 2 vols. (New York: S. Coleman, 1839), pp. vii.

19. *Ibid.*, p. viii.

20. Julian Hawthorne, *Nathaniel Hawthorne and His Wife: A Biography*, 2 vols. (Boston: James Osgood, 1885), I: 245 and 246. T. Walter Herbert, "Nathaniel Hawthorne, Una Hawthorne, and *The Scarlet Letter*: Interactive Selfhoods and the Cultural Construction of Gender," *PMLA* 103.3 (1988): 285–97, and "Part Four: Roman Fever," in *Dearest Beloved*, pp. 213–256.

21. In addition to Herbert see Joel Pfister, *The Production of Personal Life: Class, Gender, and the Psychological in Hawthorne's Fiction* (Stanford, CA: Stanford University Press, 1991).

22. See Freeman, "Honeymoon with a Stranger."

23. For Hawthorne's responses to complaints about the name from his sister Louisa and friend George Hillard see *Letters 1843–1853*, XVI: 20–22.

24. Patricia Dunlavy Valenti, "Sophia Peabody Hawthorne's American Notebook," in Joel Myerson, ed., *Studies in the American Renaissance, 1996* (Charlottesville: University Press of Virginia, 1996), p. 148. The family notebook is a single volume now at the Pierpont Morgan Library, but the history of publication has split it so that the portions in Sophia and the children's hands are printed here, while Nathaniel's portions of the journal are reproduced in the *American Notebooks*.

25. Valenti, "Sophia Peabody Hawthorne's American Notebook," p. 151.

26. *Ibid.*, p. 161.

27. *Ibid.*, p. 166.

28. Barbara Garlitz, "Pearl: 1850–1955," *PMLA* 72.4 (September 1957): 698, quoting Henry Giles, *Illustrations of Genius* (Boston, 1854), p. 76 and George P. Loring, "Hawthorne's *Scarlet Letter*," *Massachusetts Quarterly Review* 3 (September 1850): 494.

29. Child, *The Mother's Book*, p. 9.

30. Franny Nudelman, " 'Emblem and Product of Sin': The Poisoned Child in *The Scarlet Letter* and Domestic Advice Literature," *Yale Journal of Criticism* 10.1 (1997): 206.

31. Child, *The Mother's Book*, p. 4.

32. See Bercovitch, *The Office of "The Scarlet Letter,"* p. 9–10; Richard H. Millington, *Practicing Romance: Narrative Form and Cultural Engagement in Hawthorne's Fiction* (Princeton, NJ: Princeton University Press, 1992), pp. 90–93; and Nudelman, " 'Emblem and Product of Sin,' " p. 208.

33. See Franny Nudelman, "Ghosts Might Enter Here: Toward a Reader's History," in Idol and Ponder, eds., *Hawthorne and Women*, pp. 278–85.

34. Nina Baym, "Hawthorne's Myths for Children: The Author Versus his Audience," *Studies in Short Fiction* 10 (1973): 35–46; and Laffrado, *Hawthorne's Literature for Children*, pp. 66–99.

35. Valenti, "Sophia Peabody Hawthorne's American Notebook," p. 158.

36. Praise from a review in *Graham's Monthly Magazine*, quoted in *A Wonder-Book*, VII: 306.

37. See Patricia Crain, *The Story of A: the Alphabetization of America from "The New England Primer" to "The Scarlet Letter"* (Stanford, CA: Stanford University Press, 2000).

8

BROOK THOMAS

Love and politics, sympathy and justice in *The Scarlet Letter*

Describing the forest scene in *The Scarlet Letter* in which Hester and Dimmesdale "recognize that, in spite of all their open and secret misery, they are still lovers, and capable of claiming for the very body of their sin a species of justification," novelist William Dean Howells writes, "There is greatness in this scene unmatched, I think, in the book, and I was almost ready to say, out of it."[1] The emotional climax in a book of many memorable scenes, Hester's and Dimmesdale's reunion in the forest has captured readers' imaginations for generations. Despite the importance of the love story of which that scene is a part, however, some of the best recent political readings of the novel have diverted our attention from or downplayed its significance.

For instance, in "The Politics of *The Scarlet Letter*" Jonathan Arac argues that the novel's famous ambiguity needs to be understood in relation to the politics of inaction on the issue of slavery as expressed in Hawthorne's campaign biography of President Franklin Pierce. As groundbreaking as this essay was, its major mention of the love story comes when Arac notes that " 'adulterer' (or 'adultery'?) is nowhere spelled out in Hawthorne's text, just as 'slavery' is nowhere present in the Declaration or the Constitution."[2] Similarly, Sacvan Bercovitch asserts that the love scene Howells praises "is a lovers' reunion, a pledge of mutual dependence, and no doubt readers have sometimes responded in these terms, if only by association with other texts. But in *this* text the focus of our response is the individual, not the couple (or the family)."[3] Stressing the politics of gender and sexuality, Lauren Berlant does look closely at the love story. But for her it loses its political power the moment it most compellingly commands readers' sympathies. In the end, she writes, "The tale of Hester and Dimmesdale, a political scandal, is reduced to a *mere* love plot" (my emphasis).[4]

In downplaying the love story all three pay less attention to dramatically rendered scenes like the one in the forest than to narrative commentary. Especially important for Bercovitch and Berlant is the chapter "Another

View of Hester," which as the thirteenth of twenty-four chapters starts the second half of the book by describing Hester's speculations about the radical changes needed for women "to assume what seems a fair suitable position" (*The Scarlet Letter*, 1: 165). According to Berlant, when the love story is severed from that radical vision it becomes subject to "moral and literary (not political) laws."[5] In this chapter, I agree that the love story enacts Hester's fall from radicalism. I also agree with all three that to understand *The Scarlet Letter*'s significance for our own day we need to look at conditions in the mid nineteenth century when it was produced as well as at the seventeenth-century Boston that it fictionally represents. Even so, the novel raises political implications that none of these political critics considers, implications that we can understand only if we do not take a condescending attitude toward a "mere" love story or remake it into one about individualism. Those implications are linked, I will argue, to tensions we feel between feelings evoked by the dramatically rendered love story and narrative commentary about it.

In linking Hawthorne's political vision to his love story, I am not arguing, as many do today, that "the personal is political." The political, that slogan implies, cannot be confined to the traditional realm of politics but extends into all realms of social life, including the constitution of intimate relations. No truly radical reform is possible, the argument runs, without altering those relations. Although Hawthorne did not use the slogan "the personal is political," he was aware of similar arguments in his day. But even though one measure of a political system for him is its ability to provide spaces in which love can flourish and although the personal clearly influences the political order and is influenced by it, he did not need exposure to a presidential impeachment because of an adulterous affair in the White House to be aware of the dangers of conflating the personal with the political. If many today are aware of that danger, what distinguishes Hawthorne from most of them is his sense of the tragic and transgressive nature of historical change. Figured in *The Scarlet Letter* as an act of adultery that threatens the political order of Puritan Boston, such transgressions both keep history moving forward and undercut hopes of radical breaks with the past.

The possibility of radical new beginnings is a preoccupation of *The Scarlet Letter*. It starts with reflections on the Puritans' attempt to establish a fresh start in the "new world" and the narrator's whimsical comment that "The founders of a new colony, whatever Utopia of human virtue and happiness they might originally project, have invariably recognized it among their earliest practical necessities to allot a portion of the virgin soil as a cemetery, and another portion as the site of a prison" (1: 47). It then opens the second half with Hester's despairing realization that the radical reforms she imagines would require "the whole system of society to be torn down, and built up anew" (1: 165), speculations that are in turn linked to the forest scene when Hester pleads with Dimmesdale, "Leave this wreck and ruin here where it hath happened! Meddle no more with it! Begin all anew!" (1: 198).

Even though each of these efforts is frustrated, much of the story's emotional tension has to do with readers' hopes – secret or not – that one or the other – or all – will succeed. Of all the attempts, however, that of Hester and Dimmesdale has awakened most readers' hopes. Sympathy for them is so powerful that many readers overlook those passages in which the narrator condemns the lovers' sentiments. To understand *The Scarlet Letter*'s political implications we need to understand why, after martialling all of his rhetorical force to make us sympathize with his lovers, Hawthorne does not allow them a new beginning.

Puritan authorities might have answered that question by relying on John Winthrop's distinction between natural and civil liberty. "The first is common to man with beasts and other creatures. By this, man, as he stands in relation to man simply, hath liberty to do what he lists; it is a liberty to evil as well as to good." In contrast, civil liberty has to do with the "covenant between God and man, in the moral law, and the politic covenants and constitutions, amongst men themselves. This liberty is the proper end and object of authority, and cannot subsist without it; and it is a liberty to that only which is good, just, and honest."[6] Winthrop's analogy for political covenants is marriage. Assuming the common law doctrine of coverture in which husband and wife become one corporate body with the husband granted sole legal authority, Winthrop compares a woman's subjection in marriage to political members' subjection to the magistrates who govern the political covenant to which they consent. "The woman's own choice makes such a man her husband; yet being so chosen, he is her lord, and she is to be subject to him, yet in a way of liberty, not of bondage; and a true wife accounts her subjection her honor and her freedom . . . Even so brethren, it will be between you and your magistrates."[7] In turn both marriage and political covenants are analogous to "the covenant between God and man, in the moral law" in which a Christian can achieve true liberty only through total submission to Christ. For the Puritans, political institutions and the civil ceremony of marriage are governed by the moral law because they have God's sanction. A political covenant is not simply a contract among men; like the marriage contract between a man and woman, it needs God's witness.

To apply this doctrine of covenant theology to *The Scarlet Letter* is to see that for the Puritans Hester's greatest sin would not have been her adultery, whose visible evidence they see in the birth of Pearl, but a remark that Dimmesdale alone hears her make: her defiant cry that what the two lovers did "had a consecration of its own" (I: 195). Resonating with so many readers, this proclamation is sinful because it implies that Hester's and Dimmesdale's love is a self-contained act, not one in need of God's sanction. As such their love exists in the realm of natural, not civil, liberty and must be contained.

Despite the sympathy that he creates for his lovers, Hawthorne recognizes with Winthrop the dangers of natural liberty. But he also has doubts about the patriarchal and hierarchical relations between husband and wife and ruler and subject that the Puritans used to uphold the civil order. Indeed, Hawthorne continually challenges rulers' calls for absolute loyalty. That challenge is one reason that this loyal Jacksonian Democrat was seen in the 1920s by Charles and Mary Beard in their extremely popular and progressive history textbook as a deeply democratic writer. Describing Hawthorne's lack of "reverence for the infallibility of superior persons,"[8] they then quote "a moral" from *The House of the Seven Gables* about the Puritans and the witchcraft trials "that the influential classes, and those who take upon themselves to be leaders of the people, are fully liable to all the passionate error that has ever characterized the maddest mob" (II: 8). Errors of this sort occur in any society ruled by fallible human beings, but they magnify in significance when "forms of authority were felt to possess the sacredness of divine institutions" (II: 64) as they were in the Puritan theocracy of *The Scarlet Letter*.

Distrustful of granting civil authority divine sanction, Hawthorne questions the capacity of the Puritan magistrates properly to judge Hester. Their problem is not that they are evil men. "They were, doubtless, good men, just and sage" (I: 64). Their problem is that "out of the whole human family, it would not have been easy to select the same number of wise and virtuous persons, who should be less capable of sitting in judgment on an erring woman's heart, and disentangling its mesh of good and evil" (I: 64). Assuming the moral position of God, the magistrates lack Hester's "power to sympathize" (I: 161).[9] That power causes a political dilemma. If, on the one hand, Hawthorne appeals to sympathy to temper the rigid and authoritarian rule of a system in which "religion and law were almost identical" (I: 50), on the other, he warns of the dangers of having that sympathy embrace natural liberty with all of its potential dangers.

That dilemma is, of course, precisely the dilemma Hawthorne's readers confront when they sympathize with his two lovers in the forest. Hawthorne does not resolve it, as many readers assume, by championing his lovers against a repressive society. Nor does he resolve it, as a number of critics assume, by advocating absolute submission to the existing civil authority. On the contrary, Hawthorne builds the dilemma into the book's structure by generating two points of view in constant tension. One derives from the dramatic action itself, which in evoking our sympathies questions the prevailing measure of justice. The other is the narrator's commentary, which tries to subordinate our sympathies to justice as inscribed in the law.[10] Hawthorne's failure to resolve the dilemma he raises is not simply a case of his famous ambiguity. It is instead a recognition that there is no formula for determining whether our sympathies serve justice or not. As enacted in *The Scarlet Letter*, therefore, politics does not resolve the dilemma; it is a realm in which its competing claims are perpetually adjudicated. That adjudication is complicated further by the fact that the sympathies marshalled to question existing standards of justice frequently involve acts of transgression. Hester's transgression is extremely important to emphasize because even some of Hawthorne's best recent critics are prone to minimizing its importance.

For instance, T. Walter Herbert, one of the most sensitive readers of what he calls "the marital politics" of *The Scarlet Letter*, argues that "The Puritan community is guilty of enforcing a wrongful standard: Hester's youthful mistake could be corrected in a healthier social arrangement, where she could obtain a divorce from Roger and proceed to formalize at law the true marriage of her heart."[11] *The Scarlet Letter* certainly portrays a narrow Puritan society. But Hawthorne does not present us with a situation in which Hester could correct a "youthful mistake" if more liberal Puritans would have loosened divorce legislation.[12] If Hester made a mistake in marrying, she makes another in committing adultery. Hawthorne forces her to reckon with that sin. Indeed, her adultery is another example of a premature effort to begin anew. Her affair with the minister takes place with her assuming, before the fact, that her husband is dead. When Chillingworth appears he is, therefore, not only a vengeful, cuckolded husband, but also a figure from the past prepared to block Hester and Dimmesdale from achieving the dream of starting anew.

By not flinching at Hester's transgression Hawthorne raises a political dilemma related to the one concerning sympathy. Although critical of harshly repressive political orders, he, like Freud, believes that some form of repression is necessary to maintain civil order. The problem with that belief is that not all repressions are the same. How do we distinguish between necessary repressions and what Herbert Marcuse calls "surplus-repressions" that legitimate one group's domination over another? One answer to that dilemma is to seek, as did Marcuse, a non-repressive foundation to civilization, one that allows the full flourishing of eros.[13] Often associated with the 1960s, that quest had a pre-history in Hawthorne's day. Impulses fueling the fascination with experimental utopian communities in antebellum America were various, but at least some believed that true reform had to begin by liberating the sexual energy repressed by the institution of marriage. Drawing on the tradition evoked by Winthrop that uses metaphors of marriage to describe the terms of political obligation, these antebellum advocates of making the personal political felt that sexual reform would liberate society.

Hawthorne was intrigued enough by such radical sentiments that a review of *The Scarlet Letter* in the *Church Review and Ecclesiastical Register* responding to Hawthorne's portrayal of a passionate adulterous couple asked "Is the French era actually begun in our literature?" Reading the book as advocating "sympathy for [Hawthorne's lovers'] sin," the reviewer attacks Hawthorne for implying that Hester's adultery is "a natural and necessary result of the Scriptural law of marriage, which, by holding her irrevocably to her vows, as plighted to a dried up book-worm" makes "her heart an easy victim to the adulterer." Likewise, Dimmesdale's sin seems to be "not so much the deed itself" as "his long concealment of it." The reviewer attributes such scandalous sentiments to "the doctrines enforced at 'Brook-farm,'" the experimental utopian community that Hawthorne temporarily joined.[14] Having the advantage of reading *The Blithedale Romance*, Hawthorne's satiric account of his experience at Brook Farm written after *The Scarlet Letter*, we know that Hawthorne expressed great skepticism about such utopian experiments. We also know that Brook Farm was not as radical in its attack on marriage as other utopian communities. Even so, the reviewer's misreading does let us see how intimately Hawthorne understood radical reformers' arguments that the institution of marriage needed to be more responsive to the powerful force of erotic love and the sympathies that it awakens. After all, he went to Brook Farm with marriage to Sophia on his mind. But if Hawthorne shares with radicals a desire for better relations between men and women, his answer is not to abolish the institution of marriage but to reform it.

The established model of marriage in Hawthorne's day was still ruled by the doctrine of coverture. Coverture guaranteed a patriarchal lineage by having the wife lose her legal standing as an individual and willingly submit to the rule of her husband. Under it, as Winthrop makes clear, a wife's loyalty and obedience were paramount. Hawthorne's dissatisfaction with this model is expressed in *The Blithedale Romance* in his portrayal of the chauvinist Hollingsworth who would change society by reforming criminals but who maintains a reactionary view of women. "Woman," he insists, "is a monster – and, thank Heaven, an almost impossible and hitherto imaginary monster – without man, as her acknowledged principal" (III: 114). When Hollingsworth accuses the French reformer Fourier of committing "the Unpardonable Sin" for basing his reforms on – "the principle of all human wrong, the very blackness of man's heart, the portion of ourselves which we shudder at, and which it is the whole aim of spiritual discipline to eradicate" (III: 50) he is not referring to Fourier's plans to reform the system of labor, but instead to his theories about passional attractions. Skeptical as he was about radical reform, Hawthorne does not dismiss the passions, including erotic passion, as "the very blackness of man's heart." On the contrary, whereas he worries about unregulated eros, he tries to imagine institutional reform that will allow it legitimately to flourish. Authoritarian, patriarchal political systems do not allow that to happen.

For instance, in *The Marble Faun* Hawthorne opposes the despotic rule that manifests itself in trying to force the character Miriam against her will into an arranged marriage "in which feeling went for nothing" (IV: 430). Similarly, whereas authoritarian Puritan rule is not solely responsible for Hester's problems, Hawthorne is certainly critical of it and links it to Hester's unhappy marriage. Indeed, if Hester and Chillingworth represent the old model, Hester and Dimmesdale suggest a new model, which substituted coverture's image of marriage as a corporate body presided over by the husband with the image of a contractual relation between husband and wife. Rather than emphasizing the obedience and loyalty of the wife, this new domestic ideal emphasized a bond held together by love and sympathy.

According to Herbert, the "conflicts and psychic torment" of *The Scarlet Letter* result from competition in Hawthorne's day between these views of marriage.[15] Those views have political implications. For instance, Winthrop appeals to the model of coverture to bolster his claim that the primary components of political obligation should be duty and obedience. In contrast, the new model suggests a basis in love and sympathy, which because of their capacity to create bonds and establish identifications across barriers of status have great democratic potential. To be sure, the opposition between duty and obedience, on the one hand, and love and sympathy, on the other, is too simple. Love and sympathy can generate duties and obedience while obedience and adherence to one's duties can be seen as a measure of love. For instance, Elizabeth I's reign in England was successful in part because she exploited the image of a loving marriage between herself and the nation to solicit loyalty from her subjects.[16] Perhaps then the proper opposition should be between love and obedience, on the one hand, and love and sympathy, on the other. But even that opposition breaks down because sympathy, as well as love, can be channeled into obedience to the state. Indeed, effective rulers know how to command a people's support by cultivating its sympathetic identification with them.

Thus another factor affecting the political implications of competing models of marriage was the transformation of political subjects into citizens that corresponded with the overthrow of monarchies in both the United States and France. For instance, in England and colonial America, the killing of a husband by a wife was *petit treason*, analogous to regicide, although the killing of a wife by a husband was simply murder. The analogy did not, however, survive the revolution. Not wanting the symbolic slaying of the king to encourage revolution in the patriarchal family, most of the new states dropped the term *petit treason*. In granting sovereignty to "the people" as citizens, who according to Aristotle have the capacity to both rule and be ruled, the republican system of the United States challenged the hierarchical order in which sovereignty resided in a monarch – or absolute magistrates – who ruled over loving and obedient subjects. As Linda Kerber has shown, the ideal of citizenship in the revolutionary era undercut Winthrop's analogy between the wife under coverture and the subjects of a commonwealth. On the one hand, independence generated an ideological disjunction. Founded on the principle that the terms of political obligation of British subjects could be renegotiated to create United States citizens, the nation was ruled, nonetheless, by men who for the most part wanted to retain a family structure in which a wife owed her husband eternal obedience.[17] On the other hand, the rhetoric of citizenship generated a new republican model of marriage that challenged the doctrine of coverture. As Merril Smith puts it, "Tyranny was not to be considered in public or private life, and marriage was now to be considered a republican contract between wives and husbands, a contract based on mutual affection."[18]

Whereas some conceived of that contract as one of absolute equality, the majority challenging coverture, Hawthorne included, felt that the duties husband and wife brought to the union should not be identical but complementary, divided along gender lines. The marital relation was, for them, balanced by adding a form of maternalism to coverture's paternalism. In the family husbands continued to have primary responsibility for relations concerning justice and authority, whereas wives presided over affairs of moral sentiment. If that division denied women direct access to the political sphere, it entrusted to them raising children.

One challenge the new model posed to coverture is registered in the battle for custody of Pearl. Under coverture a child belonged legally to the father. In fact, in custody disputes between husband and wife a common law court did not grant custody to the mother until 1774. Even in this landmark case Chief Justice Lord Mansfield acknowledged the "father's natural right" while ruling that "the public right to superintend the education of its citizens" had more weight.[19] Mansfield's views are similar to those Hawthorne gives to his Puritan elders who feel that, for her own good and that of the commonwealth, Pearl, who had no father willing to claim her, could be taken from her mother. Hearing that some of the "leading inhabitants" are rumored to be campaigning to transfer Pearl "to wiser and better guardianship than Hester Prynne's" (1: 100–01), Hester concocts an excuse to go to the governor's hall, only to find Governor Bellingham and Reverend Wilson convinced of their plan when Pearl impiously responds to their interrogations. Desperately turning to Dimmesdale, Hester implores: "I will not lose the child! Speak for me! Thou knowest, – for thou hast sympathies which these men lack! – Thou knowest what is in my heart, and what are a mother's rights" (1: 113).

As much as readers have been moved by Hester's plea, placed in seventeenth-century Boston, it is an anachronism. Appeals to a mother's rights did not have force until the new model of marriage convinced courts that the upbringing of children – especially in their tender years – was best accomplished by their mothers. That change began in a few highly publicized cases in the United States just before Hawthorne began writing *The Scarlet Letter*. Indeed, in the D'Hauteville case, the wife's lawyers contrasted the increasingly progressive republican nature of marriage in the United States to the outmoded feudal concept of coverture maintained by her Swiss husband.[20]

Hawthorne clearly sympathizes with the new model. He is not, however, convinced that the transition from old to new model will be a smooth one. Nor is he convinced that the sympathy and love underlying it can be the sole basis for a political order. If sympathy has the power to bind people together, it can also be misdirected. In "Young Goodman Brown," for instance, Hawthorne speaks of "the sympathy of all that was wicked in his heart."[21] The problems multiply when sympathy combines with eros. Love in its erotic version involves more than sympathy. Sympathy may be necessary for love and love can help breed sympathy, but love casts a much deeper spell. Love's deep absorption can lead to a self-enclosed isolation that threatens social cohesion rather than promotes it. For instance, in *The Marble Faun* the lovers Donatello and Miriam are united through their joint participation in a homicide that forges a bond "closer than a marriage-bond . . . as if their new sympathy annihilated all other ties" and released them from "the chain of humanity," creating "a special law . . . for them alone." Not emancipatory, their bond becomes as restricting as the despotic, patriarchal system that made the young Miriam against her will a victim of a "contract of betrothal" (IV: 430). Wreathing itself "like a serpent, in inextricable links about both of their souls," their crime "drew them into one, by its terrible contractile power" (IV: 174). The link between these two lovers' sympathy and their crime suggests, as does Hester's and Dimmesdale's adultery, that any new order brought about will be founded as much on transgression as on sympathy. Transgression, it seems, is a constant element in Hawthorne's sense of historical change.

Hawthorne creates a sense of that constancy by unfolding a drama in which his main characters are caught in a spell in which civil order is suspended and they find themselves between the reign of the old model and the new. The old model may be the legal standard, but it is consigned to a time before the book begins, so that in the book Hester and her husband do not even share the same name. Nonetheless, the new model suggested by Hester and Dimmesdale can be imagined only in some future beyond the book's end while the lovers' adultery evokes fears, like those expressed in *Church Review and Ecclesiastical Register*, of the radical destruction of the institution of marriage itself. Unrolling between those past and future moments, the action between and among Hester, Dimmesdale, and Chillingworth entails not only Hester's and Dimmesdale's lawless love but also a relation between Hester and Chillingworth reduced to something less than an empty, legal arrangement of marriage – and not only because of Hester's adultery.

Critics have long noted that Hawthorne does not show us Hester's violation of her marriage vows, which takes place before the book begins. But it is equally significant that Hawthorne also never presents a public ceremony of marriage. What we get instead is a parodic enactment of one when Hester's husband appears and they establish a new bond in their private, prison interview. Rather than have their agreement sanctified by the witness of the world, they agree to keep Hester's husband's identity secret. Honoring that new vow for seven years, Hester again breaks her word in her forest reunion with Dimmesdale. More than a display of erotic passion, Hester's violation of her second vow to her husband results from a new sense of loyalty based on love rather than one based on duty alone. Viewed this way, Hester's revelation of her husband's identity seems perfectly justified, especially considering the circumstances in which she gave her word to remain silent, circumstances that add to our sympathy for the plighted lovers. Nonetheless, as we have seen, Hawthorne generates sympathy for his lovers only to test its limits. Thus we need to be wary of the means by which he elicits that sympathy.

For instance, the vow Hester makes to Chillingworth in prison is not of the same order as the one she had made in marrying him. Similarly, although a comparison between Dimmesdale's and Hester's reunion in the forest and Chillingworth's and Hester's in prison clearly favors the lovers, there are structural similarities between the two. Just as Hester's new bond with her husband can be maintained only because he has taken on a new name, so Hester counsels her lover, "Give up this name of Arthur Dimmesdale, and make thyself another" (1: 198). More importantly, the secrecy in which both bonds are made isolates everyone involved from the human community. As such, both starkly contrast with the bond created by the civil ceremony of marriage whose public witness links husband and wife to the community. Finally, we need to make sure that Hawthorne's negative portrait of his villain does not make us assume that Hester's and Dimmesdale's love is pure and untainted.

From Chaucer's January to characters in Shakespeare to Charles Bovary to Leopold Bloom, the cuckolded husband has been treated with differing amounts of humor, pathos, sympathy, and contempt. Few, however, are as unsympathetic as Roger Chillingworth. Hawthorne's treatment of him starkly contrasts the sympathetic treatment some courts gave to cuckolded husbands in the 1840s when various states began applying the so-called unwritten law by which a husband who killed his wife's lover in the act of adultery was acquitted. Arguments for those acquittals portrayed avenging husbands as "involuntary agents of God." In contrast, lovers were condemned as "children of Satan," "serpents," and "noxious reptiles" with supernatural power allowing them to invade the "paradise of blissful marriages."[22] In *The Scarlet Letter* this imagery is reversed. It is the avenging husband who stalks his wife's lover with "other senses than [those ministers and magistrates] possess" (1: 75) and who is associated with "Satan himself, or Satan's emissary" (1: 128). In the meantime, we imagine Arthur, Hester, and Pearl as a family. The narrator so writes off Chillingworth as Hester's legal husband that he refers to him as her "former husband" (1: 167), causing Michael T. Gilmore to follow suit and D. H. Lawrence to designate Mr. Prynne Hester's "first" husband.[23] A legal scholar writing on adultery goes so far as to call Hester an "unwed mother."[24]

Chillingworth is easy to write off as a husband because in the book he plays the part so poorly. Much has been made of Hester's adulterous violation of her marriage vows. Not much attention, however, has been paid to her husband's violation of his, even though the narrator comments on it. For instance, in prison Hester asks her husband why he will "not announce thyself openly, and cast me off at once?" His reply: "It may be . . . because I will not encounter the dishonor that besmirches the husband of a faithless woman. It may be for other reasons. Enough, it is to my purpose to live and die unknown" (1: 76). In legal terms, Chillingworth's fear of dishonor makes no sense inasmuch as he has committed no crime. But if some antebellum courts displayed great sympathy to cuckolded husbands through the unwritten law, there was a long tradition – still powerful in the seventeenth century – of popular and bawdy rituals mocking cuckolded husbands.[25] No matter what other motives Chillingworth might have, the narrator makes clear that the man "whose connection with the fallen woman had been the most intimate and sacred of them all" resolves "not to be pilloried beside her on her pedestal of shame" (1: 118). That resolve explains "Why – since the choice was with himself – " he does not "come forward to vindicate his claim to an inheritance so little desirable" (1: 118).

According to coverture, that undesirable inheritance was not only Hester, but also her child. Fully aware of his husbandly rights, Chillingworth tells his wife, "Thou and thine, Hester Prynne, belong to me" (1: 76). Nonetheless, he refuses to acknowledge his inheritance, telling Hester in the same scene, "The child is yours, – she is none of mine, – neither will she recognize my voice or aspect as a father" (1: 72). The doctrine of coverture was clearly a patriarchal institution; nonetheless, it was not solely to the advantage of the husband. It was also a means to hold him responsible for the well-being of his wife and children. Chillingworth might not be Pearl's biological father, but he is her father in the eyes of the law. That legal status adds another dimension to the recognition scene that occurs when Chillingworth walks out of the forest and finds his wife on public display for having committed adultery. "Speak, woman!" he "coldly and sternly" cries from the crowd. "Speak; and give your child a father!" (1: 68). Commanding his wife to reveal the name of her lover, the wronged husband also inadvertently reminds us that at any moment Hester could have given Pearl a legal father by identifying him. Even more important, Chillingworth could have identified himself. But the same man who knows his legal rights of possession as a husband refuses to take on his legal responsibilities as a father.

Pearl, in other words, has not one but two fathers who refuse to accept their responsibilities. Having lost his own father as a young boy and doubting his ability financially to support his children, having just lost his job at the Custom House, Hawthorne was acutely aware of the need for fathers to live up to their name. The failure of Dimmesdale and Chillingworth to do so helps to explain what would seem to be a contradiction in the nineteenth-century legal system's handling of domestic disputes.

How, we need to ask, could the same legal system that challenged coverture by beginning to grant women custody rights evoke an "unwritten law" to give husbands the power to kill their wives' lovers – and sometimes their wives themselves? One answer is that the US legal system is not uniform because laws on domestic matters can vary from state to state. Some states were more sympathetic to wives, others to husbands. But another answer, with important consequences for the significance of Hester's and

Dimmesdale's transgression, is suggested by Herbert when he uses the model of marriage evoked by their love to explain the enlarged significance given to adultery in antebellum America.

Coverture's patriarchal lineage, Herbert notes, was threatened only when the wife committed adultery, since her infidelity could produce illegitimate heirs. "Within the [new] domestic ideal, by contrast, adultery contaminated the relation from which the marriage itself took its meaning, poisoning the intimacy on which the sacredness of the home depended; and this is equally true for husband and wife."[26] The same ideal of marriage that saw mothers as the natural guardians of young children also saw adultery as a supreme threat to new bonds of marriage based more on sympathetic affection than on obedience and duty. The adultery of Hawthorne's lovers is, in other words, not simply a transgression against an old order; it is also a violation of the very ideal that their new love represents.

Even so, Hester's and Dimmesdale's transgression makes possible the only marriage reported in the book, that of Pearl. The suggestion that Pearl ends happily married might imply that the new order denied her mother has finally prevailed, but in typical Hawthorne fashion we are not told whether her marriage conforms to the new model or the old. What we do know is that her future is guaranteed when her two fathers finally take on their proper responsibilities. At his death Chillingworth bequeaths to his once-rejected inheritance "a considerable amount of property, both here and in England" (1: 261). At his death Dimmesdale publicly acknowledges his paternity. Developing "all her sympathies," that acknowledgment elicits from Pearl tears that "were a pledge that she would grow up amid human joy and sorrow, nor for ever do battle with the world, but to be a woman in it" (1: 256).

Occurring in the last of three memorable scenes on the scaffold, Dimmesdale's revelation of his paternity and Pearl's pledge culminate the book's dramatically rendered action. If in the first scaffold scene Hester, holding the infant Pearl, must face the public alone and in the second scene, which culminates the first half of the book, Dimmesdale joins mother and child in the secrecy of night, in this one the three stand together in public. At the beginning of the book the scarlet letter "had the effect of a spell" on Hester, "taking her out of the ordinary relations with humanity, and inclosing her in a sphere by herself" (1: 54), but when Pearl consents to kiss Dimmesdale in public after refusing to do so in the forest, "A spell was broken" (1: 256). With the book's spell broken and Hawthorne's main characters restored to a world of civil order, it is tempting to read this scene, as Herbert does, as a triumph of the new model of the family.[27] The book, however, does not allow that triumph any more easily than it allows the new beginning that Hester and Dimmesdale imagine in the forest.

Arthur, Hester, and Pearl might suggest a new order for the domestic family, but, according to Dimmesdale, they cannot embody it in this world or in the next. As her lover dies, Hester asks, "Shall we not meet again? . . . Shall we not spend our immortal life together? Surely, surely, we have ransomed one another, with all this woe?" Dimmesdale, however, responds,

> The law we broke! – the sin here so awfully revealed! – let these alone be in thy thoughts! I fear! I fear! It may be, that, when we forgot our God, – when we violated our reverence each for the other's soul, – it was thenceforth vain to hope that we could meet hereafter, in an everlasting and pure reunion.
>
> (1: 256)

Far from signaling a triumph of the new model, Dimmesdale's final words echo the narrator's point of view in affirming the very order that Hester's and Dimmesdale's adultery violates.

Thus, in one of the book's many ironies, when the two lovers finally unite in public their points of view are not in harmony but in conflict. Repenting his sin, Dimmesdale asks Hester, "Is this not better . . . than what we dreamed of in the forest?" Her response, typically, turns to human relations. "I know not! I know not! . . . Better? Yea; so we both may die, and little Pearl die with us!" (1: 254). Dimmesdale devotes his love to a higher power; Hester dedicates hers to those on earth closest to her.[28] Because human beings do not sympathize with God – they love and obey Him – Dimmesdale's love entails obedience. Nonetheless, with his capacity for sympathy that other Puritan leaders lack, he knows how to channel it into the service of God, just as earlier in the election day sermon he gets the Puritan crowd to submit "with childlike loyalty" (1: 250) to its rulers by appealing to "the great heart of mankind; beseeching its sympathy or forgiveness" (1: 243), and just as he plays on Pearl's sympathies to get her to pledge obedience. Even so, at the end of the book's dramatically rendered action, it is unclear if he has succeeded in channeling Hester's sympathies in the same way.

Hawthorne, however, does not end with this final dramatic scene. Instead he presents us with the book's "Conclusion" that describes Chillingworth's sudden death, Hester's and Pearl's departure from the "new" world for the "old," and Hester's return to Boston. On her return, we learn, she has a different relation to the community that once spurned her. On the one hand, Hester acknowledges the importance of the civil order as she did not in her rebellious days. For instance, she now has the liberty to remove her "badge of shame" – "for not the sternest magistrate of the period would have imposed it" (1: 161) – but she willingly chooses to wear it. On the other hand, the scarlet letter has taken on a new significance and is no longer a stigma. Still living on the margins of society, Hester devotes herself to counseling and comforting people with "sorrows and perplexities," especially women "in the continually recurring trials of wounded, wasted, wronged, misplaced, or erring and sinful passion, – or with the dreary burden of a heart unyielded, because unvalued and unsought" (1: 263). Indeed, Hester's return is in part – and maybe fully – motivated by her desire to be near her lover's grave.

How are we to interpret the final chapter, and what does it tell us about Hawthorne's political vision? Crucial for any interpretation is Hester's final belief that "in Heaven's own time, a new truth would be revealed, in order to establish the whole relation between man and woman on surer ground of mutual happiness" (1: 263), which indicates that Hester has indeed adopted Dimmesdale's faith in a higher force controlling the movement of history. For Arac, as we have seen, that faith reveals Hawthorne's politics of inaction. If women come to Hester asking "why they were so wretched, and what might be their remedy" (1: 263), Hawthorne's answer is, according to Arac, to have "patient trust in the future,"[29] which is the same answer Hawthorne gave in *The Life of Pierce* to those hoping to abolish slavery. Slavery, Hawthorne writes while campaigning for his friend, is "one of those evils which divine Providence does not leave to be remedied by human contrivances, but which, in its own good time, by some means impossible to be anticipated, but of the simplest and easiest operation, when all of its uses shall have been fulfilled, it causes to vanish like a dream" (III: 417). This "fantasy of evanescence," Arac claims, makes *The Scarlet Letter*, like *The Life*, a work of propaganda, a call "*not* to change your life."[30]

Bercovitch also argues that *The Scarlet Letter* is propaganda, but it is "thick propaganda." "Where *The Life of Pierce* presents a certain choice, *The Scarlet Letter* represents a metaphysics of choosing."[31] Hester's choice to return to Boston and submit to the civil order against which she once rebelled illustrates what Bercovitch identifies as "the American ideology" of liberalism. Liberalism, according to Bercovitch, works by a logic of consent that channels radical dissent into a form of social cohesion. It works, in other words, not by consensus but by dissensus. Dissensus maintains social order by projecting, as Dimmesdale and Hester do at the end, the image of an alternative, better world into the future, an image of a not-yet-achieved America that can accommodate many – and at times conflicting – individual visions. A liberalism of compromise and accommodation, Hawthorne's, according to Bercovitch, conceives of historical change as gradual and continuous, not radical and disruptive.[32]

Berlant agrees that Hester's final belief is a fall from her earlier radical speculations. Hester is still focused on "love," but love now imagined in "the diminished, private 'region' often called Hester's 'feminism'."[33] Hester's interior subjectivity may be "crucial to the preservation of the utopian promise of national identity," but it is also a region in which Hester's radical vision in "Another View of Hester" about "the foundation for justice" has been replaced by one concerned with "mutual happiness." Hester, Berlant laments, "no longer convenes collective identity within the public sphere of discourse and exchange (the marketplace), but rather convenes in the home's safe space atomized subjects possessed by individual sorrows." The result is "to preserve the idea of the law, to repress the potential eruption of female antinomian energy."[34]

These brief summaries cannot do justice to the richness of these three readings. Nonetheless, one place to start establishing an alternative interpretation is with Arac's claim that *The Scarlet Letter* is an argument not to change your life. Despite his important warning that to place reform in the hands of Providence is to risk the sort of political quietism that Hawthorne displayed on the issue of slavery, Arac neglects the fact, emphasized by both Bercovitch and Berlant, that Hester undergoes a significant change from chapter 13 to the end. To understand the politics of *The Scarlet Letter*, however, we need to do more than look at a transformation within the individual Hester, which is Bercovitch's and Berlant's focus. We also have to look at transformations within the civil order to which Hester submits. *The Scarlet Letter* may affirm the need for civil order, but that order has undergone a change.

Until the final chapter Hawthorne's Puritan theocracy tries to control all activities of life. As Berlant puts it, "in theory" it allows "neither a private part to which the state is not privy, nor a thought outside of the state's affairs."[35] For instance, describing the concern over Pearl's upbringing, the narrator comments, "Matters of even slighter public interest, and of far less intrinsic weight than the welfare of Hester and her child, were strangely mixed up with the deliberations of legislatures and acts of the state" (I: 101). Similarly, Hester is allowed to live in her isolated cottage only "by the license of the magistrates, who still kept an inquisitorial watch over her" (I: 81). When Hester returns, she reoccupies the same cottage, but she does so with a difference. Not perpetually watched over by suspicious magistrates, she receives their toleration of – and even admiration of – activities that are not directly under their supervision.

Dismissed by Berlant as taking place in a privatized, apolitical space, these activities suggest the nascent formation of a relatively independent civil society, "a sphere of social interaction between economy and the state, composed of the intimate sphere (especially the family), the sphere of associations (especially voluntary associations), social movements, and forms of public communication."[36] Not the realm of politics itself, civil society is, nonetheless, necessary for a democracy to function. As Michael Walzer puts it, "It is very risky for a democratic government when the state takes up all the available room and there are no alternative associations, no protected social space, where people can seek relief from politics, nurse wounds, find comfort, build strength for future encounters." It is so risky that one function of the state in liberal democracies is to protect the space for a civil society that incorporates "many of the associations and identities that we value outside of, prior to, or in the shadow of state and citizenship."[37] In dramatizing the importance of activities in that sphere, Hester through her return to Boston indicates the kinds of non-political transformations that Hawthorne considered necessary for a democratic society to emerge from the Puritans' authoritarian rule.

The importance of a relatively independent civil society for Hawthorne complicates Bercovitch's and Berlant's account of the demise of Hester's radicalism. If unlike Berlant, Bercovitch pays little attention to the sexual nature of Hester's "female antinomian energy," he joins her in assuming that those energies are expressed in her rebellious adultery. They differ, however, in their interpretations of the significance of those energies. For Bercovitch the adultery releases radical sympathies that are eventually subordinated to a higher sense of national justice prophesied in Dimmesdale's election day sermon whereas for Berlant the adultery unleashes a radical sense of justice that is eventually repressed in favor of Hester's sympathetic concern with the mutual happiness between men and women.

What neither recognizes is that Hester's rebellious energies are contained by her love for Dimmesdale as well as expressed by it. For Hawthorne whenever eros is combined with sympathy, with or without the sanction of the existing civil order, its individualist energies are contained. An act of social but not individualistic defiance, Hester's love for Dimmesdale is an effort to find a sympathetic, interpersonal relationship of mutual happiness. Linked in both Bercovitch's and Berlant's accounts to her adultery, Hester's antinomian speculations in chapter 13 occur because isolation from her lover has turned her life "in a great measure, from passion and feeling, to thought" (I: 164). Hester is, in other words, like Miriam in *The Marble Faun*, whose "rich, ill-regulated nature" (IV: 280) is regulated by dedicating herself to her lover. "I fear not Heaven," she acknowledges to her friend Kenyon, "but – shall I confess it? – I am greatly in dread of Donatello" (IV: 283). To be sure, Hester's love for Dimmesdale eventually causes her also to fear heaven, but the fact that her lover is the vehicle for her transformation indicates that even at the book's conclusion a significant difference remains between the lovers' visions of the future. Dimmesdale's focus is on "the relation between the Deity and the communities of mankind" (I: 249) whereas Hester's is on "the whole relation between man and woman" (I: 263).

When Hester abandons her radical utopian dream in chapter 13 for her final vision of mutual happiness between men and women, she is, as Berlant argues, more concerned with the cultivation of sympathy than with ensuring justice. Nonetheless, in a paradox that is at the heart of Hawthorne's political vision, the ends of justice are not always served by those primarily concerned with it. After all, Hester in her radical speculations is not the only one concerned with questions of justice; so too are the Puritan magistrates, the narrator, and in the end Dimmesdale. Like antinomians, they derive their sense of justice from God. But, unlike antinomians, they feel that God's justice needs to be mediated through human institutions that command absolute loyalty. In contrast, Hawthorne recognizes, along with antinomians, that no human institution can perfectly embody justice. In such a world the potentially fallible judgments of justice by the state need to be tempered by sympathy.

Existing human institutions are, nonetheless, not unique in their fallibility. Antinomian visions of alternative worlds are prone to error as well. Justice may be associated with images of balance, but human history does not come out even. On the contrary, efforts to bring about perfect justice by remedying past injustices often generate new injustices, as in cycles of revenge or in Chillingworth's desire to get even with the lover of his wife, transgressions that make it impossible to achieve perfect justice in a human realm. Thus for Hawthorne utopian visions of a new form of justice, like Hollingsworth's in *The Blithedale Romance* or Holgrave's in *The House of Seven Gables*, also need to be tempered by sympathy.

And there is yet another complication to this already complicated relation between justice and sympathy. One utopian fantasy in both Hawthorne's day and ours is to eliminate the repressive control of an always fallible state by instituting a new regime of justice based on love and sympathy. Hawthorne recognizes the utopian possibilities of such a self-regulating combination of eros and sympathy in *The Marble Faun* when he portrays the Roman carnival and its temporary suspension of civil order. Consisting of role playing that transgresses existing social hierarchies to produce a "sympathy of nonsense" (IV: 439), the celebration recalls Kant's famous description of works of art having "purposiveness without a purpose."[38] But Hawthorne's work of art is not without a purpose and not innocent. Appropriately, when *The Scarlet Letter* presents us with a spell of suspended order, in which adulterer plays the role of husband and husband the role of adulterer and neither that of father, the result is anything but utopian.

Such transgressive moments might be necessary to keep history moving forward, but Hawthorne recognizes that the suspension of civil order can unleash forces thwarting the realization of justice as much as contributing to it. In "My Kinsman, Major Molineux" he imagines that paradoxical possibility through an irrational mob that dons costumes to rid the town of a dignified ruler in service of the old, hierarchical order. In *The Scarlet Letter* he reminds us that even the combination of love and sympathy is not, in and of itself, a guarantee of a just order. Even though Hester's love for Dimmesdale regulates her erotic passion by giving her a purpose in life, that purpose is not necessarily in the service of justice. On the contrary, whereas Dimmesdale's and Hester's "iron link of mutual crime . . . like all other ties . . . brought along with it its obligations," it had also severed the "links that united them to the rest of human kind" (1: 159–60). Considerations of justice cannot be confined to the duties and obligations generated by love any more than to the sympathies it awakens.

The potentially fallible judgments of justice by the state may need to be tempered by a sense of sympathy, but feelings of sympathy also need to be measured by considerations of justice. "Only a democratic state," Walzer claims, "can create a democratic civil society; only a democratic civil society can sustain a democratic state. The civility that makes democratic politics possible can only be learned in the associational networks; the roughly equal and widely dispersed capabilities that sustain the networks have to be fostered by the democratic state."[39] And, we should add, only when a space is allowed to exist between the political sphere and civil society can a productive interaction between the two take place, for it is only through the relative independence allowed in the relations of civil society that alternative possibilities to the existing basis of political rule can be imagined. Ideally, then, the interaction between civil society and the state allows for perpetual transformation that keeps the civil order from stagnating.

Walzer's description is very close to Hawthorne's view of matters in which the state creates a space for associations generating new sympathies that can in turn test the state's judgments of justice at the same time that those judgments guard against misdirected sympathies. Nonetheless, there is an important difference. Whereas Walzer's description is balanced, for Hawthorne the interaction between the state and civil society is never perfectly balanced. The result is a sense of historical change that complicates Bercovitch's and others' characterization of Hawthorne's political vision as gradualist.

To be sure, by having most of the book's action unfold as if under a spell in which time is suspended between an old order and a new one, *The Scarlet Letter* implies that we are permanently in transformative moments.

Similarly, from the God's-eye perspective that the narrator, Dimmesdale, and in the end Hester try to achieve, those transformations turn out to confirm continuity. But from the perspective of the human actors caught within those transformations they are hardly smooth, harmonious, and continuous. They are instead full of conflict, torment, and tragic loss. Dimmesdale's merciful God may guide human history toward the fulfillment of justice, but in the world of human history justice and mercy never perfectly coincide. Nor is the marriage of justice and sentiment ever perfectly achieved. In fact, the new sympathies helping to create an altered configuration of social cohesion come more from failed relations than from successful ones. Thus, in the book's final image, Hester and Dimmesdale share a common tombstone, but an eternal space remains between their graves.

This tragic, transgressive, yet forward-looking, vision of what Lionel Trilling called "Our Hawthorne" struck a chord with a post-World War II generation of critics who shared Freud's belief that maintaining civilization inevitably requires some repression of eros.[40] For instance, Arthur M. Schlesinger, Jr., the famous historian of Jacksonian America, contrasted liberal progressivism's "sentimental belief in progress" with the "tradition of Jackson and Hawthorne, the tradition of a reasonable responsibility about politics and a moderate pessimism about man." Dispensing with "the Christian myths of sin and atonement," the former believed that "Man's shortcomings, such as they were, were to be redeemed . . . by the benevolent unfolding of history." But, as Hawthorne illustrates through his portrayal of reformers, those convinced of "infallibility can sacrifice humanity without compunction on the altar of some abstract and special good." In contrast, Hawthorne's "pessimism about man, far from promoting authoritarianism, alone can inoculate the democratic faith against it. 'Man's capacity for justice makes democracy possible,' Niebuhr has written in his remarkable book on democratic theory; 'but man's inclination to injustice makes democracy necessary.' "[41]

Hawthorne's political vision, however, had less in common with the next generation of critics that in the wake of Marcuse tried to imagine a non-repressive basis of civilization. If Bercovitch offers a brilliant reading of *The Scarlet Letter* that explains how the radical dissent of that generation was channeled into dissensus and Berlant offers a reading that tries to keep its radical dissent alive, Arac importantly reminds us how a vision in which politics inevitably involves repression can too easily tolerate unjust repressions of individual groups. In contrast, I have tried to argue that for a newer generation of Hawthorne's readers what might be most important about his political vision is not the particular positions that he took. Few today, for instance, agree with his position on slavery or his gendered account of duties in the family and in the state. Instead, Hawthorne's importance for us is his dramatization of the inevitable political problem of discriminating between different manifestations of sympathy and repression.[42] Formally embodied in *The Scarlet Letter* as a tension between a point of view eliciting readers' sympathies and one concerned with judgments of justice, that problem is not solved in the pages of the book. What we do get is a world in which mutual happiness between lovers does not necessarily correspond with justice and justice does not necessarily lead to happiness, although to abandon the quest for either would be to rule out greater possibilities for both.

NOTES

1. William Dean Howells, "Hawthorne's Hester Prynne," in Gary Scharnhorst, ed., *The Critical Response to Nathaniel Hawthorne's "The Scarlet Letter"* (Westport, CT: Greenwood Press, 1992), pp. 105, 108.
2. Jonathan Arac, "The Politics of *The Scarlet Letter*," in Sacvan Bercovitch and Myra Jehlen, eds., *Ideology and Classic American Literature* (New York: Cambridge University Press, 1986), p. 260.
3. Sacvan Bercovitch, *The Office of "The Scarlet Letter"* (Baltimore, MD: Johns Hopkins University Press, 1991), p. 122.
4. Lauren Berlant, *The Anatomy of National Fantasy: Hawthorne, Utopia, and Everyday Life* (Chicago: University of Chicago Press, 1991), p. 154.
5. *Ibid.*
6. John Winthrop, *Winthrop's Journal: "History of New England,"* ed. J. K. Hosmer, 2 vols. (New York: Scribners, 1908), II: 83–84.
7. *Ibid.*, pp. 238–39.
8. Charles and Mary Beard, *The Rise of American Civilization*, vol. I (New York: Macmillian, 1927), p. 775.
9. On sympathy in Hawthorne see Gordon Hutner, *Secrets and Sympathy: Forms of Disclosure in Hawthorne's Novels* (Athens: University of Georgia Press, 1988) and Edgar Dryden, *Nathaniel Hawthorne: The Poetics of Enchantment* (Ithaca, NY: Cornell University Press, 1977).
10. David Leverenz provides an excellent analysis of the tension between the narrator's perspective and that of the dramatic action in "Mrs. Hawthorne's Headache: Reading *The Scarlet Letter*," *Nineteenth-Century Fiction* 37 (1983): 552–75.
11. T. Walter Herbert, *Dearest Beloved: The Hawthornes and the Making of the Middle-Class Family* (Berkeley: University of California Press, 1993), p. 187.
12. Puritans in fact allowed divorce.
13. For Marcuse see *Eros and Civilization: A Philosophical Inquiry into Freud* (1955; New York: Random House, 1962). My use of Marcuse is indebted to Robert Milder. But whereas Milder argues that "The crux of Hawthorne's problem in *The Scarlet Letter* – and consequently our own reading of it – is that he could envision no social or moral space between the repressiveness of Puritan Boston

and the wildness of the forest," I argue that he conceives of such a space in the nascent formation of a relatively independent civil society. Robert Milder, "*The Scarlet Letter* and its Discontents," *Nathaniel Hawthorne Review* 22 (1996): 9–25, p. 20.

14. Arthur Cleveland Coxe, "The Writings of Hawthorne," *Church and Ecclesiastical Register*. Rpt. in John L. Idol, Jr. and Buford Jones, eds., *Nathaniel Hawthorne: The Contemporary Reviews* (New York: Cambridge University Press, 1995), pp. 149–51.

15. Herbert, *Dearest Beloved*, p. 111.

16. See Claire McEachern, *"This England": Literature and the Nation, 1590–1612*, (Cambridge: Cambridge University Press, 1996).

17. See Linda K. Kerber, *No Constitutional Right "to Be Ladies." Women and the Obligations of Citizenship* (New York: Hill and Wang, 1998), p. 13, and Mary Beth Norton, *Founding Mothers & Fathers: Gendered Power and the Forming of American Society* (New York: Knopf, 1996).

18. Merril D. Smith, *Breaking the Bonds, Marital Discord in Pennsylvania, 1730–1830* (New York: New York University Press, 1991), p. 51.

19. Quoted in Michael Grossberg, *A Judgment for Solomon: The D'Hauteville Case and Legal Experience in Antebellum America* (New York: Cambridge University Press, 1996), p. 51.

20. See *ibid*.

21. "Young Goodman Brown," *Hawthorne: Tales and Sketches* (New York: The Library of America, 1996), p. 281.

22. Robert M. Ireland, "The Libertine Must Die: Sexual Dishonour and the Unwritten Law in the Nineteenth-Century United States," *Journal of Social History* 23 (1989): 32. For more on cases involving the "unwritten law," see Ireland, "Insanity and the Unwritten Law," *American Journal of Legal History* 32 (1988): 157–72; Melissa J. Ganz, "Wicked Women and Veiled Ladies: Gendered Narratives of the McFarland-Richardson Tragedy," *Yale Journal of Law and Feminism* 9 (1997): 255–303; and Hendrik Hartog, "Lawyering Husbands' Rights, and 'the Unwritten Law' in Nineteenth-Century America," *Journal of American History* 84 (1997): 67–96.

23. Michael T. Gilmore, "Hawthorne and the Making of the Middle Class," in Christoph K. Lohman, ed., *Discovering Difference* (Bloomington: Indiana University Press, 1993), p. 93, and D. H. Lawrence, *Studies in Classic American Literature* (rpt. Garden City, NY: Doubleday, 1951).

24. Jeremy D. Weinstein, "Adultery, Law, and the State: A History," *Hastings Law Journal* 38 (1986): 225.

25. Carolyn B. Ramsey, "Sex and Social Order: The Selective Enforcement of Colonial American Adultery Laws in the English Context," *Yale Journal of Law and the Humanities* 10 (1998): 202–07.

26. Herbert, *Dearest Beloved*, p. 112.

27. *Ibid*., p. 201.

28. See Michael J. Colacurcio's excellent reading of this scene in " 'The Woman's Own Choice': Sex, Metaphor, and the Puritan 'Sources' of *The Scarlet Letter*," in *Doctrine and Difference* (New York: Routledge, 1997), pp. 205–28.

29. Arac, "The Politics of *The Scarlet Letter*," p. 252.

30. *Ibid*., p. 251.

31. Bercovitch, *The Office of "The Scarlet Letter,"* pp. 89, 88.
32. In an age in which, for many, liberalism has become the "L-word," Bercovitch's claim that liberalism is *the* "American Ideology" might seem strange. But Bercovitch is using the term in a broader sense. He is using it much as Lionel Trilling did when he argued that in the United States "liberalism is not only the dominant but even the sole intellectual tradition." *The Liberal Imagination* (New York: Viking Press, 1950), p. ix. A gloss on both Bercovitch's and Trilling's use of liberalism comes in a 1946 *Life* magazine editorial. Contrasting liberalism to socialism on the one hand and conservatism on the other, the editorial cites three liberal principles: (1) that government needs to acknowledge some outside limit to its own power; (2) that good ends never justify dubious means; and (3) that no political system – even those based on rationality – can offer a perfect answer. Liberalism, as a result, demands endless compromise in politics at the same time that "no man can be a liberal who does not believe that faith and morals are independent of politics, more important than politics and essential to political liberty." "What Is Liberalism?," *Life* 5.20 (7 January 1946): 26.
33. Berlant, *The Anatomy of National Fantasy*, p. 154.
34. *Ibid.*, p. 156. Berlant's understanding of Hester's female antinomian energies is indebted to Colacurcio, who over three decades ago wrote a groundbreaking essay comparing Hester to Ann Hutchinson that warned of the danger of turning "away from the richness and particularity of Hester's own love story." "Footsteps of Ann Hutchinson: The Context of *The Scarlet Letter*," *ELH* 39 (1972): 461.
35. Berlant, *The Anatomy of National Fantasy*, p. 98.
36. Quotation from Jean Cohen and Andrew Arato, *Civil Society and Political Theory* (Cambridge, MA: MIT Press, 1992), p. ix. Informed by events in the former Soviet bloc in 1989 where the economic sphere was controlled by the state, this and other current definitions do not include the economic in civil society as did Adam Smith, Adam Ferguson, and Georg Wilhelm Friedrich Hegel. For more on civil society in *The Scarlet Letter* see Brook Thomas, "Citizen Hester: *The Scarlet Letter* as Civic Myth," *American Literary History* 13 (2001): 181–211.
37. Michael Walzer, "Introduction," in Walzer, ed., *Toward a Global Civil Society* (Providence, RI: Berghahn Books, 1995), p. 1.
38. On the carnival scenes in *The Marble Faun* see Robert Levine, " 'Antebellum Rome' in *The Marble Faun*," *American Literary History* 2 (1990): 19–38.
39. Walzer, "The Concept of Civil Society," in *Toward a Global Civil Society*, p. 24.
40. Lionel Trilling, "Our Hawthorne," in Roy Harvey Pearce, ed., *Hawthorne Centenary Essays* (Columbus: Ohio State University Press, 1964), pp. 429–58.
41. Arthur M. Schlesinger, Jr., *The Vital Center: The Politics of Freedom* (Boston: Houghton Mifflin, 1949), pp. 38, 165, 38, 161, and 170.
42. From today's perspective Hawthorne clearly committed a major error in discrimination when he wrote a friend in July 1851: "I have not, as you suggest, the slightest sympathy for the slaves; or, at least, not half so much as for the laboring whites, who, I believe, as a general thing, are ten times worse off than the southern negros [sic]" (*Letters*, XVI: 456). Despite that alignment of sympathies, I disagree with Eric Cheyfitz's argument that Hawthorne's attitude on slavery should make us stop reading his works. And not simply because in the same

letter Hawthorne indicates that he signed a Free-Soil document on the new Fugitive Slave Law or that once Civil War broke out Hawthorne imagined "fighting for the annihilation of slavery" and "future citizenship" for blacks as the lone compelling reason to continue the war (*Letters*, XVIII: 381). See Eric Cheyfitz, "The Irresistibleness of Great Literature: Reconstructing Hawthorne's Politics," *American Literary History* 6, 3 (1994): 539–58.

9

CHRISTOPHER CASTIGLIA

The marvelous queer interiors of
The House of the Seven Gables

"Marvelous"

The House of the Seven Gables is obsessed with law. In his preface, setting
out the distinction between novels and romances, Hawthorne associates the
former with realism, in which imagination, denied the possibility of fanciful transformation, becomes enslaved to "the probable and ordinary course
of man's existence." Romance, on the contrary, need not "rigidly subject
itself to laws," but, demonstrating "a very minute feeling" for "the possible," is able "to mingle the Marvelous" (II: 1) with the probable events of
everyday life. "Law" functions here for Hawthorne on several levels. Most
immediately, he means "convention," the things "normal" people expect to
happen in a "typical" day, life lived, not as a possibility for invention, but
within the comfort of predictable pattern. Yet Hawthorne also attaches convention to more recognizable legal constructs, such as contracts: the preface itself takes on a contractual tone, establishing the terms that, if readers agree to them, will enable the romance to be understood and enjoyed.
Hawthorne also invokes the legal protection of property, "by laying up a
street that infringes upon nobody's private rights, and appropriating a lot of
land which had no visible owner, and building a house of materials long in use
for constructing castles in the air" (II: 3).[1] In the preface, then, Hawthorne
attaches the juridical functions of law (the contractual protection of property rights) to the conventions of everyday life (the predictable life-patterns
carried out, presumably, within the privately owned home), both laws represented in the plot by the officious, grasping, and literal-minded lawyer, Jaffrey
Pyncheon.[2]

In *The House of the Seven Gables*, law is not only multiform, but undergoes a historical change over the course of the narrative. Initially, law works
upon the outward appearance of things, on the evidentiary basis of which it
names a "truth" that will ultimately solve any apparent mystery. By the end
of the novel, however, truth resides, not on the outside of things, but in the

186

inner spaces of personality, character, and psyche. As criminality becomes manifest, not in disruptive or violent actions, but in pathologized emotions, affections, and desires, the law, too, takes an inner turn, insisting upon inner orders that are the purview, not of harsh jurists like Judge Pyncheon, but of benevolent reformers like Holgrave, who, at the novel's conclusion, replaces the Judge as the patriarchal head of the House of the Seven Gables. This transfer of power, which I address in the next section of the chapter, symbolizes the triumph, in the decades just before Hawthorne wrote *The House of the Seven Gables*, of reform movements that targeted inner characters over the coercive mandates of external law.

Hawthorne's principal interest – his sympathy, as he might say – is not with the law or its representatives but with those outside the law. Although he claims that the writer of romances "can hardly be said . . . to commit a literary crime" (II: 1), the fate of those who *are* judged to have broken the law – whether the juridical law of private property, the external law of social convention, or the inner law of orderly emotion and proper character – is at the center of *The House of the Seven Gables*. Hawthorne presents such characters as "queer," not in the twentieth-century sense of "homosexual" (although the desires of almost all of these characters fall outside the realm of conventional heterosexuality), but rather in the sense of "deviant." The queer characters of Hawthorne's romance – and almost all the characters are described, at some moment, as queer, although some (Hepzibah, Clifford, Uncle Venner) more consistently than others – deviate not by breaking the law (Clifford has been wrongly imprisoned for murdering his uncle), but by virtue of their excessive and inscrutable emotions, their melancholic devotion to the past, their antisocial reclusiveness, even their lack of control over bodily functions (Jaffrey's "queer and awkward ingurgulation" [II: 124], Hepzibah's near-sighted frown). While authoritative legal and medical theories of the nineteenth century would characterize these behaviors and traits as pathological, predicting their culmination in criminality, misery, illness, and death, they enable Hawthorne's characters to sustain hopes and aspirations, however impossible or ill-fated. The mechanisms that allow characters to maintain hope – as he says in describing the romance as a genre, to mingle the marvelous with the mundane – become the basis of what I would call "queer interiority" in the novel, a deviation from the public and inner orders mandated by law. As we will see, queer interiority allows a different form of sociability – what Richard Millington calls "the democratization of the tragic" – to emerge in *The House of the Seven Gables*.[3]

Phrenology, purporting to read bumps on the head as signs of inner character traits such as one's propensity to marry for life, to labor manually, or to dutifully serve one's country, exemplifies the inward turn I am describing in nineteenth-century America. Although we would recognize these traits as outgrowths of social conditioning rather than of biological determination, phrenology insisted on their generation from within the interior of one's body and one's character. If one deviated from virtue – by masturbating, philandering, shirking one's work or one's civic duty – one was not just criminal, but ill, making the regulation of character not coercive, but benevolent (instilling "health" among the citizenry). The social order phrenology imagined therefore came to seem natural, serving the interests of God, not men. At the same time, phrenology opened up the possibility for the very queer excesses it sought to regulate, excesses such as the one Hawthorne places at the heart of romance. In phrenology handbooks, "marvelousness" names the power to see what is not visible in the external world, like ghosts and phantoms (terms Hawthorne frequently uses to describe the existence of his queer characters), but also works of imagination that, like the soap-bubbles Clifford delights in blowing from an upper window of the House, create "Little, impalpable worlds . . . with the big world depicted, in hues bright as imagination, on the northing of their surface" (II: 171). The ability to make "brilliant fantasies" (II: 171) out of nothing might well appear delusional, yet Hawthorne makes it essential to the processes both of art-making and of hopeful world-making.

At the same time, such marvelous creations are also critiques, renderings of the "big world" that, through distortion, show its limitations and cruelties. As such, they challenge the operations of law that normalize only those modes of life that serve the interests of private property and orderly public life. Little wonder, then, that Judge Pyncheon "prided himself on eschewing all airy matter and never mistaking a shadow for a substance" (II: 118). The marvelous – growing from the queer interiors of those who would deviate from normalcy so as to imagine new social configurations, new aspirations, and new democratic interactions – becomes the Other, even the enemy, of the law. When phrenologists analyzed the craniums of the Great Men of the Republic (John Quincy Adams, Daniel Webster, Andrew Jackson), using portraits, death masks, and busts, they found them rich in Enlightenment virtues that make public order possible: common sense, reason, civic responsibility, self-control. Yet to a man, these men were lacking in one trait: marvelousness. What makes them – and the legal structure through which they rule – less than marvelous is their faith in order over excess, of evidence over fantasy, of calculation over imagination. Such hierarchical orderings allowed them to stabilize the establishment and generational perpetuation of private property.[4] Yet the law failed to contain invention, which arises perpetually in *The House of the Seven Gables* to challenge the "common sense" of antebellum America and the rules of property it upheld (in fact, one of the earliest meanings of "queer" is, as Will Fisher has shown, "counterfeit" or "swindle," a betrayal of the orderly transmission of property or economic value).[5] Marvelous hope persists, turning the charge of deviance against those advocates of the law who, like passers-by on Pyncheon Street, delight in bursting bubbles, "perversely gratified, no doubt, when the bubble, with all its pictured earth and sky scene, vanished as if it had never been" (II: 171). But it never vanishes entirely, not while the stuff of romance asserts its marvelous presence, lurking in the queer interiors of *The House of the Seven Gables*. "So much of mankind's varied experience had passed there – so much had been suffered, and something, too, enjoyed – that the very timbers were oozy," Hawthorne writes of the house, "as with the moisture of a heart. It was itself like a great human heart, with a life of its own, and full of rich and sombre reminiscences" (II: 27). Registering the human experiences that make predictable patterns seem flat and inexpressive, the House of the Seven Gables becomes, like the characters who inhabit it, the guardian of queer interiority. Despite the law's desire to make inner life public and orderly, the house always "had secrets to keep" (II: 27).

Outside/in

One of the oddest features of the plot of *The House of the Seven Gables* is that, over two centuries, with the outcome so doubtful, the Pyncheons go on searching for the deed that they believe will give them legal right to Waldo County in Maine; equally bizarre is the fact that the Maule descendants go on actively frustrating the Pyncheons' efforts to find that deed, despite the fact that Waldo County has long since been farmed out, making the Pyncheons' expectation of a baronic acquisition quixotic, to say the least. Perhaps representatives of both families go on with their customary choreography – the Maules tantalizing the Pyncheons with further mystery, the Pyncheons responding with frenzied study of dubious evidence – because what both parties gain from this dance is more important to them than the land itself. What this dynamic sustains – apart from the drive for material gain – is the legitimacy of law itself, which similarly rests on the dialectic of evidence and mystery, of scrutiny and speculation. Despite their different positions in relation to the law (the Pyncheons generally acting as judges while the Maules serve repeatedly as criminals), both families profit from the legitimacy of law. Both families are wedded to their right to inheritance – of real estate on the part of the Pyncheons, of "secrets" on the part of the Maules – that requites the legal transmission of property across death and generation. The children of both families – Phoebe Pyncheon and Holgrave (a Maule in disguise) – can therefore peacefully wed at the conclusion of the novel.

Each family justifying the other's existence through time, the Pyncheons and the Maules create between them a legal world-view – a cosmic search after evidence that will solve timeless and metaphysical "crimes" – that neither family has an interest in bringing to an end.

Hawthorne seems to invite the readers of *The House of the Seven Gables* to share this legalistic world-view, tantalizing us with the possibility of penetrating the secrets of the novel just as the townspeople gaze upon the forbidding exterior of the ancient Pyncheon homestead, which seems to promise so much mystery and musky malevolence within. From the beginning, readers are invited to identify with a host of characters trying to solve some mystery. The formidable Jaffrey Pyncheon seeks to discover the ancient deed, hidden now for almost two centuries. His infirm cousin, Clifford Pyncheon, recently released from prison, strives, like a Transcendental esthete, to discover Ideal Beauty beneath the moth-eaten relics of his ancestral home. Sunny, young Phoebe Pyncheon, come from the country to care for her elderly relatives, attempts to uncover the source of their profound melancholy. Perhaps most of all, Holgrave, a boarder in the Pyncheon home, as a daguerreotypist seeks to bring forth the inner character of his sitters through their posed exteriors, as a mesmerist seeks to bring forth historical secrets repressed in the psyches of his impressionable clients, as a suitor seeks to elicit a confession that Phoebe Pyncheon returns his affection, and as a Fourierian reformer attempts to bring forth the socialistic world order only barely obscured by the materialistic scramblings of the modern age. Around these characters struggling to see what lies just inside (history, the body, crass materiality, inscrutable sadness), we are invited, like the townspeople who continually hover around the Pyncheon home, gossiping about the centuries of strange goings-on within, to muse on the eternal mystery of what makes this odd family tick. It is important to note, though, that not everyone is looking in the same place for the evidence. Some believe the outsides of things are more telling; others look inward.

The faith that external signs will lead to the full revelation of Truth is most essential to the legal structure represented by Judge Pyncheon, one of those "ordinary men to whom forms are of paramount importance" (II: 229). Having arranged "clues" so as to frame his cousin Clifford, who will otherwise inherit the family fortune Jaffrey covets, Judge Pyncheon knows how much the law relies on external signs. His faith that external "facts" will lead, invariably, to hidden "meaning" leads Judge Pyncheon not only to trust in the evidentiary logic he manipulates to Clifford's detriment, but also to his conviction that the deed to the Maine lands, if discovered, will once and for all resolve the Pyncheons' dispute over the rightful ownership of the land. Contracts – which themselves take signatures as signs of good character and good faith – are the lawyer's stock-in-trade, and by insisting that deeds can reverse the course of history, clearing land long settled by independent farmers and returning the Pyncheons to an aristocratic grandeur now democratically distasteful, Judge Pyncheon rationalizes as well his Franklinesque trust that an outward show of good character will disguise a host of inner blemishes.

Such external systems of interpretation support, in turn, a normative social order based upon – and further promoting the interests of – wealth and property. Of the Judge, Hawthorne writes: "you could feel just as certain that he was opulent, as if he had exhibited his bank account" (II: 57). So insistently does the Judge wear his character – and his wealth, the two being one and the same – on his sleeve, that Hawthorne quips, "He would have made a good and massive portrait" (II: 57). Oddly, the Judge's faith in externals and the orders they uphold is seconded by a character with apparently less to gain from that faith, one who shrinks from the Judge at their first meeting: his cousin Phoebe, described by Hawthorne as: "so orderly and so obedient to common rules" (II: 68). "She shocked no canon of taste," Hawthorne insists; "she was admirably in keeping with herself, and never jarred against surrounding circumstances" (II: 80). At the same time, Phoebe's faith that all is what it seems produces its supplemental excess in the form of nagging doubts and suspicions. Watching the Judge in action, Phoebe begins to speculate "whether judges, clergymen, and other characters of that eminent stamp and respectability, could really, in any single instance, be otherwise than just and upright men. A doubt of this nature," Hawthorne concludes, "has a most disturbing influence, and, if shown to be a fact, comes with a fearful and startling effect on minds of the trim, orderly, and limit-loving class" (II: 131). "But Phoebe, in order to keep the universe in its old place, was fain to smother, in some degree, her own intuitions as to Judge Pyncheon's character" (II: 131–32), Hawthorne assures his readers. In repressing her own "intuitions," however, Phoebe, who previously prides herself on the utter superficiality of her character, becomes possessed of an unconscious, a broody interiority that makes her subject to the inward-looking law represented by Holgrave, but that also enables her sympathetic attachment to her dark and mysterious cousins.

The Judge, too, is not without his interiority, so much so, in fact, that he makes his outward-gazing law obsolete. Jaffrey not only embodies the shift in law from jurisprudence to social convention, as a reformed rake he also demonstrates the potential rewards for reshaping one's private vices along the lines of representative public virtue. The Judge operates through the public revelation of private shame (the same authority Hawthorne critiques in *The Scarlet Letter*):

"My dear Cousin," said Judge Pyncheon, with a quietude which he had the power of making more formidable than any violence, "since your brother's return, I have taken the precaution (a highly proper one in the near kinsman and natural guardian of an individual so situated) to have his deportment and habits constantly and carefully overlooked. Your neighbors have been eye-witnesses to whatever has passed in the garden. The butcher, the baker, the fish-monger, some of the customers of your shop, and many a prying old woman, have told me several of the scenes of your interior." (II: 237)

The Judge functions as a transition between punishment (the imposition of physical force) and discipline (the regulation of "interior" behaviors through the benevolent discourses of health).[6] Having released Clifford from the constraint of the jail, the Judge threatens to confine him, "probably for the remainder of his life, in a public asylum for persons in his unfortunate state of mind" (II: 236). In doing so, he renders his own juridical control over external actions and signs superfluous, replaced, now, by the institutional regulation of private character and inner states.

Hawthorne challenges both forms of regulation, however, by repeatedly showing outward things to be highly unpredictable, unreliable, and manipulatable markers of hidden depths. What Hawthorne states of the Pyncheons' efforts to discover the hidden deed – "Some connecting link had slipt out of the evidence, and could not anywhere be found" (II: 18) – is equally applicable to every effort in the novel to discover truth through external signs. Not only does the evidence leading to the possession of the Maine lands remain elusive, the material existence of the land itself eludes its external representation, "the natural history of the region being as little known as its geography, which was put down so fantastically awry" (II: 33). The "fantastic" (we might say the "marvelous") here queers the legitimate possession of land, just as Hawthorne's romance satirizes the quest for that possession. "There is something so massive, stable, and almost irresistibly imposing, in the exterior presentment of established rank and great possession," Hawthorne writes, "that their very existence seems to give them a right to exist, at least, so excellent a counterfeit of right, that few poor and humble men have moral force enough to question it, even in their secret mind" (II: 25). Showing externals to be, automatically, their own counterfeits, Hawthorne queers property rights – and the external evidence that establishes them – beyond any Pyncheon's power to reclaim.

Hawthorne turns the Judge's body itself into a counterfeit, gleefully needling Jaffrey for his smile, "the sultry, dog-day heat, as it were, of benevolence, which the excellent man diffused out of his great heart into the surrounding atmosphere, – very much like a serpent, which, as a preliminary to fascination, is said to fill the air with his peculiar odor" (II: 119). The snake in this democratic garden is precisely the counterfeit cheer bestowed so promiscuously upon the people, highborn and low, that it becomes a hollow token of fellow-feeling, a parody of the democratic equality of the pursuit of happiness bestowed by the ur-contract, the Constitution. Denying the truth-value of external symbols, Hawthorne uses legal language to condemn the Judge, whose smile "afforded very little evidence of that genuine benignity of soul, whereof it purported to be the outward reflection" (II: 116). The Judge's smile becomes, not what it purports to be on the surface, but the sign of hidden greed and guilt: "As is customary with the rich when they aim at the honors of a republic, he apologized, as it were, to the people, for his wealth, property, and elevated station, by a free and hearty manner towards those who knew him" (II: 130).

The original sin visited on the contemporary inhabitants of the House of the Seven Gables – Colonel Pyncheon's conviction of Matthew Maule as a witch, resulting in the judge's acquisition of Maule's land holdings – highlights from the beginning the abuses of juridical evidence, arising from a naïve faith that things are as they appear. This originary crime sets in play a tradition of disguise, counterfeit, and swindle, of which judges – the adjudicators of the law – are the worst perpetrators. The solution, for Hawthorne, is not a more truthful alignment of surface and depth, of evidence and criminal "truth," but rather an awareness that surfaces signify only other surfaces: the portrait of Colonel Pyncheon does not give way to the historical personage, but to another text – the deed to the lands in Maine – which, in turn, does not materialize into baronial wealth, but simply into the narrative of the novel itself. Unable to recognize that they inevitably live within a web of surfaces, the characters are driven nearly mad in their desires to break the shell of external signs to reach the kernel of truth within – a process the novel repeatedly figures as "possession." Hawthorne makes this sadistically clear in one of the most bizarre chapters in the novel, "Governor Pyncheon," which describes, in excruciating detail, the atmosphere surrounding Jaffrey's corpse as it sits, undiscovered, in the abandoned house. As it circles the body, facetiously giving it various metaphoric casts and allegorical significances, the narrative voice's macabre delight highlights the materiality of death, rendered ironic by the fact that the Judge, now a lifeless symbol, made his life by insisting upon his power to make externals speak their "truth." In killing off "Governor" Pyncheon, Hawthorne kills off as well the legitimacy of external order over citizens who are more than juridical subjects, and who therefore continually exceed the law's ability to name them in ways that produce shame and guilt for the named, and power and profit for the namer. Judge Pyncheon, "seldom or never looking inward" but "resolutely taking his idea of himself from what purports to be his image as reflected in the mirror of public opinion" (II: 232), makes himself obsolete, capable of producing only "a counterfeit of right" (II: 25).

Having killed off the Judge, however, Hawthorne's trouble with the law begins anew. In representing the Judge's hypocrisy, his "inward criminality" (II: 312) that negates his public self-regulation, Hawthorne orients the reader toward a presumably more recognizably "natural" law based not on external convention but on the inner order of what Harriet Beecher Stowe called "right feeling." Early in the novel, the innocent Phoebe has just learned that the daguerreotypist, Holgrave, associates with "reformers, temperance-lecturers, and all manner of cross-looking philanthropists" (II: 84). " 'But if Mr. Holgrave is a lawless person!' remonstrated Phoebe, a part of whose essence it was, to keep within the limits of law. 'Oh,' said Hepzibah carelessly – for, formal as she was, still, in her life's experience, she had gnashed her teeth against human law – 'I suppose he has a law of his own' " (II: 85). Although both women speak of law, neither refers to the legal documents, deeds, and titles typically associated with jurisprudence. Rather, Phoebe means outward conventions, while Hepzibah understands that Holgrave, as a reformer, has an *inner* law, regulating not public behaviors but "deep" emotions (the "confession" he elicits is not of criminal acts, but of love). While Phoebe believes firmly in the mutual dependence of (outward) law and order, Holgrave, who challenges conventions and "acknowledge[s] no law" (II: 84), can remain, insofar as he insists on the inner consistency of "identity" (II: 177), an "orderly young man" (II: 84). If Phoebe's moral system requires the subordination of private anomaly to public order through identification with established norms, Holgrave's renders public rituals of conformity obsolete, since his self-regulating affects internalize the public orders maintained, in Jaffrey's law, by external regulation and censure. Depicting the transformations of "law" from strictures to the regulation of interior states, *The House of the Seven Gables* reveals how civil apparatuses such as domesticity and reform (embodied in the ultimate marriage of Phoebe and Holgrave) led citizens to misrecognize "the social" as an expression of individual and private feeling rather than as a function of labor and profit. In return for their self-regulations, citizens are promised an illusory control, not over the law, but over *the law written in their own natures*.

In addition to being a reformer, Holgrave is a daguerreotypist, a profession that allows him to profit by bringing out his sitters' inner selves: "There is a wonderful insight in heaven's broad and simple sunshine. While we give it credit only for depicting the merest surface, it actually brings out the secret character with a truth that no painter would ever venture upon, even could he detect it" (II: 91). As a daguerreotypist, Holgrave continues the mesmeric tradition of his Maule ancestors, whose "family eye was said to possess strange powers," including that "of exercising an influence over people's dreams" (II: 26). The Maules' power of human interiority is most clear in the narrative of Alice Pyncheon, brought first to humiliating servitude and finally to death by the Maules' mesmeric control over the affective dialectic of desire and shame. Just as Matthew Maule brings forth the insecurity and guilt lurking behind Alice Pyncheon's haughty exterior, so the inner "truth" behind generations of Pyncheon counterfeits is brought forth when the Maules work their magic on the family well, making "its inner region all alive with the departed Pyncheons; not as they had shown themselves to the world, nor in their better and happier hours, but as doing over again some deed or sin, or in the crisis of life's bitter sorrow" (II: 21). While the contemporary Maule, Holgrave, shuns such fabulous displays in favor of technological skill, he too strategically exhorts confessions of affective states. At the conclusion of the novel, Holgrave cements his place as the head of the Pyncheon family by looking into Phoebe and calling forth her feelings: " 'You look into my heart,' replied she, letting her eyes droop. 'You know I love you!' " (II: 307).

When Holgrave gains Phoebe's confession of love and thereby her hand in marriage, the law of inner life produces the commercial success that neither the law of reputation nor legal deeds gained for the Maule descendants. This outcome is hardly surprising, since throughout the romance Holgrave repeatedly advocates the same work ethic one might expect to hear from the Judge. When Hepzibah, forced to open a cent-shop to earn a living, bemoans her fate to Holgrave, the young reformer romanticizes effort for its own sake, not in relation to payoffs in profit or privilege, but of health and civic union: "Henceforth, you will at least have the sense of healthy and natural effort for a purpose, and of lending your strength – be it great or small – to the united struggle of mankind" (II: 45). Hawthorne facetiously echoes this sentiment soon thereafter, attributing labor-for-its-own-sake not just to nature, but to God: "As a general rule," he writes, "Providence seldom vouchsafes to mortals any more than just that degree of encouragement, which suffices to keep them at a reasonable full exertion of their powers" (II: 52). Working not because they fear public scorn but because it is what their healthy nature requires, not for profit but for the inner sense of God's endorsement, the inner law Holgrave represents proves an even more effective force for social order than the external one endorsed by the Judge, since the order Holgrave represents is policed by each citizen in his or her own body. The passing of the law from Jaffrey to Holgrave does not represent an idealized release from the law's repressive coercion, then; "the authorian impulse is not dead," as Millington notes, "but, in analogy to the marketplace, it is becoming more widely distributed."[7] Naturally, then, the Judge's profits pass to the daguerreotypist.

While Holgrave's insistence on inner truth apparently supplants the Judge's reliance on external conventions, Hawthorne suggests the two men are more similar than they initially appear: while Holgrave's conversation with Phoebe "had generally been playful, the impression left on her mind was one of gravity, and, except as his youth modified it, almost sternness" (II: 94). For all his talk about social progress, furthermore, Holgrave does as little to improve the material conditions of the poor as does the Judge, preferring not "to help or hinder; but to look on, to analyze, to explain matters to myself" (II: 216). Hawthorne suggests that reform and conservativism, both serving the interests of middle-class social order, are close kin: "I have a presentiment," Holgrave tells Phoebe, "that, hereafter, it will be my lot to set out trees, to make fences – perhaps, even, in due time, to build a house for another generation – in a word, to conform myself to laws, and the peaceful practice of society" (II: 307). "You find me a conservative already!" (II: 315), Holgrave happily declares.

The shift from outward to inner law has several effects in American culture, as *The House of the Seven Gables* demonstrates. Inner law makes the regulation of personal emotion and desire appear not coercive or manipulative but benevolent and self-initiated, transforming the experience of the "social" in ways that left citizens isolated and without an embodied sense of shared public interest. Inner law, therefore, allows questions properly understood in relation to public institutions to detach from that base, wandering in the citizen's body and beyond it in ways that serve an increasingly mobile economy already national and quickly becoming global. But as Hawthorne suggests by having the "secret character" of the House of the Seven Gables become the subject of gossip among neighbors, tradesmen, and so on, inner life is not located in the interior at all, but is the effect of a shared discourse of order seemingly divested of the very publicity that is its operational core. Hence, at the conclusion of the novel, the House of the Seven Gables can be abandoned, its interiority produced anew in the Pyncheon estate.

Yet some mysteries – some inner riddles – are never "solved" through the public confession of emotional "truth." Why does Phoebe, initially so skeptical about Holgrave, suddenly come to love him? Why does Judge Pyncheon, who surely recognizes the futility of his hope to yet claim the Maine lands, continue to hunt the deed? What is the nature of Hepzibah's attachment to Clifford? These questions – and others that have kept critics coming back to this novel decade after decade – attest to the inability of inner law to ever resolve the unruly, disruptive, and abstruse affective life of citizens into neat and regulated orders. It is in those spaces of *dis*order that the House of the

Seven Gables, and the romance that is its namesake, maintains its secrets and its allure. In those marvelous spaces, as well, its queerness flourishes.

Queers

What does it mean to say that there are "queers" in *The House of the Seven Gables*?

Hawthorne's romance, to be sure, offers glimpses of what, by the late nineteenth century, would emerge as "homosexual identities." Hepzibah, who refuses to attend church, becoming, in her isolation, a comically bad housewife and an old maid in whom "the love of children had never been quickened" (II: 39), falls far outside nineteenth-century conventions of femininity, which rested on piety and domestic nurturance. If Hepzibah is a "bad" woman, Clifford's "beautiful infirmity of character" (II: 60) comes from his being *too* feminine, as Hepzibah acknowledges in claiming that the town "persecuted his mother in him!" (II: 60). An "old bachelor" of "an eccentric and melancholy turn of mind" (II: 22), possessed of "gentle and voluptuous emotion" (II: 32), Clifford, in his attraction to beauty, his obsession with youth, and his "womanly" sensibilities, is, as Neill Matheson argues, a proto-Wildean aesthete.[8] Insofar as modern homosexual identity gained public intelligibility as an inversion of Victorian gender roles, Clifford and Hepzibah, refusing to hold to their "proper" genders, are arguably among American literature's first homosexual characters.

My interest, though, is not in locating the characters' queerness in sexual identity, since it is precisely their status as fakes, counterfeits, bad copies – subjects who do not embody "natural" identities and whose emotional excesses defy inner order – that makes the characters "queer." I use "queer" here to suggest opacities or excesses within the self that suggest that *all* identities are in essence counterfeits. Judith Butler argues that identity, far from being a static essence that emerges *out from* a person's inner being, is in fact a series of repeated stagings (what Butler calls "performatives") of identity-conventions *on* the body.[9] Performatives posit an original – the "essence" of "who one *really* is" – of which, Butler contends, subjects are always judged to be incomplete or inadequate reproductions. The suspicion that one has not manifested completely the truth of one's identity drives the compulsive enactment of what can never be gotten right: the manifestation, as identity, of an inner truth that, in the end, is never inner at all, but exists in a discursive – and hence social – realm that changes historically, as, therefore, will the "identities" it produces.[10] Phoebe Pyncheon, for instance, in her efforts to align herself perfectly with social norms, recognizes implicitly that her "identity" is a matter of convention, not, as she frequently asserts, of innate "character." At the same time, her awareness of the distance – the never entirely bridgeable gap – between "conventions" and the "self" striving to correlate herself with those conventions suggests that Phoebe will repeatedly experience failure. At the same time that Phoebe's efforts to embody convention leave her at a loss (vulnerable to the reformer, Holgrave), those same efforts generate the illusion that identities exist, as originals, prior to the subject's efforts to achieve them. Although Phoebe asserts that conventions have the social force of law, one might well ask who, in her world, lives the "normal" life she strives for? Only her assertions that conventions exist and must be adhered to allow those "laws," or the conventions they supposedly govern, to exist.

Phoebe, to a lesser degree than Clifford and Hepzibah but in ways that allow her to sympathize with them, finds herself a not-quite Pyncheon, a bad copy of the family essence. The reiterative performance of the tense non-alignment of ordinals and (bad) copies is a central plot structure of *The House of the Seven Gables*, played out in repeated ruptures between inheritance and representation. All through the romance, characters comment on the degree to which others do or do not look like "real" Pyncheons. The ur-Pyncheon, in these evaluations, is the founder of the House of the Seven Gables, Colonel Pyncheon, whose disapproving face presides over the inevitable failure of his descendants to measure up to the Pyncheon essence. Hepzibah scowls a bit like her ancestor, but of course she is a woman. Clifford is also too much of a woman, favoring his mother to a degree that leads Hepzibah to exclaim, "He never was a Pyncheon!" (ii: 60). Jaffrey claims to see a family resemblance in Phoebe's mouth, but she too resembles her mother too much to really be one of the clan (mothers repeatedly get blamed for disrupting identity, and hence inheritance, in the novel). Even Jaffrey, who most resembles his ancestor, has gesturally transformed his appearance in ways his Puritan forefather would condemn (his too-benevolent smile, for instance, would ill suit the persecutor of witches). Each descendent, in short, is deemed a bad copy of the ancestral original. Yet the determinations of successful or failed "identity" (their identity as Pyncheons) is made through comparison, not with the original ancestor, but with his portrait, itself an interpretation shaped by historically changeable aesthetic conventions. The portrait, that is, is necessarily a counterfeit of its necessarily absent original. It is not coincidental that the deed to the Maine lands, obtained through a foundational act of deception, is hidden behind the portrait; Hawthorne thereby suggests (with his usual allegorical finesse) that behind the assertion of origins one will always find a counterfeit, a false deed. It is precisely identity's status as counterfeit that must be hidden if what is outside (convention) is to appear as if coming from within, for identification to be misunderstood as identity. The Pyncheons' claim to social superiority rests on the assertion of undeviated and un*mediated* inheritance, that all subsequent Pyncheons, being the true reflections of the Pyncheon original, are entitled to the same property willed through a direct line of succession (a line Jaffrey, by framing Clifford and hence circumventing his uncle's will, has already undermined). If the generational transmission of property (including one's principal property, "identity") rests on the truthful representation of a representation, a counterfeit of a fake, however, then the law of inheritance is as deceptive as the Colonel's justice. Put another way, if the original was already a fake, how can Hepzibah and Clifford possibly be bad copies, failed Pyncheons?

That question becomes unaskable – indeed, unthinkable – in the world of the romance precisely because of the social and *legal* authority of those who claim the privilege of sanctioned identity. In declaring his relatives bad copies, the Judge attempts to make them socially invisible, disappeared behind the obscuring walls of the family home. He thereby enacts the form of oppression Butler writes of, working "not merely through acts of overt prohibition, but covertly, through the constitution of viable subjects and through the corollary constitution of a domain of unviable (un)subjects – *abjects*, we might call them – who are neither named nor prohibited within the economy of the law."[11] Refusing to acknowledge, much less regulate, the innate "identity" that resides in the body's interior, Clifford and Hepzibah must repeatedly find themselves abjected. But who does not experience this failure, Hawthorne's romance seems to ask? If Hepzibah and Clifford, who felt "mankind's great and terrible eye on them alone" (11: 169), seem extraordinary in their abjection, Hawthorne hastens to remind the reader that the Pyncheon siblings are exemplary in their discordant identification, "a ruin, a failure, as almost everybody is" (11: 158).

Because they do not make common cause in their abjection, however, Hepzibah and Clifford are kept from asserting their presence, not by prohibition, but by shame, the characteristic state of those without socially sanctioned identities. Hepzibah, when her cent-shop forces her to face the outside world, experiences "overwhelming shame, that strange and unloving eyes should have the privilege of gazing" (11: 46) and later feels "a painful suffusion of shame" (11: 112). When Hepzibah tries to dissuade her brother from going into public, warning him of the townspeople's inevitable judgment, Clifford, whose life has been a series of mortifications, exclaims, "What shame can befall me now?" (11: 113). Shame is a potent force, keeping the siblings locked away from the world and thereby preventing them from challenging their cousin's right either to the family wealth (Clifford might assert his innocence in the murder of his uncle) or to public respectability (by publicizing his cheating and lying). In so doing, Clifford and Hepzibah would challenge the laws of normative public order, both by discrediting the Judge's status as representative of public virtue and by showing that *other* forms of identification are possible, forms capable of producing more love, kindness, and creativity than the Judge and his laws ever dreamed of. Because shame operates at the level of emotion and results in self-punishment, it serves the Judge's interests better than any juridical sentence, since his cousins, finding *themselves* lacking and experiencing their punishment not on the outside, where it might elicit sympathy, but on the inside, far from public view, become self-imprisoning subjects. As Hawthorne writes, the couple "could not flee; their jailor had but left the door open, in mockery, and stood behind it, to watch them stealing out. At the threshold, they felt his pitiless gripe upon them. For, what other dungeon is so dark as one's own heart! What jailor so inexorable as one's self!" (II: 169).

While shame works to keep Hepzibah and Clifford – and the challenges they embody – off the streets, it also enables an alternative collective life – a queer sociability – among those sentenced to shame. Creating a world of unpredictable emotions, surprising affinities, and powerful challenges, the errant Pyncheons and their allies turn their failures into an example of what Michael Warner calls the ethics of queer life:

> I call its way of life an ethics not only because it is understood as a better kind of self-relation, but because it is the premise of the special kind of sociability that holds queer culture together. A relation to others, in these contexts, begins in an acknowledgment of all that is most abject and least reputable in oneself. Shame is bedrock. Queers can be abusive, insulting, and vile toward one another, but because abjection is understood to be the shared condition, they also know how to communicate through such camaraderie a moving and unexpected form of generosity.[12]

We can use these terms to understand how an alternative sense of social connection is shaped within the romance by "sympathy," a word widely used in the nineteenth century to describe what we today might call "empathy": the ability of more apparently privileged citizens (those extending sympathy) to acknowledge (at least to themselves) their own experiences of abjection in order to imaginatively place themselves in the position of the socially wounded.[13] What sympathy attests to, then, is the ubiquitous experience of shame, transformed, through sympathy, into a potential enactment of fellow-feeling. Hawthorne implies as much when he writes that "Clifford saw, it may be, in the mirror of his deeper consciousness, that he was an example and representative of that great chaos of people, whom an inexplicable Providence is continually putting at cross-purposes with the world"

(II: 149). Living at cross-purposes generates Clifford's and Hepzibah's shame; yet through them shame becomes re-exteriorized as a social connection, a way of life, an ethics.

All who share the ethics of Hawthorne's romance – Clifford, Hepzibah, Phoebe, Uncle Venner, and, at least initially, Holgrave, who possesses "queer and questionable traits" (II: 154) – are at cross-purposes with the world. Describing the elderly jack-of-all-trades, for instance, Hawthorne writes that Venner "was commonly regarded as rather deficient, than otherwise, in his wits. In truth, he had virtually pleaded guilty to the charge, by scarcely aiming at such success as other men seek, and by taking only that humble and modest part in the intercourse of life, which belongs to the alleged deficiency" (II: 61). Casting Venner's social abjection in the language of legal judgment, Hawthorne not only creates a bond between Clifford and Venner that puts both men at odds with Judge Pyncheon, he places Venner, like Clifford, outside the "common sense" of his social world in part because he refuses a coherent identity (those being associated, by Hawthorne, with the capitalist narratives determining "such success as other men seek"). Venner is "a miscellaneous old gentleman, partly himself, but, in good measure, something else; patched together, too, of different epochs; an epitome of times and fashions" (II: 62). Rather than condemning Venner for his patchwork persona and consigning him to the shame his cross-purposeful life would seem to require, Hawthorne credits to it a rather marvelous counter-wisdom, noting that the old man had "a vein of something like poetry in him" (II: 61).

Venner's "vein of poetry" – the lifeblood of Hawthorne's queer ethics – has a transformative power over even the most apparently "normal" of the Pyncheons. Initially, Phoebe "was not one of those natures which are most attracted by what is strange and exceptional in human character. The path which would best have suited her, was the well-worn track of ordinary life; the companions in whom she would most have delighted, were such as one encounters at every turn" (II: 142–43). Before long, however, Phoebe "grew more thoughtful than heretofore." Finding herself curious about Clifford's past, she "would try to inquire what had been his life" (II: 143). When his history becomes clear to her – partly through what she is told, but also with the help of "her involuntary conjectures," suggesting Phoebe's imagination contains the stuff of gothic cross-purposefulness – "it had no terrible effect upon her" (II: 144). Phoebe's ability to "conjecture" about Clifford – to place herself imaginatively in his shoes – cements her bonds with her outcast cousins, an outcome Phoebe senses from the start of her visit, when she tells Hepzibah, "I really think we may suit one another, much better than you suppose" (II: 74).

The strongest indication of Phoebe's sympathetic bond with her cousins, however, is her adoption of Clifford's characteristic emotional state, "a settled melancholy" (II: 135). "It is perhaps remarkable, considering her temperament," Hawthorne reports, that Phoebe, singing in the evening to Clifford, "oftener chose a strain of pathos than of gaiety" (II: 138). Melancholy, according to Freud, arises from a person's refusal to surrender a lost loved one, object, or ideal, incorporating its qualities into his or her own body, where the anger and ambivalence surrounding loss are experienced as self-revilement.[14] Clifford and Hepzibah clearly fit this pattern: the former struggles with the loss of his youth, while the latter refuses to reconcile herself to her beloved brother's incarceration, both experiencing loss by reviling their own bodies (Hepzibah is ashamed of her unpleasant scowl, while Clifford fantasizes about re-entering society by breaking his body in a self-willed tumble from an upper window). Although Phoebe seems far from this pattern, she too struggles with loss. Recall that when Phoebe first understands that persons of "eminent stamp and respectability, could really, in any single instance, be otherwise than just and upright men," she is "fain to smother, in some degree, her own intuitions" (II: 131–32). Phoebe learns to repress ("smother") the disparity between social custom and her own experiences, thereby constituting a rupture within her understanding of identity. Realizing that the hypocritical Judge Pyncheon might not be "identical" to himself, Phoebe acknowledges the counterfeit nature of those customs upon which she rests her own identity. If that moment of loss risks Phoebe's identity, however, it generates new options for *identification*, not with the public world whose canons of taste she previously upheld, but with the shameful communities created by the socially abject of the House of the Seven Gables. While her desire to identify with the Judge leads her only to failure (he points out to her that she does not look much like a Pyncheon), her embrace of shame – her imaginative sympathy with Clifford and Hepzibah – leads her to melancholic bonds that, if sometimes pensive and pathetic, are also generous, caring, and poetic. Hawthorne shows us, then, that melancholia is not simply nostalgic – a pessimistic longing for a hopelessly lost past – but is productive as well. One might even say that Hawthorne's characters engage melancholy as a "vein of poetry" that allows them to disavow the sanctioned identities of the public world: Clifford's "griefs were a touch-stone of reality that few feigned emotions could withstand" (II: 146), Hawthorne writes, reversing the ususal dichotomy of real/imagined, of genuine/feigned, usually deployed to Clifford's detriment. At the same time, melancholy allows characters to inscribe in the *present* forms of identification authorized, not by the Pyncheon past, but by the assertion of the inevitable loss contained within that past. Using shameful loss to enliven modes of affiliation not yet visible in the "real world," the Pyncheons' melancholy is rather marvelous.

While Clifford and even Phoebe's melancholia are interpretable, other emotions become queer because they are unnameable, even, apparently, by Hawthorne. In this sense, the queerest character in *The House of the Seven Gables* is Hepzibah, whose inner states remain so elusive that, as Millington rightly notes, the narrative "can only represent [her] by misrepresenting her."[15] Hawthorne refers repeatedly to her "queer scowl" (II: 50), to "the sad perversity of her scowl" (II: 133), to her "queer and quaint manners" (II: 135), even to her "queer" chickens, who share Hepzibah's "queer, sidelong glances" (II: 89). Hepzibah keeps "the strong passion of her life" in a "secret drawer" (II: 31), never giving it a public name. In that, she is, in this world of confessed inner states, "a queer anomaly" (II: 37). Although her passions are one of the most persistent, if understated, mysteries of the romance, Hepzibah, refusing to acknowledge that she even *has* a "secret," resists the public orders of domestic self-sacrifice and commercial competition. For all its unnameability, Hepzibah's passionate interiority – "the vivid life and reality, assumed by her emotions" (II: 66) – becomes, like Clifford's grief, a pointed commentary on the "realities" of the external world, making "all outward occurrences unsubstantial, like the teasing phantoms of a half-conscious slumber" (II: 66). Although Hawthorne calls Clifford and Hepzibah a "queer couple of ducks" (II: 289), only the latter can reverse the law's demand for confession, ordering the Judge, apropos his motive in persecuting Clifford, "speak it out, at once!" (II: 228).

Hepzibah thus represents what might be the romance's most promising insight: the "interior" contains nothing at all, no "essence" to validate the public scrutiny of shameful secrets. If, as Hawthorne claims, "the reader must needs be let into the secret" (II: 28), the secret may turn out to be that there *are* no secrets, at least none that can be brought forth by public law and reconciled with its nominal orders. As Hepzibah defiantly claims in answer to the Judge's demands for her brother's confession, "Clifford has no secret!" (II: 237). In the face of such emptiness, one finds in oneself only one's desire to know, as Hawthorne suggests in one of his first descriptions of the House of the Seven Gables: "As regards its interior life, a large, dim looking-glass used to hang in one of the rooms, and was fabled to contain within its depths all the shapes that had ever been reflected there" (II: 20). In the end *The House of the Seven Gables* shows us what the mirror reveals: the desires of those who would look, the law's dim gaze. Emotions, passions, melancholy all become, in Hawthorne's romance, not interior states, but the external means to a more sustainable, if more provisional, sympathy that is, in turn, the basis of an alternative social affinity. "Mellow, melancholy, yet not mournful," Hawthorne writes, "the tone seemed to gush up out of the deep well of Hepzibah's heart, all steeped in its profoundest emotion. There was a tremor in it, too, that – as all strong emotion is electric – partly communicated itself to Phoebe" (II: 96).

Because emotions became named in antebellum America in part through the binary of public/private (the former being the realm of "masculine" emotions like competitiveness and anger, the latter marking "feminine" emotions like reverence and nurturing affection), the queer community of *The House of the Seven Gables* necessarily flourishes in a space neither private nor public. Every Sunday, Hawthorne relates, his "oddly composed little social party" (II: 155) gathers in the garden, a site that anthropomorphizes the characters' queer transformation of shame into sociability. Made up of "such rank weeds (symbolic of the transmitted vices of society)" (II: 86), the garden becomes, like those who enjoy its at-first-unapparent beauties, a haven from social abjection, where "Nature, elsewhere overwhelmed, and driven out of the dusty town, had here been able to retain a breathing space" (II: 87). Generating a space outside the shameful interior of the house yet making "an interior of verdant seclusion" (II: 145), the garden fosters "the sympathy of this little circle of not unkindly souls" (II: 157).

Just as the garden's "vagrant and lawless plants" (II: 86) bring forth a marvelous sociability, so too the queer passions of its inhabitants bring forth, through what Millington calls "the shared risks of transformative interchange,"[16] not the remorseful self-revilements Freud associates with melancholy, but remarkable testimonies of hopefulness and perseverance.[17] Uncle Venner voices the group's characteristic optimism, defiantly claiming, "I'm not going to give up this one scheme of my own, even if I never bring it really to pass" (II: 155–56). Although Hawthorne asserts that croaky voices like Hepzibah's "have put on mourning for dead hopes" (II: 135), the old woman, left for thirty years to long for her brother, keeps alive "in the dungeon of her heart . . . the imprisoned joy, that was afraid to be enfranchised" (II: 102), but which maintains "her undying faith and trust, her fresh remembrance, and continual devotedness" (II: 32). Similarly, "Clifford had willfully hid from himself the consciousness of being stricken in years, and cherished visions of an earthly future still before him, visions, however, too indistinctly drawn to be followed by disappointment" (II: 155). "Individuals, whose affairs have reached an utterly desperate crisis," Hawthorne writes, "almost invariably keep themselves alive with hope, so much the more airily magnificent, as they have the less of solid matter within their grasp, whereof to mould any judicious and moderate expectation of good" (II: 64). This becomes evident in one of the most poignant scenes in the novel. Having sat quietly in his half-somnolent state while his companions socialize in the garden, Clifford suddenly announces, "I want my happiness! . . . Many, many years have I waited for it! It is late! It is late! I want my happiness!" (II: 157).

Ironically, Clifford's happiness is already around him, in the hopeful imagination, the faithful devotion, the caring sympathy – in the queer sociability – of his companions. If the public world is full of citizens who, due to their "judicious . . . expectation of good," are continually confronted by disappointment and shame, if public paradise is lost through the duplicitous snake of sanctioned, but counterfeit, identity, Hawthorne holds out a garden where one can find, in queer inscrutability and unruly passion, what Robert S. Levine has called "the regenerative and redemptive possibilities of reconstituted family."[18] Does the sociability shared by his queer characters, Hawthorne asks, "deserve to be called happiness?" His answer whimsically appropriates the language of counterfeit, not to adjudicate shameful failure, but to reveal the marvelous fantasies that permit the continued life of hope: "Why not? If not the thing itself, it is marvellously like it, and the more so for that ethereal and intangible quality, which causes it all to vanish, at too close an introspection" (II: 158). If Clifford laments to his sister, "We are ghosts!" (II: 169), referring to the civil death that characterizes the socially abject, Hepzibah, for her part, knows all too well that, supported by queer sympathy, "dead people are very apt to come back again!" (II: 76). Finding that they "belong nowhere" (II: 168), Hawthorne's characters show us that happiness is all around us, if only we had their ability to embrace our shame and, recognizing with Clifford how late it is, demand its marvelous outcomes *now*.

NOTES

1. On Hawthorne and property law, see Walter Benn Michaels, "Romance and Real Estate," in Walter Benn Michaels and Donald E. Pease, eds., *The American Renaissance Reconsidered: Selected Papers from the English Institute* (Baltimore, MD: Johns Hopkins University Press, 1985), pp. 156–82.
2. On the contractual nature of Hawthorne's preface, see Fredric Jameson, "Magical Narratives: Romance as Genre," *New Literary History* 7. 1 (1975): 135–63.
3. Richard H. Millington, *Practicing Romance: Narrative Form and Cultural Engagement in Hawthorne's Fiction* (Princeton, NJ: Princeton University Press, 1992), p. 113.
4. Noyse Wheeler, *Phrenological Characters and Talents* (Boston: Dow & Jackson, 1844).
5. Will Fisher, "Queer Money," *English Literary History* 66 (1999): 1–23.
6. I am building here on the distinction between discipline and punishment made by Michel Foucault in *Discipline and Punish: The Birth of the Prison*, trans. Alan Sheridan (New York: Vintage, 1979).

7. Millington, *Practicing Romance*, p. 149.
8. Neill Matheson, "Clifford's Dim, Unsatisfactory Elegance," unpublished paper, MLA Convention, December, 2000.
9. Judith Butler, "Imitation and Gender Insubordination," in Diana Fuss, ed., *Inside/Out: Lesbian Theories, Gay Theories* (New York: Routledge, 1991), pp. 13–31.
10. *Ibid.*, p. 18.
11. *Ibid.*, p. 20.
12. Michael Warner, *The Trouble With Normal: Sex, Politics, and the Ethics of Queer Life* (New York: The Free Press, 1999), p. 35.
13. On sympathy in Hawthorne's romances, see Gordon Hutner, *Secrets and Sympathy: Forms of Disclosure in Hawthorne's Novels* (Athens: University of Georgia Press, 1989).
14. Sigmund Freud, "Mourning and Melancholia," in *General Psychological Theory* (New York: Simon & Schuster, 1991).
15. Millington, *Practicing Romance*, p. 111.
16. *Ibid.*, p. 139.
17. On Hawthorne's hopefulness, see also Brook Thomas, "*The House of the Seven Gables*: Reading the Romance of America," *PMLA* 97. 2 (1982): 195–211.
18. Robert S. Levine, *Conspiracy and Romance: Studies in Brockden Brown, Cooper, Hawthorne, and Melville* (Cambridge: Cambridge University Press, 1989), p. 159.

10

ROBERT S. LEVINE

Sympathy and reform in *The Blithedale Romance*

For a participant in a reform association that aspires to regenerate society, Miles Coverdale, the first-person narrator of Hawthorne's third novel, *The Blithedale Romance* (1852), spends very little time actually doing the work of social reform. Instead, he seems content simply to look at people, imagine their private circumstances, and fantasize about their sexual proclivities and histories. Does this mean that the narrator of Hawthorne's novel of social reform is merely a voyeur whose only true commitment is to the pleasures of his private imagination? In a key moment about two-thirds into the novel, Coverdale offers his own reflections on his moral imagination just after dreaming that Hollingsworth and Zenobia are kissing over his bed while Priscilla shrinks away, and just before he peers through the boardinghouse window where he discovers Zenobia, Priscilla, and Westervelt together for some mysterious purpose. Initially he judges his imagination in negative terms, proclaiming, "That cold tendency, between instinct and intellect, which made me pry with a speculative interest into people's passions and impulses, appeared to have gone far towards unhumanizing my heart." But then he rejects that negative assessment, declaring that his voyeuristic tendencies have everything to do with what he regards as the excess of his sympathetic imagination: "But a man cannot always decide for himself whether his own heart is cold or warm. It now impresses me, that, if I erred at all, in regard to Hollingsworth, Zenobia, and Priscilla, it was through too much sympathy, rather than too little" (III: 154). Sympathy is the key word here. As a number of critics have emphasized, sympathy is a crucial thematic in Hawthorne's fiction, imparting "a romantic ideal of communication . . . an understanding that passes beyond words."[1] There are several moments in *Blithedale* when Coverdale appears to possess this sort of exquisite sympathetic understanding of others, such as when he drinks with Moodie in the tavern, and even during some of his interactions with Zenobia and Hollingsworth. But there are many other moments when Coverdale's expressions of sympathy suggest a failure of communication and understanding, and point to his distance from those impulses that might help to bring about social reform. One of the large questions raised by Hawthorne's first-person narrator, then, is this: does sympathy help to connect the self to the other (and in this way contribute to social reform) or does sympathy create barriers between the self and other (and in this way thwart social reform)?

In putting the sympathetic imagination at the center of his novel about a community of social reformers, Hawthorne chose to interrogate a basic tenet of 1850s sentimental culture, particularly as expressed in reformist discourse of the time, which celebrated the power of sympathy to link the self to unfortunate others. This belief had important sources in eighteenth-century Scottish moral philosophy, particularly writers such as Francis Hutchinson and Adam Smith, who argued that the human predilection to sympathize provided a crucial foundation for the virtuous society. Hawthorne was familiar with those philosophers, and in many of his writings, particularly the sketches and *The House of the Seven Gables*, he drew on and engaged the Scottish sentimental tradition of moral and social thought.[2] In this respect, he shared much with the popular sentimental and reformist writers of the American 1850s. This chapter will examine *Blithedale* in relation to antebellum constructions of sympathy and reform and will be arguing that, despite its apparently satirical perspective on reform, *Blithedale* is not so disdainful of reform (or sympathy) as it might initially seem, and that in certain respects *Blithedale* offers a more capacious perspective on the possibilities of social change than many of the more explicitly reformist sentimental novels of the period.

In considering novels of social reform of the 1850s, it would be difficult not to regard Harriet Beecher Stowe's *Uncle Tom's Cabin* and Hawthorne's *Blithedale Romance*, both published in 1852, as works that develop completely different perspectives on the power of sympathy to affect social reform. Whereas Hawthorne seems to urge readers of *Blithedale* to recognize the impossibility of achieving any sort of meaningful identification with those whom social reform might benefit, Stowe deploys rhetorical strategies intended to get her middle-class readers to identify emotionally with the specific objects of her reformist novel: the nation's slaves. Like many sentimentalists of the 1850s, Stowe was indebted to Adam Smith's belief that a constituent part of being human was the ability to empathize with and even apprehend the pain of others through the workings of the moral imagination. In a passage that has become the *locus classicus* of current critical debate on the promise and limits of sympathy, Smith writes in his 1759 *The Theory of Moral Sentiments*:

> Though our brother is upon the rack, as long as we ourselves are at our ease, our senses will never inform us of what he suffers. They never did, and never can, carry us beyond our own person, and it is by the imagination only that we can form any conception of what are his sensations . . . By the imagination we place ourselves in his situation, we conceive ourselves enduring all the same torments, we enter as it were into his body, and become in some measure the same person with him, and then form some idea of his sensations, and even feel something which, though weaker in degree, is not altogether unlike them.[3]

Now, Smith does go on to allow that these sentimental identifications are always imperfect and can be elicited as much by theatricalized as authentic suffering. But it is the promise of emotional communion that has led Jane Tompkins and many other critics to celebrate Stowe's sentimentalism for having stimulated antislavery action along humanitarian lines by creating in the reader (particularly the white middle-class female reader) a sense of commonality with the black slave – an emotional connection that was often gendered in terms of domestic ideals of motherhood and family.[4]

Some recent criticism on sentimentalism in Stowe and reform discourses of the 1850s, however, has emphasized the more problematical nature of that sympathetic identification. For Karen Sánchez-Eppler, social reform as practiced by white middle-class women, who lamented their own "enslavement" in patriarchal culture, was less about the suffering other than about the suffering self. As Marianne Noble trenchantly puts the case in *The Masochistic Pleasures of Sentimental Literature*:

> In the sentimental ideal . . . [o]ne does unto one's neighbor as unto oneself, because one's neighbor *is*, in a sense, oneself. But the physical gratification associated with that experience does not necessarily extend the observer outward to a communion with the sufferer; it may turn the observer inward, compensating with a self-satisfying *illusion* of humanitarian altruism that may well not be acted upon at all.

In response to Noble, Glenn Hendler defends Stowe by arguing that, however fragile the connections between subject and object may have been, sentimentalism worked in the nineteenth century to create fictions of "experiential equivalence" that resonated emotionally and prompted the cultural work of antislavery and other social reforms. Noble comes close to conceding that point, but ultimately regards what she terms "masochistic fantasies" of identification as "efforts to find power and wield it – with mixed benefits and mixed political ramifications."[5]

Drawing on what can be regarded as the dialectic enacted by the current critical debate on sympathy and reform in Stowe, I would agree with sympathy's advocates that it was precisely the illusory sense of becoming and understanding the other that gave such a rich emotional resonance to sentimental fictions of the time, and that those fictions probably did work to inspire some reform efforts. But I would also agree with sympathy's dissenters that the efforts of white middle-class readers to project themselves into the situations of others (by viewing the other through the lens of evangelical Christianity or the discourses that portrayed slaves in the middle-class terms of domestic culture as suffering mothers, fathers, sisters, brothers, daughters, sons, and so on) could sometimes work to elide differences between black and white, slave and free, rich and poor, and thus may have forestalled social reforms that would have truly attended to difference. In this respect, sentimentalism may have undermined readers' abilities to apprehend the other as truly other, encouraging readers instead to take stock in narcissistic fantasies of communion. Such identificatory fantasies, which are not all that different from Coverdale's modus operandi in *Blithedale*, ultimately work to uphold rather than break down distance and difference. Our recognition of the limits of Coverdale's sentimental efforts to make connections to others – the recognition, that is to say, that the other in *Blithedale* is to a certain extent a projection of Coverdale's self – points to the limits of Stowe's sentimental strategies as well.

The argument that I want to develop in this chapter, then, is that *Blithedale* is participating in the sentimental project of the 1850s of imagining the other in terms of the self, while at the same time developing a critique of that project. In crucial ways, *Blithedale* looks forward to, indeed anticipates, recent critiques of sentimental reformism by Noble and others. Though *Blithedale* does not address the debate on slavery, except implicitly in its portrayal of mesmerism as a form of enslaving patriarchal power, it does address a number of the central concerns of antebellum reform. Reading with and against the grain of Coverdale's scopic, narcissistic narrative, we confront the problem of class inequalities and tensions, as we learn about and imagine Priscilla's and Moodie's personal histories, and of gender inequities, as we imagine Zenobia's resistant feminist perspective. But because Hawthorne does not give readers full access to those perspectives, he does not allow alterity to be short-circuited. Pushing the reader to imagine the other by resisting Coverdale's voyeuristic fantasies, Hawthorne, through Coverdale, pushes us as well to recognize that people have secret and individual histories, histories that could be very different from those imagined by privileged sympathizing reformers. Although recent commentators on *Blithedale* have been emphasizing the novel's satirical tone and conservative politics, I will be arguing that the overall novel presents us with a potentially promising reform culture consisting of myriad individuals with complex, hidden, and not so easily appropriated lives that all too often elude Coverdale's grasp.

Moreover, there are suggestions that, despite his satirical aims, Coverdale may be covering up the very commitment to reform that he affirms at the opening of his narrative: "Whatever else I may repent of, therefore, let it be reckoned neither among my sins nor follies, that I once had faith and force enough to form generous hopes of the world's destiny" (III: 11).

Coverdale's declaration of his hopes and aspirations ought to be taken seriously, for it speaks to Hawthorne's own attraction to the possibilities of reform. Though Hawthorne in an 1835 notebook entry compared the "modern reformer" to an escaped lunatic, he nevertheless chose to join the socialistic Brook Farm community in West Roxbury, Massachusetts, for seven months in 1841 (VIII: 10). Founded by a group of Transcendentalist reformers who would become increasingly swayed by the socialistic theories of the French political theorist Charles Fourier, Brook Farm was one of a number of fairly vital communitarian groups in antebellum America during the 1840s that hoped to restructure social and economic relationships. (The group disbanded in 1846 after a fire destroyed its buildings.) Hawthorne's motivation for participating in the project is not completely clear. His letters from Brook Farm to his future wife, Sophia Peabody, suggest that he may have joined the community with the hope that it would provide him with the quiet and repose of a writers' community; hence his subsequent disillusionment with the "drudgery" of the "manual labor" that was required of him.[6] But given his short-term commitment to the community, one imagines that he was not entirely cynical about the possibility that the Brook Farmers, by posing a challenge to the competitive practices of market culture, could help to make New England into a better place. In his Preface to *Blithedale*, Hawthorne for the most part affirms his earlier commitment to Brook Farm, remarking that he had "the good fortune, for a time, to be personally connected" (III: 1) with the communitarians, and that he regards his participation as "the most romantic episode of his own life" (III: 2). To be sure, Hawthorne is notoriously unreliable in his prefaces, regularly insisting as a romancer on his fiction's disconnection from the "reality" (III: 2) that he nonetheless invokes. But perhaps we should take at face value his generally positive statements about his participation in Brook Farm, and his statement as well that in writing about the associative community he does not wish to "put forward the slightest pretensions to illustrate a theory, or elicit a conclusion, favorable or otherwise, in respect to Socialism" (III: 2). Rather than praise or damn the reform impulse, Hawthorne in his retrospective *Blithedale* reveals his conflicted attitudes toward the aspirations that he himself had once embraced.[7]

And yet satire and skepticism, at first glance, would appear to outweigh any sort of commitment to reform. According to Coverdale, the participants at Blithedale tend to be self-important, elitist, and just plain selfish, generally regarding those outside the community from "a position of new hostility, rather than new brotherhood" (III: 20). Despite his recurrent gestures of solidarity, Coverdale takes pains to suggest that hostility, rather than fellow-feeling (or sympathetic communion), governs the actions of virtually all of the reformers in the book: Hollingsworth seeks to undermine the Blithedale community so that he might gain the community's land for his prison-reform project; the feminist reformer Zenobia, partly modeled on Margaret Fuller (and perhaps Hawthorne's sister-in-law Elizabeth Peabody), seems in search of the limelight and a man, and throughout seems hostile to the one woman (Priscilla) who yearns for sympathy from her feminist sister; Westervelt, while talking of universal reform, seems little more than a patriarchal enslaving master. Though the Blithedale community embraces gender reforms, women continue to do the cooking and men the physical labor, and Coverdale (and Westervelt) strongly suggest that Zenobia commits suicide out of her frustrated love for Hollingsworth (whereas Fuller in *Woman in the Nineteenth Century* [1845] had mocked the idea that women live only for the love of a man).

Hawthorne's representation of spiritualism and mesmerism further contributes to the apparently skeptical portrayal of reform at Blithedale farm. Whereas some Americans of the 1840s and 1850s regarded mesmerism – a species of hypnotism – as a reformatory science potentially bringing individuals and nature into a state of perfect harmony, Hawthorne presents it, particularly through Westervelt's and Hollingsworth's manipulations of Priscilla and Zenobia, as the selfish enactment of hyperintrusive patriarchal power. (Hawthorne's anxieties about the invasive, controlling aspects of mesmerism had important sources in his concerns about Sophia's use of a mesmerist to treat her recurrent headaches, and inform as well his depiction of Matthew Maule's cruel domination of Alice Pyncheon in *The House of the Seven Gables*.[8]) Similarly, while some Americans regarded the 1848 "spirit-rappings" of the adolescent Fox sisters of Rochester, New York, as a sign that spiritualism as a social reform could help to link the visible and invisible worlds, in *Blithedale* Hawthorne analogizes Westervelt's decadent spiritualistic (and mesmerical) practices, which link mediums in "one great, mutually conscious brotherhood" (III: 200), to the communitarian practices at Blithedale, which link reformers in a "general brain" (III: 140) – with the large intention of suggesting both groups' propensities toward anarchic revolutionism. This is especially clear near the end of the novel when the scene shifts from Westervelt's lyceum display to the festive masquerade at Blithedale, where the communitarians, as Coverdale describes them from his hiding place in the hermitage, whirled "round so swiftly, so madly, and so merrily, in time and tune with the Satanic music, that their separate incongruities were blended all together" (III: 210). In his imaging of communitarianism and spiritualism as forms of demonic revolutionism, Hawthorne would seem to be in the same reactionary camp as the Roman Catholic convert Orestes Brownson, whose novel *The Spirit-Rapper* (1854) portrayed spiritualism as Satan's invisible tool for bringing forth the French Revolution, the European Revolution of the 1840s, and the emerging women's rights movement. In addition to satirizing women's rights, spiritualism, mesmerism, and communitarianism, Coverdale (or Hawthorne) over the course of the novel also suggests the limits of other key social reforms of the period, such as temperance and prison reform.[9]

But *Blithedale* is more than a merely satirical (or reactionary) novel, in large part because of Hawthorne's use of the first-person narrator Coverdale to enact both a suspicion of and desire for reform. As presented in the novel, Coverdale is simultaneously an insider and an outsider, a fully energetic participant and a more ironic retrospective narrator, a character who, leading an aimlessly drifting life in the anomic city, deeply desires the structure, the community, and perhaps even the reforms offered by Blithedale.[10] He is a narrator, too, whose sexual anxieties and insecurities, and chronic cynicism, make him an unreliable critic of reform, particularly given that, as he confesses at the end of the novel, "I exaggerate my own defects" (III: 247). (One of his exaggerated "defects," of course, is his chronic cynicism.) The novel, to a large extent, is a study in desire and anxiety, as the voyeuristic Coverdale, simultaneously attracted to and frightened by Zenobia's sexuality, Hollingsworth's patriarchal fixedness of purpose, and, indeed, the carnivalesque energies of the festive Blithedalers, weaves melodramatic tales of flight and entrapment suggestive of his own wavering desires. One way of reading Coverdale's exaggeratedly self-critical confessional narrative, then, is to regard it as his somewhat coy and embarrassed effort at reading himself as a reformer. In this respect, the novel both puts on display and attempts to cover up the emotional life of a sentimental man.[11]

With its emphasis on tropes of interiority, Coverdale's confessional narrative can be taken as an extended representation of the problem of sympathy in sentimental culture. Very specifically, the novel foregrounds in the workings of Coverdale's first-person narrative what Christopher Castiglia has identified as one of the obsessive concerns of antebellum reform culture: "the middle-class subject engaged in the act of reform."[12] That focus makes *Blithedale* as profoundly *about* reform as any reformist novel of the period, even as the matter of Blithedale's specific reform mission is often occluded by Coverdale's tendencies toward a voyeuristic self-reflection. In *Blithedale*, Coverdale affirms his identity as a sentimental reformer by repeatedly reflecting on his efforts to sympathize with others. Because of the apparently selfish and narcissistic form that Coverdale's efforts take, the problem of sympathy remains at the thematic center of the novel – or perhaps it would be more precise to say that sympathy remains the central problem of Coverdale's narrative, given how little his sympathetic imaginings would appear to accomplish.

Consider the opening of the novel, which for the most part can be taken as a study of the failure of sympathy. On the day before heading off to Blithedale farm, Coverdale attends the public performance of the Veiled Lady. Watching her from a distance with the other male spectators, he describes himself as "wrought up by the enigma of her identity" (III: 6), but he remains content to regard the display as mere entertainment. As we soon learn, however, the Veiled Lady (Priscilla) could have used the help of a rescuer. Shortly after the performance, Coverdale is beseeched by the downtrodden Moodie, who would like him to be that rescuer, and Coverdale fends him off with a show of sympathy so false ("But it is late! Will you tell me what I can do for you?" [III: 8]) as to prompt Moodie to turn to Hollingsworth for help. Coverdale continues to express sympathy while holding himself apart in his account of his next day's journey to Blithedale farm, in which he both expresses his allegiance to the communitarians while pointing to their (and his) distance from the villagers whose interests they claim to be advancing. Encountering a traveler who refuses to return their friendly greeting, Coverdale laments with megalomaniacal flair: "This lack of faith in our cordial sympathy, on the traveller's part, was one among the innumerable tokens how difficult a task we had in hand, for the reformation of the world" (III: 12). As an insider, Coverdale betrays no sympathy for those who fail to appreciate the Blithedalers' beneficent designs.

Coverdale's feelings about reform and sympathy remain at the center of the narrative with the arrival of Hollingsworth and Priscilla. How should he respond to the sad situation of the newly arrived Priscilla? At first he feels some sympathy for her plight, but upon reflection, he exhibits a proto-Oscar Wildean amusement at such bathetic sufferings, confiding to the reader "that I could not help smiling at this odd scene of unknown and unaccountable calamity" (III: 29). Subsequently, while being nursed by Hollingsworth during his illness, Coverdale reflects on the male tendency, which he had exhibited in relation to Priscilla, *not* to be able to sympathize. "Most men," he claims, "have a natural indifference, if not an absolutely hostile feeling, towards those whom disease, or weakness, or calamity of any kind, causes to faulter and faint amid the rude jostle of our selfish existence," though he suggests that "the sympathy of a like experience, and the example of women, may soften, and possibly subvert, this ugly characteristic of our sex" (III: 41).

Despite his initial hard-headed (ostensibly male) inability to sympathize with Priscilla, Coverdale quickly distances himself from such conventional notions of sympathy, regularly insisting on his ability to cross the traditionally gendered lines of affect. And he suggests that the same is potentially true for Hollingsworth, whom he states has "something of the woman moulded into [his] great stalwart frame" (III: 42).

Coverdale's meditation on the prison reformer's sympathies and womanly qualities can thus be regarded as a displaced meditation on his own relation to sympathy and reform. The large question on his mind is whether Hollingsworth's reformist desires will reveal him to be the sort of sentimental man Coverdale imagines himself to be, and for the most part his answer is no. Hollingsworth, Coverdale asserts, joined the Blithedalers "actuated by no real sympathy with our feelings and our hopes" (III: 54–55). (Note the implication here that Coverdale *was* actuated by real sympathy for the Blithedalers' feelings and hopes.) He refers to Hollingsworth's "divine power of sympathy" (III: 55) when tending to Priscilla, and Coverdale himself is privy to that same apparent sympathy when he is convalescing from his illness. But he soon comes to regard Hollingsworth's "more than brotherly attendance" (III: 41) at his sickbed as motivated less by sympathy than by his efforts to gain converts to his prison-reform cause. Regarding himself, Priscilla, and Zenobia as all the potential victims of Hollingsworth's false sympathy, he presents him as typical of certain types of reformers who, rather than using their imaginations to build connections between themselves and others, try to take in others as part of their imperial project. As he bluntly remarks on the philanthropist as a moral and social type: "They have no heart, no sympathy, no reason, no conscience" (III: 70).

And yet Coverdale admires Hollingsworth as a leader with whom he would like to share a common cause. He also experiences an extraordinary attraction to the charismatic philanthropist: "I loved Hollingsworth, as has already been enough expressed" (III: 70). The homoerotic subtext of Coverdale's attraction to Hollingsworth is consistent with the portrayal of unconventional Blithedale as a site of erotic freedom, which "seemed to authorize an individual, of either sex, to fall in love with any other, regardless of what would elsewhere be judged suitable and prudent" (III: 72).[13] But during the key scene at Eliot's Pulpit, Coverdale attempts to differentiate himself from Hollingsworth and reinstate the heteronormative by invoking traditional notions of the gendered quality of sympathy. Coverdale portrays himself to Priscilla and Zenobia as a sentimental man who would gladly allow himself to be guided by women, while Hollingsworth, John Eliot redux in his desire to gain converts, is depicted as so manly, so in the tradition of the New

England Pilgrims whom the Blithedalers regard as their holy progenitors, as to be untouched by sympathy (or the womanly). Declaiming from Eliot's Pulpit, Hollingsworth states that woman's principal role is to follow male leaders as sympathizers: "Her place is at man's side. Her office, that of the Sympathizer" (III: 122). And he asserts that he would use force to keep women in their assigned place – thereby making sympathy into little more than the handmaiden to patriarchy. Presenting Zenobia as offering a tortured consent to Hollingsworth's proposition through her surreptitious pressing of his hand to her bosom, Coverdale uses the scene, in part, to deflate Zenobia's feminism by revealing her inability to transcend the personal. He also antic- ipates the presentation of his own personal crisis with Hollingsworth and the Blithedale community by depicting the drooping Priscilla, woman as unthinking sympathizer, as under thrall not only to Westervelt but also to Hollingsworth.

Given Coverdale's sense of himself as a womanly sympathizer, or male sentimentalist, he realizes that there are disturbing similarities between his and Priscilla's attraction to Hollingsworth. Like Priscilla, he desires to be the sort of sympathizer that Hollingsworth describes: free of ego, a true believer. Hollingsworth appeals to those very desires shortly after his speech at Eliot's Pulpit, approaching Coverdale in private and promising to reinvest the life of the drifter with what he has all along been seeking, "a purpose in life, worthy of the extremest self-devotion – worthy of martyrdom, should God so order it!" (III: 133). His hands outstretched, his eyes welling with tears, Hollingsworth beseeches in Christ-like fashion: "Coverdale . . . there is not the man in this wide world, whom I can love as I could you. Do not for- sake me!" (III: 133). Seemingly a Veiled Lady on the verge of entering the trance state, Coverdale makes the monumental effort and wills a response to the mesmerical philanthropist's direct demand for an unquestioning sym- pathizer: "No!" (III: 135). Subsequently feeling "an absolute torture of the breast" (III: 135), he soon after takes leave of Blithedale, returning to the city as an outsider.

In Adam Smith's model of sympathy, as Castiglia explains, "self- transformation lies with the person who extends sympathy," the person who interiorizes the other. But such self-transformation risks becoming "the basis of differential power: the sympathizer extends agency over the sufferer, while the latter controls only him or herself."[14] In the crucial scenes with Hollingsworth that precipitate his flight to the city, Coverdale presents him- self as the sufferer, the possible victim of a sympathetic relation that would rob him of his selfhood. In contrast, he presents his own efforts at sympathy as existing apart from power. Perched aloft in his hermitage while watch- ing Westervelt with the despairing Zenobia, for example, he had compared himself to "the Chorus in a classic play" governed by a deep concern for others in which "sympathy is the only bond" (III: 97). But is sympathy a "bond" or a form of bondage? That is the question begged by Coverdale's relationship with Zenobia, which from beginning to end is defined by acts of viewing, performance, and interiorization that make it difficult to say who controls whom.

In the depiction of the mesmerical power that Westervelt wields over Priscilla and Zenobia, and of Hollingsworth's assumption of analogous forms of power over the two women, Hawthorne shows an acute awareness of how the male gaze can keep women in literal and metaphorical forms of bondage. As the voyeuristic pursuer of secrets, Coverdale participates as well in the novel's depiction of what Lori Merish calls "the gendered disequilibrium in social power that structures relations of vision."[15] But things are not quite so asymmetrical in the specific relationship between Coverdale and Zenobia. Coverdale obsesses on Zenobia's bare shoulder, hothouse flower, and sensual body, but his looking is often elicited by Zenobia's deliberate design. Her artful ability to display her body and theatricalize her sufferings allows her to retain more than a modicum of control over Coverdale, who never has access to her private imagination and history. Regarding Zenobia from his sickbed as "womanliness incarnated" (III: 44), he concludes that she lacks the virginal innocence that he demands of True Womanhood: "There is no folded petal, no latent dew-drop, in this perfectly developed rose" (III: 47). But even as he meditates on her supposed lack of innocence, he feels himself to be a kind of Veiled Lady, a "mesmerical clairvoyant" (III: 47), with the suggestion, then, that Zenobia is to him as, say, Westervelt is to Priscilla – the dominant subject who has cast her spell on the hapless innocent (Coverdale), who knows next to nothing of her sexual past or present circumstances. He nonetheless persists in attempting to make her the object of his sympathy, even as she challenges him to sympathize not by "becoming" her through scopic appropriation but by listening to her story. She tells part of that story in her utterance of "a helpless sort of moan" (III: 104) that Coverdale apprehends while watching her from his hermitage as she interacts with Westervelt, and that moan does have an impact on him, "affect[ing] me more than if she had made the wood dolorously vocal with a thousand shrieks and wails" (III: 104). She tells her story a second time in her legend of "The Silvery Veil," which is usually read as an allegory of Coverdale's failure to help Priscilla but is also Zenobia's own story of her painful temptation to betray her sister to a patriarchal master, whether Westervelt or Hollingsworth. Even here, though, she chooses to theatricalize her confession rather than make herself vulnerable to Coverdale's sympathetic embrace.

Tensions between Coverdale's violating sympathetic imagination and Zenobia's theatricalized resistance culminate in a confrontation in the city that stages a debate on sympathy in terms straight out of Adam Smith. Attempting to peer through the window of Zenobia's drawing-room, where she, Priscilla, and Westervelt are gathered, Coverdale affirms his

> quality of the intellect and the heart, which impelled me (often against my own will, and to the detriment of my own comfort) to live in other lives, and to endeavor – by generous sympathies, by delicate intuitions, by taking note of things too slight for record, and by bringing my human spirit into manifold accordance with the companions whom God assigned me – to learn the secret which was hidden even from themselves. (III: 160)

In Stowe-like fashion, he conceives of his spying in providential terms; God assigned him to his task of doing good. But when this self-celebrating sentimentalist confronts Zenobia to express his beneficent wish to bring his spirit into accord with her own, the other talks back, denouncing his "indefatigable human sympathy" (III: 163) as little more than a grotesque projection of his ego:

> I know precisely what it signifies. Bigotry; self-conceit; an insolent curiosity; a meddlesome temper; a cold-blooded criticism, founded on a shallow interpretation of half-perceptions; a monstrous skepticism in regard to any conscience or any wisdom, except one's own; a most irreverent propensity to thrust Providence aside, and substitute one's self in its awful place – out of these, and other motives as miserable as these, comes your idea of duty! (III: 170)

This exchange enacts the dialectic of sympathy informing the novel, though Zenobia's complaints about the egotistical limits of Coverdale's imperial fantasies of communion seem mostly on the mark. Coverdale's efforts at sympathy, at least with respect to Zenobia, are very much grounded in (and undone by) his private confusions about identity, sexuality, gender, and desire.

The one moment in which Coverdale does manage to make a connection through sentimental identification occurs in a tavern with another man, Moodie, which may seem odd given that the book begins with Coverdale fending off Moodie. But it is Moodie as much as any of the other characters who interests Coverdale, arguably because Coverdale shares more with Moodie than he would like to allow. Both men are drinkers and drifters in search of fraternal community, and in drinking, as Hawthorne's punning suggests, these topers share in a form of utopian desire. Coverdale earlier had mentioned his effort to view the world through Moodie's eyes – "I tried to identify my mind with the old fellow's, and take his view of the world" (III: 84) – and at the tavern he is able to achieve this sympathetic identification. Guided, he says, by "a sort of sympathetic impulse that often controlled me" (III: 179), Coverdale plies Moodie with wine, and he does so in secret sympathy as he marvels at the alcohol's ability to make toper into utopian. During the time that they drink together, they both experience camaraderie and regeneration, "the renewed youth and vigor, the brisk, cheerful sense of things present and to come" (III: 178). Whether at tavern or at Blithedale, communitarian inebriation induces regenerative "associations" (III: 181) possessing "an indescribable, ideal charm" (III: 176).

These particular "associations" – Moodie-Fauntleroy's tale of his two fragmented families and economic fall – allow the sympathetically responsive Coverdale both to fill in details of the family plot and to heighten the sentimental contrast between Priscilla and Zenobia. The offspring of Moodie's superficial first marriage to a wealthy beauty, Zenobia is regarded by Moodie as just "another jewel" (III: 182). After perpetrating a secret economic crime in an attempt to preserve his dwindling wealth, Moodie retreats to the cramped Irish quarters of a colonial governor's degenerate mansion, marries a feeble seamstress, and fathers feeble Priscilla, whose renowned spiritualistic gifts eventually attract the attention of the spiritualist Westervelt. While Zenobia grows to adulthood amidst great wealth, Priscilla "was enthralled in an intolerable bondage, from which she must either free herself or perish" (III: 190). Underscoring the contrast between Zenobia's power and Priscilla's vulnerability, Coverdale appends to Moodie's history a sketch of a meeting between Zenobia and Moodie, drawn, Coverdale confesses, "mainly from fancy, although with some general grounds of surmise in regard to the old man's feelings" (III: 190). As Coverdale imagines the scene with respect to Moodie's "feelings," Moodie beholds the bejeweled Zenobia, asks the puzzled heiress to treat Priscilla kindly as a sister, and upon her departure, shouts in his lonely chamber: "Zenobia take heed! Priscilla shall have no wrong!" (III: 193). Linking this imagined scene to the unfolding narrative of Priscilla's entrapment, Coverdale suggests that Zenobia may well have betrayed her familial trust: "that very evening, so far as I can adjust the dates of these strange incidents – Priscilla – poor, pallid flower – was either snatched from Zenobia's hand, or flung wilfully away!" (III: 193).

As the adoption of Moodie's point of view makes clear, the account of Moodie's precipitous loss of financial and familial stability quite unexpectedly makes an impact on Coverdale, who in his own way had been adrift in the democratic marketplace before finding temporary sanctuary at Blithedale. While with Moodie, Coverdale, almost against his will, experiences his strongest sense of fraternity in the romance. His intuition of his kinship with the broken Moodie staggers him: "Well! I betook myself away, and wandered up and down, like an exorcised spirit that had been driven

from its old haunts, after a mighty struggle" (III: 194). In his responsive-
ness to Moodie, which derives from a rather moving moment of imaginative
communion, he seems to realize why he had thrown in his lot with the communitarians in the first place, and he subsequently privately reaffirms his
connections to Priscilla, Zenobia, and Hollingsworth. Even so, only a for-
tuitous meeting at the lyceum hall performance of the Veiled Lady recalls
Coverdale to the vortex of community, and he once again prefers to watch.

In choosing to watch, Coverdale joins the crowd – the restless, bored New
Englanders whose distance from the other (the Veiled Lady) points to the
failure of sympathy in antebellum culture.[16] The crowd's "straining eyes"
(III: 201) take in the scene, but there is no human connection to the mesmer-
ized Veiled Lady, just the demand that the spiritualist Westervelt provide his
paying customers with entertainment. To some extent, then, the scene replays
Coverdale's viewing of the Veiled Lady in the opening chapter. As in that earlier chapter, Westervelt attempts to spiritualize the entertainment, presenting
the display not just as an occasion for the predominately male eyes to gaze
upon a spectacular female body, but as a reformist fulfillment of desires for
communion between self and other with millennialist implications. Priscilla,
he claims, "is, at this moment, in communion with the spiritual world"
(III: 201), and that world, he predicts, shall soon be available to the masses:
"He spoke of a new era that was dawning upon the world; an era that would
link soul to soul, and the present life to what we call futurity, with a closeness
that should finally convert both worlds into one great, mutually conscious
brotherhood" (III: 200). That image of a utopian, spiritualistically linked
brotherhood echoes Coverdale's more critical view of the Blithedalers as
linked through "a species of nervous sympathy," so that "[i]f one of us happened to give his neighbor a box on the ear, the tingle was immediately felt,
on the same side of everybody's head" (III: 139). Presenting sympathy and
reformism as equivalent to a decadent spiritualism, Coverdale manages to
undercut Hollingsworth's "rescue" of Priscilla by suggesting that the philanthropist's desire for a sympathizer does not greatly differ from the depraved
Westervelt's desire for a medium. From his position as a watcher who claims
to sympathize with Priscilla's plight, Coverdale rather meanspiritedly suggests that whether on stage or at Eliot's Pulpit, Hollingsworth seeks to keep
his own medium within her "proper bounds."

For all of his protestations of sympathy, however, Coverdale never seems
to connect with anybody for very long, or to find a way of moving from sympathy to some sort of action along the lines of Hollingsworth's bold move
at the lyceum. But perhaps that is the whole point of sympathy: to feel good
about one's virtuous sympathetic imagination while realizing that nothing
much can be done for the other beyond simply proffering sympathy. In

The Theory of Moral Sentiments, Adam Smith suggests as much, proclaiming that sympathy generally cannot significantly help "those who have suffered," precisely because they *are* other, and sympathy "is always extremely imperfect." And not only does sympathy usually prove not to be terribly efficacious for those in need, but according to Smith, the failure of sympathy only adds to the emotional pain of the sentimentalist, who is already "burdened" by an imaginative conception of the sufferings of the object of his or her gaze: "That our sympathy can afford them no consolation seems to be an addition to their calamity; and to think that all we can do is unavailing, and that, what alleviates all other distress, the regret, the love, and the lamentations of their friends, can yield no comfort to them, serves only to exasperate our sense of their misery."[17] That exasperation becomes the very mark, indeed the redemptive cross (as it were), of the virtuous sympathizer.

Coverdale's own virtuous exasperation is precisely what is activated and displayed in his final exchange with Zenobia, which occurs soon after he returns to Blithedale farm. Apparently distressed that her imminent loss of Moodie's wealth has motivated Hollingsworth to jettison her in favor of Priscilla, she is a character in need of sympathy. Though Coverdale views Zenobia in very conventional terms as a jilted woman, he rises to the occasion, doing his best to summon a sympathetic response to her sufferings (no matter that he lacks full access to what those sufferings might be). Convinced of his heartfelt understanding of her "tearless agony" (III: 222), Coverdale rhetorically asks his readers: "Was it wrong, therefore, if I felt myself consecrated to the priest-hood by sympathy like this, and called upon to minister to this woman's affliction, so far as mortal could?" (III: 222). Zenobia implies that the answer is yes, because she regards Coverdale as narcissistically imprisoned in his imagination and blind to her sufferings. She ironically states that "you have really a heart and sympathies, as far as they go" (III: 226), and then mocks the man who aspires to be her priestly confessor by mocking his metaphors, declaring her intention of taking on a veil and "going into a nunnery" (III: 227). In response, Coverdale professes himself exhausted by his virtuous emotional interactions, "worn-out with emotion on my behalf, and sympathy for others" (III: 228). The implication of the syntax here, as throughout the novel, is that Coverdale's "sympathy for others" is primarily based on and advances only "emotion on my behalf" – which is why he is the model sentimentalist.

But is the model sentimentalist the model reformer? On the basis of Coverdale's own self-representation in his confessional narrative, the answer would appear to be no, for it is clear to most readers that Coverdale is a self-celebrating and for the most part deluded voyeur whose efforts as reformer and sympathizer remain ineffective. But here is where things get tricky.

Coverdale clearly knows this about himself, and seems to take a perverse pleasure in exaggerating his defects. Those exaggerations, which regularly depict Coverdale as an uncomprehending prig, are central to *Blithedale*'s humor. It could be argued, then, that if we were to evaluate Coverdale in completely negative terms with respect to sympathy and reform, we would be missing the joke, falling into the trap of a narrative that seems calculated to elicit from readers a self-congratulatory, self-righteous outrage.[18]

We need to move beyond such outrage. I would suggest that Coverdale's retrospective (anti)sentimental narrative is comically informed by his acute awareness of his limitations as a reformer (even as he clings to desires for reform) and as a sympathizer (even as he desires closer and more efficacious connections to others). Viewed in this way, his confessional narrative can be read as both an implicit critique of the limits of sympathy in the sentimental reform culture of the 1850s and as a provocation to readers who resist the terms of his deliberately limited confessional narrative (that is, the majority of readers) to consider alternative models of sympathy and reform.

Certainly there are characters in the novel who adopt different, less imperial perspectives on sympathy and reform, most notably Zenobia, whose feminist reform vision survives as an embodied perspective that ultimately resists appropriation by either Coverdale or Hollingsworth. Theatrical to the very end, Zenobia masks her inner self and desires, even as she calls attention to how difficult it is for women to challenge the assumptions of patriarchal culture. Any attempt to imagine Zenobia's point of view apart from Coverdale's would lead readers toward a radical critique of the patriarchal authority assumed by the mesmerical Westervelt and Hollingsworth, and by Coverdale's gaze.[19] Such a critique would have the potential of encouraging readers to think more seriously about the kinds of structural changes that would be needed to enhance women's power and possibilities in the culture. Though Priscilla and Moodie are hardly radicals, efforts to imagine their situations apart from Coverdale's appropriations would likewise encourage thinking about the need for economic reforms that would address the problem of urban poverty, which is precisely one of the aims of the Blithedale community (and of Brook Farm).

Hawthorne does give us at least one character capable of a nonappropriative form of sympathy, and that is the working-class farmer Silas Foster. In a provocative discussion of *Blithedale*, Russ Castronovo presents Foster as a "radical democrat" who "acknowledges contingency" and recognizes the specificity, the *otherness*, of embodiment and materiality.[20] It is Foster who realizes that Priscilla needs food and sustenance, while Coverdale contents himself to fantasize about her origins and desires, and it is Foster who voices what could be taken as the most sincere (and non-interiorizing) moment of sympathy in the novel. This occurs when he helps to retrieve Zenobia's dead body from the pond. Here is Coverdale's account of all that Foster has to say upon laying her body out on shore: " 'Poor child!' said Foster – and his dry old heart, I verily believe, vouchsafed a tear – 'I'm sorry for her!' " (III: 235). The simplicity of his statement and tear provide an attractive alternative to the other forms of sympathy depicted in the book. While Westervelt scornfully comments on Zenobia's "heart" (III: 240), and Coverdale works at making her into a feminist manqué, Foster as a male sentimentalist recognizes her pain while not claiming to feel her pain. In this respect, despite his sometimes brash masculinity, he can be linked with the tire-women, who quietly take Zenobia's body away from the gaze of Coverdale and Hollingsworth.

Arguably, Foster provides Coverdale himself with a model of sympathy that holds out the promise of making him a better reformer, an aim that he suggests he has in the final chapter. Though Coverdale jokingly reflects on the limits of his social reformist energies, proclaiming that he would join hands with Hungarian revolutionaries if the revolution were brought "within an easy ride of my abode" (III: 247), he asserts just before his melo-dramatic and pointless confession of his love for Priscilla that the reader must not "believe me altogether changed from the young man, who once hoped strenuously, and struggled, not so much amiss" (III: 247). We should take this statement of his reformism seriously, because in important ways Coverdale has learned how to sympathize in the manner of Silas Foster. He displays that less appropriative form of sympathy in his final encounter with Hollingsworth. Journeying to visit Hollingsworth and Priscilla a number of years after the death of Zenobia and the failure of Blithedale, Coverdale con-fronts a reformer who is intent on self-reform. In response to Coverdale's cutting question of "how many criminals have you reformed?" (III: 243), Hollingsworth says, "Not one! . . . Ever since we parted, I have been busy with a single murderer!" (III: 243). Coverdale's reaction is both moving and confused: "Then the tears gushed into my eyes, and I forgave him" (III: 243). The spontaneity of the tears suggests a non-violative form of sympathy that is honest and potentially productive. The confusion lies in the question of who should be forgiving whom.

In light of this closing image of tears and retreat, we might ask, then, where is social reform at the end of the novel? For many readers, it is dead in the water, an impossibility in a world of decadent spectacle, materialism, and selfishness. Gordon Hutner states that Coverdale's "beleaguered first-person narrative replicates the very disintegration of self which reformist movements mean to correct but which ultimately, for Hawthorne, exhibits their fail-ure"; Richard Millington remarks on the novel's depiction of the "emptiness at the center of the self and of the culture that enfolds it"; Gillian Brown and Lori Merish see in Coverdale's (and the Blithedalers') reformism little more than a consumerism that reenforces the culture's misogyny, homophobia, and materialism.[21] The same year that Hawthorne published *Blithedale* he also published his campaign biography for his Bowdoin College friend Franklin Pierce. Hawthorne's reactionary attack on abolitionists in that volume, along with his apolitical assertion that God will cause slavery "to vanish like a dream" at the point when "all its uses shall have been fulfilled," have further contributed to a general consensus that *Blithedale* has to be read in conservative terms as an attack on the sentimental culture of reform.[22]

But such a thoroughgoing conservative or apolitical reading, as I have been suggesting, would only replicate the surface cynicism of Coverdale's knowing, ironic, self-protective, and self-parodic narrative. (It would also make too much of a campaign biography that was more a letter of recommendation for a friend than an impassioned statement of Hawthorne's political convictions.[23]) In the figures of Silas Foster and Zenobia there are attractive representatives of reform and sympathy; and in Coverdale's retrospective declarations of his solidarity with the aspirations of the Blithedalers, there remains a commitment to the possibilities of reform. What Hawthorne is challenging through Coverdale's narrative are the untroubled connections between sympathy and reform that permeated sentimental culture. In *Blithedale*, Hawthorne gives life to radical possibilities of reform, particularly through the magnificent characterization of Zenobia. It is of course characteristic of Hawthorne that he seeks to contain precisely the radical forms of dissent and alterity that engage his fictional imagination. As he famously intones after boldly limning Hester Prynne's feminist revolutionism in chapter 13 of *The Scarlet Letter*: "The scarlet letter had not done its office" (1: 166). In Coverdale's narrative, Hawthorne attempts similar forms of containment and control, particularly with respect to Zenobia, but ultimately his imaginative and political sympathies are too complex and contradictory to be reduced to a simple conservatism or reactionism.

In a pioneering essay published in 1968, "*The Blithedale Romance*: A Radical Reading," Nina Baym made claims for *Blithedale*'s radicalism by underscoring the novel's "attack on repressive social organization," its celebration of "the creative energy both of nature and the self," and its feminism, which "outperforms the feminists in the decisive way in which [Hawthorne] links the liberation and fulfillment of the male to his understanding of and relation to women."[24] In my own effort to re-radicalize *Blithedale* in the wake of much critical writing that insists upon its conservatism and cynicism, I have been making two large arguments: (1) that Coverdale's limitations as a critic of reform are part of a deliberate narrative strategy of self-presentation that is intended to provoke negative responses from his readers and to mask his genuine commitment to reform; and (2) that in working with sentimental notions of sympathy, Hawthorne through his narrator exposes the limits of contemporaneous formations of sympathy, encouraging his readers to imagine a subaltern world of the poor and disenfranchised that eludes the appropriative gazes of reformers. A recognition of otherness, of difference, Hawthorne suggests, is what is missing from antebellum reform as sentimentally conceived. It is only from within that world, which needs to be apprehended in a manner very different from Coverdale's, that meaningful social change can come about. That prospect both engages and frightens Coverdale (and Hawthorne), but it gives life and energy to *Blithedale*.

In many respects *Blithedale* is one of the boldest reform texts of the 1850s, powerfully exposing the hazards of trying to make the other into what Zenobia calls "all self!" (III: 218). In simultaneously participating in and critiquing sentimentalism by reminding us of the great distance between self and other, *Blithedale* has the potential to provide its readers with a more compelling understanding of what could be called the socio-emotional dynamics of reform than a work like *Uncle Tom's Cabin*, precisely because of its perverse insistence on regularly frustrating the reader's desires for some sort of communion with the other. Unlike readers of *Uncle Tom's Cabin*, the reader of *Blithedale* has to recognize difference and the existence of alternative histories and perspectives, and to that extent *Blithedale* importantly clears the ground for the possibility of social reforms that are not simply the reflections of imperial selves. To be sure, *Uncle Tom's Cabin* may have helped to inspire a war against slavery while *Blithedale* has had a more rarefied existence as a novel that seems simply to satirize reform. But if *Uncle Tom's Cabin* truly inspired a war against slavery by encouraging white middle-class readers to feel close imaginative connections to black people, then the continuing racial prejudice and violence during and after the war – for instance, the New York City draft riots, the resistance of prominent feminists to the Fifteenth Amendment, the failure of Reconstruction – do not make much sense. Stowe's sentimentalism exacerbated contemporaneous sectional conflicts, but it did not bring blacks and whites together, a fact she recognized by positing at the end of her novel that Liberian colonization may prove to be the best solution for a nation facing intractable racial conflicts. Hawthorne had very different designs on the world than Stowe, and his novel of social reform has provoked current critics to wrestle with the problem of sentimentalism's dependence on sympathetic identification.[25] If *Blithedale* did not accomplish much cultural work in its own time, it has the potential, through its insistence on the reality of a recalcitrant otherness, to do some cultural work in our own, even if it is work that Hawthorne, with his fairly conservative views, would probably find himself unable to sympathize with.

NOTES

1. Gordon Hutner, *Secrets and Sympathy: Forms of Disclosure in Hawthorne's Novels* (Athens: University of Georgia Press, 1988), p. 8. See also Roy R. Male, "Hawthorne and the Concept of Sympathy," *PMLA* 68 (1953): 138–49; and John Stafford, "Sympathy Comes to America," in *Themes and Directions in American Literature: Essays in Honor of Ray B. Browne and Donald Pizer* (Lafayette, IN: Purdue University Studies, 1969), pp. 24–37.

2. On Hawthorne and Adam Smith, see Lester H. Hunt, "*The Scarlet Letter*: Hawthorne's Theory of Moral Sentiments," *Philosophy and Literature* 8 (1984): 75–88; and Lori Merish, *Sentimental Materialism: Gender, Commodity Culture, and Nineteenth-Century American Literature* (Durham, NC: Duke University Press, 2000), ch. 3. According to Marion L. Kesselring, *Hawthorne's Reading, 1828–1850: A Transcription and Identification of Titles Recorded in the Charge-Books of the Salem Athenaeum* (1949; rpt. New York: Haskell Books, 1975), p. 61, Hawthorne borrowed Smith's *Theory of Moral Sentiments* from the Salem Athenaeum in 1827. My argument on connections between antebellum sentimental culture and eighteenth-century notions of sympathy and sensibility is indebted to June Howard, "What is Sentimentality?," *American Literary History* 11 (1999): 63–81. See also Julia Stern, *The Plight of Feeling: Sympathy and Dissent in the Early American Novel* (Chicago: University of Chicago Press, 1997); Elizabeth Barnes, *States of Sympathy: Seduction and Democracy in the American Novel* (New York: Columbia University Press, 1997); and Julie Ellison, *Cato's Tears and the Making of Anglo-American Emotion* (Chicago: University of Chicago Press, 1999).

3. Adam Smith, *The Theory of Moral Sentiments*, ed. D. D. Raphael and A. L. Macfie (London: Oxford University Press, 1976), p. 9. For a useful discussion of the theatrical dynamics of Smith's notion of sympathy, see David Marshall, *The Surprising Effects of Sympathy: Marivaux, Diderot, Rousseau, and Mary Shelley* (Chicago: University of Chicago Press, 1988), esp. pp. 4–7.

4. See Jane Tompkins, *Sensational Designs: The Cultural Work of American Fiction, 1790–1860* (New York: Oxford University Press, 1985), ch. 5. On sentimentalism and reform, see also Shirley Samuels, "Introduction," in Samuels, ed., *The Culture of Sentiment: Race, Gender, and Sentimentality in Nineteenth-Century America* (New York: Oxford University Press, 1992); and Joanne Dobson, "Reclaiming Sentimental Literature," *American Literature* 69 (1997): 263–88.

5. Marianne Noble, *The Masochistic Pleasures of Sentimental Literature* (Princeton: Princeton University Press, 2000), p. 144; Glenn Hendler, "The Structure of Sentimental Experience," *Yale Journal of Criticism* 12 (1999): 147; Noble, "Response to the Responses," *Yale Journal of Criticism* 12 (1999): 167. (Hendler had responded to Noble's chapter on Stowe, "The Sentimental Ecstasies of Sentimental Wounding in *Uncle Tom's Cabin*," which was first printed in *Yale Journal*

of Criticism 10 [1997]: 295–320.) Karen Sánchez-Eppler writes: "At stake in the feminists' likening of women to slaves is the recognition that personhood can be annihilated and a person owned, absorbed, and unnamed . . . The difficulty of preventing moments of identification from becoming acts of appropriation constitutes the essential dilemma of feminist-abolitionist rhetoric" (*Touching Liberty: Abolition, Feminism, and the Politics of the Body* [Berkeley: University of California Press, 1993], pp. 19–20).

6. Hawthorne to David Mack, letter of 18 July 1841, in *Letters*, xv: 552. As he wrote Sophia Peabody from Brook Farm on 1 June 1841: "It is my opinion, dearest, that a man's soul may be buried and perish under a dung-heap or in a furrow of the field, just as well as under a pile of money" (xv: 545). For background on Brook Farm, see Henry W. Sams, ed., *Autobiography of Brook Farm* (Englewood Cliffs, NJ: Prentice-Hall, 1958); Richard Francis, "The Ideology of Brook Farm," in *Studies in the American Renaissance* (Boston: Twayne, 1977); Joel Myerson, ed., *The Brook Farm Book: A Collection of First-Hand Accounts of the Community* (New York: Garland Publishing, Inc., 1987); and the materials in the Bedford Cultural Edition of Nathaniel Hawthorne, *The Blithedale Romance*, ed. William E. Cain (Boston: Bedford Books, 1996).

7. Similar conflicts inform Hawthorne's presentation of reform in "The Hall of Fantasy" (1843), a sketch written shortly after his experience at Brook Farm. Though the sketch satirizes reformism as a narcissistic fantasy that, like the edifice of the Hall of Fantasy, "give[s] the impression of a dream, which might be dissipated and shattered to fragments, by merely stamping the foot upon the pavement," central to the complexity and power of the sketch is the narrator's admiration for the idealism, energy, and commitment of actual social reformers: "I love and honor such men" (*Hawthorne: Tales and Sketches*, ed. Roy Harvey Pearce [New York: Library of America, 1982], pp. 734, 740).

8. See Hawthorne to Sophia Peabody, letter of 18 October 1841, *Letters*, xv: 588–91. On Hawthorne and mesmerism, see Maria M. Tatar, *Spellbound: Studies on Mesmerism and Literature* (Princeton, NJ: Princeton University Press, 1978), pp. 189–229; Taylor Stoehr, *Hawthorne's Mad Scientists: Pseudoscience and Social Science in Nineteenth-Century Life and Letters* (Hamdon, CT: Archon Books, 1978); and Samuel Chase Coale, *Mesmerism and Hawthorne: Mediums of American Romance* (Tuscaloosa: University of Alabama Press, 1998).

9. On antebellum reform and the novel, see my "Fiction and Reform 1," in Emory Elliott *et al.*, eds., *The Columbia History of the American Novel: New Views* (New York: Columbia University Press, 1991), pp. 130–54. My discussion of *Blithedale* and reform draws on several paragraphs in that chapter. See also Ronald G. Walters, *American Reformers, 1815–1860* (New York: Hill and Wang, 1978).

10. For a reading of Coverdale's insider/outsider narrative strategies in the context of antebellum nativism, see my *Conspiracy and Romance: Studies in Brockden Brown, Cooper, Hawthorne, and Melville* (New York: Cambridge University Press, 1989), ch. 3.

11. On male sentimentalism, see Mary Chapman and Glenn Hendler, eds., *Sentimental Men: Masculinity and the Politics of Affect in American Culture* (Berkeley: University of California Press, 1999).

12. Christopher Castiglia, "Abolition's Racial Interiors and the Making of White Civic Depth," *American Literary History* 14 (2002): 37.

13. On the novel's sexual politics, see Lauren Berlant, "Fantasies of Utopia in *The Blithedale Romance*," *American Literary History* 1 (1989): 30–62; and Benjamin Scott Grossberg, " 'The Tender Passion Was Very Rife Among Us': Queer Utopia and *The Blithedale Romance*," *Studies in American Fiction* 28 (2000): 3–25. See also Barabara F. Lefcowitz and Allan B. Lefcowitz's still provocative "Some Rents in the Veil: New Light on Priscilla and Zenobia," *Nineteenth-Century Fiction* 21 (1966): 263–75.

14. Castiglia, "Abolition's Racial Interiors," p. 39.

15. Merish, *Sentimental Materialism*, p. 172. See also Gillian Brown, *Domestic Individualism: Imagining Self in Nineteenth-Century America* (Berkeley: University of California Press, 1990), ch. 4.

16. For a reading of the public entertainment of the Veiled Lady in the context of the increasingly privatized nature of domestic life, see Richard H. Brodhead, *Culture of Letters: Scenes of Reading and Writing in Nineteenth-Century America* (Chicago: University of Chicago Press, 1993), ch. 2.

17. Smith, *The Theory of Moral Sentiments*, pp. 13, 11, 13.

18. See, for example, David Leverenz's lively (but self-righteous) recoil from Coverdale in *Manhood and the American Renaissance* (Ithaca: Cornell University Press, 1989), pp. 247–58. For a useful discussion of Hawthorne's deliberate efforts to alienate his readers from Coverdale, see E. Shaskan Bumas, "Fictions of the Panopticon: Prison, Utopia, and the Out-Penitent in the Works of Nathaniel Hawthorne," *American Literature* 73 (2001): 121–45. See also Jonathann Auerbach, *The Romance of Failure: First-Person Fictions of Poe, Hawthorne, and James* (New York: Oxford University Press, 1989), ch. 2; and Dana Brand, *The Spectator and the City in Nineteenth-Century American Literature* (New York: Cambridge University Press, 1991), ch. 7.

19. See, for example, Mary Suzanne Schriber, "Justice to Zenobia," *New England Quarterly* 55 (1982): 61–78; Beverly Hume, "Restructuring the Case Against Coverdale," *Nineteenth-Century Fiction* 40 (1986): 387–99; Leland S. Person, Jr., *Aesthetic Headaches: Women and a Masculine Poetics in Poe, Melville, and Hawthorne* (Athens: University of Georgia Press, 1988), pp. 146–60; and Joel Pfister, *The Production of Personal Life: Class, Gender, and the Psychological in Hawthorne's Fiction* (Stanford, CA: Stanford University Press, 1991), ch. 3.

20. Russ Castronovo, *Necro Citizenship: Death, Eroticism, and the Public Sphere in the Nineteenth-Century United States* (Durham, NC: Duke University Press, 2001), p. 142.

21. Hutner, *Secrets and Sympathy*, p. 103; Richard H. Millington, *Practicing Romance: Narrative Form and Cultural Engagement in Hawthorne's Fiction* (Princeton, NJ: Princeton University Press, 1992), p. 172; Brown, *Domestic Individualism*, ch. 4; Merish, *Sentimental Materialism*, ch. 3. For a seminal study of the novel as a meditation on the breakdown of the authority and values of New England culture, see James McIntosh, "The Instability of Belief in *The Blithedale Romance*," *Prospects* 9 (1984): 71–114.

22. Nathaniel Hawthorne, *Life of Franklin Pierce* (1852), in Hawthorne, *Miscellanies: Biographical and Other Sketches and Letters* (Boston and New York: Houghton Mifflin Company, 1900), p. 166.

23. When Hawthorne hooked up with Franklin Pierce and other future Democrats at Bowdoin College during the 1820s, Jacksonian Democrats were socially progressive, anti-elitist, and, like most other whites of the time, irrespective of party, racist. Over time, Hawthorne's passions were more for his friends, whom he loved, than for their politics.

24. Nina Baym, "*The Blithedale Romance*: A Radical Reading," *Journal of English and Germanic Philology* 67 (1968): 546, 553.

25. Hawthorne's *Blithedale* has an important place in recent studies of sentimental culture, such as Brown's *Domestic Individualism* and Merish's *Sentimental Materialism*. Noble's *Masochistic Pleasures* concludes with a discussion of *Blithedale* (pp. 195–98). Recent critical assessments of sentimental culture would appear to have been inspired by Hawthorne's.

11

EMILY MILLER BUDICK

Perplexity, sympathy, and the question of the human: a reading of *The Marble Faun*

By almost all accounts, *The Marble Faun* is the most obscure of Hawthorne's four full-length romances. Not only does it break stride with the other long romances and most of the short fiction by being set outside the United States ("Rappaccini's Daughter," the notable exception, is also set in Italy), but it seems even to violate Hawthorne's own carefully specified definition of romance fiction. This is the definition put forth in the preface to *The House of the Seven Gables*, in which Hawthorne establishes the basic features of what becomes an influential, perhaps definitive American genre:

> When a writer calls his work a Romance, it need hardly be observed that he wishes to claim a certain latitude, both as to its fashion and material, which he would not have felt himself entitled to assume, had he professed to be writing a Novel. The latter form of composition is presumed to aim at a very minute fidelity, not merely to the possible, but to the probable and ordinary course of man's experience. The former – while, as a work of art, it must rigidly subject itself to laws, and while it sins unpardonably, so far as it may swerve aside from the truth of the human heart – has fairly a right to present that truth under circumstances, to a great extent, of the writer's own choosing or creation...He will be wise, no doubt, to make a very moderate use of the privileges here stated, and, especially, to mingle the Marvellous rather as a slight, delicate, and evanescent flavor, than as any portion of the actual substance of the dish offered to the Public. He can hardly be said, however, to commit a literary crime, even if he disregard this caution.
>
> (II: I)

Though *The Marble Faun* does, like *The Scarlet Letter* and *The House of the Seven Gables*, not to mention many of the short stories, come under the "Romantic definition . . . in the attempt to connect a by-gone time with the very Present that is flitting away from us," nonetheless it violates in the extreme the far more important caution that informs Hawthorne's definition: "to mingle the Marvellous rather as a slight, delicate, and evanescent flavor" (II: 2, 1). This is the aspect of the Hawthornean definition that Henry James also emphasizes when he cautions the romancer "to cut the cable" that tethers the text to the real world in such a way that the reader cannot "detect" the break.[1] Hawthorne's last work of fiction, published a good eight years after the other three full-length romances and after both a significant hiatus in Hawthorne's writing career and a change of abode as he served as American consul in Liverpool, does nothing if not cut the cable so as to bring the gap between real and non-real into full view of the reader. So inundated is the text with unresolved and sometimes implausible mysteries that his readers actually demanded he add a demystifying postscript to the second edition of the novel. This postscript, however, clarifies almost nothing, leaving *The Marble Faun* his most fully mysterious text. What, we might ask, prompted Hawthorne to produce as the culminating work of his career a narrative that, in a word that repeatedly and in varying contexts circulates throughout the text, is so thoroughly and unmitigatingly *perplexing*?

Perplexity and the question of the human

Romance fiction, as practiced and defined by Hawthorne and the tradition he founds (Melville, James, and Faulkner, to name the key players) is a form of skepticist inquiry. The fiction asks, interrogates, and plays out the central inquiry of philosophical skepticism: how do I know the world exists? How do I know that I exist in it? Unlike other forms of skepticism, however, including some contemporary versions of it within the field of literature and literary criticism, romance fiction asks this question, not in order to dismiss out of hand the possibilities of human knowledge or (even more importantly) of human action in a not-completely knowable world. Rather it pushes this inquiry forward in order to insist on the exquisite difficulty of making just those moral judgments as we human beings, despite the inadequacy of our evidences, are nonetheless required to make but which, because of our doubts, also require that we always take into account our own and other peoples' subjectivities. It is in order to display the unknowability of the world and thereby to produce the proper moral pressure to make decisions in the absence of absolute knowledge that Hawthorne's fiction veers toward the historical and the supernatural, sometimes both: for the past, more vividly than the present, impresses upon us an awareness that reality is literally unknowable and unverifiable. It is far easier for us to accept that we can never know for sure what happened *then*, in the past, not before our very eyes, than to accept what is also true and perhaps even more pertinent: that the evidences of our senses in the here and now are hardly more reliable.

Yet this is the point of Hawthorne's fiction over and over again. There is no relying on sense evidence for our knowledge of the world or, therefore, for the moral evidences by which we would conduct our lives. Goodman

Brown assumes that, if he sees Faith's pink ribbons fluttering down from the heavens, they must be real and they must mean what he thinks they mean. He acts accordingly. We think the opposite, and hence we know what to think of Goodman Brown's (not to mention the Puritans') mental and emotional disposition and how to respond. But what, the story makes us ask, if those ribbons are real? How do we know for sure that such things do not happen, or, at least, did not happen then, since the story is set two hundred years before the moment of its composition, and three hundred years before its interpretation by contemporary readers? Goodman Brown's condition is our condition. Even if we are convinced that, in reversal of Brown's position, Faith's ribbons violate the laws of physics as we in the nineteenth, twentieth, or twenty-first centuries "know" them to be and to have been even then, what do we do with the fact that for Goodman Brown in his world (which is to say, not only for this individual human being but for the entire community of which he is a part) these ribbons might quite logically, realistically be just what they appear to be? There are certainly things that we in the twenty-first century also take for epistemological truths that will one day be proven uninformed misperceptions. How, then, do we know on what bases to determine our conduct in the world, and how to respond to what is, to our own perception, clearly revealed to us to be sin or moral misbehavior?

The possibility of the ribbons' realness produces for the reader the same dilemma, albeit in reverse, confronted by the protagonist himself, whom the story seems so clearly to set up for ridicule and blame. Therefore, we may have to judge Brown without knowing for a certainty whether his evidences, or ours, are spectral or otherwise. And once we take the step of imagining for a moment that those ribbons, as figures within a crafted fiction, are less material objects than symbols for something else – knowledge and truth themselves, perhaps – then the power of the story explodes with stunning force. How do we even know how to understand words spoken or written to us by others, whether in life or as fiction? What do we do with other people's incomprehensible and oft-times fantastic stories?[2]

Hawthorne does provide us, in much of his work, with a complicated answer to the dilemma of acting morally within an unknowable, undecidable, and "mysterious" reality, which, one way or another, is the subject of most romance fiction. That answer has to do with maintaining a self-conscious knowledge of the undecidability of physical phenomena and therefore the subjectivity of all human perception. In other words, by making ourselves into philosophical skeptics, aware of the unknowability of the world and the uncertainty of our judgments, and yet recognizing that we need to act in that world by principles both ethical and intellectual, whether or not they are founded on provable evidences, we at very least proceed with a kind of caution and tolerance that may well spell the difference between moral, social, and political tyranny, on the one hand (such as the Puritans represent), and, on the other, generosity and goodness. Thus, also, the arguments of such major works as *The Scarlet Letter* or "Rappaccini's Daughter," to cite two of the works expressly alluded to in *The Marble Faun* (*The Marble Faun* is something of a retrospective, scanning back over Hawthorne's entire literary career). Could the protagonist, or the culture, only say *perhaps* – perhaps I have misperceived, perhaps my moral dictates are too absolute, too unyielding to take into account all the circumstances here represented, perhaps I do not understand – then *perhaps* human beings might conduct themselves toward each other in kinder, more benevolent ways. Looking back over the lifetime of his achievement, from the distance of time and space, Hawthorne recasts in *The Marble Faun* the great ethical and esthetic insights of his career but plays them out on less explicitly philosophical grounds, thereby bringing into focus another aspect of his thought. This is recognition that the hardest and most precious goal of civilization, in all its various forms of expression (culture, religion, politics), depends on something so simple, so slight, as to hardly seem a matter for intellectual or literary contemplation: the sympathetic understanding of one human being for another. For if there is a word that circulates in the story as insistently as the word "perplexity," it is the word "sympathy." *The Marble Faun*, more than any other of Hawthorne's work, explores the problem of sympathy, or more precisely its failure, not, as in *The Scarlet Letter* or *The House of the Seven Gables* or the major tales (such as "Young Goodman Brown" or "The Minister's Black Veil") as an expression of political corruption or religious or intellectual fanaticism, but rather, and more basically, as a rather unexceptional unwillingness on the parts of ordinary people to listen and hear what another human being is saying and to thereby acknowledge another person's suffering and pain. Sympathy, in Hawthorne's view, is a receptivity to others that, as Gordon Hutner has argued, enables the compassionate comprehension of and empathy with another person's suffering.[3] It is an attitude of mind, I suggest, that eschews the necessity for, perhaps even precludes the possibility of, concrete action in the world taken in response to that other individual's pain. Sympathy, as Hawthorne means the term, is passive, quiet, like art itself. Therefore, it is very basically associated with the tradition of art, though not necessarily with every variety of art work nor, more importantly, with the tradition of interpretation, which tends to insert an ethical, even a religious, dimension that art itself assiduously evades.

One of the most distinctive features of *The Marble Faun* is that it features no villains as major protagonists. There is of course the Model, who is the origin of Miriam's suffering in the tale and her tormentor, the model (as it were) of all torment and distress. It is the Model who finally becomes her or more precisely Donatello's victim. But the Model plays a minor role and is kept largely off-stage for most of the novel, even before he is killed. Similarly, we are occasionally reminded, as if in an afterthought and in order to explain some of the pressure on the characters, of the existence of the tyrannical government in present-day Rome – a precursor of Henry James's less political but equally malign aristocracy. But there is in *The Marble Faun* no world of Puritan clergy and colonial governors, no fanatical religious types like Goodman Brown or Father Hooper, no power-hungry liars or manipulators like Judge Pyncheon or Westervelt or even misconceived social reformers like Holgrave or Coverdale. Rather we have as our major protagonists four rather congenial, well-meaning young people, three of whom are artists, all of whom get trapped not by the conspiracies and dictates of others but by their own failure simply to listen to and sympathize with and help one another – not materially but emotionally and psychologically. Indeed, these young artists cannot take the measure of their own life's work: they are poor interpreters of the tradition of painting and sculpture to which they themselves contribute their considerable talents. *The Marble Faun* is essentially a story of missed moral opportunities, of moments when ordinary human beings might in very simple ways have eased each others' paths through life. It is also the story of the failure of art, and of how that failure is implicit in the limitations of human beings and their creative powers.

The plot of *The Marble Faun*, for all its inexplicable events, is really quite simple. It tells the story of four young people in Rome in the middle of the nineteenth century. Hilda, Kenyon, and Miriam are the artists of the tale; Donatello is a native of Italy, a count by family lineage but also a simple and naïve rustic, the "faun" of the title. For reasons that remain incompletely explained even at the end, Miriam is being pursued in Rome by a man, to whom she is joined in a prior crime involving her broken betrothal to an arranged and unsuitable partner and of which she is innocent. This man (the Model) is thrown off a cliff by Donatello at Miriam's largely unconscious bidding – a scene of murder that is witnessed by Hilda and that finally comes to the knowledge of Kenyon as well. How the four young people, the perpetrators and witnesses of crime (involved either actively or passively, consciously or unconsciously), come to cope with the fact of crime (and sin) in their lives, and its consequences for the other individuals about whom they care, forms the substance of the novel. Indeed, a major preoccupation of the novel is the difference, if any, between sin and crime, on the one hand, and, on the other, the simple, more passive knowledge of evil, which we might think of simply as experience, and how this difference helps define the ethics and esthetics of culture.

The four protagonists also form two sets of somewhat antithetical romantic couples, even though all of them are mutual friends and the two men have a special relationship to each other as do the two women, producing another set of couples defined along lines of gender. The two sets of romantic couples, furthermore, constellate around national and, importantly, religious affiliations, such that the two couples incorporate a sharp division between religious, national identities. The New Englander Kenyon, a sculptor, is in love with the pale, innocent, saintly copyist Hilda, who (as if to drum the point home and add a somewhat contemptuous aspect to this fact) is throughout the novel referred to as a "daughter of the Puritans." No one who knows Hawthorne's earlier fiction can for a moment doubt that, despite the other characters' adoration of her, Hilda is being set up for condemnation on some level or other. Indeed, by the end of the novel Hilda is perhaps the most disappointing of all the characters, the one who falls furthest from the ideal of sympathy the novel is setting up. Donatello, the Italian rustic/count, who is Catholic, is in love with the passionate, beautiful painter Miriam, whose origins are murky but who is throughout the book associated with a faith that one would not expect to emerge within Hawthorne's fiction at all (especially not in Rome): Judaism. Eventually Miriam is specifically identified as being partly Jewish (IV: 429), but from the beginning she is associated with rumors of her Jewish ancestry (IV: 22), she is obsessed with vengeful Old Testament Jewesses (IV: 43), she looks Jewish even in her own self-representations (IV: 48), and her name is given as Miriam Schaefer (IV: 39), though this is not her real name. The text also abounds with references to things Jewish and Old Testament (IV: 53, 159, 370–71).

The coupling of Roman Catholicism and Judaism in a novel set in Rome and having to do with pagan antiquity as well is not as odd as it might at first appear. Roman Catholicism, Judaism, and paganism are all ancient, old-world religions when compared with Protestantism, which just might be thought of, to invoke Hilda's profession, as a largely American copy or even a plagiarism (IV: 124) of these ancestor faiths. Whatever this novel has to say to us on the level of personal ethics, its message is equally socio-political and cultural. Paralleling both the tensions within each of the couples and the opposition between them is a story concerning the history of moral thought within three of the world's major religions (four if one counts classical antiquity) and within the two major communities of Western civilization: Europe and America.

Religion and nation turn out to be as much protagonists in this novel as the characters themselves, as do nature and culture as apparently contending but

finally mutually reinforcing arenas of human experience. Of utmost importance to the thematic valence of the book is this structure of distinct, separate containers of human civilization – nation, religion, culture, nature –
in their pairings and interrelationships, mutually reinforcing and antagonistically opposing one another. All of these forces come together in the two
love stories. At the end of the novel, in the pattern of Shakespearean comedy
and in reverse of Adam's and Eve's expulsion from the garden (which is one
of the myths around which the novel circulates), the two Americans take
their peaceful but distinctly pale, pallid way together back home. The two
Europeans, more in the manner of tragedy and charting the actual course of
world history, find themselves eternally divided but passionate and deeply
devout penitents, ever exiled from Eden but somehow in the world itself in
a way that Hilda and Kenyon are not.

Another bifurcation in the novel, which proves crucial to its interpretation,
is this divide between comedy and tragedy as literary genres. Anticipating
and likely providing the very foundations for such novels as Henry James's
Daisy Miller and *The Portrait of a Lady*, *The Marble Faun* concerns sin and
retribution as embedded within mythic, political, and psychological scenar-
ios beyond any simple exposition of them, and which quite possibly are only
to be resolved, when they are, by some sort of spiritual, emotional lobotomy
that leaves behind only the shell of culture – that is, unless culture itself,
particularly literature, can discover some more illuminating, perhaps even
cheering role to play in the lives of human beings. How might telling stories
(writing them, reading them) become a bolstering, if not an ethical activity
that eschews the kind of moralistic tyranny of religion itself? As in both *The
Scarlet Letter* and *The House of the Seven Gables*, the title of the romance is
more than a simple pointer to the major subject or theme or even symbol of
the narrative. *The Marble Faun* as text does nothing less than replace some
object within the text that is the source of suffering or oppression. Like *The
Scarlet Letter* and *The House of the Seven Gables*, it names itself as text as the
new (novel) narrative version of the subject or symbol it thus replaces. What
is the difference between the marble faun cut in stone that is the object of
inquiry both for the protagonists of the novel and for the narrator, if not the
novelist himself, and the romance fiction entitled *The Marble Faun*, which
is the text that Hawthorne produces? Throughout the novel the faun is a
subject that, in the often repeated word I have already cited, *perplexes* the
characters. So, we are told in the final chapter, is Hawthorne's novel. Indeed
Hawthorne uses the same word to describe his own response to the painting of Beatrice that is the central portrait of the novel, the painterly (and, it
turns out, feminine) counterpart to the statue of the marble faun, just as
Miriam is the painterly, female alternative to the male artist/sculptor Kenyon.

What, the novel forces us to ask, are we to do with the perplexities not simply of the physical world but of human nature, perplexities that are often expressed to us through the perplexing stories people tell and the perplexing demands those stories make on us? Do we attempt to interpret, comprehend, and act on what seems to us our knowledge of other people and their stories? Or is there some other way, a way of compassionate not-knowing, by which we might apprehend, acknowledge, and hold other people's emotional lives? Insofar as the central perplexity in this novel is the status of the faun as human being, which is doubled more darkly in the "Man-Demon" Model (who is, we are told, "the last survivor of [the] vanished race" of Satyrs [IV: 33, 30]), the question of what we do with the perplexities of creation is hardly academic. It raises no lesser a question than the question of the human, of how we know another human being to be a human being and not a creature of some other sort. In the context of the slave controversy raging in the United States during the decade when *The Marble Faun* was being written and published, it is hard to see this question as not having a very specific national-moral aspect to it, a feature of the text's investigation that is reinforced by the fact that Miriam herself is reputed to have "African blood" (IV: 23) in her "mixed race" (IV: 430) heritage. Race is a subtext in *Marble Faun*. The human race is its very subject.

Embracing innocence, evil close at hand

The novel begins and ends, not with some large philosophical or religious subject, but with "four individuals": "Miriam, Hilda, Kenyon, Donatello" as announced by the chapter head of the first chapter (this is also the title of the last chapter, raising the question of what, if anything, happens between the beginning and the end of this story; indeed, raising the question whether the entire meaning of this very long novel is not already contained in the opening scene). This is how the novel begins:

> Four individuals, in whose fortunes we should be glad to interest the reader, happened to be standing in one of the saloons of the sculpture-gallery in the Capitol, at Rome. It was that room (the first, after ascending the staircase) in the centre of which reclines the noble and most pathetic figure of the Dying Gladiator, just sinking into his death-swoon. Around the walls stand the Antinous, the Amazon, the Lycian Apollo, the Juno; all famous productions of antique sculpture, and still shining in the undiminished majesty and beauty of their ideal life, although the marble, that embodies them, is yellow with time, and perhaps corroded by the damp earth in which they lay buried for centuries. Here, likewise, is seen a symbol (as apt, at this moment, as it was two thousand years ago) of the Human Soul, with its choice of Innocence or

Evil close at hand, in the pretty figure of a child, clasping a dove to her bosom, but assaulted by a snake . . . Of these four friends of ours, three were artists, or connected with Art; and, at this moment, they had been simultaneously struck by a resemblance between one of the antique statues, a well-known master-piece of Grecian sculpture, and a young Italian, the fourth member of their party . . . " . . . Our friend Donatello [says Miriam] is the very Faun of Praxiteles" . . . In truth . . . Donatello might have figured perfectly as the marble Faun, miraculously softened into flesh and blood. (IV: 5–8)

The chapter is typical, quintessential, Hawthorne. Here, with utmost casualness, we are presented with the characters who will concern us over the course of the narrative. And they just happen to be standing alongside what might well constitute not merely a symbol in its own right but the symbol most central to the novel itself. This is the marble faun, which the novel itself, as I have begun to suggest, transcribes, or in its own word transforms (the original title of the novel was *The Transformation*). But there are more statues to be seen than this one, and to be seen first. As much as anything else, *The Marble Faun* concerns these statues as statues, in other words, as works of art. It concerns the tradition that these statues collectively represent. A major subject of the text is how art illuminates human being and how we can become adequate interpreters of this tradition of artistic representation.

Therefore, one of these statues, which the four protagonists ignore, has particular relevance not only to the story about to unfold but to the characters' very interpretation of the other statue that does attract their attention. This is the statue of the "child clasping a dove to her bosom, but assaulted by a snake." One is tempted to argue that, had they tried to understand this other depiction of the "Human Soul," they might never have been dragged into the tragic events that ensue. For what is this "choice of Innocence or Evil close at hand" but exactly the "choice" – more apparent than real, it turns out, and this is part of what the statue conveys to us the readers, though not to the novel's principle actors – that befalls the characters themselves and that each, in his or her way, so badly manages. The question that the statue of the child prompts, which the characters never ask, and which is revealed in Hawthorne's skillful management of his language here, is: in what sense is innocence, or for that matter, experience, a choice? Evil, to be sure, is something one might flee or embrace. But isn't innocence rather a condition or state of mind, and one that precludes the possibility of choice altogether: for how can one either flee or embrace evil so long as one remains in the embrace of the absence of knowledge that defines innocence, a subject made integrally a part of American self-consciousness by Melville in *Billy Budd*? Experience and good are the two terms that seem to fall away here, each one of them the adequate and appropriate complement of one of the two terms cited and the necessary antithesis of the other cited term, only one of the pairs (good and evil) fairly signifying a choice. We do not ordinarily choose innocence and if we were somehow to choose it, as does the "dove" of this novel, Hilda (IV: 59; she is everywhere associated with doves), what might choosing it mean other than simply pushing away or ignoring experience, making oneself not innocent but ignorant. By the same token experience as such cannot be chosen or not. Experience simply happens to us, as it does to each of the characters in Hawthorne's romance. To even interpret the statue properly one must have entered the world of experience, which enables us to recognize evil when we see it.

What, then, is this "choice close at hand" in the figure of the child "clasping" a dove in her hand? Perhaps it is an interpretive rather than or as much as a moral choice. In typical Hawthorne fashion, the passage forces us to articulate a proposition not directly presented in the passage itself. If the statue of the child symbolizes a choice, then that choice must be between good and evil. And that means the child must relinquish her hold on innocence. What we choose in life, the statue suggests, is what to *do*, not with innocence but with experience, how we *grasp* the meanings and facts of things, to use the word that emerges as the scene unfolds and that almost immediately imports into the concept of interpretation negative connotations. The contraries, paradoxes, and dilemmas embodied by the fault lines of the statue of the child match the complexity of sculpture itself as an art form, which has come to be reduced over time and through faulty interpretation made to resemble nothing so much as moral law cast in stone, much like Mosaic law itself. Even though they are still shining undiminished and as apt today as it was two thousand years ago, these statues are, we are told, nonetheless also yellowed and corroded with time. They are completely inappropriate (the text suggests) for modern purposes, and perhaps even cause some distortion, since they give a false appearance of endurance and immortality where there is only time and change. They seem, in their survival over time, to solidify a moral law that does not indeed exist in quite so solid or substantial or permanent form and that was not necessarily what the statue itself was intended by the original artist to represent, when the statue had less of the authority of antiquity.

Properly understood, the statue of the child, like the statue of the marble faun, constructs a paradox or "perplexity" (IV: 12, 13). This is the same paradox or perplexity enacted in the text through the figure of Donatello and through the moral drama that unfolds around and through him. In fact, it is because the characters in Hawthorne's romance cannot interpret the statue adequately that they must experience, albeit vicariously, in their own lives the painful "riddle" (IV: 10) of the Human Soul, of which Donatello and Miriam become the tragic vehicles. Rather than accept the riddle of the human as a riddle not to be resolved, they choose instead, in the first instance at least, to make it, not even a scene of interpretation, which for all its problems might at least render them some insight into the moral life and its relationship to innocence and evil, but a site of merriment and frolic. From the first the group fails at what might be considered the first and primary responsibility of the moral life (perhaps also the last and final requirement as well): simple kindness and respect for another human being.

It is the troupe of young artists themselves who, before any of the events in the story unfold, cast Donatello in the role that will seal his doom. "Donatello, my dear friend," says Kenyon the sculptor, who will later try literally to cast a bust of Donatello, "pray gratify us all by taking the exact attitude of this statue" (IV: 8). Gratifying his friends (the word "gratifying" is loaded) Donatello becomes as trapped as the faun itself by what emerges as at least a potential feature of art itself, or at least of a certain kind or aspect of art, which is figured in the text through the medium of sculpture: the way in which it seems to grasp truth (to pick up one of the text's words again) only by solidifying and stultifying it, killing it as surely as Donatello himself, concretizing and acting on his feelings and those of Miriam, kills the Model. "Only a sculptor of the finest imagination, the most delicate taste, the sweetest feeling, and the rarest artistic skill – in a word, a sculptor and a poet too – ," says the narrator, "could have first dreamed of a Faun in this guise, and then have succeeded in imprisoning the sportive and frisky thing, in marble." The problem is not the sculptor's imagination but the swerve to artistic representation, which imprisons delicacy of taste and sweetness of imagination in stone. Thus, the text continues, even more damningly, "Neither man nor animal, and yet no monster, but a being in whom both races meet, on friendly ground! The idea grows coarse, as we handle it, and hardens in our grasp" (IV: 10).

Resolving ambiguities and producing sharp lines of definition and resolution, the art of sculpture is said throughout the book to be "cold and hard" (IV: 105), like Kenyon himself (cf. IV: 129). Hawthorne is producing here an opposition between painting on the one hand (which is said to soften and warm – IV: 105) and sculpture on the other, and he is associating the one, through Kenyon, with masculinity and the presumed ethical imperatives of art, and the other, through Miriam and Hilda, with femininity and the emotions (of the feeling portrayed in Guido's Beatrice, Miriam comments that she "cannot seize it" – IV: 65). Not that gender guarantees the one set of qualities or the other. Much to our disappointment and dismay, Hilda is the sternest moralist in the novel. Coming to embody in herself the figure of the child in the statue, Hilda the Dove clasps the dove so firmly to her breast as to become one herself. The only moral doves, we must come to understand, are stone ones, since real doves have the capacity neither for morality nor sympathy: they are just birds. As a copyist, Hilda cannot comprehend the painterly feeling she can nonetheless so exquisitely reproduce. Moreover, there is a gender differentiation being proposed in the text which distinguishes one type of art from another.

In this opposition between male and female varieties of art, the statue of the marble faun occupies a unique position, in particular vis-à-vis the male author of what we just might think of as a female form of narrative, the romance. Donatello, we are told, does indeed seem a "softened" version of the statue (IV: 8). Yet the statue itself contains a certain degree of softness, which has as much to do with indeterminacy of gender as of species. Like its counterpart, the statue of the (female) child, it depicts a riddle rather than a truth concerning the human soul. But also like this other statue, it contains the potential for a moral-allegorical interpretation that exactly betrays what is the essence of art and human nature both: the impossibility of translating perplexities into moral creeds. In the statue of the child, the dangerous transformation of art or riddle into moral law is contained in the allegory that the statue's implied drama seems to enact: the child embracing innocence, assaulted by evil. Simultaneously, however, and this is what the mismatching of terms in Hawthorne's interpretation exposes, the statue resists its own allegorization. Clasping innocence to her breast the child threatens to remain eternally blocked from the possibility of the moral knowledge that is contained in the swerve of terminology from innocence to evil (rather than the proper term "experience"). This child will never be capable of good, which is finally what we might have to say concerning Hilda at the end of the story. She preserves her innocence at the expense of her goodness.

In somewhat different terms, the marble faun is also a figure for the same triumph and same potential failure of the moral imagination and art. Holding in his hand "the fragment of a pipe, or some such instrument of sylvan music" (IV: 8), the faun is both a prototype of the budding (male) artist and also a commentary on the antiquity of art and how that antiquity is a part of its artistic value – not in the authority it supplies the work of art but, the opposite, in its deterioration over time. Unlike the female child who clasps innocence (in the form of a natural creature) to her breast, thus taking herself out of the realm of moral meaning-making, the faun, as himself a creature of nature, seizes the much more phallic yet still natural, snake-like pipe. This pipe is (like the child) not yet fully mature, which is to say, not yet fully potent, not yet fully male. It is also, in the present moment, fragmented, eroded by time, representing not, like the child or like the pipe in the original pristine statue, the potential of sexuality but its aftermath or demise. Like the faun's quality of sympathetic relation between the human and other races, the statue itself stands for the ambiguity that is art, as art translates and communicates between different times and conditions. This ambiguity is childlike, pre-sexual. It is also, as it were, post-sexual, a consequence of the erosion, over time, of power and potency, a feature that pertains to the whole collection of time-worn and therefore poetical statues in Rome and perhaps to the aging artist, Hawthorne himself. Looked at from the right perspective, these statues communicate the truth, not of permanence and endurance and power but of tentativity and change – as embodied in the child herself. As a figure for deficiency or inadequacy – both prepubescent and post-sexual, the pipe images the triumph of art, which is to say, its capacity to figure forth suggestively and non-coercively, non-masculinely. This is the romance that precedes sexual coupling. It is what romance as a genre is about, even in its Shakespearean origins.

But Kenyon, Hilda, and even Miriam cannot abide such ambiguity or unsatiated desire (what human being can?). The young people's urge to settle the perplexity of Donatello is represented as virtually pornographic, at very least voyeuristic, in its drive to define their friend either as faun or human being, in particular as a man in the gendered sense of the word. Thus, Donatello's ears, which the young artists would like so much to see so as to settle their doubts about him, are in the statue also a softened, "furry" substitute for some other member by which the faun would be defined less in terms of species than of gender, a reference which is also made by way of displacement through the word "leaf-shaped" in relation to these ears and through the concealed but equally phallic tail. The "riddle" of the faun in this particular statue "is indicated . . . only by two definite signs . . . the two ears . . . which are leaf-shaped [and] a certain caudal appendage – which, if the Faun of Praxiteles must be supposed to possess it at all, is hidden by the lion's skin that forms his garment" (IV: 10). Politely refraining from even the coarseness of the word "tail," Hawthorne suggests that he is unwilling to name another member as well, which is often (though in this case not) hidden by the "leaf" associated with Adam after the fall. Prelapsarian, the faun's penis is in full view. It is also limp. The question that emerges is not only, is the faun with his ears and tail fully human, but is he fully male? Does the erect penis, perhaps, come to replace the tail as the defining feature in the evolution from male faun to human male? The "idea" of the man/faun "hardens in our grasp" (10), we are told, especially through the "cold and hard" male art-form, sculpture. The unerected penis of the faun in the statue corresponds with the female, childlike innocence with which the faun is also associated and which is associated with painting as a female form and with all art as artistic precisely in its withdrawal from clasping, grasping, and otherwise determining issues of doubt.[4]

What the faun as faun embodies is the friendly meeting ground of antithetical realms of being – adult/child man/creature human/animal male/female ancient/contemporary person/artist. And it is this intermingling that, by being cast in marble by human hands, is imprisoned in the hardening grasp of human handling, to become truth, and moral truth at that. This is phallic power, and it does not have to come into play. Like painting, the written word, in Hawthorne's thought, handles truths differently, grasps ideas less coarsely and with less stultification. "Nature needed, and still needs, this beautiful creature, standing betwixt man and animal, sympathizing with each, comprehending the speech of either race, and interpreting the whole existence of one to the other," says Kenyon to Hilda. Just as Donatello may, within the real world within the novel, be the reincarnation of the faun, "softened into flesh and blood" (IV: 8), so the romance might well be the resurrection of the statue within the new and more democratic genre of the nineteenth-century novel. As Hawthorne notes in the preface to *The Marble Faun*, and in keeping with similar statements throughout his career, "The author proposed to himself merely to write a fanciful story, evolving a thoughtful moral, and did not purpose attempting a portraiture of Italian manners and character" (IV: 3). Although Richard Brodhead, in his wonderful introduction to the Penguin Classics edition of the book, finds this odd and troubling, it may be exactly the point of the romance to evade portraiture and commit itself to communicating something far less precise and detailed in the interrelation between human beings, what we just might call, using a word that, as I have already noted, recurs throughout the novel, "sympathy."

The friends' taunting of Donatello about his ears (and/or tail/phallus, or lack of the one or the other) is nothing if not a failure of sympathy. "'Donatello,' playfully cried Miriam, 'do not leave us in this perplexity! Shake aside those brown curls, my friend, and let us see whether this marvellous resemblance extends to the very tips of the ears. If so, we shall like you all the better!' 'No, no, dearest Signorina!' answered Donatello laughing, but with a certain earnestness. – 'I entreat you to take the tips of my ears for granted . . . It has always been a tender point with my forefathers and me'" (IV: 12). The one mystery that Hawthorne refuses to clear up at the end of the romance is this same "tender point" – singular – the mystery of Donatello's ears:

> The idea of the modern Faun . . . loses all the poetry and beauty which the Author fancied in it, and becomes nothing better than a grotesque absurdity, if we bring it into the actual light of day. He had hoped to mystify this anomalous creature between the Real and the Fantastic, in such a manner that the reader's sympathies might be excited to a certain pleasurable degree, without impelling him to ask how Cuvier would have classified poor Donatello, or to insist upon being told, in so many words, whether he had furry ears or no. As respects all who ask such questions, the book is, to that extent, a failure.   (IV: 463–64)

This passage appears in the postscript to the text, which is added to mollify his readers' displeasure with the mystifying first ending. Essentially, however, it repeats what Hawthorne had already written in the original final chapter:

> The gentle reader, we trust, would not thank us for one of those minute elucidations, which are so tedious, and, after all, so unsatisfactory, in clearing up the romantic mysteries of a story. He is too wise to insist upon looking closely at the wrong side of the tapestry, after the right one has been sufficiently displayed to him, woven with the best of the artist's skill, and cunningly arranged with a view to the harmonious exhibition of its colours . . . The actual experience of even the most ordinary life is full of events that never explain themselves, either as regards their origins or their tendency.   (IV: 455)

Presumably this includes the author himself, who is represented at the very end of the postscript as asking one of his protagonists this very question, to which Kenyon responds "I know, but may not tell . . . On that point, at all events, there shall be not one word of explanation" (IV: 467).

But from Kenyon's first bidding Donatello to gratify his somewhat salacious, perhaps even mildly pornographic, homoerotic desire to assume the pose of the faun (an idea concerning the voyeurism of art that is picked up as well in Miriam's statement that "an artist . . . cannot sculpture nudity with a pure heart, if only because he is compelled to steal guilty glimpses at hired models" [IV: 123]), to Miriam's more directly flirtatious, seductive, request to see his ears, or, rather, his tips (do the tail and penis give the faun two tips?), to the other inquiries into Donatello's nature, or, for that matter, the attempts by each of the characters to settle the natures of the others, the individuals in Hawthorne novels are precisely unwilling to let mystery go and to live in the perplexity of incomplete and inadequate human knowledge. If the faun represents the quality of human sympathy, which Hawthorne's romance would attempt to reconstitute textually, what is lacking in each and every one of the characters, at least at some point or other in the narrative, is exactly such sympathy. Sympathy, as it emerges in the novel, is the capacity to listen and hear the expressions of another person's pain, which is to say to experience his or her humanness, *without* in any way acting on that knowledge, without making the possibility of action a precondition for such listening and hearing and acknowledging. The strategy of Hawthorne's fiction, argues Michael Dunne, is to keep us reading, for it is in the reader–writer relationship, in the ongoing negotiation or conversation between the individual and his culture (as many of Hawthorne's best critics such as Kenneth Dauber, Richard Millington, and Edgar Dryden, for example, have argued) that is contained both the aesthetic force and moral power of Hawthorne's art.[5]

Justice, mercy, and the sympathetic listener

Hawthorne would require neither "confession," which is the Roman Catholic form of listening (represented in the scene in which Hilda makes confession at St. Peter's and is rebuked by the priest for availing herself of a religious form the consequences of which she is not ready to assume), nor justice and vengeance, which are the Judaic modes of conduct represented by Miriam's paintings of the Old Testament figures Judith and Yael, by the Roman political bureaucracy, and by Donatello's murder of the Model. Thus, when Miriam first approaches Kenyon to confess her secret to him, Kenyon does not exactly refuse to hear it, but, rather, he declines to hear it *unless* he is reassured that he can do something about it:

> "Oh, my friend," cried she, with sudden passion, "will you be my friend indeed? I am lonely, lonely, lonely! There is a secret in my heart that burns me! – that tortures me! Sometimes, I fear to go mad of it! Sometimes, I hope to die of it! But neither of the two happens. Ah, if I could but whisper it to only one human soul! . . . Perhaps – perhaps – but Heaven only knows – you might understand me! Oh, let me speak!"
>
> "Miriam, dear friend," replied the sculptor, "if I can help you, speak freely, as to a brother."
>
> "Help me? No!" said Miriam.
>
> Kenyon's response had been perfectly frank and kind; and yet the subtlety of Miriam's emotion detected a certain reserve and alarm in his warmly expressed readiness to hear her story. In his secret soul, to say the truth, the sculptor doubted whether it were well for this poor, suffering girl to speak what she so yearned to say, or for him to listen. If there were any active duty of friendship to be performed, then, indeed, he would joyfully have come forward to do his best. But, if it were only a pent-up heart that sought an outlet? In that case, it was by no means so certain that a confession would do good.   (IV: 128–29)

Listening for Kenyon is a part of the "active duty of friendship," where by active duty he means some action to be "performed" which might yield some "good" – the internal and devastating logic, exactly, of Donatello's acting on Miriam's wish that the Model be dead. What indeed if this were only a pent-up heart (a glint in the eye) seeking an outlet? What "good" would come of her speaking it? Kenyon is quite right that "unless he could give her all the sympathy, and just the kind of sympathy, that the occasion required, Miriam would hate him, by-and-by, and herself still more, if he let her speak" (IV: 129). But what prevents Kenyon from giving her "just the kind of sympathy" she requires is his inability simply to sympathize with rather than advise or help her. And this he must do, he indicates, dispassionately, as a "brother," as if he must rid the relationship between them of all possible sexual, passionate ambience. The consequence of Miriam's confiding in Kenyon even the little that she reveals is to raise suspicions in his mind concerning her moral character, which he almost immediately expresses to Hilda. "You are as cold and pitiless as your own marble," Miriam says to him at the time, and later, referring back to the scene, she explains her behavior in similar terms: "finding you cold to accept my confidence," she says, "I thrust it back again" (IV: 433). Miriam is perhaps overly severe in judging Kenyon, especially since Miriam herself is as deficient in the powers of sympathy as any of the other characters. Nonetheless there is a compelling truth in her accusation, as there is in her earlier saying to Kenyon's counterpart in the novel, Hilda, that her "innocence is like a sharp steel sword" (IV: 66).

What occasions this comment on Miriam's part are Hilda's reflections on Guido's painting of Beatrice Cenci, which she has copied with impeccable perfection. As an artist, a copyist, Hilda achieves a fully sympathetic mode of relationship to the objects to which she is responding, as indeed does Kenyon as a sculptor, when he produces, without either full intentionality or consciousness, the one bust of Donatello that authentically, lovingly, conveys the young man's spirit. But what Hilda and Kenyon achieve as artists they can in no way achieve as human beings in real human relationships nor as critical interpreters of art. Indeed, it is when Hilda attempts to play art critic, to interpret the "subtle mystery" of the Beatrice (IV: 67) that her "sympathy" as an artist (IV: 59) turns into moral brutality. "Ah," says Hilda, beginning compassionately enough, "I really had quite forgotten Beatrice's history, and was thinking of her only as the picture seems to reveal her character. Yes, yes; it was terrible guilt, and inexpiable crime, and she feels it to be so. Therefore it is that the forlorn creature so longs to elude our eyes, and forever vanish away into nothingness!" And then she delivers the resounding verdict: "Her doom is just" (IV: 66).

Justice is exactly what Hawthorne's novel, let alone the painting, is *not* about. Of all the failures of moral response in the novel, it is Hilda's in relation to Miriam that is, I think, the most troubling. In a sense, Hilda and Miriam, after the murder, replay the scene between Miriam and Kenyon, drawing into greater clarity the moralistic quality that functions as a barrier to sympathetic listening within Kenyon as well. "Do not bewilder me thus, Miriam," Hilda exclaims, the word "bewilder" recalling the word "perplex" that everywhere punctuates this text;

> I am a poor, lonely girl, whom God has set here in an evil world, and given her only a white robe, and bid her wear it back to Him, as white as when she put it on. Your powerful magnetism would be too much for me. The pure, white atmosphere, in which I try to discern what things are good and true, would be discoloured.

Miriam's response to Hilda's casting herself as something like the innocent young girl in the statue at the beginning of the text (as she, albeit not the text, interprets that statue) recalls her response earlier to Kenyon: "Ah, this is hard! Ah, this is terrible! . . . As an angel, you are not amiss; but as a human creature, and a woman among earthly men and women, you need a sin to soften you!" (IV: 208–09). Hilda is no living faun but a dove cast in stone.

Both Hilda and Donatello raise the same question raised by the statues of the young child and the marble faun, the question that has seemed to many critics the central issue of *The Marble Faun*: the issue of the Fortunate Fall. Kenyon articulates a version of this doctrine in the final chapter of the novel proper (i.e., the chapter preceding the postscript which Hawthorne adds later): "Here comes my perplexity," continues Kenyon, once again using that signal word; "Sin has educated Donatello, and elevated him. Is Sin, then – which we deem such a dreadful blackness in the Universe – is it, like Sorrow, merely an element of human education, through which we struggle to a higher and purer state than we could otherwise have attained. Did Adam fall, that we might ultimately rise to a far loftier Paradise than his?" to which Hilda, true to form, responds: "Oh, hush! . . . This is terrible . . . You have shocked me beyond words" (IV: 460).

By the end of the novel, the alternative to "innocence" seems to be, not evil or its religious counterpart sin, but "sorrow" – a far more suitable antithesis to innocence, which, like sorrow, is not a moral category but a state of mind or an emotion. But Hilda cannot imagine anything but choices and ethical judgments. "Beyond words" are exactly the right words for the text to use here. For Kenyon's words come from the tradition of words, in this case the Miltonic tradition of literature, which, like the tradition of art which the characters also so imperfectly understand and which they would flee, has provided an alternative to the moral, religious language represented by Hilda and Rome. Thus, Kenyon will withdraw his words ("I never did believe it," he says of his words, which are Milton's words as well), and Hilda and Kenyon, in reverse of Adam and Eve's progression into exile, will wend their way home to an America that has seemed to many itself the new Eden of the modern world. But rather than represent a recovery of paradise lost, or even of the "reality of life" which the text, taking up Kenyon's and Hilda's perception, imagines it to be, America comes to seem to the reader a final banishment from the only reality that matters: the perplexed and perplexing world of innocence and evil. Hilda and Kenyon do not prevent their entry into the world of experience. They do, however, push that world aside for something far more tepid and simplistic – the innocence that is simply the denial of what they themselves might have learned and come to understand.

Miriam's hands, extended in "a gesture of benediction," "repel," we are told, even as they "blessed" the pair, "as if Miriam stood on the other side of a fathomless abyss, and warned them from its verge" (IV: 461). This culminating moment of benediction repeats several such moments in the text, including the moment when Kenyon, doubled by the statue of the pontiff in the square of Perugia, blesses what can only be termed a marriage (of "conversation sweet," in Milton's phrase) between Miriam and Donatello. For a moment we think, along with Hilda and Kenyon, that on the other side of the abyss from which Miriam is warning them is the place of exile that she and Donatello now inhabit, wandering Jewess and lapsed Roman Catholic, in a hell within them unhappier far. Yet might we not understand just the opposite? Perhaps it is Kenyon and Hilda who are being thrust into exile out of the only human world there is. In light of the text's severe condemnation of Roman Catholicism, which she herself, not to mention Kenyon, rejects, Hilda's "coming down from her old tower, to be herself enshrined and worshipped as a household Saint, in the light of her husband's fireside" (IV: 461) does not seem like much of an achievement, moral or otherwise. Nor does Hilda's rather sentimental obliviousness to Miriam's and Donatello's suffering:

> And, now, happy as Hilda was, we are told in the concluding words of the drama, the bracelet [Miriam has given her as a wedding present] brought the tears into her eyes, as being, in its entire circle, the symbol of as sad a mystery as any that Miriam had attached to the separate gems. For, what was Miriam's life to be? and where was Donatello? But Hilda had a hopeful soul, and saw sunlight on the mountain-tops.

Whatever the sad mysteries of life, they are for Hilda purely ornamental, not, as for Miriam a "connecting bond" in whose "circle" of suffering one is necessarily bound. Indeed it is by no means clear whether, "laid on Hilda's table" by Miriam, the bracelet will even be picked up and worn by Hilda, whose sights are cheerfully focused elsewhere: up, out of, and beyond the present scene of Rome (IV: 462).

Though Hilda and Kenyon (and thereby America and American Protestantism) seem to resist everything most objectionable about Rome, they in fact realize its most disheartening principles. Everything in Rome is centered on a concept of unforgiving "justice." Thus, when Hilda makes her confession to the priest at St. Peter's she is rebuked by the priest for not recognizing the priest's "duty to make the story known to the proper authorities; a great crime against public justice being involved, and further evil consequencies [*sic*] likely to ensue" (IV: 360). Roman Catholicism emerges as something very like its conception of Judaism, which it imagines itself as resisting: a religion of justice and vengeance, bound to duty. Not for naught is sculpture represented as the art of hardness. Cast in stone, sculpture recalls the faith cast in stone, which commands absolutely and without any shadow of a doubt what thou shalt and shalt not do. Yet Protestantism, it emerges, is no more forgiving than its Jewish and Roman Catholic predecessors. If anything it is only more ignorant in its sternness, more in flight from the realities of human being that both Roman Catholicism and Judaism are at least willing to acknowledge.

It is virtually by accident that Kenyon finally produces a bust of Donatello that is a match for the marble faun of Praxiteles and that is also an accurate reflection of Donatello's sweet and intelligent nature (IV: 273). "Unfinished," this statue "perplexes" the spectator with "the riddle that he sees propounded there; the riddle of the Soul's growth" (IV: 381). According to the narrator of *The Marble Faun* it is this statue that constitutes the inception of the narrative (IV: 381), which Hawthorne felt to be both a literary failure *and* his best work.[6] Failing to resolve the riddle of the human, *The Marble Faun* is to some degree "unfinished," like the human soul itself. In this way, it remains in the place of perplexity where what is achieved is not moral law cast in stone, but the sympathetic listening that is romance fiction itself.

NOTES

1. *The American, The Novels and Tales of Henry James*, 13 vols. (Fairfield, NJ: August M. Kelley Publishers, 1976), II: xvii–xviii.
2. For a further development of this argument see my *Fiction and Historical Consciousness: The American Romance Tradition* (New Haven, CT: Yale University Press, 1989) (my reading of "Young Goodman Brown" is on pp. 79–97); *Engendering Romance: Women Writers and the Hawthorne Tradition 1850–1990* (New Haven, CT: Yale University Press, 1994); and *Nineteenth-Century American Romance: Genre and the Construction of Democratic Culture* (New York: Twayne Publishers, 1996). See also Evan Carton, *The Rhetoric of American Romance: Dialectic and Identity in Emerson, Dickinson, Poe, and Hawthorne* (Baltimore, MD: Johns Hopkins University Press, 1985), who defines American romance as "a specific and urgent kind of rhetorical performance, a self-consciously dialectic

enactment of critical and philosophical concerns about the relation of words to things and the nature of the self . . . American romance . . . is . . . an artistic enterprise that engages and transforms post-Cartesian epistemological questions" (p. 1). In *Nineteenth-Century American Romance* I review the history of romance criticism (pp. 1–23 and 138–73).

3. Gordon Hutner, *Secrets and Sympathy: Forms of Disclosure in Hawthorne's Novels* (Athens: University of Georgia Press, 1988).

4. On the relationship of skepticism, romance, and gender see my *Engendering Romance*.

5. Michael Dunne, *Hawthorne's Narrative Strategies* (Jackson: University Press of Mississippi, 1995); Kenneth Dauber, *Rediscovering Hawthorne* (Princeton, NJ: Princeton University Press, 1977) and *The Idea of Authorship in America: Democratic Poetics from Franklin to Melville* (Madison: University of Wisconsin Press, 1990); Richard H. Millington, *Practicing Romance: Narrative Form and Cultural Engagement in Hawthorne's Fiction* (Princeton, NJ: Princeton University Press, 1992); Edgar Dryden, *Nathaniel Hawthorne: The Poetics of Enchantment* (Ithaca, NY: Cornell University Press, 1977); and again Gordon Hutner, *Secrets and Sympathy*.

6. See Roy R. Male, *Hawthorne's Tragic Vision* (Austin: University of Texas Press, 1957), p. 158.

12

GORDON HUTNER

Whose Hawthorne?

"Our" Hawthorne

As the afterword to the Hawthorne Centenary volume of essays, Lionel Trilling contributed "Our Hawthorne," an essay he later republished as "Hawthorne in Our Time."[1] Although Hawthorne specialists have never been particularly enamored of it, the essay is one of the most important studies of the author during the 1960s, not because it introduces any new scholarship or because it offers some methodological advance. Instead, its interest lies in the way it crystallizes a way of thinking about Hawthorne, his importance to US society as well as to academic values. Trilling's second title may have improved over the first, since it minimizes the issue of ownership and insists, however gently, on the historicity of reception. The first title, however, resonates aptly, evoking as it does how much a generation's reading of Hawthorne, or, indeed, any classic author, lays claim to possession, i.e., the owning of critical rights. "Our" moment, for Trilling, was the post-war era of New Critical predominance, the generation whose Hawthorne has given us the one that the post-1980s generations have needed to overturn or recast.

This sense of critical proprietorship is usually disclosed in scholarly skirmishes through questions of propriety – the protocols of interpretation. Generally claims of possession are made by individuals or by societies, perhaps keepers of the flame who may be outraged by some new revisionist. Trilling's title reminds us that possession is more nuanced and that a generation, even a whole literary culture, can have a great deal invested in seeing an author in a particular light, perhaps in the way that the post-World War II generation had so much invested in Ernest Hemingway, a veteran of World War I, whose example filled a romantic need to exalt the author as both virile and sensitive. It was not Trilling's point that such investment risks a blindness that gives later readers insight, but it might as well have been: Hawthorne's example illuminates how we may respond to a world filled with paradoxes and mutually exclusive dilemmas, a world filled with wrongdoing that reader-citizens could learn to negotiate through their increased power of moral awareness. Moreover, reading Hawthorne showed us that too much introspection could distance us from our relations, rendering us isolated in a world already too friendless but for one or two sympathetic souls. As much as any writer of the mid twentieth century, Hawthorne taught us how to retreat into a private sphere and how not to. In the post-war Hawthorne, America discovered its classic author as a "one-dimensional man," to use Herbert Marcuse's phrase for the identity that late industrial society creates.

Reading Hawthorne as ours – not some previous generation's – enables us to understand how the fight his fiction stages over cultural meaning also helps us to read our critical moment. As a result of Hawthorne's status as America's first fully recognized artist of genius, his writing has always elicited a critical reaction that fairly well encapsulates the prevailing social tendencies and critical preoccupations embedded in our rhetorics of interpretation and appreciation, especially academic discourse: in the twentieth century, Hawthorne scholarship and criticism provided an ample field for old historicist inquiry, including source-hunting, along with formalism, psychoanalysis, and deconstruction, as well as feminist critique, new historicism, and cultural studies. However scholars and critics decide to discuss literature, Americanists eventually test their principles through Hawthorne's fiction; after all, he was the very first American writer to be the subject of a critical monograph – Henry James's 1879 volume for the English Men of Letters Series. Trilling's title, whatever else it implies, means to locate a sense of Hawthorne's liberal imagination that this famous critic believed crucial for grasping a decisive moment in the history of American cultural understanding.

At the same time, Trilling's inveterate first-person plural causes even more trouble today than it did in his time. He was sometimes chided for his insistent use of "our" and "we," particularly for the pronoun's power of arrogation. Nor is it ever altogether clear to whom his "we" and "our" refer – the educated reading public that delighted in Trilling's prose (his death was front page news in the *New York Times*), or the community of scholars, critics, and teachers who followed his work, or his colleagues in the New York intellectual circles where he spent his entire professional life. Perhaps his first-person plural references were meant to cajole readers into granting his sometimes tendentious arguments and to flatter them into including themselves as fellow citizens, whatever their affiliations, of the intellectual cosmopolis over which Trilling's erudition and art of persuasion presided. His readers then resisted the inclusion, not out of the current sense of identity politics as a complex premise of interpretation, but out of displeasure with this coercive gesture. Today, academic readers are as likely as not to think of themselves as too diverse, too different from each other, to find much space within Trilling's conception of their relation to one writer – any writer.

Contemporary critics neither imagine themselves enjoying the solidarity of an academic community nor think that they share a larger social project with which most can comfortably identify. Even Toni Morrison, who generates as much allegiance as Hawthorne ever did, fails to elicit such a commitment, despite her position (following Hemingway and Mailer) as the media's image of the premier contemporary American novelist and the contemporary American writer that the academy most warmly embraces. Too many different kinds of readers want to possess her. So unitary an understanding of an American classic as Trilling's will even seem foreign to many who read, teach, interpret, and theorize for a living, since contemporary critical purposes will now seem very unlike his guiding spirit. Americanists now are less committed to discovering how reception actually discloses their likeness than was the generation Trilling addressed. Today's academic critics will care less for seeing how their reaction to a writer marks them as a generation and more for seeing how it highlights the ways they distinguish themselves, within that generation, as critics and scholars with different, often competing agendas. Surely some contemporary literary historians roll their eyes, alternately amused and annoyed, by his characteristic effort to rationalize culture, amid all its modern forces of entropy and destruction (which he describes so eloquently), even as Trilling might well have considered the celebration of heteroglossia and hybridity as naïve, even weak-minded, since these values are so self-evident that they are beneath a truly acculturated person's notice.

The Hawthorne who is ours, according to Trilling, is also the American writer that the academy was reading in 1964. Trilling's Hawthorne, the Hawthorne with whom so many readers of the post-war era had grown so familiar – in the high schools and colleges especially – modeled a skepticism at times genial and corrosive, as well as a morality of sympathetic engagement altogether consonant with the privileges conferred on liberal compassion, tolerance, and beneficence that made the mid-1960s seem like such a golden hour of democracy, no matter how illusory that moment would ultimately prove. Trilling's Hawthorne is very much the story-writer and novelist of the critical quarterlies and the case-books; his enshrinement in such places also expresses the way his tragic sense had become assimilated, accommodating a generation's need to obscure its complicity with guilt and corruption, its unacknowledged associations with bourgeois conformity or material well-being – the pieties that would be exploded in the coming years. In the post-war years, Americans may have lost a communal sense of sin so important to Hawthorne, but they still had not seen as well as they would – in the turbulent times immediately following Trilling's meditation – their cohabitation with evil, in Vietnam.

In 1964, Hawthorne was read for his power of endorsing the era's liberal consensus even as he was asked to give it the depths of his tragic awareness. This Hawthorne, of course, is the New Critical author to a large extent, a Hawthorne recommended for his powers of ambiguity, a profound, relentless, and unerring ironist who dwells in contradiction and paradox and who forces us to do the same. Typically, he reveals his characteristic doubts about the place of art and culture in a materialistic society, especially in a host of artist fables. Indeed, virtually everything Hawthorne wrote seemed transformable into that favorite New Critical formula of allegorizing the writer's burdens, anxieties, conflicts, and betrayals. This Hawthorne was not radical or religious in any orthodox way. Instead, he loved beauty, history, and human powers of introspection, and especially their overlap, though of both he was fiercely skeptical, trusting as he did in the democratic spirit he found in the "great heart of mankind" rather than the egotism that isolation risks. Hawthorne's passion for history was typically invoked rather than waged during this era, so that the campaign to decontextualize him could proceed without much ado. Trilling's Hawthorne had not yet been the object of Frederick Crews's groundbreaking psychoanalytic study, which provided a vocabulary for making Hawthorne seem even more modern, though readers of the darker fiction, such as Lionel Trilling himself, had already comprehended how Hawthorne had intuited, in a proto-psychoanalytic way, the workings of obsession, repetition compulsion, ambivalence, and repression. Still, seeing these motifs projected as prominently and as vividly as Crews's study permitted was like meeting an even gloomier, lonelier Hawthorne than had been known, a writer well qualified, a century after his death, to help readers find their way through the morass – the chaos and violence – of their inner life and their culture's.

Moreover, this sense of Hawthorne corresponded with some of the earliest ways of reading the haunted writer and was precisely the one Henry James wanted to put in perspective. (James too would be subject to a similar kind of modernist revisionism.[2]) For James, it was especially important to reascertain Hawthorne's authority as an artist, leading many scholars to study a kind of Oedipal relation between the two.[3] To reinscribe that authority, James needed at once to see Hawthorne as an American, talented enough to be a worthy predecessor whose overthrow would be meaningful, yet weak enough to leave room for an American writer who could be an artist of international standing, as James – having recently enjoyed the success of *Daisy Miller*, his biggest hit – thought himself poised to become. So James highlights for his British readers the limits that a European reader could predictably find in Hawthorne for being an American author. James's Hawthorne could not be a citizen of the world but must be rooted in the US, the place that, for James's purposes, he must really know; so the younger novelist tries his hardest to exhibit Hawthorne's stature as a regionalist as well as his confounded playfulness, that faculty of whimsy that Hawthorne thought imparted a certain lightness to his imagination by relieving it of the somberness that he feared would otherwise preside. James makes that pitch precisely at that point of his study that marks its most famous page. After the notorious catalogue of things missing in American life that a French or English novelist would find "appalling," James urges European readers to grant Hawthorne the "consolation" of his "national gift," the "American humour of which of late we have heard so much."[4] The note reeks of a younger man's unearned condescension, but its wrongness is even more wrong for its effort to class Hawthorne among the new post-Civil War local color humorists. Wrong as the gesture is – James, a year away from writing *Portrait of a Lady*, did not need to diminish his predecessor this way, nor should he have let his own ambitions lead him to misrepresent his American master for an English audience – there *is* a Hawthorne who writes with this comic, regionalist intention, the author of "Passages from a Relinquished Work," which retells the satiric tale "Mr. Higginbotham's Catastrophe," a story that may have been intended as part of a projected collection, one that would have predated *Twice-told Tales* (1837) by a year or two, "Seven Tales of My Native Land." Such a volume would have born comparison, however, not with the wit of a Bret Harte or Samuel Clemens, who were rising to fame in the 1860s and 1870s, as James suggests, but with Southwestern humorists of a generation before, such as Augustus Longstreet or T. B. Thorpe, who were more exactly Hawthorne's contemporaries. Indeed, while Hawthorne came to worry about the female novelists of the 1850s who easily outsold him, perhaps his chief competitors for critical esteem were males – regionalists, like William Gilmore Simms in the South and Daniel Thompson, a popular historical romancer in New England.

In the complex dynamics of the critical biography, James means both to praise Hawthorne and to undermine him, in this case by restoring to the author his reputation for wit and by building up and even overdoing the obstacles facing a writer who stayed in the US, the bankruptcy of resources against which that ingenious humor must contend. That power of wit, what James calls Hawthorne's "playing" with the "pigments" of history, further diminishes the claim to seriousness that an internationally recognized artist should have. Never mind that James throughout his career never got over Hawthorne, enlisting him as one of several mentors – and the only American – whose challenge he deemed crucial to surpass. For James turned to Hawthorne again and again if only to test his self-conception as an author.

Here James invents Hawthorne as a writer who absorbed his time and place so completely that we might read American cultural history through his corpus and his works through that history. Thus as a writer knowledgeable about all matters of local color, wit, and wisdom, Hawthorne stands as an insufficiently serious precursor of the realist imperative. With Hawthorne cast in this light, James could then understand himself as a true cosmopolite, immersed in the great world, unencumbered by American provincialism. It was this Hawthorne, the romantic artist par excellence, that F. O. Matthiessen recuperates: New England, and especially its past, was a subject and place vital to Hawthorne's imagination as well as to his world-view, but, unlike James, who tried to make this connection into an implicit liability, Matthiessen aimed to restore the moral depth and aesthetic brilliance of Hawthorne's engagement with his locale and its potential for cultural myth-making. Thus, readers could understand just how truly seminal was the hour of intellectual and literary rebirth that Matthiessen called *American Renaissance: Art and Expression in the Age of Emerson and Whitman* (1941).[5]

By contrast, Trilling's purpose, and critical challenge, was to transform these earlier Hawthornes into an appropriate American classic whose resonance with European masters could be articulated and properly measured. So he reads Matthiessen's Hawthorne through the lens of a writer who had witnessed the Second World War as well as one who had heard the blandishments of American bourgeois conformity through the 1950s. Trilling's Hawthorne perhaps would have eschewed any partisan commitment in the 1930s (as Trilling did), making him a comfortable fit with some critics in the 1950s who had relinquished the claims of their radical pasts. This Hawthorne had not yet been heard to utter his curses about the "mob of scribbling women," and if he had, he was to be praised for his integrity and his indomitable will to triumph over a degraded, because feminized, marketplace, not criticized for his uncomprehending disdain for sentimental writing. Nor had Trilling's Hawthorne yet been intimately associated with an essay like "Chiefly About War Matters" and thus subjected to the embarrassing disclose of his indifference to questions of race, as he was in the 1980s and 1990s, when complacent excuses about conventional beliefs lost their sway.

Indeed, Trilling's interpretation of Hawthorne's prestige exhumes from our critical consciousness the dynamic whereby Hawthorne ceased to be a question and became a solution, i.e., the answer to the question of what American author before the Civil War was worth the attention of modern, educated readers. (Cooper? not sophisticated enough; Melville? too invested in the metaphysics of his times.) So Trilling searches for a worthy progenitor of the modernists that liberal opinion favored, but also someone whose intense psychologism could accommodate an ever-expanding private sphere.

This vision of Hawthorne as a precursor of modernity also had to be made to mesh with his status as an American classic. To that end, Trilling's Hawthorne was generally understood to inhabit the dark side, what the novelist might have called the "dusky corner" of history and fantasy. One could scarcely speak of a Beat Hawthorne; such were the limits of his playfulness on one hand, or his religious tenor, on the other, though Hawthorne's isolatoes could sometimes be confused with that fifties' figure of alienation, William Barrett's "irrational man" or some other existential doubter. Besides, for all their single-minded lunacy, Hawthorne's mad doctors or obsessed artists morphed readily enough into genial villager storytellers, like the narrators of "A Rill from the Town-Pump" or "A Bell's Biography," insofar as these whimsical sketches, and their fascination with mutability, often echoed faintly the more pessimistic pieces, like "Monsieur du Miroir." Moreover, several of Hawthorne's homespun tales, like "The Great Carbuncle," enacted his formula of combining "jest and earnest," as he describes his own characteristic sensibility on so many occasions. This Hawthorne put readers in touch with a modern American self that knew about the perils of nonconformity; Hawthorne's lessons in the costs of estrangement challenged the individualist values at its very core – a core whose health demanded spirited watchfulness. So fundamental to the post-war sense of American cultural psychology as well as of the state of the polity did Hawthorne become that *The Scarlet Letter* was inscribed as a high school chestnut, along with stories like "The Minister's Black Veil" or "My Kinsman, Major Molineux," to name two stories Matthiessen does not even mention over the course of the nearly 200 pages on Hawthorne in his landmark study. Perhaps he does not mention them because in 1940 the culture did not yet know how to read them, certainly not in the ingenious ways high school juniors, twenty or thirty years later, would be expected to interpret their ambiguities and, forty or fifty years later, their indeterminacies. Yet, at ages when few students could be imagined to empathize with self-tormenting hypocrisy, crazed vengeance, suppressed adulterous passion, and resolute penitence, American teenagers were asked to appreciate the mind that staged their interaction as imbricating, in *The Scarlet Letter*, a tragic lesson in human frailty, historical vitality, ideological conviction, and spiritual conflict.

For all of the many reasons no longer to read Hawthorne as he once was read that we have now, Hawthorne remains a stalwart of the doctoral prelim reading list, though *The Blithedale Romance*, with its lessons in the failure of democratic community, seems now to have more cachet than it once did and perhaps rivals that of *The Scarlet Letter*. Professors no longer require as many novels and as many story titles as they once did, however. Even if he no longer is enlisted as the nineteenth-century author most likely to initiate students in the complex terms of cultural citizenship – an honor that might now go to Frederick Douglass – Hawthorne is still called upon to instruct the young in close reading, so his works remain part of the college prep curriculum as well as undergraduate survey and the major's course. "Our" Hawthorne, however, has lost the status of being what Trilling confers upon him, the writer from the past who remains vivifying and indispensable to the present. We seem to have lost, as a culture, an appreciation for whatever "equipment for living" Hawthorne might have proffered, the lessons in negotiating modernity that Kenneth Burke thought literary works should provide.[6] Such equipment as a previous generation's Hawthorne imparts may even seem inappropriate, as if students were being outfitted for a journey they are no longer asked to take. Hawthorne's loss of status may suggest that our culture does not care as much as it once did for sustaining a capacity for living with ambiguity, self-doubt, and estrangement as fundamental psychological circumstances or abiding social or political values, a loss that perhaps marks our move from a modern to a post-modern society. If contemporary American culture really has become as bloodless, as superficial, as much a pastiche of faux commitments as its most appalled critics have said it has, then the virtues that reading Hawthorne were supposed to transact really may not matter much at all. His appeals to the idea of interiority and the complexity of human motives, his worries about the risks of individualism and the costs of freedom, his skepticism about worldly success, his ambivalence about the obduracy of the material world, all seem, by contrast, in America forty years after Trilling wrote, much too irrelevant.

"Our" Hawthorne, as Trilling evokes him, is a writer, now that his bicentenary has arrived, that we, as a critical era, have lost to our peril. By generating a self equally at home in the world of "substance and shadow" (to use another of Hawthorne's favorite locutions), this Hawthorne perhaps enabled his own decline by rendering himself nearly trivial for a critical culture that sees "shadows," not as productive uncertainties but as obfuscations of his complicity with the forces of reaction. To the extent that "our Hawthorne" came to signify to contemporary readers the limits of American democracy, the willingness to make peace with the forces of corruption, as in Hester's return or in Holgrave's end, this new recognition has led to Hawthorne's critical undoing, maybe even his passing. Nor is it too much to aver that it was Trilling's Hawthorne – or Hawthorne as he came to be read during the years roughly between the end of World War II and the beginning of

American war in Vietnam – who helped to teach the culture how to read him into this irrelevance.

To an important extent "our" Hawthorne – the author Trilling thought to matter so mightily – became "their" Hawthorne, the Hawthorne who now sometimes no longer matters at all, an author whose great purpose is to expose his own inauthenticity and debility, thereby unveiling the corruption of the critical world that enshrined him as the classic who could be recovered as a connoisseur of "dark affections," the romantic author who, like Baudelaire, anticipates the terrors of modernity, the Puritan legatee who, like the critics of the first quarter of the twentieth century, could document the sterility of his forefathers. Instead, "our Hawthorne" has evolved, gradually and persistently, into a chilling model of the dead white male of European origin, whose classic status now seems best suited to exemplify the alternative, often contestatory framework through which our cultural imagination was sustained. At his worst, this Hawthorne is a writer too often racist and sexist, a writer who trusted too little in the very powers of sympathy he exalted and who may well owe much of his stature to a network of publishing friends and influential critics. Yet as much as this overstates the case among critics, the Hawthorne that students read today is surely someone else's Hawthorne. Our Whitman, yes; Our Douglass and Our Stowe, perhaps; even Our Melville to an extent, but Hawthorne now belongs to critics who see themselves resisting the excesses of pluralism – some sympathetically, others antagonistically. Trilling's Hawthorne, the great romantic American predecessor of modernism, is now stuck with all the baggage that is implied in the canonicity that modernist literary historiography conferred. This assessment may make us tired, but, whatever else Hawthorne criticism has revealed since the mid 1980s – with Jane Tompkins's *Sensational Designs*, Richard Brodhead's *The School of Hawthorne*, Sacvan Bercovitch's *The Office of "The Scarlet Letter,"* and Lauren Berlant's *Anatomy of National Fantasy* – our Hawthorne – i.e., Trilling's Hawthorne – was once the only one to be read. So forceful has been the revision since then that we might ask, whose Hawthorne are we reading?

Your Hawthorne

Your Hawthorne, today's Hawthorne, matters largely because he used to and thus stands as very nearly the central figure that revisionist Americanist literary historians have had to confront. Other authors have faced radical reassessment, especially Faulkner, but perhaps only Hemingway rivals Hawthorne in the degree to which his canonical status has been challenged. It is not so much that contemporary critics hate Hawthorne – only what he represents. Most of all, he represents the complacency of previous generations, their bland assurance that worth could be gauged and disseminated without "complication," that classic status not only even needed to be awarded, but could be. Such investment in works over texts blurred the very ideology implicit in a canon. Such a Hawthorne was an affront to the historical reality of the multiple communities of readers. Curiously, the book of essays in which Trilling publishes the revision of "Our Hawthorne" has a title that seems farcical to contemporary ears – *Beyond Culture*. What, contemporary critics would like to know, is even passingly beyond cultural study?

Your Hawthorne comes out of a brilliant diptych that, on the one side, portrays the overthrowing of the authority of the author, through Tompkins's reading of the works' reception, along with Brodhead's research into the Hawthorne culture industry. Tompkins's work in some ways complements Brodhead's, though the latter undertakes his own inquiry for his own purposes – to show how Hawthorne has come to dominate the interpretation of mid nineteenth-century culture through the 140 years or so after his literary career was completed. Brodhead's research reminds readers just how forcefully Hawthorne's culture capital was circulated. For Tompkins, Hawthorne became Hawthorne as a result of the way criticism and cultural authority transmute and elevate the properties they want to propagate, as part of the canon-making process she labels "masterpiece theater"; the values that they do not support are relegated to the remainder bin of literary history, no matter how vivid and prominent their expression once was. In granting privilege to works like *The Scarlet Letter* and *Moby-Dick*, a half-century of Americanists unjustly degraded the achievement of other writers: most notably, Harriet Beecher Stowe, whose preeminent work, *Uncle Tom's Cabin*, had, by the mid-1980s, not only suffered the loss of its once colossal prestige, but, as a victim of New Critical dominion in the 1950s and 1960s, it had become perhaps the least read of the truly influential American novels. As part of a brilliant effort to recapture the claim that Stowe's famous novel used to make on the American psyche, Tompkins develops her signal contribution to the new historicist reading of nineteenth-century American fiction, in the tenet of "cultural work," or the ways that fiction's design galvanizes and constellates sensation, the world of affective relations, thereby imparting to these private worlds more public significance, more historical resonance, more social weight than previous generations of scholars had understood. *Uncle Tom's Cabin* is only one of several test-cases, but it is the most pivotal and consequential one, since the cultural work Tompkins sees it performing, in accord with Lincoln (who so famously referred to its author as the woman who wrote the book that started the Civil War) is nothing less than

the righting of the most infamous wrong in American history, the legal imple-
mentation of chattel slavery. In addition, Tompkins's Stowe takes up this
challenge insofar as she also shared in a female tradition of domestic fiction.
Hawthorne's novels, whatever else they do, do not perform a negotiation
of such public magnitude in the lives of ordinary citizens. Why, we want to
know now, does the writer reputed to be our most accomplished author, by
international standards, have so little to say about slavery and race in the
four novels he wrote between 1850 and 1860? The valuation of the private
life, the new materialism, and the movement for social reform are worthy
enough topics, but there is nothing remotely like *Benito Cereno* in his oeuvre.
Instead, the putative appeal of Hawthorne's novels, as the argument went,
can be found in how, in their scrutiny of the psychological and moral circumstances of freedom and responsibility, these novels discover the tragic
cast of our social dilemmas, an appeal that Tompkins finds largely invented.

The second panel of the diptych that portrays your Hawthorne comes out
of Bercovitch's study of the workings of liberal compromise and Berlant's
"anatomy" of the national fantasy coiled in Hawthorne's fiction, most
especially *The Scarlet Letter*. Together, these studies combine to reshape
Hawthorne's vision as an object of cultural critique, but to an extent unacknowledged, their Hawthorne needs Trilling's sense of the author in order to
take on the consequence they assign. For both, however, it is not Hawthorne
the author who is the object of inquiry, but the social and political discourses
of his texts, and, for both, the status of democratic possibilities is supremely
what is at stake in Hawthorne's fiction. Both critics need to dismantle the
Hawthorne Trilling enshrines, not the petty Democrat who schemed to keep
his political sinecure, but the author whose novels and stories have since
been seen as creating a repository of democratic possibilities.

Bercovitch enlists the author of *The Scarlet Letter* as perhaps the key
figure in the prosecution of his "dissensus" theory of American literature.
This Hawthorne is fundamentally compromised insofar as his notorious
ambivalence, rather than the psychic virtue a previous generation had distinguished, ties him to political tendencies as conservative as any he may have
thought himself to oppose. As savvy a reader of Hawthorne as any predecessor, Berlant develops a Hawthorne also resembling Trilling's: an iconic
figure, less an artist than a presence, a scribe whose report is a palimpsest on
which is written the key to American liberal visions of "utopia and everyday
life." Inevitably, something of equation then comes into being; Hawthorne's
writings become the very languages of American faith, both good and bad.

One could certainly argue that not since the 1940s through the mid 1950s
had Hawthorne truly engaged, as he had in these several critics between
1985 and 1992, the most searching critical intelligences of a decade. These

critics brought both their genius and the lessons of critical theory to bear on Hawthorne, changing him for years to come. No longer does Hawthorne's name immediately invoke what it used to mean – an agreed-upon American genius, an author who could stand next to English writers or any from the continent, America's first recognized literary master, whose commanding prose and whose bold psychological portraits could be haunting.

Instead, your Hawthorne's magnitude has been revised downward to more manageable proportions than previous generations'. Part of that is the general devaluation of authorship that has occurred in the last twenty-five years. This Hawthorne is a writer whose stories and novels give readers a glimpse of some interesting social developments of their time and whose proto-psychoanalytic portraits of various obsessive personalities give a deeper sense of a culture's capacity to distort individuals, showing us how the warping of their motives yields some disastrous consequences. Moreover, your Hawthorne is oddly out of touch with the dominant ways of reading the nineteenth-century American novel, although once he was central to any theory of the genre and American practice. Hawthorne's novels used to appear on college syllabi in between Cooper and Melville; now he is perhaps just as likely to be read somewhere next to Catherine Sedgwick, or Stowe or Fanny Fern or Harriet Wilson or William Wells Brown, where the contrast is likely not to be in his favor.

The Hawthorne who descends to you from the 1980s is a novelist whose limits are even too apparent. To a critical generation more concerned with recuperating unfairly excluded or silenced writers or in discerning the political and social engagements in canonical authors, the position Hawthorne once enjoyed will seem dangerous. The perils of reading Hawthorne were once, like Young Goodman Brown's, the anxiety of losing faith and the resultant void. Readers may once have teetered over such a precipice and looked down to see the pit of moral disconnection. Now, the anxieties are different: the new Hawthorne too little prepares us for the great inequities of the mid-century – slavery, the rights of women, the rights of labor. Instead, his example upholds the structures whereby those moral wrongs are promoted, accepted, and even secured. An earlier generation once may have admired so mechanical a tale as "Wakefield," seeing it as a less accomplished "Bartleby, the Scrivener"; now it seems all too simply a lesson in the anxieties of domesticity and male-coded fears of a loss of self, incited and accommodated as they are by the rush of urbanization. "Alice Doane's Appeal" was once an unjustly neglected meditation on the vitality of the historical imagination; now it reads just as truly as a sort of psychic rape case. One may always be touched with Hawthorne's grief over a daughter stricken with Roman fever, but critics will search in vain for much direct evidence of his compassion for the Lowell mill girls. The cruel humor that animates his characterization of Hepzibah Pyncheon, or even Clifford, strikes us now as unfunny, an even brutish failure of empathy. Once tales like "The Celestial Railroad" and "Main-street" were understood as potentially loaded social documents; now they are uninspired sketches that show the limits of Hawthorne's political and social engagements. "Roger Malvin's Burial" was once a frightening story of compulsively murderous behavior, an Oedipal drama so unsettling critics rarely knew what to make of it; now it is a tale that indicates the limits of our understanding of colonial aggrandizement like the Pequot War.

Your Hawthorne was a damaged young man, perhaps even sexually abused, who yearned for the bourgeois respectability that his marriage to Sophia Peabody was to supposed to certify. In the past, he was understood as Byronic; today, Hawthorne is more likely to be read for the ways his vision embraces masochism, fear of women, and homosexual panic. Our Hawthorne was diffident and unworldly; your Hawthorne used his literary connections to further his career and actively pursued his connections to maintain his political appointment as Surveyor, a post he may have even mismanaged by permitting a common practice of minor graft to continue under his willfully inattentive watch. Today's Hawthorne had too little to say to Margaret Fuller and, after a while, not enough to say to Melville. An earlier Hawthorne found Fuller to be a dreary pedant and Melville an overly excited young man who too urgently sought an intimacy of communication that the older writer surely considered inappropriate.

One great service that contemporary criticism has performed is to bring a new, more subtle interest to Hawthorne's social writings: criticism of the *The House of the Seven Gables*, *The Blithedale Romance*, and *The Marble Faun* has flourished, no longer dominated, as it once was, by nice determinations of crucial formal issues. Instead, their richness as deliberations over the public sphere is only now being appreciated. Just as happy has been the shift from the overwrought urns that such stories as "The Minister's Black Veil," "Rappaccini's Daughter," and "Ethan Brand" had become to less studied works, like "Legends from the Province House." Also to be admired is the renewed attention to previously neglected works like *Our Old Home* and the children's tales. Yet this Hawthorne has none of the purchase on contemporary imaginations that Trilling cited; Hawthorne's charm, to use the word that James deployed so problematically, is at present his susceptibility to new historicist reading, as his texts create a testing ground, not for "sins of the fathers" but for arguments over history and the fate of liberal politics. *The Scarlet Letter* becomes important not for the profundity of its research into human motives or even its detailing the complexity of the private sphere and its doomed confrontation with the public, but as a foundational text for cultural citizenship in pre-Civil War America; *The House of the Seven Gables* is less about the presence of the past or the legacy of misery that one generation brings on the next and more about changing demographics; *The Blithedale Romance* less a satire of the excesses of reformist zeal and communitarianism than it is a troubled meditation on voyeurism; *The Marble Faun*, less about art than the struggle for Italian reunification.

Many of the new readings really do create a more interesting author than the one cast so readily as a moralist of the imagination. And nowhere is the new reading more poised and perhaps more urgent than in reconstructing Hawthorne's representations of the relations between men and women. One does not have to read a great deal of the fiction to realize that throughout his career, Hawthorne distrusted women, even as he invested a great deal in their authority. Nearly every one of his adult women is punished – usually unduly – unless they escape adulthood by being perpetual virgins, like Phoebe in the *The House of the Seven Gables*. Hawthorne's problem with women, to a significant extent, has become as fundamental a fact of Hawthorne criticism as the interplay of light and dark ever was. Today's Hawthorne needs to be recognized not as a result of his skill in creating Hester Prynne, but despite it.

Hawthorne no longer signifies what he once did – the liberal visionary par excellence, the author who, internalizing the forces of affirmation and of negation in his culture, came even to embody the dialectic of his civilization, both its past and its present, and who can thus be read to foretell presciently that culture's future. Yet Hawthorne can now teach you, his current students, something of their own time, something perhaps more salient and useful than he taught Lionel Trilling and his other post-war readers.

NOTES

1. Roy Harvey Pearce, ed., *Hawthorne Centenary Essays* (Columbus: Ohio State University Press, 1964). Lionel Trilling, *Beyond Culture: Essays on Literature and Learning* (New York: Viking Press, 1965).
2. See Ross Posnock, *The Trial of Curiosity: Henry James, William James, and the Challenge of Modernity* (New York: Oxford University Press, 1991).
3. See John Carlos Rowe, *The Other Henry James* (Durham, NC: Duke University Press, 1998), among others.
4. Henry James, *Hawthorne* (London: Macmillan, 1879), pp. 42–43.
5. Decades later, in his magisterial reading of the early short stories, Michael Colacurcio took seriously James's sense of Hawthorne's expert witness of his region's history. See *The Province of Piety: Moral History in Hawthorne's Early Tales* (Cambridge, MA: Harvard University Press, 1984). Colacurcio aims to recover the wealth of Hawthorne's fascination with the early history of New England, not for psychological or mythic purposes, but as part of the author's complex

negotiation with the America he inherited. To that end, Colacurcio means to establish Hawthorne as a "moral historian," the chronicler of the new republic's ethical imagination. This Hawthorne is the author who, by examining more minutely than anyone had heretofore supposed the political and social history ingrained in his works, enables himself to assess not only the legacies of the Puritans and their successors, but also the moral character of his own times.

6. Kenneth Burke, "Equipment for Living," in *Language as Symbolic Action: Essays on Life, Literature, and Method* (Berkeley: University of California Press, 1966).

SELECTED BIBLIOGRAPHY

Hawthorne has been a central figure for as long as American literature has been an academic subject, and critical studies of his work are accordingly numerous. This bibliography emphasizes book-length studies published in the last twenty years, though seminal early works and a sampling of significant recent articles are also included.

Hawthorne's writings

The Centenary Edition of the Works of Nathaniel Hawthorne (1962–97), published by Ohio State University Press and a labor of many years, is now complete and supplies an exhaustive and definitive scholarly edition of Hawthorne's writings. (The General Editors for the Edition were William Charvat, Roy Harvey Pearce, Claude M. Simpson, and Thomas Woodson.) Readers can find many of the *Centenary* texts in good paperback editions, published by Penguin, Oxford University Press, and The Library of America, among other publishers. In the following list, the first publication date, where appropriate, is provided parenthetically.

The American Claimant Manuscripts. Ed. Edward H. Davidson, Claude M. Simpson, and L. Neal Smith. *The Centenary Edition of the Works of Nathaniel Hawthorne,* vol. xii. Columbus: Ohio State University Press, 1976.

The American Notebooks. Ed. Claude M. Simpson. *The Centenary Edition of the Works of Nathaniel Hawthorne,* vol. viii. Columbus: Ohio State University Press, 1972.

The Blithedale Romance and Fanshawe (1852, 1828). Ed. Fredson Bowers, Matthew J. Bruccoli, and L. Neal Smith. *The Centenary Edition of the Works of Nathaniel Hawthorne,* vol. iii. Columbus: Ohio State University Press, 1964.

The Consular Letters, 1853–1857. Ed. Bill Ellis. *The Centenary Edition of the Works of Nathaniel Hawthorne,* vols. xix–xx. Columbus: Ohio State University Press, 1988.

The Elixir of Life Manuscripts. Ed. Edward H. Davidson, Claude M. Simpson, and L. Neal Smith. *The Centenary Edition of the Works of Nathaniel Hawthorne,* vol. xiii. Columbus: Ohio State University Press, 1977.

The English Notebooks, 1853–1856. Ed. Thomas Woodson and Bill Ellis. *The Centenary Edition of the Works of Nathaniel Hawthorne,* vol. xxi. Columbus: Ohio State University Press, 1997.

The English Notebooks, 1856–1860. Ed. Thomas Woodson and Bill Ellis. *The Centenary Edition of the Works of Nathaniel Hawthorne*, vol. XXII. Columbus: Ohio State University Press, 1997.

The French and Italian Notebooks. Ed. Thomas Woodson. *The Centenary Edition of the Works of Nathaniel Hawthorne*, vol. XIV. Columbus: Ohio State University Press, 1980.

The House of the Seven Gables (1851). Ed. Fredson Bowers, Matthew J. Brucolli, and L. Neal Smith. *The Centenary Edition of the Works of Nathaniel Hawthorne*, vol. II. Columbus: Ohio State University Press, 1965.

The Letters, 1813–1843. Ed. Thomas Woodson, L. Neal Smith, and Norman Holmes Pearson. *The Centenary Edition of the Works of Nathaniel Hawthorne*, vol. XV. Columbus: Ohio State University Press, 1985.

The Letters, 1843–1853. Ed. Thomas Woodson, L. Neal Smith, and Norman Holmes Pearson. *The Centenary Edition of the Works of Nathaniel Hawthorne*, vol. XVI. Columbus: Ohio State University Press, 1985.

The Letters, 1853–1856. Ed. Thomas Woodson, James A. Rubino, L. Neal Smith, and Norman Holmes Pearson. *The Centenary Edition of the Works of Nathaniel Hawthorne*, vol. XVII. Columbus: Ohio State University Press, 1988.

The Letters, 1857–1864. Ed. Thomas Woodson, James A. Rubino, L. Neal Smith, and Norman Holmes Pearson. *The Centenary Edition of the Works of Nathaniel Hawthorne*, vol. XVIII. Columbus: Ohio State University Press, 1987.

The Marble Faun: Or, the Romance of Monte Beni (1860). Ed. Fredson Bowers and L. Neal Smith. *The Centenary Edition of the Works of Nathaniel Hawthorne*, vol. IV. Columbus: Ohio State University Press, 1968.

Miscellaneous Prose and Verse. Ed. Thomas Woodson, Claude M. Simpson, and L. Neal Smith. *The Centenary Edition of the Works of Nathaniel Hawthorne*, vol. XXIII. Columbus: Ohio State University Press, 1995.

Mosses from an Old Manse (1846). Ed. Fredson Bowers, L. Neal Smith, John Manning, and J. Donald Crowley. *The Centenary Edition of the Works of Nathaniel Hawthorne*, vol. X. Columbus: Ohio State University Press, 1974.

Our Old Home (1863). Ed. Fredson Bowers and L. Neal Smith. *The Centenary Edition of the Works of Nathaniel Hawthorne*, vol. V. Columbus: Ohio State University Press, 1970.

The Scarlet Letter (1850). Ed. Fredson Bowers and Matthew J. Brucolli. *The Centenary Edition of the Works of Nathaniel Hawthorne*, vol. I. Columbus: Ohio State University Press, 1962.

The Snow-Image and Uncollected Tales (1852). Ed. Fredson Bowers, L. Neal Smith, John Manning and J. Donald Crowley. *The Centenary Edition of the Works of Nathaniel Hawthorne*, vol. XI. Columbus: Ohio State University Press, 1974.

True Stories (1841, 1842, 1850). Ed. Fredson Bowers, L. Neal Smith, and John Manning. *The Centenary Edition of the Works of Nathaniel Hawthorne*, vol. VI. Columbus: Ohio State University Press, 1972.

Twice-told Tales (1837). Ed. Fredson Bowers, L. Neal Smith, John Manning, and J. Donald Crowley. *The Centenary Edition of the Works of Nathaniel Hawthorne*, vol. IX. Columbus: Ohio State University Press, 1974.

A Wonder-Book for Girls and Boys and Tanglewood Tales (1852, 1853). Ed. Fredson Bowers, L. Neal Smith, and John Manning. *The Centenary Edition of the*

Works of Nathaniel Hawthorne, vol. VII. Columbus: Ohio State University Press, 1972.

Listed below is a brief selection of other interesting editions of Hawthorne's writings, including several recent editions of *The Scarlet Letter* and *The Blithedale Romance* that surround the text with useful historical and critical material.

Auster, Paul, ed. *Twenty Days With Julian & Little Bunny by Papa*. New York: New York Review Press, 2003.

Cain, William E., ed. *The Blithedale Romance*. A Bedford Cultural Edition. Boston: Bedford/St. Martin's, 1996.

D'Aulaire, Ola, ed. *A Wonder-Book for Girls and Boys*. Illustrations by Walter Crane, Introduction by Ola D'Aulaire, Afterword by Joel Pfister. New York: Oxford University Press, 1996.

Gollin, Rita, ed. *The Scarlet Letter*. Boston: Houghton Mifflin, 2001.

Levine, Robert S., ed. *The House of the Seven Gables*. A Norton Critical Edition. New York: Norton, forthcoming.

Martin, John Stephen, ed. *The Scarlet Letter*. Peterborough, Ontario: Broadview, 1995.

Myerson, Joel, ed. *Selected Letters of Nathaniel Hawthorne*. Columbus: Ohio State University Press, 2002.

Turner, Arlin, ed. *Hawthorne as Editor: Selections from his Writings in the "American Magazine of Useful and Entertaining Knowledge."* Baton Rouge: Louisiana State University Press, 1941.

Weber, Alfred, Beth L. Lueck, and Dennis Berthold, eds. *Hawthorne's American Travel Sketches*. Hanover, NH: University Press of New England, 1989.

Bibliographies

Consult the list below for useful listings of earlier bibliographical material on Hawthorne. The best way to become acquainted with or keep abreast of recent or current Hawthorne scholarship is through the Hawthorne chapter in *American Literary Scholarship: An Annual* (Durham, NC: Duke University Press, 1963–); also useful are the yearly "Current Bibiliography" essays in *The Nathaniel Hawthorne Review*, and the annual MLA Bibliography. Chapters on Hawthorne in books that address a range of authors may be found in the *Essay and General Literature Index*; these works are also covered in *American Literary Scholarship*.

Blair, Walter. "Nathaniel Hawthorne." In *Eight American Authors: A Review of Research and Criticism*, ed. James Woodress, pp. 85–128. New York: Norton, 1971.

Boswell, Jeanetta. *Nathaniel Hawthorne and the Critics: A Checklist of Criticism, 1900–1978*. Metuchen, NJ: Scarecrow, 1982.

Clark, C. E. Frazer, Jr. *Nathaniel Hawthorne: A Descriptive Bibliography*. Pittsburgh: University of Pittsburgh Press, 1978.

Ricks, Beatrice, Joseph D. Adams, and Jack O. Hazlerig, eds. *Nathaniel Hawthorne: A Reference Bibliography, 1900–71*. Boston: G. K. Hall, 1972.

Scharnhorst, Gary, ed. *Nathaniel Hawthorne: An Annotated Bibliography of Commentary and Criticism before 1900.* Metuchen, NJ: Scarecrow, 1988.

Wilson, James C. *The Hawthorne and Melville Friendship: An Annotated Bibliography, Biographical and Critical Essays, and Correspondence between the Two.* Jefferson, NC: McFarland, 1991.

Biographical studies and resources

Important sites for archival material include the Hawthorne–Manning Collection at the Essex Institute, Salem, MA; The Henry W. and Albert A. Berg Collection of the New York Public Library; the Pierpont Morgan Library, New York City; and the Hawthorne–Longfellow Library of Bowdoin College. Two strong, comprehensive biographies, by James Mellow and Arlin Turner, appeared in 1980. Mellow's has been regarded as the best biography for the general reader, but Hawthornians have been eagerly awaiting the appearance of Brenda Wineapple's just published *Hawthorne: A Life* (2003). The intervening years saw the publication of several more specifically focused biographies; of these, T. Walter Herbert's exploration of the Hawthornes as a paradigmatic middle-class family has been extremely influential, while Margaret Moore's book supplies an unequalled understanding of Hawthorne's years in and relation to Salem. The list below also includes a selection of early biographies, which have the vividness of proximity and continue to be useful to scholars. Thomas Woodson's "Introduction" to the *Letters* will serve readers well as a fine brief biography.

Baym, Nina. "Nathaniel Hawthorne and His Mother: A Biographical Speculation." *American Literature* 54 (1982): 1–27.

Bridge, Horatio. *Personal Recollections of Nathaniel Hawthorne.* New York: Harper, 1893.

Conway, Moncure D. *Life of Nathaniel Hawthorne.* New York: Lovell, 1890.

Erlich, Gloria C. *Family Themes and Hawthorne's Fiction: The Tenacious Web.* New Brunswick, NJ: Rutgers University Press, 1984.

Fields, James T. *Yesterdays with Authors.* Boston: Houghton Mifflin, 1871.

Hawthorne, Julian. *Nathaniel Hawthorne and his Circle.* New York: Harper & Brothers, 1903.

 Nathaniel Hawthorne and his Wife: a Biography, 2nd edition. 2 vols. Boston: James Osgood, 1884.

Herbert, T. Walter. *Dearest Beloved: The Hawthornes and the Making of the Middle-Class Family.* Berkeley: University of California Press, 1993.

Hoeltje, H. H. *The Inward Sky: The Mind and Heart of Nathaniel Hawthorne.* Durham, NC: Duke University Press, 1962.

Homer, Bryan. *An American Liaison: Leamington Spa and the Hawthornes, 1864–1865.* Rutherford, NJ: Fairleigh Dickinson University Press, 1998.

Hull, Raymona E. *Nathaniel Hawthorne: The English Experience, 1853–1864.* Pittsburgh, PA: University of Pittsburgh Press, 1980.

Lathrop, George P. *A Study of Hawthorne.* Boston: Osgood, 1876.

Lathrop, Rose Hawthorne. *Memories of Hawthorne.* Boston: Houghton Mifflin, 1897.

Mellow, James R. *Nathaniel Hawthorne in His Times.* Boston: Houghton Mifflin, 1980.

Miller, Edwin Haviland. *Salem Is My Dwelling Place: A Life of Nathaniel Hawthorne.* Iowa City: University of Iowa Press, 1991.

Moore, Maragaret B. *The Salem World of Nathaniel Hawthorne.* Columbia: University of Missouri Press, 1998.

Stewart, Randall. *Nathaniel Hawthorne: A Biography.* New Haven, CT: Yale University Press, 1948.

Tharp, Louise Hall. *The Peabody Sisters of Salem.* Boston: Macintosh and Otis, 1950.

Ticknor, Caroline. *Hawthorne and his Publisher.* Boston: Houghton Mifflin, 1913.

Turner, Arlin. *Nathaniel Hawthorne: A Biography.* New York: Oxford University Press, 1980.

Van Doren, Mark. *Nathaniel Hawthorne: A Critical Biography.* New York: William Sloane, 1949.

von Abele, Rudolph. *The Death of the Artist: A Study of Hawthorne's Disintegration.* The Hague: Martinus Nijhoff, 1955.

Wineapple, Brenda. *Hawthorne: A Life.* New York: Alfred A. Knopf, 2003.

Woodson, Thomas. "Introduction: Hawthorne's Letters, 1813–1853." In *The Letters, 1813–1843,* vol. xv, *The Centenary Edition of the Works of Nathaniel Hawthorne.*

Critical reception

Cohen, B. Bernard, ed. *The Recognition of Nathaniel Hawthorne.* Ann Arbor: University of Michigan Press, 1969.

Crowley, J. Donald, ed. *Hawthorne: The Critical Heritage.* New York: Barnes and Noble, 1970.

Faust, Bertha. *Hawthorne's Contemporaneous Reputation: A Study of Literary Opinion in America and England, 1828–1864.* New York: Octagon, 1968.

Idol, John L., Jr., and Buford Jones, eds. *Nathaniel Hawthorne: The Contemporary Reviews.* New York: Cambridge University Press, 1994.

Scharnhorst, Gary, ed. *The Critical Response to Nathaniel Hawthorne's "The Scarlet Letter."* Westport, CT: Greenwood, 1992.

Nathaniel Hawthorne: An Annotated Bibliography of Commentary and Criticism before 1900. Metuchen, NJ: Scarecrow, 1988.

Collections of critical essays, guides, and special issues

Bell, Millicent, ed. *New Essays on Hawthorne's Major Tales.* New York: Cambridge University Press, 1993.

Bloom, Harold, ed. *Hester Prynne.* New York: Chelsea House, 1990.

Cady, Edwin H., and Louis J. Budd, eds. *On Hawthorne: The Best from American Literature.* Durham, NC: Duke University Press, 1990.

Colacurcio, Michael J., ed. *New Essays on "The Scarlet Letter."* Cambridge: Cambridge University Press, 1985.

Eberhard, Alsen, ed. *The New Romanticism: A Collection of Critical Essays.* New York: Garland, 2000. [Hawthorne and present-day writers]

Gale, Robert L. *A Nathaniel Hawthorne Encyclopedia.* Boston: G. K. Hall, 1991.

Gerber, John C., ed. *Twentieth Century Interpretations of "The Scarlet Letter":* A Collection of Critical Essays.* Englewood Cliffs, NJ: Prentice Hall, 1968.

Goddu, Teresa A., and Leland S. Person, eds. *"The Scarlet Letter* after 150 Years: A Special Issue." *Studies in American Fiction* 29 (2001): 3–128.

Idol, John L., Jr., and Melinda Ponder, eds. *Hawthorne and Women: Engendering and Expanding the Hawthorne Tradition.* Amherst: University of Massachusetts Press, 1999.

Johnson, Claudia Durst, ed. *Understanding "The Scarlet Letter": A Student Casebook to Issues, Sources, and Historical Documents.* Westport, CT: Greenwood, 1995.

Kennedy-Andrews, Elmer. *Nathaniel Hawthorne: "The Scarlet Letter."* Columbia Critical Guides. New York: Columbia University Press, 1999.

Kesterson, David B., ed. *Critical Essays on Hawthorne's "The Scarlet Letter."* Boston: G. K. Hall, 1988.

Lee, A. Robert, ed. *Nathaniel Hawthorne: New Critical Essays.* New York: Barnes and Noble, 1982.

Martin, Robert K., and Leland S. Person, eds. *Roman Holidays: American Writers and Artists in Nineteenth-Century Italy.* Iowa City: University of Iowa Press, 2002.

"The Hawthorne–Melville Relationship." *ESQ: A Journal of the American Renaissance* 46 (2000): 1–122.

Newman, Lea Bertani Vozar. *A Reader's Guide to the Short Stories of Nathaniel Hawthorne.* Boston: G. K. Hall, 1979.

Pearce, Roy Harvey, ed. *Hawthorne Centenary Essays.* Columbus: Ohio State University Press, 1964.

Reynolds, Larry J., ed. *A Historical Guide to Nathaniel Hawthorne.* New York: Oxford University Press, 2001.

Rosenthal, Bernard, ed. *Critical Essays on Hawthorne's "The House of the Seven Gables."* New York: G. K. Hall, 1995.

Thompson, G. R., and Virgil L. Lokke, eds. *Ruined Eden of the Present: Hawthorne, Melville, and Poe: Critical Essays in Honor of Darrel Abel.* West Lafayette, IN: Purdue University Press, 1981.

von Frank, Albert J., ed. *Critical Essays on Hawthorne's Short Stories.* Boston: G. K. Hall, 1991.

Studies of Hawthorne

Abel, Darrel. *The Moral Picturesque: Studies in Hawthorne's Fiction.* West Lafayette, IN: Purdue University Press, 1988.

Abrams, Robert E. "Critiquing Colonial American Geography: Hawthorne's Landscape of Bewilderment." *Texas Studies in Language and Literature* 36 (1994): 357–79.

Arac, Jonathan. "The Politics of *The Scarlet Letter.*" In *Ideology and Classic American Literature,* ed. Sacvan Bercovitch and Myra Jehlen, pp. 247–66. New York: Cambridge University Press, 1986.

Arvin, Newton. *Hawthorne.* Boston: Little, Brown, 1929.

Auerbach, Jonathan. "Executing the Model." *ELH* 47 (1980): 103–20.

Barlowe, Jamie. *The Scarlet Mob of Scribblers: Rereading Hester Prynne.* Carbondale: Southern Illinois University Press, 2000.

Baym, Nina. *"The Scarlet Letter": A Reading.* Boston: Twayne, 1986.

The Shape of Hawthorne's Career. Ithaca, NY, and London: Cornell University Press, 1976.

"Thwarted Nature: Nathaniel Hawthorne as Feminist." In *American Novelists Revisited: Essays in Feminist Criticism,* ed. Fritz Fleishmann, pp. 58–72. Boston: G. K. Hall, 1982.

Bell, Michael Davitt. *Hawthorne and the Historical Romance of New England.* Princeton, NJ: Princeton University Press, 1971.

Bell, Millicent. *Hawthorne's View of the Artist.* New York: State University of New York Press, 1962.

Bensick, Carol Marie. *La Nouvelle Beatrice: Renaissance and Romance in "Rappaccini's Daughter."* New Brunswick, NJ: Rutgers University Press, 1985.

Bercovitch, Sacvan. *The Office of "The Scarlet Letter."* Baltimore, MD: Johns Hopkins University Press, 1991.

Berlant, Lauren. *The Anatomy of National Fantasy: Hawthorne, Utopia, and Everyday Life.* Chicago: University of Chicago Press, 1991.

"Fantasies of Utopia in *The Blithedale Romance.*" *American Literary History* 1 (1989): 30–62.

Brickhouse, Anna. "Hawthorne in the Americas: Frances Calderon de la Barca, Octavio Paz, and the Genealogy of 'Rappaccini's Daughter.'" *PMLA* 113 (1998): 227–42.

Brodhead, Richard H. *Hawthorne, Melville, and the Novel.* Chicago: University of Chicago Press, 1976.

The School of Hawthorne. New York: Oxford University Press, 1986.

Browner, Stephanie P. "Authorizing the Body: Scientific Medicine and *The Scarlet Letter.*" *Literature and Medicine* 12 (1993): 139–60.

Budick, Emily Miller. *Engendering Romance: Women Writers and the Hawthorne Tradition, 1850–1990.* New Haven, CT: Yale University Press, 1994.

Cagidemetrio, Alide. *Fictions of the Past: Hawthorne and Melville.* Amherst: University of Massachusetts Press, 1992.

Cameron, Sharon. *The Corporeal Self: Allegories of the Body in Melville and Hawthorne.* Baltimore, MD: Johns Hopkins University Press, 1981.

Carton, Evan. *"The Marble Faun": Hawthorne's Transformations.* New York: Twayne, 1992.

Cheyfitz, Eric. "The Irresistibleness of Great Literature: Reconstructing Hawthorne's Politics." *American Literary History* 6 (1994): 539–58.

Coale, Samuel Chase. *In Hawthorne's Shadow: American Romance from Melville to Mailer.* Lexington: University Press of Kentucky, 1985.

Mesmerism and Hawthorne: Mediums of American Romance. Tuscaloosa: University of Alabama Press, 1998.

Colacurcio, Michael J. "Footsteps of Ann Hutchinson: The Context of *The Scarlet Letter.*" *English Literary History* 39 (1972): 459–94.

The Province of Piety: Moral History in Hawthorne's Early Tales. Cambridge, MA: Harvard University Press, 1984.

Cox, James M. "*The Scarlet Letter*: Through the Old Manse and the Custom House." *Virginia Quarterly Review* 51 (1975): 432–47.

Crews, Frederick. *The Sins of the Fathers: Hawthorne's Psychological Themes.* New York: Oxford University Press, 1966.

Daly, Robert. "'We Have Really No Country at All': Hawthorne's Reoccupations of History." *Arachne* 3 (1996): 66–88.

Dauber, Kenneth. *Rediscovering Hawthorne*. Princeton, NJ: Princeton University Press, 1977.

Davidson, Cathy. "Photographs of the Dead: Sherman, Daguerre, Hawthorne." *South Atlantic Quarterly* 89 (1990): 667–701.

Davidson, Edward H. *Hawthorne's Last Phase*. New Haven, CT: Yale University Press, 1949.

Derrick, Scott. "'A Curious Subject of Observation and Inquiry': Homoeroticism, the Body, and Authorship in Hawthorne's *The Scarlet Letter*." *Novel* 28 (1995): 308–26.

DeSalvo, Louise. *Nathaniel Hawthorne*. Atlantic Highlands, NJ: Humanities Press, 1987.

Dolis, John. *The Style of Hawthorne's Gaze: Regarding Subjectivity*. Tuscaloosa: University of Alabama Press, 1993.

Doubleday, Neil Frank. *Hawthorne's Early Tales: A Critical Study*. Durham, NC: Duke University Press, 1972.

Dryden, Edgar A. *Nathaniel Hawthorne: The Poetics of Enchantment*. Ithaca, NY: Cornell University Press, 1977.

Dunne, Michael. *Hawthorne's Narrative Strategies*. Jackson: University Press of Mississippi, 1995.

Easton, Alison. *The Making of the Hawthorne Subject*. Columbia: University of Missouri Press, 1996.

Elbert, Monica M. *Encoding the Letter "A": Gender and Authority in Hawthorne's Early Fiction*. Frankfurt, Germany: Haag & Herchen, 1990.

Fiedelson, Charles. "The Scarlet Letter." In *Hawthorne Centenary Essays*, ed. Roy Harvey Pearce, pp. 31–77. Columbus: Ohio State University Press, 1964.

Fogle, Richard H. *Hawthorne's Fiction: The Light and the Dark*. Norman: University of Oklahoma Press, 1964.

Gable, Harvey L., Jr. *Liquid Fire: Transcendental Mysticism in the Romances of Nathaniel Hawthorne*. New York: Peter Lang, 1998.

Gilmore, Michael T. "Hawthorne and the Making of the Middle Class." In *Rethinking Class: Literary Studies and Social Formation*, ed. Wai Chee Dimock and Michael T. Gilmore, pp. 215–38. New York: Columbia University Press, 1994.

Gollin, Rita K. *Nathaniel Hawthorne and the Truth of Dreams*. Baton Rouge: Louisiana State University Press, 1979.

   Portraits of Nathaniel Hawthorne: An Iconography. DeKalb: Northern Illinois University Press, 1983.

Gollin, Rita K., and John L. Idol, Jr. *Prophetic Pictures: Nathaniel Hawthorne's Knowledge and Uses of the Visual Arts*. Westport, CT: Greenwood, 1991.

Greenwald, Elissa. *Realism and the Romance: Nathaniel Hawthorne, Henry James, and American Fiction*. Ann Arbor: University of Michigan Press, 1989.

Hall, Lawrence Sargent. *Hawthorne: Critic of Society*. New Haven, CT: Yale University Press, 1944.

Harris, Kenneth Marc. *Hypocrisy and Self-Deception in Hawthorne's Fiction*. Charlottesville: University Press of Virginia, 1988.

Herbert, T. Walter. "Nathaniel Hawthorne, Una Hawthorne, and *The Scarlet Letter*: Interactive Selfhoods and the Cultural Construction of Gender." *PMLA* 103.3 (1988): 285–97.

Hutner, Gordon. *Secrets and Sympathy: Forms of Disclosure in Hawthorne's Novels.* Athens: University of Georgia Press, 1988.

Jacobsen, Richard J. *Hawthorne's Conception of the Creative Process.* Cambridge, MA: Harvard University Press, 1965.

James, Henry. *Hawthorne.* English Men of Letters Series. London: Macmillan, 1879.

Johnson, Claudia Durst. *The Productive Tension of Hawthorne's Art.* Tuscaloosa: University of Alabama Press, 1981.

Kesselring, Marion L. *Hawthorne's Reading, 1828–1850.* New York: New York Public Library, 1949.

Kilcup, Karen L. " 'Ourself behind Ourself, Concealed – ': The Homoerotics of Reading in *The Scarlet Letter*." *ESQ : A Journal of the American Renaissance* 42 (1996): 1–28.

Knadler, Stephen. "Hawthorne's Genealogy of Madness: *The House of the Seven Gables* and Disciplinary Individualism." *American Quarterly* 47 (1995): 280–308.

Laffrado, Laura. *Hawthorne's Literature for Children.* Athens: University of Georgia Press, 1992.

Levine, Robert S. " 'Antebellum Rome' in *The Marble Faun*." *American Literary History* 2 (1990): 19–38.

Long, Robert Emmet. *The Great Succession: Henry James and the Legacy of Hawthorne.* Pittsburgh, PA: University of Pittsburgh Press, 1979.

Luedtke, Luther S. *Nathaniel Hawthorne and the Romance of the Orient.* Bloomington: Indiana University Press, 1989.

Mackenzie, Manfred. "Colonization and Decolonization in *The Blithedale Romance*." *University of Toronto Quarterly* 62 (1993): 504–21.

Male, Roy R. *Hawthorne's Tragic Vision.* Austin: University of Texas Press, 1957.

Martin, Robert K. "Haunted by Jim Crow: Gothic Fictions by Hawthorne and Faulkner." In *American Gothic: New Interventions in a National Narrative,* ed. Robert K. Martin and Eric Savoy, pp. 129–42. Iowa City: University of Iowa Press, 1998.

"Hester Prynne, C'est Moi: Nathaniel Hawthorne and the Anxieties of Gender." In *Engendering Men: The Question of Male Feminist Criticism,* ed. Joseph A. Boone and Michael Cadden, pp. 122–39. New York: Routledge, 1990.

Martin, Terence. *Nathaniel Hawthorne.* Rev. edn. Boston: Twayne, 1983.

McCall, Dan. *Citizens of Somewhere Else: Nathaniel Hawthorne and Henry James.* Ithaca, NY: Cornell University Press, 1999.

McIntosh, James. "The Instability of Belief in *The Blithedale Romance*." *Prospects* 9 (1984): 71–114.

McWilliams, John P., Jr. *Hawthorne, Melville, and the American Character: A Looking-Glass Business.* Cambridge: Cambridge University Press, 1984.

Melville, Herman. "Hawthorne and His Mosses," 1850. Rpt. in *The Shock of Recognition,* ed. Edmund Wilson, pp. 187–204. New York: Modern Library, 1955.

Michael, John. "History and Romance, Sympathy and Uncertainty: The Moral of the Stones in *The Marble Faun*." *PMLA* 103 (1988): 150–61.

Michaels, Walter Benn. "Romance and Real Estate." In *The American Renaissance Reconsidered: Selected Papers from the English Institute*, ed. Walter Benn Michaels and Donald E. Pease, pp. 156–82. Baltimore, MD: Johns Hopkins University Press, 1985.

Miller, J. Hillis. *Hawthorne and History: Defacing It*. Cambridge: Basil Blackwell, 1991.

Millington, Richard H. *Practicing Romance: Narrative Form and Cultural Engagement in Hawthorne's Fiction*. Princeton, NJ: Princeton University Press, 1992.

Mitchell, Thomas R. *Hawthorne's Fuller Mystery*. Amherst: University of Massachusetts Press, 1998.

Moore, Thomas R. *A Thick and Darksome Veil: The Rhetoric of Hawthorne's Sketches, Prefaces, and Essays*. Boston: Northeastern University Press, 1994.

Newberry, Frederick. *Hawthorne's Divided Loyalties: England and America in His Works*. Rutherford, NJ: Fairleigh Dickinson University Press, 1987.

Newfield, Christopher, and Melissa Solomon. "Few of Our Seeds Ever Came Up at All: A Dialogue on Hawthorne, Delany, and the Work of Affect in Visionary Utopias." In *No More Separate Spheres!: A Next Wave American Studies Reader*, ed. Cathy Davidson and Jessamyn Hatcher, pp. 377–408. Durham, NC: Duke University Press, 2002.

Nudelman, Franny. " 'Emblem and Product of Sin': The Poisoned Child in *The Scarlet Letter* and Domestic Advice Literature." *Yale Journal of Criticism* 10.1 (1997): 193–213.

Pfister, Joel. *The Production of Personal Life: Class, Gender, and the Psychological in Hawthorne's Fiction*. Stanford, CA: Stanford University Press, 1991.

Ponder, Melinda. *Hawthorne's Early Narrative Art*. Lewiston, ME: Edwin Mellen, 1990.

Schiff, James. *Updike's Version: Rewriting "The Scarlet Letter."* Columbia: University of Missouri Press, 1992.

Smith, Allan Gardner Lloyd. *Eve Tempted: Writing and Sexuality in Hawthorne's Fiction*. Totowa, NJ: Barnes and Noble, 1984.

Stein, William Bysshe. *Hawthorne's Faust: A Study of the Devil Archetype*. Gainesville: University of Florida Press, 1953.

Stern, Milton R. *Contexts for Hawthorne: "The Marble Faun" and the Politics of Openness and Closure in American Literature*. Urbana: University of Illinois Press, 1991.

Stoehr, Taylor. *Hawthorne's Mad Scientists: Pseudoscience and Social Science in Nineteenth-Century Life and Letters*. Hamden, CT: Archon Books, 1978.

Stubbs, John Caldwell. *The Pursuit of Form: A Study of Hawthorne and the Romance*. Urbana: University of Illinois Press, 1970.

Swann, Charles. *Nathaniel Hawthorne: Tradition and Revolution*. New York: Cambridge University Press, 1991.

Thomos, Brook. "Citizen Hester: *The Scarlet Letter* as Civic Myth." *American Literary History* 13 (2001): 181–211.

"*The House of the Seven Gables*: Rereading the Romance of America." *PMLA* 97. 2 (1982): 195–211.

Thompson, G. R. *The Art of Authorial Presence: Hawthorne's Provincial Tales*. Durham, NC: Duke University Press, 1993.

Trachtenberg, Alan. "Seeing and Believing: Hawthorne's Reflection on the Daguerreotype in *The House of the Seven Gables*." In *National Imaginaries, American Identities*, ed. Larry J. Reynolds and Gordon Hutner, pp. 31–51. Princeton, NJ: Princeton University Press, 2001.

Waggoner, Hyatt H. *Hawthorne: A Critical Study*. Rev. edn. Cambridge, MA: Harvard University Press, 1963.

  The Presence of Hawthorne. Baton Rouge: Louisiana State University Press, 1979.

Wallace, James D. "Hawthorne and the Scribbling Women Reconsidered." *American Literature* 62 (1991): 201–22.

Yellin, Jean Fagan. "Hawthorne and the American National Sin." In *The Green American Tradition: Essays and Poems for Sherman Paul*, ed. H. Daniel Peck, pp. 75–97. Baton Rouge: Louisiana State University Press, 1989.

Literary and historical studies with sections on hawthorne

Some of the most influential work on Hawthorne has appeared in contextual and theoretical studies that address a range of authors. The Hawthorne texts discussed, when limited to one or two, are indicated parenthetically.

Alkana, Joseph. *The Social Self: Hawthorne, Howells, William James, and Nineteenth-Century Psychology*. Lexington: University Press of Kentucky, 1997.

Anderson, Douglas. *A House Undivided: Domesticity and Community in American Literature*. New York: Cambridge University Press, 1990.

Arac, Jonathan. *Commissioned Spirits: The Shaping of Social Motion in Dickens, Carlyle, Melville, and Hawthorne*. New Brunswick, NJ: Rutgers University Press, 1979.

Auerbach, Jonathan. *The Romance of Failure: First-Person Fictions of Poe, Hawthorne, and James*. New York: Oxford University Press, 1989. [*The Blithedale Romance*]

Bauer, Dale M. *Feminist Dialogics: A Theory of Failed Community*. Albany: State University of New York Press, 1988. [*The Blithedale Romance*]

Bell, Michael Davitt. *The Development of American Romance: The Sacrifice of Relation*. Chicago: University of Chicago Press, 1980. [*The House of the Seven Gables*]

Bellis, Peter J. *Writing Revolution: Aesthetics and Politics in Hawthorne, Whitman and Thoreau*. Athens: University of Georgia Press, 2003.

Bentley, Nancy. *The Ethnography of Manners: Hawthorne, James, Wharton*. Cambridge: Cambridge University Press, 1995. [*The Marble Faun*]

Brand, Dana. *The Spectator and the City in Nineteenth-Century American Literature*. New York: Cambridge University Press, 1991. [*The Blithedale Romance*]

Brodhead, Richard H. *Cultures of Letters: Scenes of Reading and Writing in Nineteenth-Century America*. Chicago: University of Chicago Press, 1993. [*The Blithedale Romance*]

Bromell, Nicholas K. *By the Sweat of the Brow: Literature and Labor in Antebellum America*. Chicago: University of Chicago Press, 1993.

Brown, Gillian. *Domestic Individualism: Imagining Self in Nineteenth-Century America*. Berkeley: University of California Press, 1990. [*The House of the Seven Gables, The Blithedale Romance*]

Budick, Emily Miller. *Fiction and Historical Consciousness: The American Romance Tradition*. New Haven, CT: Yale University Press, 1989.
  Nineteenth-Century American Romance: Genre and the Construction of Democratic Culture. New York: Twayne Publishers, 1996.
Buell, Lawrence. *New England Literary Culture: From Revolution Through Renaissance*. New York: Cambridge University Press, 1986.
Carton, Evan. *The Rhetoric of American Romance: Dialectic and Identity in Emerson, Dickinson, Poe, and Hawthorne*. Baltimore, MD: Johns Hopkins University Press, 1985.
Caserio, Robert L. *Plot, Story, and the Novel: From Dickens and Poe to the Modern Period*. Princeton, NJ: Princeton University Press, 1979. [*The House of the Seven Gables*]
Castronovo, Russ. *Necro Citizenship: Death, Eroticism, and the Public Sphere in the Nineteenth-Century United States*. Durham, NC: Duke University Press, 2001. [*The Blithedale Romance*]
Chai, Leon. *The Romantic Foundations of the American Renaissance*. Ithaca, NY: Cornell University Press, 1987.
Charvat, William. *The Profession of Authorship in America, 1800–1870: The Papers of William Charvat*, ed. Matthew J. Bruccoli. Columbus: Ohio State University Press, 1978. [Antebellum literary careers]
Chase, Richard. *The American Novel and its Tradition*. Garden City, NY: Gordian Press, 1957. [*The Scarlet Letter, The Blithedale Romance*]
Crain, Patricia. *The Story of A: The Alphabetization of America from "The New England Primer" to "The Scarlet Letter."* Stanford, CA: Stanford University Press, 2000. [*The Scarlet Letter*]
Dauber, Kenneth. *The Idea of Authorship in America: Democratic Poetics from Franklin to Melville*. Madison: University of Wisconsin Press, 1990.
Dekker, George. *The American Historical Romance*. Cambridge: Cambridge University Press, 1987.
Dryden, Edgar. *The Form of American Romance*. Baltimore, MD: Johns Hopkins University Press, 1988. [*The Marble Faun*]
Eigner, Edwin. *The Metaphysical Novel in England and America: Dickens, Bulwer, Melville, and Hawthorne*. Berkeley: University of California Press, 1978.
Fiedelson, Charles. *Symbolism and American Literature*. Chicago: University of Chicago Press, 1953.
Fiedler, Leslie. *Love and Death in the American Novel*. New York: Stein and Day, 1966. [*The Scarlet Letter*]
Forgie, George. *Patricide in the House Divided: A Psychological Interpretation of Lincoln and His Age*. New York: Norton, 1979. ["My Kinsman, Major Molineux," *The House of the Seven Gables*]
Franchot, Jenny. *Roads to Rome: The Antebellum Protestant Encounter with Catholicism*. Berkeley: University of California Press, 1994. [*The Scarlet Letter, The Marble Faun*]
Fussell, Edwin S. *Frontier: American Literature and the American West*. Princeton, NJ: Princeton University Press, 1965.
Gilmore, Michael T. *American Romanticism and the Marketplace*. Chicago: University of Chicago Press, 1985.

Surface and Depth: The Quest for Legibility in American Culture. New York: Oxford University Press, 2003. [*The Scarlet Letter*]

Girgus, Sam B. *Desire and the Political Unconscious in American Literature: Eros and Ideology.* New York: St. Martin's, 1990.

Goddu, Teresa A. *Gothic America: Narrative, History, and Nation.* New York: Columbia University Press, 1997. [*The Blithedale Romance*]

Hamilton, Kristie G. *America's Sketchbook: The Cultural Life of a Nineteenth-Century Literary Genre.* Athens: Ohio University Press, 1998.

Herbert, T. Walter. *Sexual Violence and American Manhood.* Cambridge, MA: Harvard University Press, 2002. [*The Scarlet Letter*]

Howe, Irving. *Politics and the Novel.* New York: Horizon Press, 1957. [*The Blithedale Romance*]

Jehlen, Myra. *American Incarnation: The Individual, the Nation, and the Continent.* Cambridge, MA: Harvard University Press, 1986. [*The Scarlet Letter, The Marble Faun*]

Kermode, Frank. *The Classic: Literary Images of Permanence and Change.* New York: Viking Press, 1975.

Kramer, Michael P. *Imagining Language in America: From the Revolution to the Civil War.* Princeton, NJ: Princeton University Press, 1992. [*The Scarlet Letter*]

Lang, Amy Schrager. *Prophetic Woman: Anne Hutchinson and the Problem of Dissent in the Literature of New England.* Berkeley: University of California Press, 1987. [*The Scarlet Letter*]

The Syntax of Class: Writing Inequality in Nineteenth-Century America. Princeton, NJ: Princeton University Press, 2003. [*The House of the Seven Gables*]

Lawrence, D. H. *Studies in Classic American Literature.* 1923. New York: Penguin Books, 1977. [*The Scarlet Letter, The Blithedale Romance*]

Leverenz, David. *Manhood and the American Renaissance.* Ithaca, NY: Cornell University Press, 1989.

Levine, Robert S. *Conspiracy and Romance: Studies in Brockden Brown, Cooper, Hawthorne, and Melville.* Cambridge: Cambridge University Press, 1989. [*The Blithedale Romance*]

Lewis, R. W. B. *The American Adam: Innocence, Tragedy, and Tradition in the Nineteenth Century.* Chicago: University of Chicago Press, 1955.

Mailloux, Steven. *Interpretive Conventions: The Reader in the Study of American Fiction.* Ithaca, NY: Cornell University Press, 1982. ["Rappaccini's Daughter"]

Marx, Leo. *The Machine in the Garden: Technology and the Pastoral Ideal in America.* New York: Oxford University Press, 1964. ["Ethan Brand"]

Matthiessen, F. O. *American Renaissance: Art and Expression in the Age of Emerson and Whitman.* New York: Oxford University Press, 1941.

Mellard, James M. *Using Lacan, Reading Fiction.* Champaign: University of Illinois Press, 1992. [*The Scarlet Letter*]

Merish, Lori. *Sentimental Materialism: Gender, Commodity Culture, and Nineteenth-Century American Literature.* Durham, NC: Duke University Press, 2000. [*The Blithedale Romance*]

Mizruchi, Susan L. *The Power of Historical Knowledge: Narrating the Past in Hawthorne, James, and Dreiser.* Princeton, NJ: Princeton University Press, 1988. [*The House of the Seven Gables*]

Newbury, Michael. *Figuring Authorship in Antebellum America*. Stanford, CA: Stanford University Press, 1997.

Pease, Donald E. *Visionary Compacts: American Renaissance Writings in Cultural Context*. Madison: University of Wisconsin Press, 1987. [*The Scarlet Letter*]

Person, Leland S. *Aesthetic Headaches: Women and a Masculine Poetics in Poe, Melville, and Hawthorne*. Athens: University of Georgia Press, 1988.

Porte, Joel. *The Romance in America: Studies in Cooper, Poe, Hawthorne, Melville, and James*. Middletown, CT: Wesleyan University Press, 1969.

Railton, Stephen. *Authorship and Audience: Literary Performance in the American Renaissance*. Princeton, NJ: Princeton University Press, 1991. [*The Scarlet Letter*]

Reynolds, David S. *Beneath the American Renaissance: The Subversive Imagination in the Age of Emerson and Melville*. New York: Alfred A. Knopf, 1988.

Reynolds, Larry J. *European Revolutions and the American Literary Renaissance*. New Haven, CT: Yale University Press, 1988. [*The Scarlet Letter*]

Romero, Lora. *Home Fronts: Domesticity and its Critics in the Antebellum United States*. Durham, NC: Duke University Press, 1997. [*The Scarlet Letter, The Blithedale Romance*]

Rowe, John Carlos. *Through the Custom House: Nineteenth-Century American Fiction and Modern Theory*. Baltimore, MD: Johns Hopkins University Press, 1982. [*The Blithedale Romance*]

Schirmeister, Pamela. *The Consolations of Space: The Place of Romance in Hawthorne, Melville, and James*. Stanford, CA: Stanford University Press, 1990. [*The Marble Faun*]

Siebers, Tobin. *The Romantic Fantastic*. Ithaca, NY: Cornell University Press, 1984.

Smith, Henry Nash. *Democracy and the Novel: Popular Resistance to Classic American Writers*. New York: Oxford University Press, 1978.

Steele, Jeffrey. *The Representation of the Self in the American Renaissance*. Chapel Hill: University of North Carolina Press, 1987.

Steiner, Wendy. *Pictures of Romance: Form Against Content in Painting and Literature*. Chicago: University of Chicago Press, 1988. [*The Marble Faun*]

Sundquist, Eric J. *Home as Found: Authority and Genealogy in Nineteenth-Century American Literature*. Baltimore, MD: Johns Hopkins University Press, 1979. [*The House of the Seven Gables*]

Tanner, Tony. *The American Mystery*. Cambridge: Cambridge University Press, 2000. [*The Blithedale Romance*]

Thomas, Brook. *Cross-Examinations of Law and Literature: Cooper, Hawthorne, Stowe, and Melville*. New York: Cambridge University Press, 1987. [*The House of the Seven Gables*]

Tompkins, Jane. *Sensational Designs: The Cultural Work of American Fiction: 1790–1860*. New York: Oxford University Press, 1985. [Hawthorne and canon formation]

Vance, William. *America's Rome*. New Haven, CT: Yale University Press, 1989. [*The Marble Faun*]

Warren, Joyce. *The American Narcissus: Individualism and Women in Nineteenth-Century American Fiction*. New Brunswick, NJ: Rutgers University Press, 1984.

Weinstein, Cindy. *The Labor of Love and the Labors of Literature: Allegory in Nineteenth-Century American Fiction*. New York: Cambridge University Press, 1995. ["The Birth-Mark"]

Williams, Susan S. *Confounding Images: Photography and Portraiture in Antebellum America*. Philadelphia: University of Pennsylvania Press, 1998. [*The House of the Seven Gables, The Marble Faun*]

Yellin, Jean Fagan. *Women and Sisters: The Antislavery Feminists in American Culture*. New Haven, CT: Yale University Press, 1989. [*The Scarlet Letter*]

INDEX

CAMBRIDGE COMPANIONS TO LITERATURE
Period and Thematic

US writers

CAMBRIDGE COMPANIONS TO CULTURE

Culture Companions